URBAN S(
AS PLACES, LINKS AND DISPLAYS

To attract investment and tourists and to enhance the quality of life of their citizens, municipal authorities are paying considerable attention to the quality of the public domain of their cities – including their urban squares. Politicians find them good places for rallies. Children consider squares to be playgrounds, the elderly as places to catch up with each other, and for many others squares are simply a place to pause for a moment.

Urban Squares as Places, Links and Displays: Successes and Failures discusses how people experience squares and the nature of the people who use them. It presents a "typology of squares" based on the dimensions of ownership, the square's instrumental functions, and a series of their basic physical attributes, including size, degree of enclosure, configuration and organization of the space within them and, finally, based on their aesthetic attributes – their meanings. Twenty case studies illustrate what works and what does not work in different cities around the world. The book discusses the qualities of lively squares and quieter, more restorative places, as well as what contributes to making urban squares less desirable as destinations for the general public. The book closes with the policy implications, stressing the importance and difficulties of designing good public places.

Urban Squares offers how-to guidance along with a strong theoretical framework, making it ideal for architects, city planners and landscape architects working on the design and upgrade of squares.

Jon Lang is an Emeritus Professor at the University of New South Wales in Sydney, Australia, where he headed the School of Architecture from 1998 to 2004. He is also the Director for Urban Design of ERG/Environmental Research Group Inc. in Philadelphia, Pennsylvania. Born in Kolkata, India, he received his early education in that city and in Kalimpong. He has a Bachelor's degree in architecture from the University of the Witwatersrand in Johannesburg and a doctorate from Cornell University in Ithaca, New York. He taught at the University of Pennsylvania from 1970 to 1990, heading its Urban Design Program in the 1980s, before settling in Australia. He has authored books on urban design, architecture in India, the relationship between people and the built environment and on architectural theory. He has served on international urban design juries and worked as a consultant throughout much of Asia as well as the United States and Latin America. He received the Reid and Malik Medal from the Institution of Civil Engineers (UK) in 2011.

Nancy Marshall is a Senior Lecturer at the University of New South Wales in Sydney, Australia, where she was Associate Dean/Education from 2009 to 2013. She has taught theory and practice in the Planning Program there since 2004 and won the UNSW Vice-Chancellor's Award for Teaching Excellence in 2007. Born and raised in Calgary, Canada, she received her undergraduate and postgraduate degrees from the University of Calgary and her PhD from the University of New South Wales. Prior to coming to Australia, she worked as a planning consultant in Canada, specializing in public involvement in urban planning and design. Her work as a planner at the local government level included efforts to more efficiently deliver high quality parks and civic spaces. She has been greatly involved in the affairs of planning – serving as a national, senior editor of the Canadian Institute of Planning's journal *Plan Canada* from 1997 to 2002 and a member of Calgary's Subdivision and Development Appeal Board from 1994 to 1997. She is currently a corporate member of the Planning Institute of Australia.

URBAN SQUARES
AS PLACES, LINKS AND DISPLAYS

Successes and Failures

JON LANG AND NANCY MARSHALL

Routledge
Taylor & Francis Group

NEW YORK AND LONDON

First published 2017
by Routledge
711 Third Avenue, New York, NY 10017

and by Routledge
2 Park Square, Milton Park, Abingdon, Oxon OX14 4RN

Routledge is an imprint of the Taylor & Francis Group, an informa business

Library of Congress Cataloging in Publication Data
Names: Lang, Jon T., author. | Marshall, Nancy (Nancy G.), author.
Title: Urban squares as places, links and displays : successes and failures /
By Jon Lang and Nancy Marshall.
Description: New York : Routledge, 2016. | Includes bibliographical
references and index.
Identifiers: LCCN 2015047624| ISBN 9781138959279 (hardcover) |
ISBN 9781138959293 (pbk.) | ISBN 9781315660707 (ebook)
Subjects: LCSH: Plazas. | City and town life. | City planning.
Classification: LCC NA9070 .L36 2016 | DDC 711/.55—dc23
LC record available at http://lccn.loc.gov/2015047624

ISBN: 978-1-138-95927-9 (hbk)
ISBN: 978-1-138-95929-3 (pbk)
ISBN: 978-1-315-66070-7 (ebk)

Typeset in Univers
by Keystroke, Station Road, Codsall, Wolverhampton

Printed in Canada

Times Square, New York
Photograph by Kate Bishop

Places do not become loved because they are great;
they become great because they are loved.
G. K. Chesterton, *Orthodoxy* (1908)

Cloud Gate by Anish Kapoor in AT+T Plaza, Chicago

CONTENTS

PART IV WHAT WORKS AND WHAT DOESN'T WORK

13 The Qualities of Lively Urban Squares

14 The Qualities of Quiet Urban Squares

EPILOGUE

Notes on the Designing and/or Upgrading of Squares

INDEX

PREFACE

Urban open spaces are fundamental to establishing the image of a twenty-first-century city and contributing to the enjoyment that people, young and old, gain from urban life. Cities, towns and villages around the world have public gardens, waterfront promenades, extensive park systems and other public amenities that provide opportunities for walking, jogging and strolling to see the sights. Famous squares adorn many cities. Fountains, sculptures, seating and place activation strategies make diverse urban squares attractive spots in which to linger. Some squares, however, do not function well; a noticeable number of recently created ones have not met what was expected of them by their designers, municipal authorities and the general public.

Much has been written on the qualities of urban public places over the past 150 years. Many books and articles have been authored by very knowledgeable observers of the urban scene. Phenomenological studies of the experiencing of urban environments have added to our knowledge of how people evaluate the public realm of cities. Systematic empirical studies on the use and meanings of streets and squares abound. These studies have significant implications for professional practice in urban design, landscape architecture and city planning. While cities and societies evolve continuously, this new research on urban squares offers many insights into what works and what does not work for different groups of people living, visiting and working in very different climatic, sociocultural, economic and political contexts.

One difficulty faced by designers is that the findings of these numerous studies are widely spread in books, journals and conference proceedings so that the existing body of knowledge is not easily accessible. The result is that, in creating squares, designers often rely on intuition shaped by personal experiences and on the casual observations they make as part of daily life. Such observations are important but they are also limiting. The design of urban open spaces, including urban squares, should be evidence-based.

Our Objective

The aim of this book is to synthesize existing research, the often forgotten observations of a large number of scholars and our own studies into a coherent collection of statements about urban squares. Our objective is to present this body of knowledge to the professional world in a form that is easy to understand and accessible for architects, landscape architects, planners, municipal authorities, students and members of the general public who are concerned about the quality of the built environment. The focus in this book is primarily on public and quasi-public open spaces in cities lying within the world's temperate climatic zones and within the social norms of Anglo-American, European and Latin American cultures. Squares in other cultures are mentioned in passing to place our observations into a broader context. Great care must be taken to avoid imposing Eurocentric ideas onto Asian and African cities.

There are often desires for more public squares in cities that have no tradition of or sociocultural use for them. For example, Kolkata has BBD Bagh (formerly Dalhousie Square), a product of the British colonial administration of India, but little else in the form of squares other than small, but important *chowks* at street intersections. One of India's leading architects, B. V. Doshi, has called for more public open spaces where people can meet "by accident." Much can be learnt from the global experience but it should be treated with caution.

We are fully aware that there is vast knowledge that exists about squares in cities of diverse cultures and climates. By no means is a complete analysis presented in this book. We discuss a representative sample of types of urban squares in order to present an understanding of what have proven to be lively and well-used places and what factors contribute to making squares quiet, restorative places and those that are unintendedly less desirable places. We have not attempted to provide a full explanation of each square that we mention, nor do we provide exhaustive scholarly citations for the sources of our information. At the end of each chapter References and Further Readings are listed. Collectively, these contain a substantial listing of subjects related to the design of squares which, we hope, will be of assistance to many readers.

The Outline of Our Argument

For the everyday life of pedestrians, squares are part of the public realm usually on the ground floor of cities. In recent years a great deal of effort and money has been expended on enhancing urban squares with some success but many of the results have incurred substantial opportunity costs. Some new squares were considered only as open areas and thoughts of what they can and should offer people were neglected in their design. This book begins with a Prologue, has a core that consists of four parts, each with several chapters, and ends with an Epilogue, all of which are described briefly below.

The Prologue brings attention to the nature of urban squares and to the number of squares being built or refurbished as the result of public policies and private initiatives around the world. It considers what has been gained from recent developments and what has been disappointing.

Part I presents an introduction to how squares should be considered, based on our understanding of how people experience them and the nature of the people who may or may not use them. We argue that any approach to describing the functioning of squares has to be based on an understanding of the perception and the role of movement through spaces in allowing an appreciation of what squares may afford. We suggest that squares can best be considered as potential behavior settings and displays, primarily visual displays. The people who use squares in either an active or passive manner vary as do their perceptions of any open space's utility. People of all abilities, the young and the old, men and women, the wealthy and the poor, tourists and local residents, scan the environment to recognize what it offers them in terms of their own interests and motivations. Individuals have differing motivations. An individual perceives the behavioral opportunities and messages contained in the built environment based on who they are, their experiences and background. While every person is unique, the manner in which diverse people scan and assess the environment is similar and can be understood.

Part II presents a typology of squares. Squares come in a seemingly haphazard range of configurations and identifying the types that exist is a complex task. There are a large number, if not infinite, dimensions on which a square could be described. The most important of these dimensions are presented chapter-by-chapter in four sub-sections. The first sub-section consists of one chapter discussing types based on ownership. The second looks at types of squares based on their instrumental functions and the third on their physical attributes: size, degree of enclosure, their configuration and organization of the space within them. We regard these characteristics as the basic attributes of squares. The fourth sub-section classifies squares based on their esthetic attributes – their meanings.

Part III consists of a single but significant chapter, Chapter 12. In it, we present a description and analysis of 20 squares. The purpose is to enhance and concretize the observations made throughout the book about types of squares. The case studies clearly illustrate what works and what does not work, for whom, in a variety of places. The combined evidence from abstract empirical theory and from case studies provides the basis for designing successful open spaces and for predicting and explaining the utility of any design when it is still on the drawing board or computer screen.

Part IV is a synthesis of our knowledge and describes how squares of various types function, based on the findings of current research and the analyses of the case studies. Although much remains poorly understood, we have the empirical knowledge to make the sound design judgments that are required to ensure that a specific design meets the goals and objectives set for it. The proviso is that the goals – always political in nature – are realistic. Chapter 13 discusses the qualities of lively squares. We also know how to make squares quieter and, possibly, more restorative places as well as what contributes to making them less desirable as destinations for the general public. That discussion is the focus of Chapter 14.

The Epilogue of the book describes the issues involved in applying knowledge about the nature and functioning of urban squares that is available to design professionals. It also discusses the design process and policy implications for municipal governments, city planners and design professionals. We hope this book will also help explain the importance and difficulties of designing good public places for the inhabitants of and visitors to a city.

The Illustrations

"What is the use of a book without pictures and conversation?" asked Alice in Lewis Carroll's (1865) *Alice's Adventures in Wonderland*. The question certainly applies to a book dealing with city design. Jane Jacobs, in *Death and Life of Great American Cities* (1961) suggested that all one had to do is look carefully around to understand the points she was trying to make. While acknowledging the veracity of her sentiment, our stance is different. We have attempted to illuminate the points we make in the text of the book with illustrations. The photographs and drawings could all have been of any one major city: Berlin, Buenos Aires, London, New York, Paris or Sydney. They are, however, drawn from a variety of cities and towns. The reason is simply to show that much of what is covered in this book is generic to a range of urban contexts.

Assembling the illustrations has been a demanding task and we would like to thank Rachel Cogger and Katie Withers for their assistance with that process. The source of every drawing and photograph for which Jon Lang or Nancy Marshall does not hold the copyright is specified. Every attempt has been made to credit the copyright holders of the other illustrations that we have used. If copyright proprietorship can be established for any work incorrectly attributed please contact either of the authors. Any error will be gladly rectified.

ACKNOWLEDGEMENTS

It will immediately be evident to the readers that the information presented in this book has relied heavily on the work of others. The names of the people whose studies and writings have been crucial to the development of our argument are referred to frequently throughout the book and listed in each chapter's Reference Lists. Special mention must be made of the studies of Camillo Sitte, Werner Hegemann and Elbert Peets, Paul Zucker, Jane Jacobs, William (Holly) Whyte, Rob Krier, Clare Cooper Marcus and Carolyn Francis, Cliff Moughton, Matthew Carmona and Jan Gehl. These authors and many others established the foundation on which we have built.

This book had its genesis in a study completed for the City of Sydney on one small public open space, Oxford Square, which we undertook with Kate Bishop and Rachel Cogger. A brief summary of the research is presented in Case Study 12, included in Chapter 12. The review of the existing state of our knowledge about what works and what does not work conducted for that study was the point of departure for this examination of urban squares.

Finally, we are grateful to the Faculty of the Built Environment at the University of New South Wales in Sydney, Australia, for providing us with the institutional support without which this book would have been impossible to produce. The support of the Faculty is much appreciated.

PROLOGUE

Heroes Square, Budapest
Photograph by Mike Sheppard.

THE CONCERN

This Prologue addresses why it is important to write about urban squares. The justification is simple. Streets and squares are the primary and, many would argue, the most important open spaces in the dense urban core of cities throughout the world. They constitute a city's ground floor: the world of pedestrians and motorists alike. Skylines can be spectacular when seen from afar but it is the nature of their ground floors that largely differentiates one city from another. The qualities of a city's ground floor create its unique sense of place and its affordances[1] for public sociability. They need to be designed well.

Urban squares are a key element in a city's network of public open spaces. They constitute part of a city's amenities and add to its character and identity. Municipal authorities in cities vying for a place in the global spotlight understand that the public spaces of their cities must be of a high standard. As a result, a lot of attention is being paid to the upgrading of the public realm in cities around the globe as they compete to be regarded as a 'world city.' Existing squares are being refurbished and new ones built in major metropolises such as Berlin, London, Paris, New York, Shanghai and Los Angeles, to note just a few. Smaller cities, towns and villages are also being revitalized. Ageing infrastructure is being upgraded – squares are being remodeled and sidewalks[2] are being widened or narrowed as the case may be and repaved, or reclaimed with 'parklets,' or temporarily activated with pop-up features.

Considerable financial resources, both public and private, are being invested in squares in order to improve the quality of the urban environment for people who live and work in cities and for visitors. Some of the new squares are the product of public policies and community processes; others have resulted from private initiatives. Some are much loved by the public; they are an integral part of a city's flow of pedestrian life and vehicular circulation. Many recently designed squares are, however, incurring substantial opportunity costs as hindsight and analysis indicate; alternative designs would have worked better. Some squares, while highly praised, are unloved and are dilapidated places only a decade after construction because the physical or social context in which they exist was misunderstood or has changed since they were designed. A number of such squares have been designed by internationally renowned architects and have received awards and widespread acclaim from professional associations such as institutes of architecture and landscape architecture. The role of these squares in the day-to-day life of a community hardly warrants their fame.

Are the disappointments of many new squares due to the belief among municipal authorities that any open space is desirable? Are some squares disappointing because of a failure to recognize the importance of a square's geographic and social context? Is it because built environment professionals fail to understand how different patterns of squares can and do function or perhaps is it because these professionals and scholars have failed to share the knowledge they have gained from experience? We can learn much from the performance of much-loved squares whether they are relatively new or longstanding. Squares that function poorly also offer us many lessons.

Open Space in Cities

Cities are full of open space which consists of streets, squares, parks, bodies of water and private courtyards and gardens, as one can see in aerial views of even very dense cities. Cities such as Rome may seem crowded from a casual glance but they are full of public and private open spaces. Giambattista Nolli mapped the public spaces of Rome in 1748, as shown in the figure–ground map in Figure 0.1. The streets, many courtyards and the interiors of buildings such as churches were seen as public spaces. A number of squares formed an important part of the public realm of Nolli's Rome. Much open space was also in private hands, some accessible to the public and some not.

Open spaces amount to close to 50 percent of the area of most cities. This book is concerned with what one type of these open spaces – urban squares – offers the inhabitants of a city. The great effort being made to enhance the quality of the public environment in many places makes it important for municipal authorities as well as designers to understand the role played by squares of different types in the life of a city. We need to know what works, where, when and for whom. There is little reason to create new open spaces in cities simply to create more open space. Many cities have enough open area, *per se*.

Figure 0.1 *Public space and open space in Rome: the Nolli plan of Rome 1748*

Many cities of Europe are replete with squares of importance for public life. In contrast, many countries in Africa and Asia, with some notable exceptions, have no history of public squares comparable to Europe or those squares that are the product of the application of the *Law of the Indies* in Spain's American and Philippine colonies (Rodriguez 2005). In these other countries squares are, however, now being created in response to changing ways of life, a globalization of cultures and the desire to have the quality of open spaces that world-class cities in other countries possess.

As metropolises around the world become more crowded and denser,[3] there is often a call for higher quality open spaces than they already possess in their core areas. Policies have been implemented in a number of cities to remodel existing squares and create new ones. The reasons vary from providing better pedestrian circulation to revitalizing urban precincts, as at Victoria Square in Adelaide (Monfries 2012), King's Cross Station in London, Public Square in Cleveland (Litt 2014) and Times Square in Midtown Manhattan, New York, or, as in the case at Châtelet les Halles in Paris, creating a new heart for a city. The renovations do not come cheaply and the results have often been disappointing. To learn from them as well as those places deemed to have been resoundingly lively and joyous places, we need to consider the pedestrian's view of the city.

The World of Pedestrians

Streets, squares and parks serve a multiplicity of functions for people and the natural world. The focus of this book is on people, squares and urban life but squares can, although to a lesser extent, like parks, serve a number of purposes other than providing for social and communal activities or restorative places to rest. They can serve to reduce the heat island effect of large amounts of hard surfaces, provide habitats for animals and birds, and be places where aquifers are replenished. Streets, squares and parks can also function as works of art, as expressions of their creators' intent, and a commentary on society. All three, however, need to function well in meeting the basic patterns of everyday urban life. Urban parks have specific design and management requirements so they need their own special attention.

Streets and squares are the primary public open spaces of cities. The two have a number of features in common: a more or less horizontal surface (or floor) and some degree of enclosure provided by surrounding buildings and/or landscaping, especially trees. Sidewalks and squares are reserved primarily for pedestrians although they may be crossed by vehicular or bicycle traffic, and in some places used as parking lots. They are, nevertheless, seen as the rightful territory of pedestrians. They also possess ambient qualities. Arguably the most important of these qualities is the nature of light, particularly sunlight. The desirability of sunlight depends on the latitude of the location of a square. Access to light depends on the height of the surrounding buildings and trees, and at night on artificial sources of illumination. As perception is multi-modal, the sources and quality of sounds and odors intrude on perceptions of the quality of urban spaces. Touch is a fundamental human sense so the haptic experience afforded by the textures of the built environment can enhance or detract from a person's experience of any open space.

What differentiates streets from squares is that the former consists primarily of links – channels of movement from one place to another – and the latter usually of places, localized sites of activities. This observation needs to be qualified because, as we show, places contain links and links contain places. Before focusing on squares, it must be recalled that the major public space of any city consists of its streets and what differentiates one city from another is often the character of its streets. "Think of a city and what comes to mind? Its streets," as Jane Jacobs (1961: 29) noted.[4]

A street consists of: a carriageway for vehicles, a sidewalk for pedestrians, the adjacent buildings and the way they meet the sidewalk, and the nature of the activities that the buildings house. A street's character comes from its physical features, the activities that take place on it as well as its architectural nature as a symbolic display. The movement of traffic and people along a street is a major factor in establishing its nature. If the traffic volume and speed are substantial, it divides one side of a street from the other. It becomes an edge and the two sidewalks along its sides become separate territories. If the traffic volume is low, the speed of its movement is slow and the street is narrow, it becomes a seam joining its two sides together into a unit (Appleyard and Lintel 1972; Appleyard et al. 1981). Shopping streets with these characteristics are often the center of the communal life of a district.

The character of a street (or a square) very much depends on the types of the surrounding buildings and the activities they generate. A residential street is very different from those in the commercial areas of cities. The character of a street changes over the course of a day, a week, as the weather changes and from season to season. These changes are more dramatic in places with continental climates where both summers and winters are severe than in places with temperate or tropical climates. In most areas with continental or temperate climates, trees lose their leaves in the fall; in the tropics, trees may be evergreen but monsoon rains can result in streets becoming rivers and squares become lakes, particularly in cities with inadequate drainage systems.

The city of Venice is unique. No city can match the network of canals that give access for deliveries of people and goods by boat to its buildings, pathways and squares. Chinatown in San Francisco, like many Chinatowns around the world, has been heavily personalized by the types of shops and the signage. If a street is narrow enough, it can serve as a ribbon shopping strip because pedestrians are able to recognize the nature of items in the shop windows across it. Parked cars and jaywalkers slow the traffic. The street, despite the traffic on it, then acts as a seam.

A hilly terrain, as in San Francisco, gives a city a clear character. The hills occlude views that open up into vistas as one walks or drives along the streets in a way that almost automatically makes the view interesting (see the discussion of serial vision/sequential experience later in this book). The narrowness of Wall Street in New York makes it unattractive to vehicular traffic. Its 'pedestrianization' adds to the international reputation that it has as home to stock exchanges. Minneapolis or Calgary, with their extensive skyway networks that partially obscure long-distance views, are unique in the large number of links they possess at second floor level.[5]

The carriageway of a street serves as a link for vehicles although some streets also serve as occasional settings for public displays such as parades and other performances. Few streets are designed specifically for these additional functions although some large squares were created to serve or have come to serve as parade grounds. The Rajpath in New Delhi, created by the British Government of India, served the imperial power and now serves the government of independent India as both a symbolic axis and as a parade route (Figure 0.2 (a)).

The sidewalks of streets are primarily links along which pedestrians travel. They also contain 'places,' particularly at intersections, at spots where casual activities such as window shopping occur, where vendors hawk their wares and where people momentarily meet, greet and say farewell to each other. The ground floor uses of buildings and the frequency of entrances to them are major variables in establishing the visual and behavioral character of an open space, whether it is a street or square. Like streets, squares benefit from strong connections to the ground floor of the adjacent buildings. Such connections can be direct or via colonnades or verandas, doors of residences or shopfronts.

The cut-away plan of the banking district in Mumbai portrayed in Figure 0.3 (a) indicates the precinct's nature and why it is full of life in a way that an aerial view cannot. The streets are lined by frequent entrances and the activities within the ground floors can be seen from streets. Horniman Circle is a landmark in the area and has a fountain as a focus of attention at its center. The circle also possesses many

Figure 0.2 Streets as settings for parades: (a) Republic Day Parade, 1996, Rajpath, New Delhi; (b) Macy's Parade, 5th Avenue, New York

Sources: (a) Photograph by R. K. Dayal; (b) Photograph by lev radin/shutterstock.com.

Figure 0.3 *The ground floor of cities – the city at eye-level. (a) The banking district and Horniman Circle, Mumbai; (b) Street front, Collins Street, Melbourne; (c) Primrose Hill, London*

Source: (a) Drawing by Oleksandra Babych.

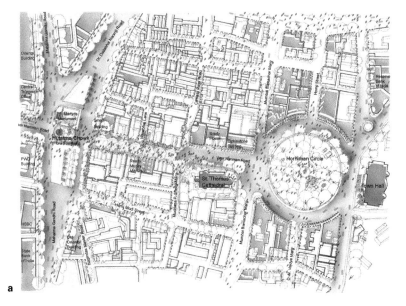

benches in a shaded environment provided by broad leaf evergreen trees. These benches are heavily used in Mumbai's tropical climate. While an aerial sketch could reveal much about the character of the precinct, the cut-away plan shows more. Dating from the 1860s, the circle now acts as a catalyst for commercial gentrification. The liveliness of the district is attracting international high-fashion shops to locate in the area. This change will lead to a change in the socioeconomic characteristic of the people visiting the precinct and add life to the square.

Squares/Plazas/Gardens/Greens and Parks

The terms gardens, parks and squares, particularly the latter two, are often used interchangeably. A square is usually considered to be a paved area surrounded by streets or at the intersection of streets and enclosed by buildings. Sometimes a square is planted with lawns and trees and used as a park. An urban park is basically defined as a public green space with vegetation and few, if any, buildings. It can range from being quite natural or well-manicured. Key functions include providing areas for recreation, green visual relief, and in some cases contributing to the local ecosystem. A public garden is a planned expanse laid out with parterres and walkways where the outdoors and nature in the form of trees and plants can be enjoyed by people. Such gardens vary in character from those with formal classical designs to those designed in the English landscape tradition. They are, nevertheless, often called squares. To confuse matters more, many shopping malls and even individual buildings are named 'Something Square.'

In many people's minds, particularly in Anglo-Saxon societies, a 'park' is regarded as more desirable than a 'square' and 'plaza' is more exotic than 'square'. 'Greens' can be added to the list. The UK *Commons Act of 2006* (Chapter 26: 1) is an "Act to make provision about common land and town or village greens; and for connected purposes." It does not state that a green has to be green and cannot be a paved area, and in fact, greens come in many forms. In England, some are cricket fields, others are market areas and others are simply visual point elements that act as a landmark. Plazas are predominantly the forecourts of buildings but the term has been applied to city squares and even to buildings.

Paternoster Square in London is clearly a square but St James's Square is a grassed area with crossing paths and an equestrian statue of William III as its central feature (Figures 0.4 (a) and (b)). It was originally a paved Italianate square. Paley Park in New York is entirely paved but replete with trees in rows. Its walls are ivy clad except its end wall which is a waterfall that drowns the sounds of the city. City Park in Bradford, like Paley Park, is almost entirely paved; we consider both of them to be squares. The recently proposed Canal Park in Washington is largely a paved place. Some of the squares we include in this book are called parks, gardens or plazas, but most are, indeed,

Figure 0.4 Squares: (a) Paternoster Square, London; (b) St James's Square, London

called squares. To complicate matters, 'squares' exist along with 'places' in Paris. While both might be regarded as squares elsewhere, the former term is generally applied to small garden squares while the latter refers to paved areas. Confusion persists. Place Vendôme is a paved square but Place des Vosges, in contrast, has a classic layout of paths and lawns with formally organized rows of trees (see Figures 8.3 (a) on p. 126 and 10.1 (b) on p. 151).

Squares may be entirely paved and treeless (for example, Paternoster Square in London), consist of both significant paved areas and significant areas of lawns and trees (for example, Rittenhouse Square in Philadelphia), or paved areas with only a few trees (for example, Martin Place, Sydney). Large settings of predominantly trees and lawns (for example, the Hyde Parks in London and Sydney), although very important in their urban contexts, fall outside the domain of consideration here.

The Design Issues of Concern

Despite cities being full of open space, it is often said that there is not enough of it. The image of the city in many people's minds is that of the dense, crowded industrial city of the nineteenth and early twentieth centuries. The Modern Movement in both city planning and urban design developed their ideas in response to the "Coketown" image of the city portrayed by Charles Dickens ([1854] 2003) in *Hard Time*s and picked up by Lewis Mumford (1961) in *The City in History*. Both the Rationalist[6] and Empiricist[7] branches of the Modern Movement sought more open space in cities as an antidote to a city's ills.

As a result of perceptions of the need for more open space, public policies have been created in a number of cities around the world to create more and better squares within them.[8] Cities that are attractive to wander through and linger in are those that draw both tourists and locals to spend time (and money) in them. Cities with highly populated squares and streets are envied by other cities which then strive to achieve similar success. To enhance urban circulation patterns and the esthetic quality of cities, streetscapes and sidewalks have been improved and many new squares built. On closer examination, the results have been mixed.

Many urban squares are very popular. Others are not used because they are poorly located with no nearby catchment of people. Some squares in dense areas may be difficult to physically reach due to intervening traffic, lack of over- or underpass access points, poor entrance signage, or have other obstacles in getting to them. Some squares are simply poorly designed. They serve no instrumental function. They are dull and boring, providing no affordances for potential users of the place. Other squares provide no public amenity on site or next to them. To compound this condition, if a square is not being used, people may think it is unsafe to be there and so do not enter the space. Figures 0.5 (a) and (b) present squares with missed opportunities.

City dwellers have benefited from many well-used and well-loved squares but, at the same time, many cities have forlorn, unloved and desolate new squares that add little to the city's prestige or liveability.

Figure 0.5 Squares with missed opportunities: (a) Adam Clayton Powell State Office Building Plaza, New York; (b) World's End Place, London

As an example, by the year 2000, New York's 1961 Incentive Zoning Resolution and subsequent amendments broadening its scope, had brought about 503 public spaces (privately owned) at 320 sites in the city in exchange for developers obtaining the right to increase the rentable floor area of their buildings (New York City Department of Planning 2007). A study by Jerold Kayden (2000) showed that many of the squares that resulted from the program have failed to add much to the quality of life of New Yorkers. They are little more than links between sidewalk and building.[9] Some squares serve little function other than to allow some sunlight to reach street level.

A cynical critic may suggest that private corporations see no benefit and have no desire to create open spaces that serve the public interest. One of a property developer's primary goals is certainly to increase the rentable commercial space in their buildings rather than to create well-loved squares. The string of squares at both sunken and street level along 6th Avenue in New York is one example of a number of recently developed areas of American cities that do little to enhance a city's public realm. The Adam Clayton Powell State Office Plaza on 125th Street in New York's Harlem has people sitting on the periphery watching the passing scene but it is a desolate space otherwise. Plans are now underway to upgrade it. The American experience is not unique. Cities all over the world have many loved squares but also those that are unused and neglected. Their intended function to improve the urban experience has not been fulfilled.

It seems that the planners and municipal authorities developing the policies to create such spaces had little idea of the factors that result in well-functioning public squares and those that do not.[10] Their policies and plans could have been more effective and had better outcomes. These findings and community opposition led to a significant curtailment of incentive programs in New York and elsewhere. We need to learn from the failures as well as the successes of such programs. We also need to learn from the performance of other squares around the world. What are the dimensions of their success or failure as perceived by whom?

The forecourt of the Guggenheim Museum in Bilbao is an example of a square that has acquired considerable notoriety in the decade since it was built. The space has its critics, suggesting it could relate more to its urban context and provide easier access to the museum entrance (Project for Public Spaces n.d.). It is surrounded by blank and textureless surfaces. On a positive note, the space is bathed in sunlight and provides a good place from which to photograph the museum. Jeff Koon's *Puppy* artwork adds a presence to an otherwise vacant space. The forecourt, however, is just that, a forecourt. Could it have been something more? An opportunity to create a lively urban space as part of Bilbao was missed.

Freeway Park in Seattle and Freedom Plaza in Washington, DC, are other examples of squares designed by internationally renowned architects and landscape architects that have not met their expectations as places in which to spend time.[11] The reasons are very different in the two cases. Both of the squares display the bold, intellectual ideas of their designers that underpin their layouts but these ideas have inadvertently created problems. Freeway Park (Figure 0.6 (a)) with its dark corners, obscuring walls, sequence of spaces and dense vegetation is an interesting place to be. However, for a long period its attractive features also gave it a reputation as a 'drug den' and location for other antisocial behavior (Mudede 2002). With some adaptations and better policing, it is now well used during the daytime. Freedom Plaza (Figure 0.6 (b)) attracts some tourists to consider the intellectual esthetic features of its paving but few linger and fewer visit it again. It is, however, featured in many architectural books and journals because of the strength of the intellectual ideas that shape its design.

In contrast to the limitations of some recently designed squares, a number of those that once flourished now languish. What made them successful places was not understood and changes were made to them and/or their surroundings that have had a detrimental effect on the way they function. Toopkhaneh Square in Tehran is an example

(see Figure 0.7). It was once the core, the heart, of Tehran with the City Hall on its north and the three-story Telecommunications Building on its south. Both buildings were built to the property line and provided not only a sense of enclosure but were also symbolically important. The buildings that framed the square have now been demolished. On the south is a new high-rise office building set back from the property line. It overshadows the square for much of the day. On the north side is a vast open air bus terminal. The buildings that enclosed it on the east and west have been largely replaced by roads. Traffic swirls around the square making it hazardous for pedestrians to access. It no longer seems like an outdoor room; the surrounding buildings fail to create a sense of enclosure. Now named Imam Khomeini Square, the equestrian statue of Pahlavi I that once was a significant feature in the square has been removed and the grand pedestal now supports a barely visible, politically acceptable art work (Figure 0.7 (c)). The sense of the square being an important place has been lost. It now primarily acts as a traffic circle.

These types of changes are seldom made maliciously but result from piecemeal pragmatic decisions made without a comprehensive understanding of or concern for their impacts. Planners and city managers should be basing their decisions on evidence and be more aware of the consequences of key decisions on how public open spaces function. Laurie Olin (2012: website), one of the leading landscape architects in the United States, in reflecting on his disappointment at the outcome of his and Ricardo Legorreta's design of Pershing Square in Los Angeles, said: "Our thinking was that we knew what we were doing in that situation, and we didn't." It is important that we get planning and design decisions right if the quality of the public realm of cities is to be enhanced.

Streets and squares are the places that provide the affordances for the sociability of a city's residents and visitors. While steps, street corners, street cafés and now pop-ups provide places for people to linger, squares are one of the centers for public life (Marshall 2016). The demise of public life has often been heralded but observations of city squares, both publicly and privately owned, show that it is alive and well despite many changes in people's everyday social practices resulting from better housing and new communications technolo-

Figure 0.6 Squares based on bold intellectual ideas: (a) Freeway Park, Seattle; (b) Freedom Plaza, Washington, DC

Source: (a) Photograph by Kate Bishop.

Figure 0.7 *The unmaking of a square through piecemeal surrounding development: (a) Toopkhaneh Square, Tehran, in 1942; (b) Imam Khomeini Square in 2012, view of the former City Hall site; (c) The pedestal of the statue*

Source: Talab (2008: 74).

gies.[12] Squares continue to make an important contribution to civic life and some have a catalytic effect on the economy of cities.[13]

Many squares have been built in cities around the world during the past 50 years; countless more have been refurbished.[14] They may have been created as the result of political pressure for more open space exerted by the public or specific interest groups. Given the amount of money being spent on them, it is important to design them well. Campus Martius in Detroit, which was redeveloped in 2004, is an example where monies appear to have been well spent. It was built on a derelict site by a public-private development partnership. The square (although now called a park) has become a popular spot for residents and workers to linger because it tapped into a latent demand for such a place. A winter ice-skating rink and a summer beach as well as formal events are activities that attract people downtown in what is regarded as a city in economic trouble (Crommelin 2016). The square has also had a catalytic effect on the development of the surrounding area. Most people overlook the intrusion of the noise from a busy road nearby. However, not everybody appreciates having a lively square nearby as some locals may have preferred a quiet oasis.

The capacity of making and/or remaking public space to enhance the quality of daily life of people has been demonstrated in the public policy efforts of municipal governments all over the world. In Medellín, Colombia, for instance, "civic pride has been buoyed by new public buildings and squares" (Kimmelman 2012: 8).[15] The state-owned Empresas Públicas de Medellín has invested its profits in the building of the city's public infrastructure, including some new squares and the refurbishment of others. While avoiding the trap of thinking deterministically about the impact of such changes in the built environment on social behavior, the correlation between the improvement in the infrastructure of the city and social indicators is impressive (Berney 2010).

Social programs and environmental design policies are often complementary. The investment in public spaces in Medellín sends a message to its residents, in particular, those who reside in its poorer neighborhoods, that they and their community are valued and worth investing in. The results show that the intellectual esthetic concerns of architects interested in squares as artistic displays and social concerns can be considered simultaneously (Kimmelman 2012). The municipal authorities who have sought prestigious squares for their cities and the designers have often failed to recognize (or have rejected) this truism when developing a number of the squares described later in this book.

As mentioned, cities such as London, Paris and New York have invested heavily in the improvement of their public environments and continue to do so. In London, Mayor Boris Johnson, in conjunction with the Landscape Institute, challenged designers to come up with ideas for innovative 'green spaces' for the city, including grids of trees (Abbott 2012). In New York, Times Square is one among many places that have been and continue to be upgraded to make them more hospitable to pedestrians. Paris will obtain 'le noveau cœur' at Châtelet with a new Place M. de Navarra and a Forum des Halles. The

Figure 0.8 Paris, a recently upgraded square: (a) Place de la République, Paris, before redesign; (b) After redesign

Sources: (a) Photograph by Carles Tomás Martí/Flickr; (b) Photograph by Clem/Flickr.

Place de la République in Paris has already been upgraded and was reopened in June 2013 (Hough 2013) (Figure 0.8).

Much effort has also been expended on upgrading existing places in many other cities, large and small, around the world. In Puigcerdà, Spain, a town with a population of fewer than 9,000 people, the deteriorated central square has been renovated. Pepe Gascón Arquitectura redesigned the square and its context by diverting the vehicular traffic that used to surround it, simplifying an irregular space and improving lighting and street furniture (Gascón 2012). It has become a pleasant place in which to linger. At the same time, other upgraded places have yet to capture the hearts of a city's citizens. They are either in a poor location or are poorly designed or both. In some cases the focus on manifesting architectural ideas – intellectual esthetics considerations – in built form has led to opportunity costs being incurred by new squares. Schouwburgplein in Rotterdam is an example discussed in Chapter 12.

New squares continue to be built. Some are being built by city governments but others form part of large-scale privately funded urban renewal and new precinct projects. In London, Granary Square, part of the redevelopment around the city's King's Cross Station and facing the University of Arts London/ Central St Martins College of Arts and Design, was opened in 2012. A private enterprise project and the result of neoliberal economic policies, Granary Square is one of Europe's largest new squares.

The cost, financial and political, of refurbishing squares or creating new ones is not trivial. For example, the redevelopment of Place de la République in Paris cost €30 million and the renovation of Piccadilly Gardens in Manchester cost £10 million. The contracted price for rehabilitating Times Square is US$40 million and may exceed that during the three years required to implement the current proposal, given that specific problems needing attention are likely to arise during the construction process. The time and money allocated to all such efforts need to be well spent.

Conclusion

Many different types of squares exist in cities. Each serves a current set of purposes that may differ from the ones intended when it was built. Over time, some have been successful in providing for the activities and enjoyment of the people who use them. Others have become forgotten and fallen into disrepair. As the world continues to urbanize and the cores of cities become more populated and dense, urban open areas and, more specifically squares, are becoming increasingly important in the urban fabric. Many squares are being built and many more refurbished. This Prologue has pointed out that some squares function well on almost any dimension of analysis but others are disappointing places. The aim of this book is to describe and explain how squares function and to present to readers our current understanding of what works and what does not work in meeting specific design objectives.

Notes

1 The term *affordance* was coined by perception psychologist James J. Gibson (1966, 1979). It signifies the potential uses to which a physical object or environment can be put, given the competence level of a person or people or any other species of concern. Although there is no such word in the English language, it has slipped easily into the vocabulary of architects and urban designers. Its use avoids trapping designers into thinking deterministically about the impact of the built environment on human behavior. For a fuller description and references to other sources, see Lang and Moleski (2010).

2 We are using the American term, "sidewalk," for what are called pavements or footpaths in other countries.

3 Many cities have more open space and are lower in residential density than they were 100 years ago. Manhattan, for instance, has had a dramatic decrease in residential density since 1910 (Yglesias 2014). They are, nevertheless, denser. The number of tall office buildings that overshadow the ground floor of cities – the pedestrians' world – has increased dramatically along with the increase in the number of more middle-class office workers.

4 Many authors have brought attention to the importance of streets and streetscapes in establishing the character of cities. Jane Jacobs (1961), Allan Jacobs (1993), Karl Kropf (1996), Michael Southworth and Eran Ben Joseph (1997) and Vikas Mehta (2009, 2013a, 2013b) are among them.

5 The US designation of floor levels is used throughout this book. First floor here would be ground floor in much of the world.

6 As represented by Le Corbusier's 'city in a park' rather than a 'park in the city' model of the future city.

7 As represented by the Garden City Movement.

8 The *Cento Piazza* Program developed under Mayor Francesco Rutelli in Rome during the 1990s and the *100 Spaces* program of Mayor Ken Livingstone (2002) in London and the *Great Spaces* program of his successor Boris Johnson (2009) are European examples; New York's incentive zoning is an American one. John Punter (2011) describes similar efforts in England and Rachel Berney (2010) the work in Bogota.

9 See Whyte (1989) and Kayden (2000) on the New York City's Incentive Program's results and, more generally, Carr *et al.* (1992). Jared Green (2012) provides examples of poor results in Europe.

10 Many controls, incentives and guidelines have not achieved the outcomes that officials sought. Emily Talen (2011) considers the role of zoning in shaping cities often in unintentional ways.

11 The former was the work of the firm of Lawrence Halprin and the latter of Robert Venturi and Denise Scott Brown.

12 The demise of publicly owned open space in the United States has been observed by Michael Sorkin and others (Sorkin 1992). While much publicly accessible space is now controlled by private organizations, much still remains public and popular.

13 See Madanipour (1999) for the importance of high quality public spaces for cities.

14 London alone has some 230 proposed, new or substantially regenerated spaces with 100 since 1980 but mostly from 2000 (Carmona 2014a, 2014b).

15 Medellín was selected as "City of the Year" in March 2013 by the *Wall Street Journal* and *Citi* magazine for the civic improvements made in it over a 20-year period. The city, nevertheless, continues to have significant social problems.

References

Abbott, Joz (2012) London seeks 'high-line design'. *Architectural Record*. Available at: http://archrecord.construction.com/yb/ar/article.asp?stc

Appleyard, Donald and Mark Lintell (1972) The environmental quality of streets. *Journal of the American Institute of Planners* 38(2): 84–101.

Appleyard, Donald, M., Sue Gerson and Mark Lintell (1981) *Livable Streets*. Berkeley, CA: University of California Press.

Berney, Rachel (2010) Learning from Bogotá: How municipal experts transformed public space. *Journal of Urban Design* 15(4): 539–558.

Carmona, Matthew (2014a) The place-shaping continuum: A theory of urban design process. *Journal of Urban Design* 19(1): 2–36.

Carmona, Matthew (ed.) (2014b) *Explorations in Urban Design: An Urban Design Primer*. Farnham: Ashgate.

Carr, Stephen, Mark Francis, Leanne G. Rivlin and Andrew D. Stone (1992) Grace Plaza, New York, New York. In *Urban Space*. Cambridge: Cambridge University Press, pp. 177–180.

Crommelin, Laura (2016) Examining place-making in practice: Observations from Detroit. In *Place and Placelessness Revisited*, edited by Robert Freestone and Edgar Liu. New York: Routledge, pp.153–167.

Dickens, Charles ([1854] 2003) *Hard Times*. London: Penguin.

Gascón, Pepe (2012) Squares in Puigcerdà. Available at: www.archdaily.com/126579/squares-in-puigcerda-pepe-gascon.

Gibson, James J. (1966) *The Senses Considered as Perceptual Systems*. Boston: Houghton Mifflin.

Gibson, James J. (1979) *The Ecological Approach to Visual Perception*. Boston: Houghton Mifflin.

Green, Jared (2012) Paver power. *The Dirt*. American Society of Landscape Architects. Available at: http://dirt.asla.org/2012/07/05/paver-power.

HM Government (2006) *Commons Act (c.26)*. London: The Stationery Office.

Hough, Mark (2013) Cool happenings in Paris's urban landscape. *Planetizen*, June 25. Available at: www.planetizen.com/node/63833.

Jacobs, Allan B. (1993) *Great Streets*. Cambridge, MA: MIT Press.

Jacobs, Jane (1961) *The Death and Life of Great American Cities*. New York: Random House.

Johnson, Boris (2009) *The Mayor's Great Spaces*. London: Greater London Authority.

Kayden, Jerold S. (2000) *Privately Owned Public Space: The New York City Experience*. New York: John Wiley & Sons Inc.

Kimmelman, Michael (2012) A city arises along with its hopes. *The New York Times*, June 25, p. 8.

Kropf, Karl (1996) Urban tissue and the character of towns. *Urban Design International* 1: 247–263.

Lang, Jon and Walter Moleski (2010) *Functionalism Revisited: Architectural Theory and Practice and the Behavioral Sciences*. Farnham: Ashgate.

Litt, Steven (2014) The Public Square debate. *The Plain Dealer*, August 28. Available at: www.cleveland.com/architecture/index.ssf/2014/08/the_public_square_debate_rtas.html#incart_m-rpt-1.

Livingstone, Ken (2002) *Making Space for Londoners*. London: Greater London Authority.

Madanipour, Ali (1999) Why are design and development of public open spaces significant for cities? *Environment and Planning B: Planning and Design* 26: 879–891.

Marshall, Nancy (2016) Urban squares: a place for public life. In *Place and Placelessness Revisited*, edited by Robert Freestone and Edgar Liu. New York: Routledge.

Mehta, Vikas (2009) Look closely and you will see, listen carefully and you will hear: Urban design and social interaction on streets. *Journal of Urban Design* 14(1): 29–64.

Mehta, Vikas (2013a) *The Street: A Quintessential Social Public Space*. London: Routledge.

Mehta, Vikas (2013b) Evaluating public space. *Journal of Urban Design* 19(1): 53–58.

Monfries, Alice (2012) Adelaide City Council reveals master plan for $95 million Victoria Square redevelopment. *Sunday Mail*, May 5. Available at: www.adelaidenow.com.au/news/south-australia/adelaide-city-council-reveals-masterplan-for-95-million-victoria-square-redevelopment/story-e6frea83-1226347668984.

Mudede, Charles (2002) Topography of terror. *The Stranger*, August 22. Available at: www.thestranger.com/seattle/topography-of-terror/Content?oid =11685.

Mumford, Lewis (1961) *The City in History*. New York: Harcourt, Brace and World.

New York City Department of City Planning (2007) Privately owned public plazas: Text amendment. Available at: www.nyc.gov/html/dcp/pdf/ priv/101707_final_approved.text.pdf.

Olin, Laurie (2012) *The Architect's Newspaper*, June 15. Available at: www. archpaper.com/news/articles.asp?id=6117.

Project for Public Spaces (n.d.) Hall of Shame: Available at: www.pps.org/ great_public_spaces/list?type_id=2.

Punter, John (2011) Urban design and the English urban renaissance 1999– 2009: A review and preliminary evaluation. *Journal of Urban Design* 16(1): 1–42.

Rodriguez, Roberto (2005) The foundational process of cities in Spanish America: The Law of Indies as a planning tool for urbanization in early colonial towns in Venezuela. *Focus* 2(1): 46–57.

Sorkin, Michael (ed.) (1992) *Variations on a Theme Park: The New American City and the End of Public Space*. New York: Hill and Wang.

Southworth, Michael and Eran Ben Joseph (1997) *Streets and the Shaping of Towns and Cities*. New York: McGraw-Hill.

Talab, Hamid R. N. (2008) *Tehran: Past and Present: A Glance at the Features of Life, Art and Architecture*. Trans. by Ali F. Dana Gharavi. Tehran: Yassavoli Publication.

Talen, Emily (2011) *City Rules: How Regulations Affect Urban Form*. Washington, DC: Island Press.

Whyte, William H. (1989) *City: Rediscovering the Center*. New York: Doubleday.

Yglesias, Matthew (2014) Manhattan's population is way lower than it was 100 years ago. Available at: www.vox.com/2014/9/23/6832975/manhattan- population-density-is-way-lower-then-it-was 100-years-ago/.

Further Reading

Carmona, Matthew, Tim Heath, Taner Oc and Steve Tiesdell (2003) *Public Places – Urban Squares: The Dimensions of Urban Design*. Oxford: Architectural Press.

Cogger, Rachel (2016) Tuning in and out of Place. *In Place and Placelessness Revisited*, edited by Robert Freestone and Edgar Liu. New York: Routledge, pp. 120–137.

Dimendberg, Edward (2004) *Film Noir and the Spaces of Modernity*. Cambridge, MA: Harvard University Press.

Engwicht, David (1999) *Street Reclaiming: Creating Liveable Streets and Vibrant Communities*. Gabriola Island, BC: New Society Publishing.

Francis, Mark (2003) *Urban Open Space: Designing for User Needs*. Washington, DC: Island Press.

Krier, Rob (1979) *Urban Space*, trans. from the German by Christine Czechowski and George Black. New York: Random House.

Moughton, Cliff (2003) *Urban Design: Street and Square*, 3rd edn. Oxford: Architectural Press.

van Uffelen, Chris (2012) *Plazas, Squares and Streetscapes*. Salenstein: Braun.

PART I

INTRODUCTION

La Cours Honoré d'Estienne d'Orves, Marseille
Photograph by Gilles Martin-Raget.

The Prologue addressed the question, 'Why is it important to write about urban squares?' Part I consists of three chapters that present the way we think about squares and the people who visit them and the reasons why they visit them.

Chapter 1 presents our brief but important understanding of the processes of environmental perception and cognition. A number of competing theories of perception currently exist among psychologists. We have adopted and adapted the ecological theory of environmental perception proposed originally by James Gibson (1950, 1966, 1979) for our contemporary purposes.[1] It explains how we perceive the everyday world around us rather than the theoretical approaches that are built on research conducted in the tightly controlled environment of the research lab. Three observations drawn from the ecological theory of perception are crucial to our analysis. The first is that perception is an active process; we search the environment for information that is of use to us although some outside information impinges on our senses. The second is that perception is multi-modal, that is, we see, hear, smell and touch the world around us. This book is full of photographs that give some visual image of what squares are like; however, they are a limited representation of a world full of color, sounds, odors and tactile experiences that are partially described in words but largely have to be imagined. The third observation is that movement is fundamental to a genuine perception of our surroundings. The images in this book are all presented, however, from a single station point.

With a basic knowledge of how we perceive and understand the world around us, the question becomes, 'How then to best consider urban squares?' We maintain an ecological viewpoint by relying on the psychological approach of Roger Barker (1968) and his contemporaries.[2] In particular, the concept of behavior settings has informed our analysis. In Chapter 2, we argue that considering urban squares as places and links leads to an understanding of how they function. Squares are, however, inevitably displays that have evolved over time or been designed by architects and landscape architects. They carry explicit and implicit messages available for interpretation by the people who use or view them as recognized by environmental and social psychologists,[3] a number of phenomenologists[4] and many architects.[5]

In Chapter 3, we discuss the people who are likely to use squares and the affordances they seek. We continue with an ecological line of thought. Most cities today have highly diverse populations. Even in ethnically homogeneous societies there are considerable economic disparities. Based on different characteristics, such as age, gender, physical ability, culture or other personal attributes, people consider the affordances of squares differently. The cognoscenti, that is, those with specialist design knowledge, will examine a square in terms of a design paradigm or their knowledge of the intentions of a square's designer as an artist. All of these differences make the task of setting design goals and the means of fulfilling them difficult and often politically charged for municipal authorities and designers alike.

The thesis that we present in this part of the book is that squares can best be considered to consist of two major components: (1) effective behavior settings as places and links; and (2) as effective displays. By effective, we mean those that are used and enjoyed. Considering squares in this manner enables an observer to understand how they function for various activities and how they function as meaningful symbols for the inhabitants and visitors of a city.

Notes

1 See also Reed and Jones (1982) and Reed (1988, 1996).
2 See Gump (1971), Le Compte (1974), Barker and Schoggen (1973), Lang (1987), Kaminski (1989), Heft (2001) and Lang and Moleski (2010).
3 Gibson (1950, 1966, 1979), Wicker (2002) and Gifford (2007), for example.
4 Relph (1976), Norburg-Schulz (1980) and Seamon (1993), for example.
5 See Lefaivre (2003), for example.

References

Barker, Roger (1968) *Ecological Psychology: Concepts and Methods for Studying the Environment of Human Behavior*. Stanford, CA: Stanford University Press.

Barker, Roger and Phil Schoggen (1973) *Qualities of Community Life*. San Francisco: Jossey-Bass.

Gibson, James J. (1950) *The Perception of the Visual World*. Boston: Houghton Mifflin.

Gibson, James J. (1966) *The Senses Considered as Perceptual Systems*. Boston: Houghton Mifflin.

Gibson, James J. (1979) *The Ecological Approach to Visual Perception*. Boston: Houghton Mifflin.

Gifford, Robert (2007) *Environmental Psychology: Principles and Practice*. Colville: Optimal Books.

Gump, Paul V. (1971) The behavior setting: A promising unit for environmental design. *Landscape Architecture* 61(2): 130–134.

Heft, Harry (2001) *Ecological Psychology in Context: James Gibson, Roger Barker and the Legacy of William James*. Mahwah, NJ: Lawrence Erlbaum Publishers.

Kaminski, Gerard (1989) The relevance of ecologically oriented theory building in environment and behavior research. In *Advances in Environment, Behavior, and Design*, vol. II, edited by Ervin H. Zube and Gary T. Moore. New York: Plenum Press, pp. 3–36.

Lang, Jon (1987) *Creating Architectural Theory: The Role of the Behavioral Sciences in Environmental Design*. New York: Van Nostrand Reinhold.

Lang, Jon and Walter Moleski (2010) *Functionalism Revisited: Architectural Theory and Practice and the Behavioral Sciences*. Farnham: Ashgate.

Le Compte, William F. (1974) Behavior settings as data-gathering units for the environmental planner and architect. In *Designing for Human Behavior: Architecture and the Behavioral Sciences*, edited by Jon Lang, Charles Burnette, Walter Moleski and David Vachon. Stroudsburg, PA: Dowden, Hutchinson and Ross, pp. 183–193.

Lefaivre, Liane (2003) Critical regionalism: A facet of modern architecture since 1945. In *Critical Regionalism: Architecture and Identity in a Globalized World*, edited by Liane Lefaivre and Alexander Tzonis. London: Prestel, pp. 22–55.

Norberg-Schulz, Christian (1980) *Genius Loci: Towards a Phenomenology of Architecture*. New York: Rizzoli.

Reed, Edward S. (1988) *James J. Gibson and the Psychology of Perception*. New Haven, CT: Yale University Press.

Reed, Edward S. (1996) *Encountering the World: Toward an Ecological Psychology*. New York: Oxford University Press.

Reed, Edward S. and Rebecca Jones (1982) *Reasons for Realism: Selected Essays of James J. Gibson*. Hillsdale, NJ: Lawrence Erlbaum.

Relph, Edward (1976) *Place and Placelessness*. London: Pion.

Seamon, David (1993) *Dwelling, Seeing and Designing: Toward a Phenomenological Ecology*. Albany, NY: State University of New York Press.

Wicker, Alan W. (2002) Ecological psychology: Historical contexts, current conception, prospective directions. In *Handbook of Environmental Psychology*, edited by Robert B. Bechtel and Azra Churchman. New York: John Wiley & Sons, Inc. pp. 114–126.

CHAPTER I

EXPERIENCING PUBLIC OPEN SPACES[1]

An understanding of how we experience the world around us provides the foundation on which an understanding of the utility and meaning of public spaces can be built. The quality of any square, for instance, depends on the individual perception of a person and his or her values. What we pay attention to in the environment around us is based on our motivations and attitudes. These motivations, in turn, are directed by our knowledge of the world and what its patterns afford us. We appear to have mental schema that can be regarded as templates that guide the process of perception.[2] Without understanding the processes of perception, any commentary on human activities within the built environment and/or feelings about it is limited in scope.

Environmental Perception

Perception is the active process of obtaining information from the environment (Gibson 1979). We scan the world around us for information that is of instrumental utility for us or for its own sake because it gives us pleasure. Some information, especially that which is deviant from the norm, also impinges on our awareness; it attracts our attention.

Humans possess five perceptual systems of which the most basic is our orienting system that enables us, via the vestibular organs of the inner ear, to detect the forces of gravity and acceleration. We have little control over this perceptual system but it is fundamental to actions, activities and experiences. Our other perceptual systems also provide us with information that shapes our everyday lives. The experiencing of the world around us is multi-modal as identified by all perception psychologists but heeded by only a few architects, city planners and architectural critics.[3] Drawings and photographs, as in this book, draw attention to what we see.[4] In urban design it is no easy task to characterize sounds, odors, tactile and metabolic experiences which cannot be represented in drawing form and thus have to be imagined.

Unless visually impaired, we primarily examine the environment via our visual perceptual system that consists of the eyes and our ability to turn our head and body to focus our attention on aspects of the world around us. The system enables us to understand the source of both radiant, but more particularly and importantly, ambient, reflected light. We use our auditory system for listening. It enables us to pick up the vibrations in the air that tell us about the nature and location of what we regard as sounds. Sounds bounce off walls so they can originate outside the range of our vision. Our haptic systems enable us to obtain information through the skin, joints and muscles by touching different surfaces. What we perceive tells us much about the nature of the ground on which we stand. We also use touch to understand the shapes and textures of objects and their solidity or viscosity. Through touch and our metabolic processes that inform us of the temperature around us, we feel whether we are comfortable or not. Our smell and taste systems enable us, via our noses and mouths, to understand the nature and composition of the air that we breathe and the food and drinks that we consume. Like sounds, aromas, unpleasant or pleasing, can also originate outside our line of vision. Aromas waft in the air and form part of the ambient quality of urban squares.

The Ambient Qualities of Squares

The qualities of the ambient environment are important in people's appreciation of the world around them. Pleasant experiences are positive but we can also cope with many unpleasant qualities of the built environment that impinge on our experience. The quality of light, the sounds, smells and textures of what is around us all affect our assessments of the spaces we inhabit.

The way squares are illuminated by sunlight and/or by artificial light contributes substantially to the manner in which people experience them. The squares described in this book are located at a variety of latitudes so the angles of the sun penetrating and illuminating them vary considerably as the time of the day and the seasons change. Direct sunlight into or reflected light from the walls surrounding any open space dictates those areas that are comfortable places in which to spend time. In the tropics and during the summer in temperate climates, shaded areas will be popular. In spring and autumn, we may seek the sun; in winter, we definitely will. The quality of light in a square depends not only on the latitude of a place but also on the nature of the elements that surround it.

The height of buildings or trees surrounding a square shapes the amount of light entering it. At the higher latitudes, the sun is lower in the sky than in the tropics. In summer, the noonday sun in the northern hemisphere (where most of the examples cited in this book are located) is to the south, the sunrise and sunset are increasingly to the north as the summer solstice approaches. The opposite is true in the southern hemisphere. At the higher latitudes, the mid-summer daylight hours are extensive and the mid-winter hours limited. In the tropics, the length of daylight and the height of the noonday sun vary considerably less.

The illumination of the vegetation – trees in particular – and the walls surrounding an open square affect the perception of the place's warmth through both direct and radiant light. Sunlight creates patterns of light and shade and patches of heat and coolness as one walks through a square. Sunlight playing on the textures of the surfaces surrounding it adds much to the quality of a square. In some cases, such as Times Square in New York or London's Piccadilly Circus (or in spaces like Shibuya Crossing in Tokyo), the plethora of neon and LED advertisings lights covering the surrounding walls are as much an aspect of a square's sense of place as any other factor. While the quality of light and illumination in a square is fundamental to our experiences, it is by no means the sole factor.

The sources and levels of sounds are major factors in the appreciation of being in a square. The sources can be highly varied: some are pleasing, some unpleasant. They range from the whispering of the breeze through trees, to the voices of people talking and children playing, to the chirping of birds and music being played. Sounds, when perceived as unpleasant are called noise and can be intrusive, whatever their sources. The major urban intrusions come from the noise of machines, traffic and heating/cooling systems. Many much-loved squares are isolated from the sounds of passing traffic. Yet some of the major squares in the world, Times Square in New York and Trafalgar Square in London, for example, are noisy places although attempts have been made and are being made to ameliorate the sound levels from passing vehicles. People in squares under the flight paths of aircraft have to contend with more intermittent and higher pitched sounds.

Falling water is sometimes used to override sounds that are regarded as unpleasant. Paley Park in New York is one of the best-known examples. On occasions, such a sound can be overwhelming, as it was in Central Square in Melbourne, Australia, where the fountain has been much reduced in size. City planners have historically managed noise mitigation using city by-laws but other approaches such as landscape features are now being tried. Art installations that purposefully construct the sonic environment have been installed to provide sounds that counteract the noise coming from the surroundings of a square.[5] The quality of the soundscape is often overlooked in designing squares. The quality of odors is even less frequently considered.

Odors, like sounds, have many sources and can be pleasant or unpleasant. Odors waft into squares from traffic, buildings and passing people. The natural scent of flowers and other vegetation, perfumes and often foods, such as freshly baked bread, can be pleasant. The smells emanating from exhaust fans of kitchens or from vehicles, from passing garbage trucks and from poorly maintained toilets on site are unpleasant, although we do soon adapt to unpleasant odors to a remarkable extent. Many fountains are chlorinated as a health precaution but the smell of chlorine does not seem to deter people from frolicking in them on a hot day. If we seldom pay much attention to designing with scents in mind, designing for tactile experiences is only marginally more frequently explicitly considered.

The proposed tactile quality of the surfaces of a square is implicit in most designs. The surfaces of the environment are the fundamental elements of squares and our experience of them visually and tac-

Figure 1.1 Textural qualities of surfaces and haptic experience: (a) Granary Square terrace, London, 2013; (b) The same terrace in 2014

tilely shapes our feelings about them. The ground surface can be paved, gravel, sand, grass, rough or smooth. Each offers a different feeling underfoot and different sounds as one walks on it. Benches and retaining walls that afford seating and lying on come in materials of different insulating qualities that absorb, or generate different levels of heat. They have different levels of hardness and heights that provide differing comfort levels as one sits. There are elements, such as street furniture or vegetation, which we can explore with our hands. All of these characteristics provide affordances for human experiences. How sensitive we are to them depends on our level of interest.

Our world may be ocular-centric (focused on the visual) but our experiencing of the qualities of squares is multi-modal. Richard Sennett (1998) asserts that physical contact with the forms of the built environment – the tactile experience – is an important catalyst for creative place-making. The change of surface material of the terrace leading down to Regent's Canal at London's Granary Square between 2013 and 2014 results in a very different tactile experience for those seated there. The ambient quality was different on the two days too. The 2013 photograph was taken on a cool spring day while the 2014 photograph was taken in the summer (Figure 1.1).

Meanings of Patterns of Built Form

Places such as squares are meaningful. We have emotional feelings about being in them depending on the experiences we have had in everyday life and through our formal education or other institutions. Patterns of built form have four levels of meaning that shape our responses to the world around us. The basic is the concrete meaning. We learn the qualities of surfaces and materials as objects and environments. Are they solid or viscous? The second level is their affordances – the use to which the patterns can be put. Can they be climbed on, for instance? The patterns also act as signs that provide us with meanings through conventions by coding cultural ideas and references. At the highest level the patterns act as symbols; they have meanings that go beyond representation.

Both the physical elements of the world – streets, buildings, vegetation – and the people and their activities around us are meaningful.

These meanings are central to our liking or disliking of places. The processes that generate feelings of liking or disliking depend on our attitudes which, in turn, depend on our beliefs about what we perceive and the values we hold. Our values define what we determine to be attractive or repulsive elements of the environment. We strive to keep the values we hold of the physical and social world around us consistent with each other – that is, in balance.

Balance Theory (originally formulated by Heider 1958 and more recently adapted by Hummon and Doreian 2003) suggests that if a person is positive about a set of ideas, places or experiences (the referent), then that person's attitudes towards a similar idea, place or experience will also be positive. The reverse is the same – if a person is negative about a set of ideas, places or experiences, then when similar ones are presented, a negative response will be formed. The attitude to the association between the patterns of the environment and the referent is what establishes our feelings about the pattern of built form being perceived. Having said that, the values we hold can change over time as we are exposed to new experiences. We attempt to eliminate incongruities by changing our beliefs or values; we strive for cognitive consistency (Festinger 1962; Cooper and Fazio 1984).

A Further Note on the Perception of Affordances

People, animals and even insects scan the environment to understand the layout of the world and the objects, materials, motions, events and places that are important to them within it. We scan the world to learn more about it and to ascertain what aspects of it are of use to us – what it can afford us, that is, its utility for us (Gibson 1979; Kaminski 1989; Reed 1996; Heft 2001).

Each person looks for different affordances in the patterns of the built environment, given his or her motivations. As generalizations, children may look at a square as a potential playground, for elements to climb on, adolescents as places to skateboard (if allowed or not or just to 'hang out,' young adults as places to meet others, adults as places to rest, eat or as a meeting point and the elderly as places to chat and feel part of a community. Nancy Marshall (2016) argues that squares afford a place for public life more generally, especially in compact twenty-first-century cities.

The affordances that we actually use depend on our perceptions of the cost and rewards of engaging in a particular behavior within culturally acceptable norms (Helmreich 1974; Lang and Moleski 2010). Urban squares and other open spaces within the city provide not only the affordances for activities and the formation and development of different behaviors but they also carry symbolic meanings that we learn to understand. Some messages remain beyond our comprehension as observers although they may be meaningful to their creators.[6]

The Sequential Experiencing of the Built Environment

The role of motion and movement through spaces is central to the perception of the world around us. Walking is basic to our comprehending and enjoying (or not) the urban environment.[7] What is important in establishing visually interesting environments is the experience of movement past occluding elements to reveal new vistas. Gordon Cullen (1961) differentiated between the visual transformations that take place in the environment when a pedestrian moves around an object – a building, sculpture or fountain – and the movement through space (Figure 1.2).

Figure 1.2 (a) shows the transformation of the optic array as one moves around a series of buildings and Figure 1.2 (b) shows how new vistas emerge as one moves through a set of grouped squares. In the latter, the changes of vistas occur as the observer moves through covered gateways, or 'ports.' These ports can take any number of forms. All are comprised of opaque or translucent occluding surfaces. The transformation in the optic array through a sequence of 'station points' is slower and holds our attention less when the squares are large unless they contain specific objects of interest that we can examine as we move past or around them. Experimental studies have shown that there is a correlation between the complexity of the optic array and interestingness and also between novelty and interestingness as one moves through the urban environment. How interesting something is is also correlated with perceptions of how pleasant something is. The question to be asked is, 'When does complexity result in chaos?' It seems that perceptions of geometric order as well as

Figure 1.2 Serial vision/sequential experience as analyzed by Gordon Cullen: (a) Serial vision moving around objects; (b) Serial vision moving through an environment

Source (a) and (b): Cullen (1961: 17).

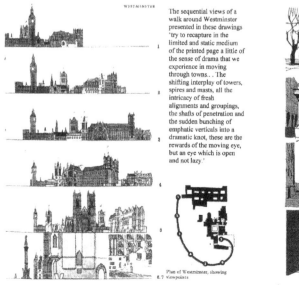

a

b

complexity are a necessary ingredient in liking or disliking the visual qualities of a square. Personality and habituation levels – what one is accustomed to seeing – are intervening variables in the equation.[8]

The details of what one can see at various distances can form the basis for creating principles for making design decisions. At a distance of 22–25 meters (73–83 feet), a person can see the facial expressions of another individual; as that person approaches, the amount of detail one can see is enhanced. The same is true of building details, sculpture and lettering.[9] What one pays attention to in any sequence depends on one's purposes and if any of one's perceptual systems is impaired (Thiel 1961).

Cullen's (1961) analysis focuses on the visual world but the information we pick up via our other perceptual systems also comes in sequences. For a visually impaired person, the sequence of sounds reverberating from surrounding surfaces and the haptic experience of those surfaces (particularly those underfoot) when they are touched become important. This information is available for the attention of the sighted but we seldom notice it to the same extent as a person who is visually impaired. It nevertheless impinges subconsciously on our experiences. It is possible to design for the sequence of sounds and odors but this is rarely done. The sequence of scents in a garden can be orchestrated as a work of art.

Experiencing Squares as Works of Art: Intellectual Esthetic Constructs

All squares have a design. The design may be the self-conscious work of a single author or group or may have emerged piece-by-piece over time at the hands of numerous people. A square may contain fountains and sculptures that are memorials to specific events or people. Sculptures may simply be placed in specific locations as abstract or realistic works of art. Perceiving them, if they are not ignored, may evoke feelings in people based on the meanings that the sculptures have for them. Different people will respond to environments and objects based on what they perceive them to represent and the value that they attach to the representation. The swastika, for instance, is a Sanskrit symbol, meaning good fortune and well-being for many people in South Asia. It also has positive connotations for the indigenous people of South America. For many in Europe, however, it is the sign of Nazism. The use of a swastika on a wall of the capital complex in Chandigarh by Le Corbusier has a very different meaning than it would have had if placed in a square in France, for example. Designers working internationally have to be conscious of the variety of meanings, sometimes subtle, of shapes, patterns and certainly colors.

Many squares are consciously designed to express an architect's personal intellectual ideas as works of fine art. To architects, landscape architects and other design experts, the manner in which a square, as a display, represents a style of design or the œuvre of its designer is important. To the general public, it seldom is. Fashions and design theories, that is, design ideologies, change over time.

At a particular point in history, there has been a general consensus among the cognoscenti as to what are good designs and what are poor designs and how a specific design expresses a particular design paradigm. In today's postmodern world with an emphasis on individual expressions, a variety of paradigms exist, each with its supporters.

An architect's work may well be recognizable because of the repetitive use of specific patterns of form in a number of designs. Design experts will evaluate a square in terms of their own attitudes to the messages the architect or landscape architect is trying to communicate, based on their own esthetic preferences. An understanding of the link between a design idea and the design pattern is thus a product of an intellectual esthetic analysis. Such analyses are an important aspect of many people's lives, particularly those of design professionals. They will analyse a square to see the extent to which it meets its designer's goals in terms of the sensory experiences it offers, the patterns it possesses and the intellectual reasoning behind them and for the associations they evoke.

Conclusion

The fundamental processes of environmental perception are essentially universal, although some physiological differences do exist among groups of people and between people. Individuals scan the environment based on their physiological abilities, motivations and knowledge. The knowledge they possess depends on their life experiences, by what is demanded of them within a geographic and cultural setting and their own motivations. How they make use of the affordances of any particular layout of built form will depend on the qualities that they perceive before them and their understanding of the consequences of any actions they may take. Their assessment of how attractive a square is will be biased by what they are used to experiencing.

Notes

1 This chapter borrows heavily from Lang (1987) and Lang and Moleski (2010).
2 For a full description of the processes of ecological perception, see Gibson (1966, 1979) and Reed (1996). For a statement on the utility of Gibson's information-based model of perception for the design of the environment, see Kaminski (1989) and Lang and Moleski (2010). The clearest commentary on the processes of cognition is that in Neisser (1976).
3 Steen Eiler Rasmussen (1959) explored the manner in which multi-modal perception affects our interpretation of the built environment. Sepe (2013) presents a recent review.
4 See Southworth (1969), Thibaud (2003), Kang (2006), LaBelle (2010) and Cogger (2011) on the sonic environment of cities.
5 See Kang and Zhang (2010) and Cogger (2011) for an analysis of sound and noise management efforts in public spaces.
6 See Rapoport (1982) among other treatises dealing with non-verbal communication from a designer's viewpoint.
7 See Gibson (1966) on the role of movement in the processes of perception and Cullen (1961), Thiel (1961, 1996), Halprin (1965), Hillier and Hansen (1984) and Gehl (2010) on its importance in the design of the built environment.

8 See the essays in Berlyne (1974) and, especially, his paper on "novelty, complexity and interestingness."

9 Hermann Maertens' studies (1877) brought attention to the role of visual acuity in perceiving the built environment and its components. His book was a major influence on the better-known work of Camillo Sitte (1889; Sitte and Stewart 1945); see also Moravánszky (2012) on Meartens and Sitte. Edward T. Hall (1969), in his Proxemic Theory, demonstrates the role of the acuity of all the senses in establishing an anthropology of manners.

References

Berlyne, Daniel E. (1974) Novelty, complexity and interestingness. In *New Experimental Aesthetics; Steps Toward an Objective Psychology of Aesthetic Appreciation*, edited by Daniel E. Berlyne. New York: John Wiley & Sons, Inc.

Cogger, Rachel (2011) The urban symphony: Are you listening? Unpublished thesis, University of New South Wales, Sydney, Australia.

Cooper, Joel and Russell H. Fazio (1984) A new look at dissonance theory. In *Advances in Experimental Social Psychology* 17, edited by Leonard Berkowitz. Hillsdale, NJ: Lawrence Erlbaum, pp. 229–262.

Cullen, Gordon (1961) *Townscape*. London: Architectural Press.

Festinger, Leon (1962) Cognitive dissonance. *Scientific American* 207(4): 93–107.

Gehl, Jan (2010) *Cities for People*. Washington, DC: Island Press.

Gibson, James J. (1966) *The Senses Considered as Perceptual Systems*. Boston: Houghton Mifflin.

Gibson, James J. (1979) *The Ecological Approach to Visual Perception*. Boston: Houghton Mifflin.

Hall, Edward T. (1969) *The Hidden Dimension*. New York: Anchor Books.

Halprin, Lawrence (1965) Motation. *Progressive Architecture* 46(7): 126–128.

Heft, Harry (2001) *Ecological Psychology in Context: James Gibson, Roger Barker and the Legacy of William James*. Mahwah, NJ: Lawrence Erlbaum Publishers.

Heider, Fritz (1958) *The Psychology of Interpersonal Relationships*. New York: John Wiley & Sons, Inc.

Helmreich, Robert (1974) The evaluation of environments: Behavioral research in an undersea habitat. In *Designing for Human Behavior: Architecture and the Behavioral Sciences*, edited by Jon Lang, Charles Burnette, Walter Moleski and David Vachon. Stroudsburg, PA: Dowden, Hutchinson and Ross, pp. 274–285.

Hillier, Bill and Julienne Hanson (1984) *The Social Logic of Space*. Cambridge: Cambridge University Press.

Hummon, Norman P. and Patrick Doreian (2003) Some dynamics of social balance processes: Bringing Heider back into balance theory. *Social Networks* 25: 17–49.

Kaminski, Gerard (1989) The relevance of ecologically oriented theory building in environment and behavior research. In *Advances in Environment, Behavior, and Design*, vol. II, edited by Ervin H. Zube and Gary T. Moore. New York: Plenum Press, pp. 3–36.

Kang, Jian (2006) *Urban Sound Environment*. London: Spon.

Kang, Jian and M. Zhang (2010) Semantic differential analysis of the soundscape in urban open public spaces. *Building and Environment* 45(1): 150–157.

LaBelle, Brandon (2010) *Acoustic Territories: Social Culture and Everyday Life*. London: Continuum International.

Lang, Jon (1987) *Creating Architectural Theory: The Role of the Behavioral Sciences in Environmental Design*. New York: Van Nostrand Reinhold.

Lang, Jon and Walter Moleski (2010) *Functionalism Revisited. Architectural Theory and Practice and the Behavioral Sciences*. Farnham: Ashgate.

Maertens, Hermann (1877) *Der Optische-Maßstab oder die Theorie und Praxis des ästhetischen Sehens in der bildenden Kunsten. Auf Grund der Lehrer der physiologischen Optic*. Bonn: Cohen, 2nd edn, 1884, Berlin: Wasmuth.

Marshall, Nancy (2016) Urban squares: A place for public life. In *Place and Placelessness Revisited*, edited by Robert Freestone and Edgar Liu. New York: Routledge, pp. 186–203.

Moravánszky, Ákos (2012) The optical construction of urban space: Hermann Maertens, Camillo Sitte and the theories of 'aesthetic perception.' *Journal of Architecture* 17(5): 655.

Neisser, Ulrich (1976) *Cognition and Reality: Principles and Implications of Cognitive Psychology*. San Francisco: Freeman.

Rapoport, Amos (1982) *The Meaning of the Built Environment: A Non-verbal Communications Approach*. Beverley Hills, CA: Sage.

Rasmussen, Steen Eiler (1959) *Experiencing Architecture*. Cambridge, MA: MIT Press.

Reed, Edward S. (1996) *Encountering the World: Toward an Ecological Psychology*. New York: Oxford University Press.

Sennett, Richard (1998) The sense of touch. *Architectural Design Profile* 66(132): 18–22.

Sepe, Marichela (2013) Places and perceptions in contemporary city. *Urban Design International* 18(2): 111–113.

Sitte, Camillo (1889) *Der Städtebau nach seinen künstlerischen Grundsätzen*. Vienna: Karl Graesser.

Sitte, Camillo and Charles T. Stewart (1945) *The Art of Building Cities: City Building According to its Artistic Fundamentals*. New York: Reinhold.

Southworth, Michael (1969) The sonic environment of cities. *Environment and Behavior* 1(1): 49–70.

Thibaud, Jean-Paul (2003) The sonic composition of the city. In *The Auditory Culture Reader*, edited by Michael Bull and Les Black. Amsterdam: Berg, pp. 329–341.

Thiel, Philip (1961) A sequence-experience notation for architectural and urban spaces. *Town Planning Review* 32(1): 33–52.

Thiel, Philip (1996) *People, Paths, and Purpose: Notations for a Participatory Envirotecture*. Seattle: University of Washington Press.

Further Reading

Carmona, Matthew, Tim Heath, Taner Oc and Steven Tiesdell (2003) *Public Places – Urban Spaces: The Dimensions of Urban Design*. Oxford: Architectural Press.

Cooper Marcus, Clare and Carolyn Francis (1990) *People Places: Design Guidelines for Urban Open Space*. New York: Van Nostrand Reinhold.

Cuthbert, Alexander R. (2011) *Understanding Cities*. New York: Routledge.

Pergola, Cesare (1997) *La Città dei Sensi*. Firenze: Alinea.

CHAPTER 2

SQUARES AS PLACES, LINKS AND DISPLAYS

Almost inevitably any urban public open space will be used at some time by somebody for some purpose. The activities that actually take place will depend on the space's accessibility, the affordances of its design and on the predispositions of its users. The design is also inevitably a display enhanced or decreased by its nature as an environment and by the objects within it. The patterns of light and shade, movement of air, sounds and odors add or detract from what it affords people and its perceived quality. A square, its structure and what goes on within it, can also be something to contemplate for the sake of the intellectual review if it is regarded as a work of art.

Squares as Nested Sets of Behavior Settings

Behavior settings, a term originally termed by Roger Barker (1968), are analogous to the term 'activity sites' that architects use in order to think about places.[1] They consist of three components: (1) a physical milieu; (2) a recurrent activity; and (3) a time period.[2] "Behavior settings consist of a sequence of activities ... in recurrent patterns of behavior combined with appropriate objects in complex ways with clearly defined spatial and temporal boundaries in a symbiotic relationship" (Le Compte 1974: 184). An empty city square consists of a nested set of potential behavior settings that vary in scale from the whole square to the activity of a sole person in one spot within it (Figure 2.1). 'Nested' suggests that these behavior settings occur within one another; often they also overlap.

The physical milieu has to be able to afford, or enable, an activity in order for it to occur. Whether or not it will actually occur depends on the site's users' motivations, their levels of ability, predispositions, and the perceived consequences of any activity in which they might engage. The physical milieu comes in a variety of layouts, or patterns, of surfaces, of different materials possessing particular strengths, textures and colors. The basic requirement for everyday life is that the milieu has a solid, walkable surface.

Roger Barker (1968) considered the milieu to possess an 'invitational quality' for people to use the square for their own purposes

Figure 2.1 Parc Güell, Barcelona:
a potential and an effective behavior
setting: (a) Potential behavior settings;
(b) A nested set of effective behavior
settings

Source: Photograph (b) by Tupungato/
Shutterstock.com.

(Schoggen 1989; Sabar 2014). This view is slightly deterministic – just because the milieu of a square has particular patterns does not mean that the patterns coerce people to use it in a specific way. The patterns of the environment do not determine people's behaviors. It is better to think of those patterns in terms of their 'affordances,' or, in architect Louis Kahn's terms, "availabilities" (Lang and Moleski 2010: 50). Certainly if a pattern of built form does not enable a particular pattern of behavior to occur, it cannot. Hence, it is possible to preclude certain activities from taking place. However, even though the designer of a square may think that certain activities cannot occur in it, someone else may see the affordances for them.

It is important to recognize that people of varying cultural backgrounds use space differently; the behavior settings they inhabit differ. Edward T. Hall (1969: 162–163), in his original study of the anthropology of space, differentiated between *monochronic* and *polychronic* behavior settings. The former consists of standing patterns of behavior in which participants have a low level of involvement with the activities taking place in the setting and the latter those with a high level of involvement (ibid.). The difference does not correlate directly with the patterns of the layout of the environment but the Italian piazzas and Spanish plazas are settings of polychronic space but such squares need 'nooks and crannies' that create the affordances for the easy formation of polychronic settings.[3] Upper Sproul Plaza at the University of California, Berkeley, has a number of them along its sides.

The design of a square is likely to afford many different activities. What takes place may change as its inhabitants change over the course of a day, week, season or years. The behavior setting thus changes; it has a temporal existence. Rockefeller Center in New York was designed as a setting for the enjoyment of local and international visitors alike. A restaurant often exists there in summer and in the winter a public ice-skating rink is created. The milieu of the square affords many types of standing patterns of behavior nested within each other, as can be seen in the two scenes shown in Figure 2.2. Added moveable items in the form of tables and chairs, seasonal decorations and the lighting in the two settings vary but otherwise the fixed features of the milieu are the same. The standing patterns of behavior are very different.

The Two Major Types of Behavior Settings

Squares consist of the two major types of behavior settings: places and links. Places almost inevitably contain links that contribute substantially to their functioning and people tend to underestimate the number of ephemeral places that occur in pedestrian links. Many squares serve as both places and links. Places and links come in many forms that serve different functions (Figure 2.3). These functions vary by their situation, and different cultural and climatic settings. They change over the course of the day and the seasons, but their essential nature and what they afford remain the same. Some squares are

Figure 2.2 Rockefeller Center, New York as two different behavior settings: (a) One behavior setting as a restaurant; (b) Another as an ice-skating rink

Sources: (a) Photograph by Sean Pavone/ Shutterstock.com; (b) Photograph by Andrew F. Kazmierski/Shutterstock.com.

Figure 2.3 Grassmarket, Edinburgh: a square that is primarily a place although used as a link

primarily places but others were designed to be and are primarily links. The forecourts of buildings are a prime example of the latter.

The Nature of Places

The theory and understanding of the meaning of 'place' are contested. Urban planners and geographers often define places as geographical locations that have become socially constructed with meaning and value (Tuan 1977; Cresswell 2009). For designers, one way to understand squares as places is to consider them to be behavior settings in which the standing, or regularly recurrent, patterns of behavior are localized. There are two overarching types of standing patterns of such behavior: the formal and the communal. The former are organized and designed; the built environment can be created to accommodate them well. The latter just happen but are constrained by the affordances provided by the geometric structure and materials of a built environment.[4]

The formal, such as memorial services, theater productions or protest marches, are organized, purposefully created events. Municipal governments often actively program activities in squares, especially in climatically congenial months. The layout of a square and the objects within it can be designed or adapted with the specific formal activity in mind. More usually, however, the ceremony or performance is adjusted to the configuration of an existing square. On many occasions the activity can be said to be shoehorned into the square because its size or layout does not afford it easily.

Communal organizations develop from the public itself. Communal activites, by definition, are grassroots efforts (see Lang and Moleski 2010: 174 for Gottschalk's summary of the research). Communal activities can be either monochronic or polychronic in Hall's terms (1969). People see the affordances for the activities in which they wish to engage and avail themselves of those opportunities. Some of these behaviors are regarded as antisocial but most contribute positively to the development of a sense of community in the surrounding areas.[5] Jan Gehl (1987, 2010) refers to these activities as "social." He contrasts social activities with the "necessary" – those activities required to fulfill a specific task in everyday life – and the "optional" – those that we choose to do. Recently, community groups have taken to using 'guerrilla urbanism'[6] tactics to redesign or to provide temporary designs and events to enliven a space.

The market in Salernes (see Figure 5.7 (b) on p. 91), despite its haphazard appearance, is a formal activity; it is organized and the recurrent patterns of behavior can be identified. Within it many activities are communal in nature. The minimum requirement for such activities is, as noted, a solid horizontal surface. Most squares have seats, steps and/or ledges which can serve a number of purposes. Places for specific activities such as skateboarding have their own requirements. Today squares often include coercive design features in an attempt to preclude such activities (see Figure 14.6 on p. 278). It is important to recognize that while designers can purposefully create the settings for formal activities, they can only create a potential environment for communal activities.

The Nature of Links

Links are behavior settings in which the activity is movement from one location to another. In a square they can be thought of as open corridors. Sometimes the corridors are well-defined pathways (Figure 2.4 (b)) and sometimes the line of movement is shaped by the entrances formed in a low-walled enclosure or simply by differentiation in the paving pattern. The Seagram Building Plaza in New York (see Figure 14.4 on p. 273) serves as a foreground to the building and a link between it and the sidewalk. While regarded as an architectural masterpiece, the plaza affords little for other than pedestrian movement.[7] Other squares that may be less obviously a link may have many and great variety of pedestrians passing through them at various times of day.

Links between horizontal surfaces at different heights can be in the form of stairs, ramps, elevators and escalators. The important built-form consideration in the design of a link is that horizontal surfaces should be easy to walk on by people of all abilities and easy to use by people using mobility devices, wheelchairs and people pushing strollers. This requirement need not clash with esthetic objectives but often does. The much admired pavement patterns in Rio de Janeiro (see Figure 9.7 (a) on p. 142) are a tripping hazard for those people who have walking difficulties or are wearing high heels.

The most obvious pedestrian space akin to a square and serving as a link is the pedestrian mall. These malls are only highly used if they have many entrances to housing or retail/commercial space opening onto them. They also need to have attractions at both ends (that is, a dumbbell design) and be designed to have smaller places within them. Many pedestrian malls that were formed by closing streets have now been reopened to traffic because they were underused and the commercial enterprises located on them failed to flourish.[8]

Spaces shared by vehicles and pedestrians are ambiguous. Exhibition Road in London, opened in 2011, has received accolades for the simplicity of its curbless design. It has also been criticized for being dangerous for pedestrians because of the territorial ambiguity of the patterned surfaces. Pedestrians, sensibly, need to be cautious in stepping out into the traffic even though they have the right of way

Figure 2.4 Two squares that are primarily links: (a) Albert Luthuli Place, Cape Town; (b) 1221 Avenue of the Americas Plaza, New York

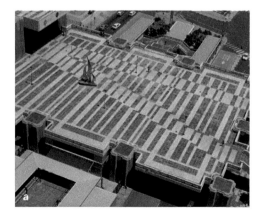

Figure 2.5 Shared spaces:
(a) A designed shared space, Collins
Street; Melbourne; (b) An assumed
shared space, Bangkok

(Prynn 2012). The *woonerf* is a prime example of a self-consciously designed shared space. Developed originally in the Netherlands as a place for cars and pedestrians and even for children to have a place in which to play, it is a model that has been widely used in residential areas around the world. In many economically developing countries most streets end up being an intermingling of moving vehicles and pedestrians (Figure 2.5 (b)).

Daily, Weekly and Seasonal Change

Patterns of human activity vary over the course of the day, week and changing seasons. The nested set of behavior settings that constitute any square may thus vary from moment to moment.[9] Much depends on the square's location and who its potential users are. Squares are more likely to be used as links at rush hours and to be places at lunchtime if they are surrounded by commercial buildings. If the weather is warm and dry, they may be packed with people eating and drinking. Places, such as Trafalgar Square in London or Piazza San Pietro in the Vatican, are tourist destinations; they too will see the daily and seasonal ebb and flow of visitors and as special events take place or important dates are celebrated (see Figure 12.10 (a) on p. 207).

Many squares are very different places during the day and night, depending on the way they are illuminated. Times Square in New York, always busy, comes alive at night when its bright lighting dazzles (Figure 2.6). The same is true of cities not renowned as tourist destinations. City Park in Bradford, England, completed in 2012, is an example. In the tropics, many squares are empty of people during the day but come to life in the evenings when the heat of the day has dissipated.

In temperate climates, the physical change in squares containing deciduous trees will be substantial as trees gain leaves in spring and lose them in the autumn. The direction of the sunrise and sunset and the height of the noon sun in the sky change over the course of the year and consequently so do patterns of light and shade in a place. In Sydney, Australia, the midday height of the sun is 83° above

the horizon at Christmas time but at the winter solstice it is only 33°. The difference changes the character of the city's open spaces, particularly those with an east–west orientation. Consider the extent of the shade in Sydney's Italian Forum at midday at the summer solstice and in mid-winter (Figure 2.7).

As the seasons change, so do the affordances of squares. In cold climate cities, the ground will be covered with snow during the winter, possibly for months. Cities with continental climate have to deal with extremes of cold and heat: freezing cold in the winter and hot in summer. The affordances of a square will change as its physical nature changes. Ice and snow make surfaces slippery. Benches and ledges will be cold to sit on. Olympic Plaza in Calgary, originally designed solely for the duration of the medal presentation ceremonies at the XV Winter Olympic Games of 1988, proved to be so popular that it is now transformed from an ice-rink during the winter into a special events stage also in the winter (Figures 2.8 (b) and (c)), noting changes within one season.

In summer, heat from the sun and radiant heat from the surfaces of a square may make a place stifling hot, even in the shade. Many such places come to life in the evenings. The square, really a courtyard, in the Dutch Hospital Shopping District, in Colombo, is empty of people

Figure 2.6 Times Square, New York during the day and at night: (a) A daytime view; (b) A night-time view

Figure 2.7 The Italian Forum, Sydney, at midday: (a) In December, at the summer solstice; (b) In June, at the winter solstice

Figure 2.8 Seasonal change and the change in the nature of behavior settings: (a) Flooded Piazzetta San Marco, Venice; (b) Olympic Plaza, Calgary as an ice skating rink in winter, (c) and holding a New Years Eve event in winter

Source: (a) Photograph by javarman/ Shutterstock.com. (b) Photograph by Erin Jones.

at noon (see Figure 4.5 (b) on p. 77) but is subtly illuminated and full of people during the evening. During the day people stick to the shade provided by the surrounding veranda. In the tropics the character of a square changes depending on whether it is under a scorching sun or being drowned in a thunderstorm or monsoonal rains. The situation in Venice can be very different. In winter, an *acqua alta*, which occurs when winds funnel waters up the Adriatic Sea, can flood Piazza San Marco and surrounding areas (Figure 2.8 (a)). Amusing for some tourists who frolic in the water, it creates considerable hardship for others, particularly locals who use the square as a link.

Many squares, with relatively minor seasonal interventions afford very different behavior settings in summer and winter. Strollers enjoy walking in London's garden squares during their opening hours on a sunny winter day. The change in use at the sunken Rockefeller Center Plaza in New York is similar. At the ground level above, spectators, although more warmly dressed in winter than in summer, engage in much the same behavior year-round. Rainy days usually inhibit the use of any public space.

The perception of seasonal changes enhances the development of the sense of a locale. A square can be designed to emphasize the changes or obscure them. The decision depends on the purpose a square is expected to serve. In general, we are advocates for the clear demonstration of seasonal changes in a place. The changes create affordances for different activities. They can enrich life, provide for a varied and inclusive public life and mark the passing of time.

Squares as Displays and as Settings for Displays[10]

The milieu of a behavior setting always has a design, whether it is the result of self-conscious thought or it evolved unself-consciously by individual actions over time. It can be designed purposefully to contain works of art and be a setting for performances. It can thus be a work of art or a setting for works of art such as fountains, sculptures, installations or memorials. The objects themselves may have emotional associations for a square's users, individually or collectively.

Squares as Works of Art

The layout of the environment can be seen as a display of contemporary ideas of what constitutes a good design. A square can thus be seen as a work of art itself symbolic of the era in which it was built and/or the œuvre of its designer or the architectural paradigm employed in their design (Figure 2.9). The associations that the patterns evoke in the minds of observers are what is important.

The intellectual or emotional associations that a person may have with the patterns of a square or any object within it can be people, a single event or recurrent events of consequence to a group of people, or with the square's creator and the ideas that the creator wishes to

Figure 2.9 *Schouwburgplein, Rotterdam, a square as a work of art itself*

express. The square itself becomes an object to contemplate rather than an environment to enjoy. The contemplation requires particular attention. The perception may be controversial because the design may evoke different associations in the minds of its various viewers. For some, the associations may be positive and for others negative, as cognitive balance theory suggests, as noted in Chapter 1.[11] Other people may have no response to the design at all; it fails to attract their attention.

The enclosing elements of a square – the walls that surround and give it much of its quality – can also be the surfaces for advertising and light shows. Times Square in New York and Yonge-Dundas Square in Toronto are internationally known examples where the enclosing elements are, in essence, billboards.

Squares as Settings for Works of Art

Squares are often settings for displaying art works. The world is replete with such examples. They can also be the settings for performances and gatherings – spontaneous or orchestrated – that are displays. Many public open spaces contain amphitheaters specifically designed to house such activities (Jewell 2003). Many more performances occur in places where there is simply a good surface on which to perform and a surrounding layout that provides sight lines for good watching and, ideally, good acoustics for listening. Such performances act as a catalyst for attracting people to a place.

While being careful with generalizations, it is safe to say that the general public relates more to figurative arts works such as the *Cervantes* memorial in Madrid (see Figure 5.11 (b) on p. 96) than abstract structures. Few New Yorkers loved Richard Serra's *Tilted Arc* in New York's Jacob K. Javits Federal Building Plaza (see Figure 12.17 (a) on p. 230). Some admired it. Despite the ambiguity of Picasso's unnamed abstract sculpture in Daley Plaza in Chicago, it has a warm place in the heart of many citizens of that city (Figure 5.11 (a) on p. 96).

The Rights and Obligations of Artists

The right of artistic expression is subject to tensions, particularly when an art object fails to enhance the quality of people's experience of a setting.[12] People who are not members of the art community may see a work as an artist's intrusion into a space, as was the case with the *Tilted Arc* which made a poorly functioning square even worse in its users' estimation. The work has long since been removed. Artists generally regard the removal as an invasion of their right of self-expression; most viewers, in contrast, were happy to see the art removed (Hill 2007). The subsequent seating designed by Martha Schwartz, another work of art, but with a social objective, was selected to replace it. It too has given way to a new design.

The quality of public spaces, such as streets and squares, while potentially important as works of art and as settings for art, is measured largely as places for the general public to enjoy actively or passively. The position of members of the art world may differ. The nature of squares as displays is important. What squares afford people as esthetic displays is fundamental to their design.

Conclusion

A square, we have stated, contains links and places. To be inhabited at all, a square needs to be tied into its surrounding environment. Unless it is located in a cul-de-sac or surrounded by heavy traffic, a square is likely to be criss-crossed by people moving from one destination to another. When does the function of a square as a link detract from its function as a place? A conceptual framework is required to make sense of how squares function. Thinking of squares as places and displays captures the essence of their nature. This view can stand as the basis for discussion and debate until a more useful one for planning and design is developed.

Many critics think a good design from an artistic viewpoint and good layout for activities are separate issues. A typical comment regarding the latest design for the Jacob K. Javits Center Plaza is that "the new design looks much more people-friendly while still being a good design" which implies that being user-friendly cannot, in itself, be regarded as a good design (Green 2010: website). A square can serve the ends of both users and creators and, we believe, should do so.

Many designers believe that providing people with a square as a work of art is its most important function. This perspective, they claim, challenges and educates those who use a square. Breaking new intellectual esthetic grounds and being in fashion are certainly important to designers and the cognoscenti but these individuals are seldom the users of the spaces they design or admire.[13] "Most people don't want what architects want" (Michelson 1968: 37). New design patterns can frustrate the local residents by interfering in their routines and expectations. The debate continues as to whether a square should be primarily a 'good design' from an architectural theory viewpoint or 'people-oriented.' The question in evaluating existing squares or creating a brief, or program, for a new one is: 'Which concerns should be given priority?' We believe that the art defense used to defend a square that functions poorly on other dimensions of analysis on the grounds that it is a 'good design' is undesirable.

Notes

1. See Haviland (1967) and Chapin (1968) on activity sites.
2. Much has been written on behavior settings as the basis for observing human behavior in the field rather than in the laboratory. Barker (1968), Schoggen (1989), Wicker (2002) and Popov and Chompalov (2012), for example, describe the theoretical background for behavior setting analysis. Le Compte (1974) and Lang and Moleski (2010) describe the utility of the concept of behavior setting for architectural programming and design. Although they do not use the term 'behavior settings' explicitly, other scholars are concerned with space temporality in the flow of urban life. See, for instance, Cosco and Moore (2010) and Wunderlich (2013).
3. See Li (2014) on Chinatowns in the United States.
4. The clearest exposition on the similarities and differences between 'formal' and 'communal' organizations is found in Gottschalk (1975). See also Lang and Moleski (2010).

5 Squares are often perceived to contribute to a sense of community. Some planners argue for more squares on this social ground. Believing that squares lead to the development of communities must be taken with caution. People who go to squares do so on their own or with acquaintances. They very seldom go to squares to bond with strangers. It may happen but should not be expected to occur.

6 Also referred to as 'user-centered urbanism,' 'city-repair' and 'Do-It-Yourself: DIY urbanism.'

7 See Deutsche (2003), Dimendberg (2004) and Jordy (2005) for analyses of the plaza.

8 For a case study of Oak Park Center Mall, see Lang (2005): 81–83.

9 See Wunderlich (2013) for an analysis of one open space: Fitzroy Square, London.

10 See Chapter 11 for a fuller exposition of the esthetic qualities of squares and for a discussion of types of squares based on the architectural paradigm employed in their design.

11 See Hummon and Doreian (2003) and Lang and Moleski (2010) for recent statements on balance theory. The point is that we attempt, consciously or subconsciously, to keep our attitudes to the relationships among our perceptions of an object, its associations with a referent and our attitude towards the referent itself congruent with each other.

12 For a detailed analysis of the history of the Serra and Schwartz designs and reactions to them, see Hill (2007).

13 Much architectural ideology downplays considerations of the quality of everyday life in establishing architectural theories that shape what architects actually do. See Conrads (1970) and Hayes (1998).

References

Barker, Roger (1968) *Ecological Psychology: Concepts and Methods for Studying the Environment of Human Behavior*. Stanford, CA: Stanford University Press.

Chapin, F. Stuart, Jr (1968) Activity systems and urban structure: A working scheme. *Journal of the American Institute of Planners* 34(1): 11–18.

Conrads, Ulrich (ed.) (1970) *Programs and Manifestoes on 20th-Century Architecture*, trans. from the German by Michael Bullock. Cambridge, MA: MIT Press.

Cosco, Nilda G. and Robin Moore (2010) Behaviour mapping for designing healthy outdoor environments for children and families; conceptual framework, procedures and applications. In *Innovative Approaches to Research Excellence in Landscape and Health*, edited by Catherine Ward Thompson, Peter Aspinall and Simon Bell. London: Routledge, pp. 33–74.

Cresswell, Tim (2009) *Place: A Short Introduction*, 2nd edn. Oxford: Blackwell.

Deutsche, Rosalyn (2003) *Tilted Arc* and the uses of democracy. In *Designing Cities: Critical Reading in Urban Design*, edited by Alexander R. Cuthbert. Oxford: Blackwell Publishing, pp. 160–168.

Dimendberg, Edward (2004) *Film Noir and the Spaces of Modernity*. Cambridge, MA: Harvard University Press.

Gehl, Jan (1987) *Life between Buildings: Using Public Space*. New York: Van Nostrand Reinhold.

Gehl, Jan (2010) *Cities for People*. Washington, DC: Island Press.

Gottschalk, Shimon S. (1975) *Communities and Alternatives: An Exploration of the Limits of Planning*. Cambridge: Schenkman.

Green, Jared (2010) Jacob Javits Plaza gets a redesign with recovery funds. *The Dirt*. American Society of Landscape Architects. Available at: http://dirt.asla.org/2010/02/03/jacob-javits-plaza-gets-a-redesign-with-recovery-funds.

Hall, Edward T. (1969) *The Hidden Dimension*. New York: Anchor Books.

Haviland, David (1967) The activity/space, a least common denominator for architectural programming. Paper presented at the American Institute of Architect-Researcher Conference, Gatlinburg, Tennessee.

Hayes, Michael K. (1998) *Architecture Theory since 1968*. Cambridge, MA: MIT Press.

Hill, John (2007) Jacob Javits Plaza: Reconsidering intentions. Prepared for *Anthropology of Place and Space: Locating Culture*, edited by Setha Lowe and Denise Lawrence-Zúñiga. Malden, MA: Blackwell.

Hummon, Norman P. and Patrick Doreian (2003) Some dynamics of social balance processes: Bringing Heider back into balance theory. *Social Networks* 25: 17–49.

Jewell, Linda (2003) The American outdoor theater: A voice for the landscape in the collaboration of site and structure. In *Re-envisioning Landscape/Architecture*, edited by Catherine Spellman. Chicago: Actar Publications.

Jordy, William H. (2005) *'Symbolic Essence' and Other Writings on Modern Architecture and American Culture*. New Haven, CT: Yale University Press.

Lang, Jon (2005) *Urban Design: A Typology of Procedures and Products Illustrated with Over 50 Case Studies*. Oxford: Architectural Press.

Lang, Jon and Walter Moleski (2010) *Functionalism Revisited: Architectural Theory and Practice and the Behavioral Sciences*. Farnham: Ashgate.

Le Compte, William F. (1974) Behavior settings as data-gathering units for the environmental planner and architect. In *Designing for Human Behavior: Architecture and the Behavioral Sciences*, edited by Jon Lang, Charles Burnette, Walter Moleski and David Vachon. Stroudsburg, PA: Dowden, Hutchinson and Ross, pp. 183–193.

Li, Chuo (2014) Ethnicity, culture and park design: Case studies of urban parks in American Chinatowns. *Journal of Urban Design* 19(2): 230–254.

Michelson, William (1968) Most people don't want what architects want. *Transactions* 5(8): 37–43.

Popov, Lubomir and Ivan Chompalov (2012) Crossing over: The interdisciplinary meaning of behaviour setting theory. *International Journal of Humanities and Sciences* 2(19): 18–27.

Prynn, Jonathan (2012) Exhibition Road: An 'exemplar' of how to make a city liveable. *Evening Standard*, June 21, p. 32. Available at: www.standard.co.uk/news/london/exhibition-road-an-exemplar-of-how-to-make-a-city-liveable-7872404.html.

Sabar, Ariel (2014) *The Outsider: The Life and Times of Roger Barker*. Kindle.

Schoggen, Phil (1989) *Behavior Settings: A Revision and Extension of Roger G. Barker's Ecological Psychology*. Stanford, CA: Stanford University Press.

Tuan, Yi-Fu (1977) *Space and Place: The Perspective of Experience*. Minneapolis, MN: University of Minnesota Press.

Wicker, Alan W. (2002) Ecological psychology: Historical contexts, current conception, prospective directions. In *Handbook of Environmental Psychology*, edited by Robert B. Bechtel and Azra Churchman. New York: John Wiley & Sons, Inc. pp. 114–126.

Wunderlich, Filipa Matos (2013) Place-temporality and urban place-rhythms in urban analysis and design: An aesthetic akin to music. *Journal of Urban Design* 18(3): 383–408.

Further Reading

Douglas, Gordon C. (2014) Do-It-Yourself urban design: The social practice of informal 'improvement' through unauthorized alteration. *City and Community* 13(1): 5–25.

Green, Jared (2012) Paver power. *The Dirt*. American Society of Landscape Architects. Available at: http://dirt.asla.org/2012/07/05/paver-power.

Harvey, David (1993) From space to place and back again. In *Mapping the Futures: Local Culture, Global Change*, edited by John Bird, Barry Curtis, Tim Putnam, George Robertson and Lisa Tickner. London: Routledge, pp. 3–29.

Harvey, David (1997) The New Urbanism and the communitarian trap. *Harvard Design Magazine* (Winter/Spring): 68–69. Available at: http://wsm.wsu.edu/stories/2008/Spring/1harvey.pdf.

Kyttä, Marketta (2004) The extent of children's independent mobility and the number of actualized affordances as criteria for child-friendly environments. *Journal of Environmental Psychology* 24(2): 179–198.

Lydon, Mike, Dan Bartman, Ronald Woudstra and Aurash Khawarzad (2010) *Tactical Urbanism Beta Short-Term Action//Long Term Gain*, vol. 1. New York: The Street Plans Collaborative.

Lydon, Mike, Dan Bartman, Ronald Woudstra and Aurash Khawarzad (2012) *Tactical Urbanism Beta Short-Term Action//Long Term Gain*, vol. 2. New York: The Street Plans Collaborative.

Marshall, Nancy (2009) Retreat from the city: Representations of sense of place. Paper presented at the State of Australia Cities Conference, November 25–27, Perth, Australia.

Relph, Edward (1976) *Place and Placelessness*. London: Pion.

Wicker, Alan. W. (1984) *An Introduction to Ecological Psychology*. New York: Cambridge University Press.

CHAPTER 3

SOCIOCULTURAL CONSIDERATIONS

Squares afford a sociability of public life. They offer us a place to celebrate, protest, mourn and play. They can host small events for locals and welcome international visitors to major occasions. The art of living in a twenty-first-century city which has public squares includes engaging with people who come from a range of ethnic, cultural, socioeconomic and religious backgrounds. People have different value sets and go about their lives in varying ways.

Around the globe, people of different cultures experience squares as settings in dissimilar seasons and seasonal changes, temperatures, precipitation amounts and wind levels. Cultural and climatic factors are inextricably linked so that the way squares function has to be seen within specific geographic contexts. In cooler climates, people may choose to sit in the sun (Figure 3.1 (a)) but in areas where the sun beats down on paved areas, on a summer day a square will be deserted as in Marzamemi (Figure 3.1 (b)).

People have a desire to be comfortable, physiologically and psychologically, but tolerances for different norms vary and are influenced by personal values and life experiences (Apley 1971). It must be recognized that ways of life, the ideals and the tastes of people vary from society to society. They are transmitted from one generation to the next by the manner in which children are socialized. Thus, a culture provides the rules that define what is acceptable and what is not and also how activities are expected to be carried out by whom.[1]

Figure 3.1 Afternoon in two squares: (a) Copley Square, Boston; (b) Piazza R. Margherita, Marzamemi, Sicily

Source: (b) Photograph by Joanne Taylor.

Figure 3.2 *Cultural context and the use of squares (a) Street market, Cairo; (b) Asan Square, Kathmandu in 2012*

Sources: (a) Photograph by 360b/ Shutterstock.com; (b) Photograph by Monica McNamara.

Substantial differences in ways of life and attitudes to what is public and what is private space occur among different societies.[2] Attitudes to what activities can and cannot be carried out in public differ. Gender roles, the image of what it means to be a child, a teenager or an older person within their communities vary from culture to culture. Many cities have a global and pluralistic citizenry and thus are a collection of people with very different approaches to life, patterns of behavior and attitudes. Clashes in opinions about the appropriate qualities of any open space in a city can and do arise because people have differing visions of what constitutes acceptable behavior. These differences should be neither exaggerated nor ignored in the assessment and design of city squares. The use of public squares flourishes in the cosmopolitan cities of Islamic Turkey but in the former colonial areas of North African Islamic cities, there is little such use of public space except for markets. The street market in Cairo shares spatial similarities to street markets everywhere even though the goods and the people selling them are unique to Egypt (Figure 3.2 (a)). The situation in Kathmandu's Asan Square prior to the earthquakes of 2015 may seem chaotic to people from Western Europe but the actions of people are governed by unwritten rules understood by the city's population (Figure 3.2 (b)).

Some societies are relatively homogeneous with common agreement about appropriate ways of life, manners and tastes; others are highly diverse with varying degrees of tolerance for deviations from a society's expectations of how people should behave. The public life of cities thus has to be seen within the norms of a social context in a postmodern and globalizing world in which communication technologies are reshaping how people relate to each other. The various inhabitants of a city may or may not tolerate the behavior of people of certain subcultures whose activities do not conform to what is generally acceptable. Examples of these subcultures include skateboarders, the homeless, gangs and guerrilla urbanists. The purposes that squares serve for different people thus vary from city to city and within a city. Although some functions that a square might fulfill are clear to planners, the latent demand for opportunities to engage in public life may exist unexploited in a particular place.

India had no tradition of public open spaces in the European sense before the colonial era, but the spaces, where they exist, have been embraced in cities such as Kolkata. Denmark did not have the tradition of outdoor cafés as in Italy until introduced as the result of work of Jan Gehl (1987, 2010) and his colleagues. It was generally accepted that such outdoor life would not occur in the Danish climate but outdoor cafés have proven to be popular even though they require artificial heating for part of the year. Nevertheless, cultures differ and climate and culture are intertwined, although not in a deterministic manner. Within any society there are groups of people who share values based on a set of characteristics such as socioeconomic status, stage in the life cycle or religious background or, as mentioned above, based on common interests.

Cultures are in a constant state of flux. Changes in everyday social practices are constantly occurring and altering the use of public spaces and they will continue to do so. In this digital age, ways of life and experiencing 'the urban' are changing. Most communication is facilitated through electronic media, such as the internet, email and social networking and takes place on portable, personal devices. Many streets and squares now have open access Wi-Fi and hardware connection points for digital users. These modes of communication do not mean that face-to-face contact in public places is disappearing. The need for such contact may well be increasing and urban squares remain a place for meeting friends or simply for passing a few leisurely moments, provided they have the amenities that people seek. Despite all these changes, many patterns of behavior have remained remarkably consistent.

A number of the squares discussed and illustrated in this book are from France, Spain, Italy and Latin America, where palaces and churches face squares that were and still are used for markets and religious festivals. In countries such as Australia, Canada, the United Kingdom and the United States, public life is generally considered to be on the rise, as cities become more dense (Marshall 2016). Much public life, however, occurs not only in city squares or public open spaces but in semi-public or quasi-public shopping malls, bars and restaurants. The same observation can be made about the behavior of the burgeoning middle class in many cities in Asia. Squares in developing countries tend to be more complex. They contain a greater variety of uses, including more individual vendors encouraged by fewer regulations.

Group and Individual Differences in Experiencing Public Squares

The population which could potentially use a public space can be disaggregated in a number of ways. We have chosen to consider the differences and similarities of people's use of squares by their stage in the life cycle, their physical ability, gender, socioeconomic status, ethnicity, and other personal characteristics, such as sexuality and personality type. We also look at subcultures and how groups of people, with a shared set of alternative value sets, use public space. Subcultures construct their own local moral order and thus dictates which behaviors are acceptable and expected in public spaces and which are not.

Stage in Life Cycle

Several ways of differentiating people by life stages can be identified; we have chosen to highlight how children, adolescents, middle-aged adults and the elderly typically use squares. Generally, when people think of children and public spaces, they think of playgrounds with swings, slides and sandpits. Some pocket parks are just that; they have play equipment for young children and benches for their parents or carers. All public space is, however, perceived by children to be a potential play area, as seen in Figure 3.3a where a child is dancing on the steps of the Sydney Opera House.

As many squares are located in the commercial cores of cities, they are not perceived as places for children. Children, nevertheless,

Figure 3.3 The affordances of flat surfaces, fountains and stairs for children: (a) Parliament Square, Bern Switzerland; (b) Sydney Opera House forecourt, Sydney, Australia

Source: (a) Photograph by Lee Yiu Tung/Shutterstock.com.

are often present either because they live nearby or they are accompanying their parents on excursions. Some squares, without much consideration for children, have a great array of affordances of objects – statues, benches, and retaining walls – for climbing on and fountains to play in (Figure 3.3). Others have few affordances but children still discover them. For instance, in Rotterdam's Schouwburgplein, they clamber on the covers to the entrances to the parking garage below (see Figure 12.14 (b) on p. 221). There is little else to challenge them or attract their attention.

Participation in the public life of a city provides children with the opportunity to vicariously learn about the worlds of other people and develop their own competencies.[3] They face challenges from which they can learn; they are constantly testing themselves. Cultural attitudes towards the presence of children in public places vary among societies. In some cultures, they are welcomed by adults. In others, they are tolerated but not made welcome while in yet others they are simply, by social convention, not allowed to be there (Lennard and Lennard 2001; Churchman 2003).

Adolescents often gather in a square; it is a meeting space away from home. Depending on what they are doing, their presence is enjoyed, tolerated or frowned on by older adults but perhaps admired by younger children. Two major standing patterns of behavior are characteristic of adolescents: hanging-out and engaging in self-testing activities such as skateboarding or roller-blading. 'Hanging out' behavior is often seen as threatening (Efroymson *et al.* 2009). Engaging in such activities acts as a catalyst for socializing but few squares are designed for use by young people. Many are designed to inhibit skateboarding on the grounds that the activity is noisy and causes damage to curbs and ledges (Figure 3.4).[4] Recently, formal and informal pop-up activities, such as listening to DJ music or enjoying temporary place activations (pop-up cafés and bars) have become attractive to young adults.

Adults use squares for a number of reasons. Typically they are places to eat and have a drink, to pass time, as a meeting point or to attend a special event. In general, they use squares for passive leisure purposes, as can be seen in Figure 3.5. There are, however, many

Figure 3.4 *Prohibiting young people's activities (a) Do NOT sign, San Francisco; (b) Designing out skateboarding, San Francisco*

Figure 3.5 Adults in public squares: (a) Paternoster Square, London; (b) Elderly men in the Plaza de España, Madrid

other places such as coffee shops, pubs and clubs within certain cultures that are more attractive places to gather. Squares and streets are often used by adults for formal occasions such as markets, protest meetings or street performances. If in downtown districts, squares are generally used as places during lunchtime and just after office hours or as links to and from work.

A disproportionate number of older people live in the centers of many cities attracted by a wide range of easily accessible cultural institutions and health services. Squares that have pleasant, sunny ambient qualities are often replete with the elderly. Most visitors to squares believe that elderly habitués add a spark of life to the quality of a square and provide an added sense of security. In a number of societies, elderly men in particular are frequent users of local squares.[5] The major activity of the elderly in squares is talking with others like themselves and watching the activities taking place.[6] In public spaces, such as Paley Park in New York and Rittenhouse Square in Philadelphia, that are perceived to be safe, many women are present. 'Hanging-out' is not generally regarded as acceptable behavior for teenagers but it is an important activity for the older adults. In some cultures, specific activities are organized for pensioners in squares such as dancing in Latin America or Tai Chi in China.

Some squares have been designed specifically with the elderly in mind. The Praça Sarah Kubitschek and the Praça de Ludo in Copacabana, Rio de Janeiro, are squares dedicated to the 'terceira idade,' i.e. the elderly. The two squares have a pavilion at the center with tables for playing cards, checkers and chess. Guards join the activities from the periphery. They are there because the squares also attract younger people, with potentially threatening behaviors. The Praça de Ludo has exercising equipment for the elderly in one corner with a sign that states (in Brazilian Portuguese) "Give priority to people of the third age" but in reality, it is used by men and women of all ages.

People with Disabilities

In western countries approximately 20 percent of the population is said to be managing a disability at any one time. This figure includes

Figure 3.6 Flat surfaces and mobility

people who have a physical, intellectual or sensory disability that persists for more than six months. Many countries have comprehensive legislation aimed at providing social and physical access to public life for people with disabilities. These standards address access and include the provision of ramps, tactile ground surface indicators, handrails and clearly visible and legible signage. The standard specification is for there to be at least one level-entry to any public space. Unfortunately, few designers know how to go beyond the basic legal access standards while others believe inclusive design conflicts with the desired esthetics.

For people who have difficulty in walking or use a mobility device, such as a cane, crutches, a walker, a wheelchair or a scooter, a smooth walking surface is required (Figure 3.6). In designing squares, accessibility for all abilities is a constant consideration.

Gender Differences

Neither men nor women are a homogeneous group. Men and women in general use squares differently although the variance differs considerably by the expected gender roles within a culture as well as the location and design of a place. All societies have different expectations of how boys and girls and young men and young women should behave in public. These restrictions are often contested and change with the generations.

In many countries, fewer adult women than men are seen in public squares. In some societies women are very rarely seen in city squares. Such spaces are regarded as men's territory. Attitudes change with time and result in new social norms and local laws. In Turkey, for instance, the presence of women in cafés in squares was unusual only 40 years ago but is now commonplace in the country's major cities. In the villages of Asian Turkey, however, squares remain strictly for the use of men. In countries with strict beliefs and defined gender roles, women must be accompanied by a male relative when in public places.

Differences in the use of urban squares also depend on the role a man or woman plays at different stages in their life cycle. For instance, the affordances of a square perceived by young parents are not necessarily those seen by older men or women (Figure 3.7). Older women are often accompanied by family members or carers who are looking for a quiet outdoor area and fresh air. These observations suggest that most public squares still do not provide women with a range of settings in which they feel comfortable. The current research on gender-based differences in the use of squares in the Americas and European countries is indicative of gender differences in preferences.[7] It shows that women prefer quieter places, where they can have "the back yard experience" compared to men who prefer the "front yard experience" (Mozingo 1989: 46). Women also appear to be more sensitive to urban noise, crowding and traffic than men. Men, in general, tend to sit 'closer to the action.'

Women tend to come in pairs or groups to a square (or arrange to meet someone there) and demand a sense of security once there. As Louise Mozingo (1989) noted, they generally sit in spots that are somewhat secluded from the flow of pedestrians. From there they can survey the whole site easily. Women generally do not want to be on display or open to being hassled by men. As a result, some seating needs to be placed to reduce this possibility (or it should be moveable); steps with low risers are not good places to sit for women wearing skirts/dresses (ibid.). If on their own, women may be reading,

Figure 3.7 Women in public squares: (a) Place Forez, Lyon; (b) 101 California Plaza, San Francisco

working on a personal electronic device or have something else that is the focus of their attention rather than gazing around at the passing scene (Cooper Marcus and Francis 1990).

Socioeconomic Status

People of different socioeconomic groups consider the affordances of public squares in different ways and many of the analyses of squares contain significant economic class biases (Becker 1972).[8] Records of the differences in attitudes to utility of squares by socioeconomic status have a long history. Covent Garden Piazza, the first square built in London, was originally a paved square open to the public. Created in 1630 by the Fourth Earl of Bedford, it was based on Italian precedents. Surrounded by wooden posts and rails, it was enclosed on three sides by arcades and houses for 'people of distinction.' Vendors started to use the square so the wealthy moved away (Richardson 1995).[9] Squares that were built subsequently in London were the semi-private garden squares open only to the residents of the surrounding houses (Longstaffe-Gowan 2012).

Middle-aged, high social status men and women do not use squares as much as younger people and those of low socioeconomic status (Boyer 1992). When they do, the squares are located in high status areas. Despite this observation, the design of many new squares is targeted to and based on the tastes of middle-class consumers. Lower-economic groups tend to use squares more often because they often live in smaller residential units with smaller private outdoor spaces; their lives extend into the public realm turning it into semi-public space[10] or an 'outdoor living room.'

People who are of high socioeconomic status expect and demand a higher level of privacy for their activities. They usually choose locations inside buildings for eating and drinking. They might meet at specific spots in public places but they tend not to linger there. Squares may still be important to them as landmarks and may give a sense of identity to a city in the eyes of the wealthy. Children from wealthy families are often not permitted to frequent public squares but instead have access to private and semi-private garden squares for recreation. Due to a range of sociopolitical and environmental changes and growing fears, largely unfounded, of 'stranger-danger' during the past few decades, middle-class children in wealthy societies are now rarely allowed to be in public streets and squares unsupervised by adults.

Public squares lined with restaurants and cafés or those near shops and art galleries/museums tend to be spaces inhabited by the middle classes. Mandela Square in Sandton, near Johannesburg, South Africa, has had restaurants added along its sides to meet middle-class demands (Figure 3.8 (b)); these additions fracture the pattern of the floor paving and the symmetry that the square once had. The working class, predominantly black men and women, are often seen sitting on the ledges on the periphery of the square opposite the restaurants. Quasi-public spaces such as Paternoster Square in London, because of the surrounding commercial firms and institutions (for example, the Stock Exchange) are the domain of younger middle-class adults

Figure 3.8 Squares for the middle class: (a) Place de la Bourse, Lyon, France; (b) Mandela Square, Sandton, South Africa

(see Figure 3.5 (a) on p. 53). Pop-up bars and cafés provide a catalyst for predominantly middle- and upper-economic groups to visit urban squares. Socioeconomic status does, however, cut across ethnic lines.

Ethnicity and Culture

All cities have a degree of socioeconomic and cultural diversity. Many have some level of ethnic, racial and/or religious segregation. Sometimes the borders between the residential areas of specific ethnic groups are definite as, for example, when they are divided by a railway line. More often, the borders are ambiguous and based on a range of historical factors. In some of these enclaves, such as the predominantly Italian-American area of South Philadelphia, Greeks in Toronto, Chinese in many cities, or the predominantly African-American precinct of Harlem in New York, the public spaces tend to be well used, but the presence of a different ethnicity, 'the other,' is noted. Areas in predominantly Anglo-American communities have lower usage of public space.

In culturally diverse societies, certain groups of people are frequently seen as threatening by others. African-American men in public places, particularly young men, often fall into this category in the United States, as do the indigenous populations of Australia and Canada.[11] These prejudices may be changing but they, unfortunately, still persist. In multicultural societies where prejudices exist, the design of public spaces has particular problems especially if the intention is for a square to be inclusive and serve as a place to bring people together. Prejudices and fears co-exist. In Johannesburg, Martin Murray (2011: 19) observes that after the end of the apartheid era, chance encounters in public places are "tainted with suspicion and unease because they are framed by stereotypical images of imminent danger, embodied in the unemployed black youth. Tension, anxiety and fear are the new hallmarks of public intercourse and social interaction." In contrast, in Kuching in Sarawak, Malaysia, the promenade of Waterfront Park is the one place in the city where ethnic Malays and Chinese mix freely (Lang 2005).

Although generalizations can bring the attention of designers to how people of different cultures use squares and the types of questions that they need to raise when designing the programs for new squares or refurbishing existing ones, users of squares are still individuals. Their free will and unique personalities can override other factors in the way they perceive the affordances of public open spaces.

Personal Characteristics

Not much has been written about individual personality types and the use of open spaces in postmodern cities. A distinction is, however, often made between people's psychological characteristics, that is, whether they are extraverts or introverts. People can be classified as one or the other type, based on their openness to the world around them and on how willing they are to act on it. Extraverts tend to spend time out in the world with other people whereas introverts are said to enjoy an inner world of ideas and images (Briggs Myers et al. 2009).[12] Introverts and extraverts do have different concepts of privacy but it is unclear if these differences are translatable into open space design principles. Extraverts are said to use public places to display themselves and introverts to watch others and be more inward-looking but there is little hard evidence to confirm or reject this hypothesis put forward by Michael Balint (1955) more than 60 years ago.

Subcultures

Municipal authorities and researchers rarely consider non-traditional subcultures when considering the nature of public places and public life despite these groups having rights to the city. Subcultures consist of sociological groups who have behaviors that are other than the norm. Noticeable subcultures include the homeless, the skateboarders, guerrilla urbanists, the 'emos,' the 'goths' and gangs, to mention but a few (Figure 3.9). These non-traditional groups often claim so-called placeless squares as their own (Relph 1976). Some groups are seen by the municipal authorities and others as problems

Figure 3.9 *Squares and specific communities: (a) A homeless man at Battery Park, New York; (b) Skateboarders, 345 Park Avenue, New York*

and are often asked to move out of the space. There is little evidence to show that squares have to be designed in particular ways to meet the specific needs of any of these groups but we do know that these factors influence the use of open space.

The lesbian, gay, bisexual, transgender and intersex (LGBTI) communities often have districts within cities where there are friendly shops, restaurants and open space which are either highly inclusive or dominated by similar people. Squares in these districts are often identified with LGBTI symbols such as flags and the rainbow painting of ground surfaces. Cultural geographers have studied the effect of the "pink dollar" on built form, place identity and belonging (Murphy and Watson 1997). They have also studied how these segments of the population use aspects of public open space (Aronson 1999).

The homeless and transient groups of people are generally regarded as undesirables in public squares. In quasi-public spaces members of this group of people are likely to be asked to move on by third parties (typically police or private security guards) who control the space. The same may happen in public areas. They move on until they find a more tolerant place or one undesired by anybody else. The generally accepted wisdom is that if a park or square is made attractive to the general public, the homeless will move on. Alternatively, they blend in at a distance, outnumbered by the general population (Weber 1995). Bryant Park in New York is often cited as an example of such a public space. Many public squares, such as Paley Park and Marcus Garvey Park in New York, are fenced and locked at night, restricting hours of entry. Such measures are usually aimed at the subcultures that use open spaces in a way different to that intended by city managers.

Skateboarders, mostly young in age, belong to a subculture that defines them but one that can be viewed negatively by the general public. The possibility to use skateboards easily is purposefully designed-out of many public spaces by city administrators (see Figure 3.4 (b)). Squares or building forecourts that are bland, stark and non-descript, or concrete open spaces, are often a veritable paradise for skateboarders. If they have stairs, steps and ledges, they are sought-after locations for skateboarding. The skateboarding subculture claims these spaces as their own, especially on weekends or at night (Jones 2013).

Guerrilla urbanists (also known as tactical urbanists, DIY urbanists) are appropriating seemingly unused city spaces, including squares. They are part of the relatively robust 'placemaking' movement afoot in a number of cities, particularly in the United States. Pop-ups, markets and other temporary place activations such as "lighter, quicker, cheaper" developments (such as parklets) are being built or programmed, with or without the consent of planning authorities, in order to enliven unused spaces or to create places where people can meet.[13] These groups were initially 'anti-planning,' community-minded, middle-class 'rebels' who were unhappy with their local neighborhoods so they started to make changes themselves. The results are varied in both construction quality, utility and longevity but continue to alter the built form of cities, including some squares (Marshall and Bishop 2015).

The Utility of Open Spaces for Birds and Urban Wildlife

Depending on geographic location, the presence of animals (such as squirrels, monkeys or, in Venezuela, even sloths) and birds (from ducks in ponds to songbirds to intrusive ibis and crows) can enhance the experience of people in squares. Some urban wildlife attract passing attention, some interact with people while others are creatures to watch. They can amuse and educate. Some species are, however, simply unwelcome.

Native birds and songbirds generally please the public in localities where they exist. Pigeons and seagulls have an ambiguous position. Children enjoy feeding them, but while they add life to many squares, they are also considered to be pests when they flock in large numbers as pigeons once did in Trafalgar Square. Their droppings are both unsightly and unhealthy. Today, as the consequence of systematic efforts to eradicate them, many fewer pigeons inhabit Trafalgar Square than in the past. Authorities have now taken the same steps in Venice where pigeons were and still are causing considerable damage to the buildings and squares of the city. Feeding pigeons is no longer allowed in Piazza San Marco. Some birds, such as ibis and crows, while amusing to watch, wreak havoc with the content of rubbish bins and are generally unwelcome and difficult to manage.

Squirrels, butterflies or even fish in a pond, where they exist, usually delight the users of squares. Monkeys too can be amusing but also be dangerous if mistreated. Although rats are mostly unwelcome in public spaces, in some locales, they are tolerated and even venerated. Baiting to get rid of rats in other places has had unintended consequences when the bait is eaten by people's pets. Attracting welcome birds, animals and butterflies usually requires specific indigenous types of vegetation – trees, shrubs and flowers that may well struggle for life in the urban environment.

The presence of animals, like the presence of birds in urban squares, needs to be managed. Dogs, probably the most common domestic animal in public places, can be a positive catalyst for the meeting of their owners, but their presence can be unwanted by non-dog owners. In some garden squares in London the hours that dogs can be present are severely restricted. In some other squares, such as Tompkins Square Park in New York, separate zones are provided for dogs to run freely. Dog runs can be odorous and unhealthy if pet owners do not clean up after them; their droppings can attract rats as they do in Tompkins Square (Maurer 2012). In yet other squares the presence of dogs is totally prohibited.

Conclusion

As Jan Gehl (2010) notes, better city space equates to more city life. Urban squares designed with a range of publics in mind afford a sociability of public life. People lead different kinds of life and have different social practices; they also have a variety of motivations that lead them to discover different affordances for their use in the physical patterns of squares. It may seem that the diversity of interrelationships between people's predispositions and the use of squares is so arbitrary that it is impossible to predict with any degree of probability whether a square will be used or not. Squares designed with the people who are likely to use them or who live in the surrounding areas in mind will work well. The difficulties designers face is that they often, if not always, have to speculate about the latent desires of potential users – the activities that people would engage in if the opportunity was available. The ways people use squares is constantly changing although not as rapidly as we are often accustomed to believe. Squares need to be robust enough to adapt to the new contexts that the future provides. Public participation and engagement strategies can assist in making these conjectures. Often, however, decisions are made solely by the municipal authorities.

Notes

1 See Rapoport (2005), for a short but comprehensive look at the role of culture in the use of the built environment and a view of how architects should respond.
2 Jyoti Hosagrahar (2005) describes the differences between British colonial authorities and indigenous attitudes to what constitutes *public* open space. Many of the spaces that the British considered to be public were considered to be semi-public by the locals. See Chapter 4.
3 See Ward (1978), Michelson and Roberts (1979), Lennard and Lennard (1984, 2001), Churchman (2003) and Lang and Moleski (2010).
4 See the discussion in Woolley *et al.* (2011) and Jenson *et al.* (2012).
5 See Li (2014) for a discussion of the use of public space by American Chinese elderly.
6 The description of elderly men in Plaza Park written by Robert Sommer and Franklin Becker in 1969 is still valid today. It shows the enduring nature of such behavior, particularly among men of southern European heritage.
7 See Franck and Paxson (1989), Lofland (1984), Mozingo (1989), Cooper Marcus and Francis (1990), Duncan (1996) and Scranton and Watson (1998).
8 Franklin Becker (1972) provides an analysis of the biases in the evaluation of one such public place, Sacramento Mall, California.
9 The London squares and class concerns are described by John Richardson (1995) and Todd Longstaffe-Gowan (2012).
10 See Loukaitou-Sideris (1995), Rios (2010) and Li (2014), for instance, on cultural groups and the use of urban open spaces in the United States.
11 See Staples (1986) on the American context.
12 See Keirsey (1998) and Briggs Myers *et al.* (2009) for a discussion on the Myers-Briggs assessment of "temperament types" or personality types.
13 Parklets are an example of authorized light development undertaken by Do-It-Yourself urbanists to help develop and improve a city's public realm. The first parklet was piloted in 2010 in San Francisco. See City of San Francisco, Department of Public Works (2013).

References

Apley, M. H. (ed.) (1971) *Adaptation Level Theory: A Symposium*. New York: Academic Press.
Aronson, J. (1999) Homosex in Hanoi? Sex, the public sphere, and public sex? In *Public Sex/Gay Space*, edited by William Leap. New York: Columbia University Press, pp. 203–231.
Balint, Michael (1955) Friendly expanses – horrid empty spaces. *International Journal of Psycho-analysis* 36(4–5): 225–241.
Becker, Franklin (1972) A class-conscious evaluation: Going back to Sacramento pedestrian mall. *Landscape Architecture* 64: 448–457.

Boyer, M. Christine (1992) Cities for sale: Merchandising history at South Street Seaport. In *Variations on a Theme Park: The New American City and the End of Public Space*, edited by Michael Sorkin. New York: McGraw-Hill, pp. 181–204.

Briggs Myers, Isabel, Mary H. McCaulley, Naomi L. Quenk, Allen L. Hammer and Wayne D. Mitchell (2009) *MBTI Step III Manual: Exploring Personality Development Using the Myers-Briggs Type Indicator Instrument*. Mountain View: Consulting Psychologists Press.

Churchman, Arza (2003) Is there a place for children in the city? *Journal of Urban Design* 8(2): 99–111.

City of San Francisco, Department of Public Works (2013) *Parklet Manual*. The Authors. Available at: http://pavementtoparks.sfplanning.org/docs/SF_P2P_Parklet_Manual_1.0_FULL.pdf

Cooper Marcus, Clare and Carolyn Francis (1990) *People Places: Design Guidelines for Urban Open Space*. New York: Van Nostrand Reinhold.

Duncan, Nancy (1996) Renegotiating gender and sexuality in public and private spaces. In *BodySpace: Destabilizing Geographies of Gender and Sexuality*, edited by Nancy Duncan: London: Routledge, pp. 127–145.

Efroymson, Debra, Tran Thi Thanh Ha and Pham Thu Ha (2009) *Public Spaces: How They Humanize Cities*, edited by Lori Jones. Dhaka: Health Bridge-WBB Trust.

Franck, Karen A. and Lynn Paxson (1989) Women and urban public space: Research, design, and policy issues. *Human Behavior and Environment* 10: 121–146.

Gehl, Jan (1987) *Life between Buildings: Using Public Space*. New York: Van Nostrand Reinhold.

Gehl, Jan (2010) *Cities for People*. Washington, DC: Island Press.

Hosagrahar, Jyoti (2005) *Indigenous Modernities: Negotiating Architecture and Urbanism*. London: Routledge.

Jenson, Adam, Jon Swords and Michael Jeffries (2012) The accidental youth club: Skateboarding in Newcastle-Gateshead. *Journal of Urban Design* 17(3): 371–388.

Jones, Sam (2013) Can a skateboarding area be classed as a village green in order to save it? *The Guardian Weekly*, July 5, pp. 40–41.

Keirsey, David (1998) *Please Understand Me II: Temperament, Character, Intelligence*. Del Mar, CA: Prometheus Nemesis.

Lang, Jon (2005) *Urban Design: A Typology of Procedures and Products Illustrated with Over 50 Case Studies*. Oxford: Architectural Press.

Lang, Jon and Walter Moleski (2010) *Functionalism Revisited: Architectural Theory and Practice and the Behavioral Sciences*. Farnham: Ashgate.

Lennard, Henry and Suzanne H. C. Lennard (2001) *The Forgotten Child: Cities for the Well Being of Children*. Carmel, CA: Gondolier Press.

Lennard, Suzanne H. C. and Henry Lennard (1984) *Public Life in Urban Places*. Carmel, CA: Gondolier Press.

Li, Chuo (2014) Ethnicity, culture and park design: Case studies of urban parks in American Chinatowns. *Journal of Urban Design* 19(2): 230–254.

Lofland, Lyn H. (1984) Women and urban public space. *Women and Environment* 6: 12–14.

Longstaffe-Gowan, Todd (2012) *The London Square: Gardens in the Midst of Town*. New Haven, CT: Yale University Press.

Loukaitou-Sideris, Anastasia (1995) Urban form and social context: Cultural differentiation in the uses of urban parks. *Journal of Planning Education and Research* 14(2): 89–102.

Marshall, Nancy (2016) Urban squares: A place for public life. In *Place and Placelessness Revisited*, edited by Robert Freestone and Edgar Liu. New York: Routledge, pp. 186–203.

Marshall, Nancy and Kate Bishop (2015) Is there any correlation between place-making and place attachment? *International Journal of Interdisciplinary Social and Community Studies* 9(3–4): 1–10.

Maurer, Daniel (2012) Have rats returned to Tompkins Park? *The New York Times*, August 3. Available at: http://eastvillage.thelocal.nytimes.com/2012/08/03/37659/comment-page-1.

Michelson, William and E. Roberts (1979) Children in the urban physical environment. In *The Child in the City: Changes and Challenges*, edited by William Michelson, Saul V. Levine and Ellen Michelson. Toronto: University of Toronto Press.

Mozingo, Louise (1989) Women and downtown open spaces. *Places* 6(1): 38–47.

Murphy Peter and Sophie Watson (1997) *Surface City*. Sydney: Pluto Press.

Murray, Martin J. (2011) *City of Extremes: The Spatial Politics of Johannesburg*. Durham, NC: Duke University Press.

Rapoport, Amos (2005) *Culture, Architecture, Design*. Chicago: Locke Science.

Relph, Edward (1976) *Place and Placelessness*. London: Pion.

Richardson, John (1995) *London and Its People: A Social History from Medieval Times to the Present Day*. London: Barrie and Jenkins.

Rios, Michael (2010) Claiming Latino space: Cultural insurgency in the public realm. In *Insurgent Public Space*, edited by Jeffery Hou. London: Routledge, pp. 99–110.

Scranton, Sheila and Beccy Watson (1998) Gendered cities: Women and public leisure space in the 'postmodern city.' *Leisure Studies* 17(2): 123–137.

Sommer, Robert and Franklin Becker (1969) The old men in Plaza Park. *Landscape Architecture* 59(2): 111–113.

Staples, Brent (1986) Black men and public spaces. *Harper's Magazine*, December. Available at: http://harpers.org/archive/1986/12/black-men-and-public-space.

Ward, Colin (1978) *The Child in the City*. London: Architectural Press.

Weber, Bruce (1995) Town square of Midtown; drug dealers' turf is now an office oasis. *The New York Times*, August 25. Available at: www.nytimes.com/1995/08/25/nyregion/town-square-of-midtown-drug-dealers-turf-is-now-an-office-oasis.html.

Woolley, Helen, Teresa Hazelwood and Ian Simkins (2011) Don't skate here: Exclusion of skateboarders from urban civic spaces in three northern cities in England. *Journal of Urban Design* 16(4): 471–488.

Further Reading

Bishop, Kate and Linda Corkery (eds) (2016) *Designing Cities with Children and Young People: Beyond playgrounds and skate parks*. New York: Routledge (in press).

Hall, Edward T. and Mildred R. Hall (1990) *Understanding Cultural Differences – Germans, French and Americans*. Yarmouth: Intercultural Press.

Iveson, Kurt (2013) Cities within the city: Do-it-yourself urbanism and the right to the city. *International Journal of Urban and Regional Research* 37(3): 941–956.

Landry, Charles (2006) *The Art of City Making*. London: Earthscan.

Low, Setha (2000) *On the Plaza: The Politics of Public Space and Culture*. Austin, TX: University of Texas Press.

Malone, Karen (2002) Street life: Youth, culture and competing uses of public space. *Environment and Urbanization* 14(2): 157–168.

Marshall, Nancy and Kate Bishop (2015) Is there any correlation between place-making and attachment? *International Journal of Interdisciplinary Social and Community Studies* 9(3–4): 1–10.

Whyte, William H. (1980) *The Social Life of Small Urban Spaces*. Washington, DC: The Conservation Foundation.

PART II

TYPES OF URBAN SQUARES AND THEIR DESIGN

Paternoster Square, London

Categorization systems are useful in drawing attention to the similarities among seemingly disparate elements of a topic; the differences among them can, however, easily be obscured. A number of approaches to the categorization of squares have informed the one we use here. In 1959, Paul Zucker identified types of squares in a manner that enabled him to analyze what works and what does not work within them. His categorization, which is shown the figure below, is more abstract than ours but we refer to it with some frequency.

Like many observers, Zucker (1959) focused on the historic squares of Europe built during medieval or Renaissance times and whose present character emerged over time. He differentiated among squares based on their enclosing elements and the location of features that added to their quality. The self-contained *closed square* was his "ideal" type. The *nuclear* square has a feature at its center; the *dominated square* serves as a foreground for a building, while, in some cities, open spaces are linked to form *grouped squares*. Other scholars have categorized squares differently.

Jan Gehl and Lars Gemzøe (2000) distinguish among *main city squares, recreational squares, promenades, traffic squares* and *monumental squares*. This classification is based on the instrumental function that squares serve. Nigel Coates (2003) identified squares that are *ceremonial, cathedral/church, social, residential, courtyards, with parks,* and *street shopping*. He draws attention to what goes on around squares. Stephen Carr and his colleagues (1992) studied *central squares, corporate plazas* and *memorial squares*. Aleksandar Janicijevic's (n.d.) system is similar. These categorizations of types may, on the surface, seem very different but they are really quite alike. Our focus is different but our debt to these previous efforts is obvious.

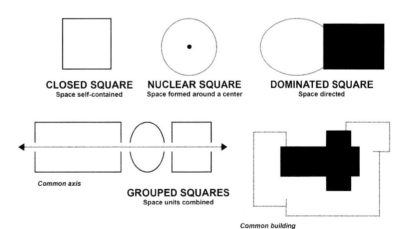

CLOSED SQUARE
Space self-contained

NUCLEAR SQUARE
Space formed around a center

DOMINATED SQUARE
Space directed

Common axis

GROUPED SQUARES
Space units combined

Common building

Paul Zucker's categorization of types of squares (1959: 2–3)

Source: Redrawn by Rachel Cogger.

A Categorization of Types: A Typology of Squares

The typology used here is based on the decisions that urban design-ers, architects, landscape architects and city planners have to make in refurbishing public spaces and in creating new ones in our con-temporary world. We pick up on most of the characteristics identified in the earlier approaches of our colleagues but we look at squares in a somewhat different and more detailed manner. The design pro-cess almost always follows a mimetic set of steps so we look at the concerns of decision-makers.

In creating a categorization system, we have taken an active posi-tion. We have striven to identify the common attributes of squares. Good examples are those closest to the definition of the category and the poorest examples are the furthest from the defining charac-teristic. Nevertheless, squares that fall into one category will also be members of others based on a different set of attributes. Thus, each square that forms part of the selection of case studies we present in this book is categorized along several dimensions. The categories may be fuzzy at the boundaries but their focus is clear.

Focusing on urban squares, designers are principally concerned with their purposes and physical character. Their primary goal is to ensure that the built environment functions well and "that nothing should interfere with its fitness to fulfil its purpose" (Fleming *et al.* 1999: 210). Deciding on how a square functions depends on its spon-sors, that is, the people funding a square and the decision-makers – either private companies or government authorities. Thus, squares may be private or public in their ownership. We also make a distinc-tion among squares based on their instrumental functions and their geometries. Their layouts differ based on their overall shape and the degree to which they are enclosed and the nature of their enclos-ing elements. Squares carry meaning and so we have cautiously developed a typology of meanings knowing full well that symbolic meanings remain a difficult subject matter.

Recognizing the Types of Ownership of Squares

The terms 'public space,' 'public realm' and 'open space' are often used interchangeably but there are nuanced differences. Planners, architects and landscape architects all question, as a matter of practice, who owns different spaces in the city and who owns the space between buildings and, particularly, which spaces can the general public freely access. People have the right to enter fully public squares that are owned by government agencies on behalf of and in the interest of the public. They can be entered at any time of day and any activity, other than those that fall outside the law and the moral code of a culture, can legally be carried out in them. Many such public squares have, however, restricted hours of entry and a list of restrictions on what kind of behaviors can take place in them.

Many recently completed and proposed squares are being built by private developers and will remain privately controlled by a profit-making corporation. In some of the squares, the public can enter at any hour but in others the hours of admission are restricted. As they are built and managed by private enterprises, they are usually well maintained and privately policed. In some squares, publicly or privately owned , the occupiers of adjacent buildings regard the squares as belonging to them. They thus exert another layer of control over what can happen in them. Does this control have an impact on how a square functions? Does it affect how squares are designed? We turn our attention to these questions in Chapter 4 where we differentiate among three principal types of ownership of squares: public, quasi-public and semi-public. In addition, we introduce a fourth category: semi-private squares. We only mention a fifth type, private, in passing because they are not open to the public. They are, nevertheless, part of a city's ground floor.

Recognizing the Fundamental Purposes Served by Squares

Squares serve many overlapping functions, ranging from the provision of behavior settings, or activity sites, to giving an identity to a locale or reinforcing the self-image of a people. The range of instrumental purposes that squares fulfill is the point of departure in differentiating one square from another. It is the basic difference among squares as Gehl and Gemzøe (2000) and also Coates (2003) recognize in the way they categorize squares. Our categorization differs because we consider a square's basic use from a social and an architectural programming viewpoint. We present our approach in Chapter 5.

Squares have been used to give a logical configuration to the plan of a city. Historically this function has only been characteristic of pre-planned cities. We take this function as our point of departure. Most cities have grown in a piecemeal fashion. Some squares have been formed either self-consciously or unself-consciously to act as the hearts of precincts or even cities. Historically, many squares were, for instance, market places. There has been a recent revival of weekly markets in many places where they had ceased to operate. Many squares can provide for large gatherings of people either in celebration or protest. Some that do so are attractive places when they are empty; others are not.

Few squares were specifically designed to be landmarks but have become well-known ones. Others are merely forecourts to buildings. A significant number of squares are memorials to heroes or heroic events. Others, particularly some recent ones, were simply created as works of art. It is clear that a relationship exists between the physical characteristics of a square and the instrumental purposes it can serve.

Recognizing the Basic Physical Attributes of Squares

Squares come in a variety of basic physical forms that can serve different instrumental functions. They come in a range of basic geometries; they vary in size, degree of enclosure, configurations and internal designs that affect their affordances. We categorize the types of each in Chapters 6–9 to show municipal authorities and designers the vast range of physical types of squares that can and do exist for their consideration. We also describe what the various patterns of built form afford diverse groups of people.

Recognizing the Meanings of Squares

Squares also serve advanced functions – they have a role in establishing a sense of identity, belonging, legitimacy and pride in their users. Squares can be analyzed in term of the symbolic meanings they convey and by the ideas of their architects as embodied in their design – their intellectual esthetic underpinnings. We thus address two topics under the rubric of advanced functions. The first is in Chapter 10, "Types Based on Symbolic Functions" and the second is in Chapter 11, "Types Based on Design Paradigms." The former deals with the problems and issues in creating a sense of place and the latter with the way designers have striven to create an identity for themselves that establishes their niche in the competition for recognition and for design services.

We ultimately argue that designing purely to fulfill the artistic expression of their designers should be treated with caution because many such squares have proven to serve little other purpose. They lie empty most of the time, visited only by architects who may well then copy the organizing ideas underlying them in their own designs and achieve similar, limited results.

Conclusion

We have divided this part of the book into four highly interrelated sub-sections. The first deals with the ownership of squares and their implications (Classifying Squares Based on Ownership Type: Chapter 4). The second considers the basic functions a square serves (Classifying Squares Based on Their Purposes: Chapter 5). The third focuses on the physical attributes of squares (Instrumental Functions and the Basic Physical Attributes of Squares: Chapters 6–9), and the fourth the symbolic functions of squares (Classifying Squares Based on Their Esthetic Attributes – Meanings: Chapters 10 and 11). The distinction adds some clarity to the discussion of the utility of squares, but it will be clear that the four concerns are very much intertwined. Ultimately it must be recognized that any categorization system classifies the categorizer; the system we have adopted, as Pierre Bourdieu (1984) reminds us, classifies us the authors. It also shapes and thus biases the way we look at and discuss our subject (King 2004).

References

Bourdieu, Pierre (1984) *Distinction: A Social Critique of the Judgement of Taste*, trans. from the French by Richard Nice. Cambridge, MA: Harvard University Press.

Carr, Stephen, Mark Francis, Leanne Rivlin and Andrew Strauss (1992) *Public Space*. Cambridge: Cambridge University Press.

Coates, Nigel (2003) *Guide to Ecstasy*. London: Laurence King.

Fleming, John, Hugh Honour and Nikolaus Pevsner (1999). *The Penguin Dictionary of Architecture and Landscape Architecture*, 5th edn. London: Penguin Books.

Gehl, Jan and Lars Gemzøe (2000) *New City Spaces*. Copenhagen: Danish Architectural Press.

Janicijevic, Aleksandar (n.d.) Urban squares. Available at: www.urbansquares.com/index.html.

King, Anthony (2004) *Spaces of Global Cultures: Architecture, Urbanism, Identity*. London: Routledge.

Zucker, Paul (1959) *Town and Square: From the Agora to the Village Green*. New York: Columbia University Press.

Further Reading

Carmona, Mathew (2010) Contemporary public spaces, Part Two: Classification. *Journal of Urban Design* 15(2): 157–176.

Franck, Karen A. and Lynda Schneekloth (1994) *Ordering Spaces: Types in Architecture and Design*. New York: Van Nostrand Reinhold.

Gehl, Jan (2010) *Cities for People*. Washington, DC: Island Press.

Jacob, Elin K. (2004) Classification and categorization: A difference that makes a difference. *Library Trends* 52(3): 515–540.

CHAPTER 4

PUBLIC, QUASI-PUBLIC AND SEMI-PUBLIC SQUARES

The areas of cities that are deemed to be open space and those deemed to be public may seem to be self-evident. Open space often, however, means parks, and public simply means that people are allowed to enter without having to obtain permission. One option, which we take here, to understand how open spaces function as part of urban life is to show that there is a hierarchy of open space types based on the degree of power and control that various groups of people have over them. Urban open spaces vary on a continuum from being public to being private in their nature. In between these ownership types come quasi-public, semi-public and semi-private spaces (Newman 1972).

Public Space

All societies have restrictions on what kind of activities can occur in public. Some are more restrictive than others and are regulated differently, varying from by unwritten social norms, to local by-laws and zoning, to state and national legislation. Urban open spaces that are truly public are those in which people have total unrestricted right of access at any time but not for any activity that they wish.[1] This definition may seem obvious but it is insufficient. Although presumed to be public, many parks and squares have restricted hours of access and major restrictions on what a person can do in them. Generally we still regard them as public spaces. Municipally owned streets and squares may always seem to be fully public but this categorization should be treated with some caution. Some may well be entirely public while others are only semi-public. Neighbors exert some control over semi-public spaces because they feel that they have a degree of ownership over them and thus the right to limit what happens in them. Indeed, 'guerrilla urbanists' extend this right to changing or programming temporarily a space in their own interests.

Cities are full of genuine public spaces (see Figure 4.1). Some are ostensibly *places* such as squares made for lingering but the major

Figure 4.1 Typical genuinely public open spaces in cities: (a) A street: N State Street, Chicago; (b) A square: Thibault Square, Cape Town

public open spaces – the streets – are designed primarily as *links* – channels of movement. The carriageway is for vehicular and bicycle traffic and the footpaths/sidewalks are for pedestrians. Streets vary in dimensions from major thoroughfares to narrow alleys. The latter, mainly a relic of past delivery systems and for clearing sewage, have now often been turned into pedestrian ways. In Melbourne, Australia, many laneways are now lined with open-air cafés and shops and are a feature of the central area of the city and a destination for both locals and tourists. Few people, however, consider streets as public open space but they are very important because they are heavily used; they are the location from where a city is seen. The characteristics of a city's streets thus contribute greatly to the overall image of a city. For pedestrians, the streets, squares and parks represent the public open space of a city that is immediately available to them.

Privacy, Security and the Publicness of Public Places

As mentioned in Chapter 3, people need to feel psychologically secure and safe before they will use a public space (Németh and Schmidt 2007, 2011). Potential visitors to a square scan the environment to see whether their desire for privacy,[2] as individuals or as a group, as well as their need to feel secure from antisocial behavior can be met. A degree of privacy must be given up to attain that sense of security.[3] Too few people in a square can be a problem as safety is seen in numbers. Over-crowding, however, is not desirable. Crime Prevention Through Environmental Design (CPTED) guidelines have been applied to the design of public open spaces since the 1960s in order to design-out opportunities for criminal behavior with some success (Lang and Moleski 2010).

Over-crowded spaces may provide pickpockets with the opportunity to prey on the people in those spaces. The presence of others in public space does, however, generally provides people with a sense of safety. People have the expectation that others will come to their aid if necessary. Certainly the presence of a number of people in a square acts as a deterrent to would-be offenders. Squares such Olympic Plaza in Calgary are regarded as safe in the public's eye when an event is being held or at lunchtime when there are many people there. In the evenings when the surroundings are largely deserted, it is regarded as one to avoid.

Quasi-Public Spaces: Privately Owned Public Open Spaces

Quasi-public spaces are those that are open to the public but are in private ownership. They are known as POPS (Privately Owned Public Spaces) or POPOS (Privately Owned Public Open Spaces). The growth in number of POPS reflects the widespread privatization of the control of public space.[4] Cities are full of quasi-public spaces; some are indoor spaces such as arcades and winter gardens. The assembly area at Grand Central Station in New York is essentially a privately owned interior square open to the public at all hours. The Winter Garden of Brookfield Place (the World Financial Center) in New York, in contrast, is open only at restricted although generous hours (Figure 4.2 (a)). The same is true of the skyway linkage bridges and walkway systems linking buildings as in Calgary and Minneapolis (Figure 4.2 (b)).

Skyway systems connecting POPS within buildings enable pedestrians to move around much of the centers of cities in metabolic comfort and safety at second floor or even higher levels. While open to the public for most of the day and weekends, many such links are closed at other times. Often posted sets of rules spell out what are unacceptable behaviors in these places. Handing out political leaflets is, for instance, among those activities that are prohibited. POPS are the prime example of quasi-public squares in cities.

Figure 4.2 Interior quasi-public spaces: (a) The Winter Gardens, Brookfield Place, New York: (b) The +15 walkway in downtown Calgary

Figure 4.3 Privately Owned Public
Space (POPS): (a) Siam Paragon
Plaza, Bangkok; (b) Paternoster
Square paper marker; (c) Sidewalk
marker, Los Angeles

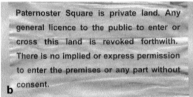

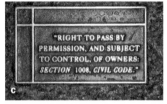

POPS range in type from the forecourts of commercial buildings to large-scale squares. Central San Francisco has 68 identifiable POPS (SPUR 2013) (Figure 4.3). POPS are often criticized because they are not fully public. Some critics consider them to be a product of neoliberalist economic policies formulated by municipal authorities attempting to pass the cost of the traditional public investment in infrastructure on to the private sector. Others believe private owner-ship and maintenance are a strategy that ensures more and better public open space in cities.[5] Some POPS are owned and maintained by public interest groups – The Friends of the High Line in New York, for example, maintain that open space.

If well designed, POPS can serve an important role in cities, par-ticularly in Central Business Districts. They can serve as transitions, or thresholds, between public and private areas, places to meet people, to have a lunchtime break or simply to rest for a while in a clean, comfortable place. To function well economically, commercial squares have to attract shoppers and businesses so they are usually well maintained. Many POPS that serve as forecourts to buildings, roof gardens or even enclosed squares, have metal markers in the paving or other signs demarcating the boundaries and announcing that the area within them is in private ownership. The largely ignored paper signs in metal holders at each entrance to Paternoster Square declare that the square is not public property (Figure 4.3 (b)). They were rapidly created after the Occupy London demonstrations of 2011. Commercial squares are in the same position.

Although one associates commercial squares with enclosed shopping malls, such squares started to appear in cities in the 1980s. Ghirardelli Square in San Francisco is an example (Carr *et al.* 1992). The square is located in what was once an open space in a complex of chocolate factories. The factories were adapted to new uses in the 1980s to create a shopping and restaurant complex. The open spaces wlthln it form part of a linked set of privately owned public squares. The public open space at 343 Sansome Street in San Francisco is on the rooftop of a secure building in the financial district. It was built specifically to be a public open space but it is only quasi-public.

Semi-Public Spaces

Semi-public spaces are those in which the people inhabiting adjacent buildings exert control over what happens on the streets or squares in front of them. They regard the space fronting their premises as if it were their own. Sidewalks are the primary examples of such spaces in cities.[6] The general public may well have the full legal right of access but the range of activities in which they can engage may be inhibited by residents in housing districts, or retailers on shopping streets. Although Cours Honoré d'Estienne d'Orves in Marseille is a public space, the restaurant owners claim 'ownership' of its edges.

Semi-public spaces, although in public ownership, may have objects placed in them that denote a claim of proprietorship over the open space. In a number of New York's residential streets, canopies and carpets, real or painted, lead from buildings to the edge of the sidewalk. In Figure 4.4 (a), carefully manicured plantings of flowers reinforce the claim. *Chowks* in India are full of the personal belongings of the adjacent residences (Figure 4.4 (b)). If large enough they become parking lots too. In other cases, lines drawn in the paving imply a degree of private ownership that does not legally exist.

Figure 4.4 Semi-public spaces: (a) 165 West 66th Street, New York; (b) A chowk, India

Source: (b) Photograph by Gritsana P/ Shutterstock.com.

Semi-Private Spaces

There are two types of semi-private open spaces. The first type is that which is clearly under private ownership but to which outsiders have access at certain times, such as the courtyard of the Victoria and Albert Museum in London (free entry) or the Sculpture Garden of the Museum of Modern Art in New York (payment required) (Figure 4.5 (a)) and, in a very different context, the Dutch Hospital Shopping Precinct in Colombo (free entry) (Figure 4.5 (b)).

The second type consists of walled or fenced open squares that have locked entrance gates and are under the private ownership of their members. Membership is usually restricted to the people whose houses face directly onto the space. Some of the fences/walls are substantial but others are minimal and largely symbolic. Examples include Bedford Square and many other squares in London, Gramercy Park in New York and Louisburg Square in Boston (Figures 4.6 (a) and (d), respectively). Although passers-by can see into the squares, they have no right of admission. Such places, often known as *garden squares*, are remnants of the nineteenth century before the era of garden suburbs.

In some of the semi-private squares, all the surrounding and enclosing buildings are products of a single development but in others (for example, Louisburg Square in Boston), they were designed by different people at different times. They were, nevertheless, executed with a sense of decorum with the new houses being built respecting the design choices made for the earlier buildings. The common materials used for the walls and the common window-to-wall ratios give a unity to the square. In Arabic-Islamic countries, similar practices were historically an unwritten but accepted building code (Hakim 1986). Garden squares that are part of large property developments created these days are, however, generally public or quasi-public spaces.

Figure 4.5 Semi-private courtyard squares: (a) Museum of Modern Art, New York; (b) The Dutch Hospital Shopping Precinct, Colombo

Figure 4.6 *Semi-private squares: (a) Bedford Square, London; (b) An interior glimpse; (c) A notice at the gate; (d) Louisburg Square, Boston; (e) A pedestrian's view*

Sources: (a)–(d) Collection of Jon Lang.

Private Spaces

Private spaces fall outside the scope of our study but they are of great importance in a city. Without them, a sense of community would be almost impossible to obtain in many cultures. Outdoor spaces such as courtyards and backyards are under the complete control of their inhabitants but many are really only semi-private because outsiders can see into them and emanating sounds and smells are difficult to control. An invasion of privacy can also occur when such places are viewed into from adjacent taller buildings. This problem is particularly acute in hot and arid climates where the roofs of buildings are heavily used in the evenings for family life.

Traffic and its Impact on the Publicness of Public Squares[7]

A distinction can be made between those squares that form courts because they are cut off from traffic, as in the traditional Italian squares, and those that have vehicles moving around them or even across them at various levels of intensity. The traffic can be regarded as an intrusion on the activities of people in the square so the square, even if legally public, takes on the form of a semi-public space especially where the traffic volumes are high. When intense, the public's right of access to such squares is compromised although not denied. The traffic swirling around Khomeini Square in Tehran, for instance, makes the square difficult to reach (see Figure 0.7 on p. 13). The same

Figure 4.7 Vehicular traffic and public squares: (a) Plaza Mayor, Madrid – no vehicle traffic; (b) Azadi Square, Tehran, swirling traffic

Sources: (a) Photograph by Vinicus Tupinamba/Shutterstock.com; (b) Photograph by Homa Rahmat.

observation can be made about many squares in cities where the volume of vehicular traffic has increased. Tahrir Square in Cairo, once a relatively quiet square, has become a busy traffic circle. During the mass protests of the 'Arab Spring' of 2011, traffic was, nevertheless, brought to a standstill. Some squares are simply large traffic circles (see Figure 5.13 on p. 98).

Plaza Mayor in Madrid is a closed square. No vehicles pass through it unless it is a delivery truck. Traffic passes on three sides of Trafalgar Square, swirls around Azadi Square in Tehran and criss-crosses Public Square in Cleveland. This type of bisecting has occurred in a number of places although when the traffic passing through the square is sporadic, the whole space functions as a single square. The sonic environment and the freedom of movement of pedestrians vary considerably in the two examples shown in Figure 4.7.

Conclusion

Squares can be public, quasi-public in the form of privately owned public space, semi-public and semi-private. Some of the fully public spaces such as Trafalgar Square in London, Piazza San Marco in Venice and Tiananmen Square in Beijing, serve an international function by giving a city a focal point for both locals and tourists. Anybody can ostensibly enter them at any time. Many critics feel uncomfortable with the existence of quasi-public squares; they would prefer such spaces to be fully public. The general public seems not to care if a square is public or a POPS if their behavior is used as the criterion for evaluation. Political activists who test the public access may have a very different view.

At a local level, it is the spaces that serve neighborhood or block purposes that are of special concern. It is important in their design, as Jane Jacobs noted, that "there must be a clear demarcation between what is public space and what is private space. Public and private spaces cannot ooze into each other" (1961: 35). If demarcations are unclear, conflicts over rights, allowable activities and control over the space may arise.

Notes

1 Several attempts have been made to define 'public space' based on how a space is administered and/or owned. See Langstraat and van Melik (2013) for a review.
2 Privacy does not mean seclusion. It has to do with the control of information – visual, sonic, olfactory or touch – about an activity that goes out of a behavior setting and the intrusion of outside information into it.
3 Many urban experts have made this point. Jacobs (1961) and Newman (1972) were among the early authors to make this observation.
4 See Sennett (1977), Buchanan (1988), Hitt (1990), Sorkin (1992) and Low (2006) among others.
5 A number of recent statements examine the concerns in much greater depth than we do here. See Krier (1979), Varna and Tiesdell (2010), De Magalhães (2010) and Langstraat and van Melik (2013). See also Minton (2012) for a fuller description of the British context and Vasagar (2012) for a commentary on it.
6 For a discussion of claims of informal private rights on public sidewalks in the United States, see Loukaitou-Sideris and Ehrenfeucht (2014).
7 See also the discussion of squares as traffic circles in Chapter 5.

References

Buchanan, Peter (1988) What city? A plea for the place of the public realm: City planning in Britain. *Architectural Review* 184(11): 30–41.

Carr, Stephen, Mark Francis, Leanne Rivlin and Andrew M. Stone (1992) *Public Space*. Cambridge: Cambridge University Press.

De Magalhães, Claudio (2010) Public space and the contracting-out of publicness: A framework for analysis. *Journal of Urban Design* 15(4): 559–574.

Hakim, Besim S. (1986) *Arabic-Islamic Cities: Building and Planning Principles*. London: KPI.

Hitt, Jack (1990) Whatever became of the public square? edited by Lewis H. Lapham. *Harper's Magazine* 281(July 1): 49–60.

Jacobs, Jane (1961) *The Death and Life of Great American Cities*. New York: Random House.

Krier, Rob (1979) *Urban Space (Stadtraum)*. Trans. from the German by Christine Czechowski and George Black. New York: Random House.

Lang, Jon and Walter Moleski (2010) *Functionalism Revisited: Architectural Theory and Practice and the Behavioral Sciences*. Farnham: Ashgate.

Langstraat, Florian and Rianne van Melik (2013) Challenging the 'end of public space': A comparative analysis of publicness in British and Dutch urban spaces. *Journal of Urban Design* 18(3): 429–448.

Loukaitou-Sideris, Anastasia and Renia Ehrenfeucht (2014) "This is my front yard!" Claims and informal property rights on sidewalks. In *The Informal American City: Beyond Taco Trucks and Day Labor*, edited by Vinit Mukhija and Anastasia Loukaitou-Sideris. Cambridge, MA: MIT Press, pp. 97–118.

Low, Setha (2006) How private interests take over public space: Zoning, taxes and incorporation of gated communities. In *The Politics of Open Space*, edited by Setha Low and Neil Smith. New York: Routledge, pp. 81–104.

Minton, Anna (2012) *Ground Control: Fear and Happiness in the Twenty-First Century City*. Harmondsworth: Penguin.

Németh, Jeremy and Stephen Schmidt (2007) Towards a methodology for measuring the security of publicly accessible spaces. *Journal of the American Planning Association* 73(3): 283–297.

Németh, Jeremy and Stephen Schmidt (2011) The privatization of public space: modelling and measuring publicness. *Environment and Planning B: Planning and Design* 38(1): 5–23.

Newman, Oscar (1972) *Defensible Space*. New York: Macmillan.

San Francisco Planning and Urban Research (SPUR) Association (2013) *A Guide to San Francisco's Privately-Owned Public Open Spaces: Secrets of San Francisco*. San Francisco: SPUR.

Sennett, Richard (1977) *The Fall of Public Man*. New York: Knopf.

Sorkin, Michael (ed.) (1992) *Variations on a Theme Park: The New American City and the End of Public Space.* New York: Hill and Wang.

Varna, George and Steve Tiesdell (2010) Assessing the publicness of public space: The star model of publicness. *Journal of Urban Design* 15(4): 575–590.

Vasagar, Jeevan (2012) Public spaces fall into private hands. *The Guardian Weekly*, June 22, pp. 16–17.

Further Reading

Longstaffe-Gowan, Todd (2012) *The London Square: Gardens in the Midst of Town.* New Haven, CT: Yale University Press.

Madanipour, Ali (2003) *Public and Private Spaces in the City.* London: Routledge.

Punter, John (1990) Privatization of the public realm. *Planning Practice and Research* 5(3): 9–16.

CHAPTER 5

TYPES BASED ON INSTRUMENTAL FUNCTIONS

Squares are either designed for a specific purpose or acquire that purpose through a later conscious design decision or as unselfconsciously determined by their users. Any square can serve a multiplicity of purposes. A flat surface affords many different behaviors, active and passive, as a casual glance at almost any square soon reveals. Squares can, nevertheless, be differentiated from one another in terms of their instrumental functions – the activities they actually serve as places and as links. We regard these purposes as their basic functions. The two functions are not independent but overlap; sometimes they are contradictory. Later we discuss the advanced functions that squares can serve as symbols.[1]

The Potential Functions of Squares as Places

Squares, as places, can serve many purposes. Many squares could just as easily be put into more than one of the categories described in this chapter. We identify a number of roles that squares can play in a city. In the first place, their distribution can give an overall structure to a city's plan. This function has not been given the attention or research it deserves as other functions have dominated the discussion. The quality of any square is enhanced by its major instrumental function being supplemented by the other purposes that it serves.

Some of the world's best-loved squares serve as the heart of a city or a neighborhood. To function this way they have to serve many purposes simultaneously. They can for, instance, be places to relax and also be landmarks and/or serve as the forecourts to buildings. If they are the foreground for a number of important institutional buildings, they can be the heart of a city but if they are forecourts for commercial buildings, they are seldom more than a link between streets and buildings. Squares that are the hearts of cities also provide for events, large and small, regularly scheduled, such as markets, or intermittently, such as for special holiday celebrations and pop-up activities. The basic function of some squares is to be a memorial, whereas others simply contain memorials and/or works of art.

The Function of Squares in Organizing the Plan of a City

Some cities have a consciously planned pattern of squares that function as part of a system as in Philadelphia, Pennsylvania, and Savannah, Georgia, in the United States and Adelaide in Australia. The most clearly articulated decree for planning city squares as a system was embodied in the *Laws of the Indies* produced by King Philip II of Spain and instigated in 1573 and developed further by King Charles II in 1680. The laws governed many aspects of life including the design of settlements in the Spanish colonies of the Americas and the Philippines (Crouch and Mundigo 1977; Crouch *et al.* 1982). Its impact is noticeable, if somewhat blurred, to this day in North American cities such as Albuquerque, Los Angeles and Tucson and more clearly throughout Latin America in squares dating back to the first Spanish settlements and in the Philippines (for example, Plaza Salcedo in Vigan City). Few other cities around the world have such planned distributions of squares. In these other cities the pattern of squares has been developed unself-consciously, piece by piece over time by property developers, public authorities or private ventures. They function as the centers of the precincts of the city despite being formed in a haphazard manner.

The Spanish colonial settlements were laid out with the *Plaza Mayor* (in Mexico, the *Zócalo*) at their center. The dimensions were specified according to the size of the settlement. The square was enclosed by the major church, the town hall and other public buildings – the center of the local area. From the square, a rectangular grid of streets was built. The directions were chosen according to the prevailing winds in order to enhance the ambient qualities of the *Plaza Mayor*. Smaller secondary squares and narrow streets were also decreed. The buildings around them had colonnades facing the square and were to be uniform in character to create a sense of harmony (Crouch and Mundigo 1977; Crouch *et al.* 1982). These squares are still used for special celebrations, markets and as everyday social spaces.

Today, Mexico City's *Zócalo* is a vast paved area with its sides often filled with traffic (Figure 5.1). In the early twentieth century it contained a garden surrounded by streets and at its center had a fountain with paths radiating from its sides and corners. *Zócalos* like that in Oaxaca, which is widely regarded by both the design experts and the general public as one of the world's finest, had trees and grassed areas added to it. It is now undergoing a controversial renovation to incorporate the region's native vegetation. Despite strong protests, the exotic, shade-giving trees are to be removed.

As mentioned, in the United States, Savannah and Philadelphia are two cities whose original plans were organized around squares. Savannah was laid out by General James Oglethorpe in 1733 with four open squares, each of which was surrounded by four residential (*tithing*) blocks and four civic (*trust*) blocks (Figures 5.2 (a) and (b)). The square and its eight surrounding blocks were known as a *ward*. The basic grid allowed for additional squares to be added as the city grew; by 1851, there were 24 of them. Twenty-one remain in place

today and give the center of Savannah much of its unique character. Each square is named after a person, persons or an historical event; many contain monuments, markers, memorials, statues, plaques and other tributes that give each ward a particular identity.

Philadelphia's original grid plan has similarities to the plan for London prepared by Richard Newcomb after the Great Fire of 1666. It contained five squares: Central Square, now the site of City Hall, Southeast Square (now Washington Square), Northeast Square (now Franklin Square), Northwest Square (now Logan Square) and Southwest Square (now Rittenhouse Square) (Figures 5.2 (c) and (d)).[2] Although they were originally used for such purposes as potters' fields, the squares have evolved into new forms and give central Philadelphia not only open spaces but hearts to its Center City neighborhoods. Central Adelaide in Australia has essentially the same plan as Philadelphia. All five of the squares of the city are still open spaces.

Unself-consciously designed systems of squares are those where the squares were designed but the relationship among them has grown haphazardly. Each of the garden squares of London was designed individually but the overall pattern is the result of piecemeal, area-by-area, property development of the city. Each square is the center of the surrounding buildings but no geometric pattern governs the relationship of one square to the others. In a very different climatic and cultural context, the small squares in North African Islamic cities and cities such as Jaisalmer in the Thar Desert of India occur at intersections of winding paths and have also been created piecemeal over time. In either case a system of squares now exists. These squares are the hearts of neighborhoods; some are the hearts of cities.

Figure 5.1 *Squares of the Law of the Indies: the Zócalo, Mexico City*

Source: Photograph by javarman/ Shutterstock.com.

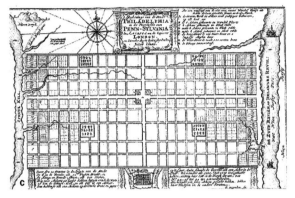

Figure 5.2 Two urban plans with a pattern of squares, USA: (a) Illustration of the 1733 Oglethorpe plan for Savannah; (b) Forsythe Square, Savannah; (c) The Penn-Holmes plan for Philadelphia, 1683; (d) Southwest Square, now Rittenhouse Square, in 2013

Sources: (a) Photograph by Everitt Historical Society/ Shutterstock. com; (b) Photograph by Sean Pavon/ Shutterstock.com.

Squares Functioning Simply as Open Space

Continuing demands for more open space can be heard from both powerful advocates for improvements in cities and the general public. In dense urban cores and high-density residential neighborhoods, any open space may fulfill a need but the demand for more open space is often misguided. Forlorn open spaces in the form of parks and squares abound – Jane Jacobs (1961: 89) described them as "dispirited city vacuums" but they can, nevertheless, still serve a purpose. Open spaces can allow more light to reach street level and allow the air to circulate but often squares are placed in a location where they do neither. Many serve little purpose other than providing light and downdrafts at street level and simply acting as open space. In complete contrast to the largely purposeless open spaces, many other squares function as the hearts of urban areas.

Squares as the Hearts of Cities or Neighborhoods

Some major squares around the world are the core open spaces of a city. They represent, in Gertrude Stein's (1937) words, a "there" there – something that was lacking in Oakland, California, her childhood city. Oakland was not alone in this regard. Many cities have no central square. Other cities, however, have squares that were designed from the beginning to be the hearts of a city; some have squares that have acquired that role. Yet other squares have been created recently, with more or less success, to play that role. To do so successfully, they have to simultaneously serve many of the functions described in this chapter.

The squares at the center of the Hispanic cities of the Americas that were laid out following the *Law of the Indies* are of the first type and most are still the hearts of cities. The Plaza des Armas in Santiago, Chile, is one of many (Figure 5.3 (a)). It has the cathedral on one side, the Portal Fernadez Concha on a second and the Museo Historico Nacional (formerly the National Congress) on a third. At the square's center is a memorial to Simón Bolívar, and on one side is a bandstand. The square is criss-crossed by links and replete with places to sit. Even on a gray, cold winter's day, it is full of people in warm coats sitting on benches or passing through. Buskers, protest marches and free-ranging dogs add to the scene. Barrows with geraniums in pots provide a touch of color to the square throughout the year but especially on a drab winter's day. New property developments, particularly

Figure 5.3 *Squares as the hearts of cities, pre-planned, evolved or created: (a) Plaza des Armas, Santiago, Chile, a pre-planned central square; (b) Times Square, New York, an evolved central square; (c) Federation Square, Melbourne, a created central square*

Source: (b) Photograph by Jenny Fitzgerald.

Neotraditional ones, are often planned around a central square; Sugar Land Town Square near Houston is the planned center of a recent (2000+) suburban design.

Times Square in New York and Trafalgar Square in London have become central squares partly due to the buildings located around them and the life they generate and partly simply due to their location. The recent pedestrianization of Times Square enhances its claim as *the* central open space of New York. Its surrounding walls, illuminated by colored and dazzling advertising and television screens, draw in visitors by the thousands. Raffles Square in Singapore has become the heart of the city's traditional Central Business District. Much the same can be said about much smaller squares. Asan Square in Kathmandu is an example (see Figure 3.2 (b) on p. 49). These squares are not the places many outsiders go to on a daily basis but workers in the surrounding buildings use them as places and links.

Federation Square in Melbourne, completed in 2002, is an example of a square fairly recently created to act as *the* central space of the city; many of the city's inhabitants believe that it is. Westlake Park in the heart of Seattle is another example (see Figure 8.10 (b) on p. 132). It was first proposed in 1968 but took 20 years to implement. It is located at a place where many paths cross, making it a true node. The plaza is considered to be Seattle's town square – a grand public place (Cooper Marcus and Francis 1990). Heritage Square in Flagstaff, Arizona, was purposefully created in 1999. People using these squares have a high degree of anonymity due to the high volume of users of these places.

Squares as Outdoor Precinct/Neighborhood Living Rooms

Akin to being the hearts of a city, squares can serve as places for local people to sit, meet people, have cups of coffee and be entertained. The campi (city squares) of Venice are an historical example. People know each other by sight at least and shopkeepers know their clients. Such squares can be the centers of neighborhoods or form the hearts of small towns and villages. A sense of belonging to a community is often engendered. This sense of community can be tight-knit at a local level but much looser at a larger urban scale. In the former case, people have many obligations to each other; in the latter, they are member of a community of "limited liability."[3] They have few but important expectations of each other when a necessity arises.

Planners like to believe that such outdoor living rooms lead to the development of a strong sense of community but this view needs to be taken with great caution.[4] Squares may afford people coming together but they cannot cause actual gatherings. Any such outcome depends on the social practice and motivations of the people living nearby. The potential for a sense of community to develop among people using a square varies from culture to culture and is strongest where people have few external resources on which they can rely. Place-making and guerrilla urbanist tactics by local citizens activating 'their place' temporarily as a community initiative are most likely to occur in these smaller squares.[5]

Some large squares are referred to as outdoor living rooms. Praça Real in Barcelona is one; Piazza San Marco in Venice is more famous, and although it is not a small square, it has the attributes of a living room and is often described as the 'greatest of them all.' Squares succeed best as outdoor living rooms when they are small in dimension and well framed by buildings, as are many traditional squares in the historic neighborhoods of Italian cities. They are particularly important in small towns where they are surrounded by high-density residential apartments and people's lives spill out into the street. The quality of light in a square is always important and those that serve as outdoor living rooms generally have an excellent quality of light penetrating them. In temperate climates, the access to sunlight is important but, in the tropics, shade is what is welcomed, as it is in Raffles Square in Singapore (1.4°N) (Figure 5.4 (a)).

Many high-density neighborhoods have squares that are located at nodes where paths meet or cross. *Chowks* in traditional Indian cities serve as collective gathering points located at odd intersections of roads or paths. In Ahmedabad, shade trees in gated caste-based *pols*, or neighborhoods, make such places small nuclear squares. Purposefully designing such places is a difficult task; many squares that serve as outdoor living rooms have evolved over time.

Figure 5.4 Outdoor living rooms: (a) Raffles Place, Singapore's CBD in the early evening; (b) Place Général Girard, Aups, France

Source: (a) Photograph by Su-Jan Yeo.

Water Squares as Places in a Sensory-Rich Environment

Another type of square acts as a sort of outdoor living room. Almost all squares have some place to sit and relax, usually on benches but otherwise on ledges; many have fountains in which the sound of falling water can be heard. Some squares were purposely designed to be places in which to relax in a sensory-rich environment. Paley Park in New York has already been mentioned. With the waterfall on its rear wall, the square does more than provide a place to relax in a dense urban setting. Its moveable tables and chairs give it a home-like quality.

Two examples of much larger squares where the sound of flowing and falling water offers a peaceful sensory experience and drowns the noises of the surrounding city are shown in Figure 5.5. Keller

Figure 5.5 *Water squares (a) Keller Fountain Park, Portland, Oregon; (b) Water Gardens, Fort Worth, Texas*

Source: (a) Photograph by Luke Marshall; (b) Photograph by Alix Verge.

Fountain Park in Portland, opened in 1970 on a 0.37-hectare (1 acre) site; the Water Gardens in Fort Worth, completed in 1974, sit on a 1.7-hectare (4 acre) site. Neither has a food outlet so people bring their own food with them; families hold picnics where the adults chat and the children wade in the water. The flow of water holds people's gaze and attention.

The Keller Fountain Park and the Water Gardens are also displays – works of art – created by well-known designers. Keller Square is the work of Lawrence Halprin while the Water Gardens were designed by Philip Johnson and John Burgee. The cognoscenti can see the two as significant examples of their designers' creativity. To others, they are simply peaceful places to be.

Squares as Places for Large Gatherings and Events

Squares where large events can take place are often the hearts of a city. Many of them have taken on the role of hosting special events, markets or concerts, although they were not specifically designed to cater for them. Squares purposely designed for holding events tend to be spacious, with enough flat surfaces for the predicted size of the gatherings. They also have electricity power points and a water supply readily available and toilets nearby or brought in when an event is held. Such infrastructure elements are now regarded as essential in new squares where pop-up activities are recurrent events. Disabled access is highly desirable and in most cities is legally required.

Any flat surface affords the holding of many of these types of gatherings. Usually the surfaces are paved but the grass surface of Yerba Buena Gardens in San Francisco has been used for many different types of events such as commemoration ceremonies and conventions. The flat area of Trafalgar Square is fragmented by fountains and sculptures but it has long been the location of protests and celebrations centered on Nelson's Column. The column's base forms a podium from which to address a large audience. The recently created North Terrace may well be a better place but does not possess the symbolic meaning created by generations of protests formed around Nelson's Column.

Some recent squares have been purposefully designed to comfortably hold large crowds. Of the cases presented in Chapter 14, Olympic Plaza in Calgary and Schouwburgplein in Rotterdam are examples. The former was originally designed specifically for the medal presentations at the 1988 Winter Olympic Games. The latter was designed for a variety of events. In contrast, in many places, crowds are simply squeezed into the available space when a ceremony is held.

Other squares specifically designed for large gatherings and major addresses are still too small for them. The crowd sometimes is so large that it spills over into the adjacent streets. Piazza San Pietro fronting St Peter's Cathedral in Rome may well have been designed for ceremonial appearances of the Pope when addressing crowds but on many occasions the crowd fills the Piazza Papa Pio XII and much of Via della Conciliazione as well. The Piazza San Pietro also serves as the foreground for the Cathedral. The architecture is meaningful in its grandeur for the general public and its design history is something for the cognoscenti to contemplate.

Some large squares were designed to accommodate military parades and other spectacular events. Red Square in Moscow and Tiananmen Square in Beijing are well-known examples. The Grand Parade in Cape Town was purposefully designed to be a parade ground in the seventeenth century (see Figure 6.1 (a) on p. 103). Horse Guards Parade in London is generally not thought of as a square but serves as such. The problem is that such squares located in the heart of cities lie empty for much of the time. Some have been converted to other uses. Yeo-ui-do Park in Seoul, once a vast, asphalt parade ground, is now a park that was opened in 1999.

Many market squares in cities were indeed created to house markets and many continue to do so. The market function no longer exists in others although their name remains a reminder of the square's past. Old Market Square (also known as Civic Square) in Nottingham once had a daily market but now hosts them less frequently. It has been refurbished as a large, usually empty, forecourt to the Town Hall and as a set of links rather than being a place. It is nevertheless the site of many formal events. Markets have been revived in many places where they had gone out of favor. Squares as diverse as Daley Plaza in Chicago, City Hall Plaza in Boston, Rittenhouse Square in Philadelphia, Nathan Phillips Square in Toronto and Market Square in Pittsburgh now have regular farmers' markets. The only requirement for a market square is a flat smooth surface and good links to surrounding areas. Electric power supply helps.

It is difficult to reconcile the requirements for sufficient space for large events and the need for the square to be a pleasant place when no event is taking place.[6] The recently renovated Market Square in Pittsburgh is a lively place when markets are held but little enlivens it on other days. Works of art are added but there is little evidence that it achieves much. In winter, a skating rink draws people as it does in Nottingham's Old Market Square. Rotterdam's Schouwburgplein is a good place for fairs and large events but it is often an empty place otherwise. Other newly designed squares are more successful in dealing with the duality of their instrumental functions.

Figure 5.6 Squares as setting for events: (a) Nathan Phillips Square, Toronto, as a potential setting for events; (b) Nathan Phillips Square, Toronto, as an effective setting

Sources: (a) Photograph by rmnoa357/Shutterstock.com; (b) Photograph by Atomazu/ Shutterstock.com.

Nathan Phillips Square in Toronto, the largest urban square in Canada, was first opened in 1965 but was revitalized through a design competition held in 2007. Plant Architects and Shore Tilbe Irwin + Partners won the competition – their design was based on the concept of an agora. The square was completely finished in 2014 and hosts many special events and festivals (Figure 5.6). Federation Square in Melbourne does better too although it is used mainly as a link between destinations when no event is taking place in it. Its southwestern orientation in the southern hemisphere means its core is poorly illuminated. Cours Theodore Bourge in Salernes is a smaller square, its trees, shops and outdoor cafés add to its daily life when no market is held (Figure 5.7). In addition, the sun streams into the space, throwing dappled shadows across it.

Parking nearby and connections to public transit are important for any square to successfully host events on a recurring basis. Of the studies presented in Chapter 12, Sproul Plaza at the University of California in Berkeley, Pershing Square in Los Angeles, Cours Honoré d'Estienne d'Orves in Marseille, La Place des Terreaux in Lyon, and Schouwburgplein in Rotterdam, have parking garages located under the square. These places also benefit by being located on busy public

Figure 5.7 Market squares: (a) Cours Theodore Bourge, Salernes, daily; (b) On market days

transportation routes. Such amenities do not, however, automatically make a square a destination.

Social Media and Gathering in Squares

Given the ease of social media and communication, people can quickly gather in public open space to protest and display their grievances en masse. Protesters are drawn together at major squares or parade down streets carrying banners and shouting slogans. The places where individuals and groups converge are those that have symbolic meaning embedded in them. The mass protests against the regime of Hosni Mubarak in Egypt in February 2011 took place in the linked open spaces that form Tahrir Square in Cairo. Tahrir Square is flanked by buildings of importance as well as being large and central. The Occupy Wall Street Movement later in the same year in New York, protesting against economic inequality in the USA, took place in Zuccotti Park, a paved area with rows of trees.

People also use squares to mourn together, publicly and often on the global stage. Trafalgar Square held a large vigil after the terrorist bombings in London in July 2005. Martin Place in Sydney became a shrine to the victims of a shooting in a café there in December 2014. Thousands of people visited the square in the first few days after the incident to lay flowers and pay tribute to the victims of the siege. Public life and a sense of community are often played out in public spaces like squares and these are often facilitated by the use of social media.

Squares as Landmarks

Landmarks are orienting devices used to locate oneself in geographic space and as the basis for giving directions. They are one of the five elements that Kevin Lynch (1960) found that form people's cognitive representation of a city; they add legibility to the city and make way-finding easier.[7] They are usually places of interest to tourists and often convenient places for them and locals to meet others.

Piccadilly Circus in London is one such square favored by Londoners and tourists as a meeting place (Figure 5.8). There is little ambiguity about the exact location of the meeting spot. It is also a good place to be a *flâneur* and watch the world pass by. The Puerta de Sol serves much the same purpose in Madrid although it lacks Piccadilly Circus's single central point and is bisected by a road. A statue of a bear with a strawberry tree is a central spot. Almost all squares are, at least, minor landmarks simply because they make a break in the continuity of buildings that form streets.

Squares that serve as landmarks, especially if they are nodes where paths cross, are important parts of any city. Place Charles de Gaulle with the Arc de Triomphe at its center is a major node in Paris; it is also an island surrounded by swirling traffic. The size of the arch makes it visible along the several axes of Haussmann's Paris that terminate there so it helps people to form a mental map of that part of Paris.

Figure 5.8 Squares as landmarks: (a) Piccadilly Circus, London; shady side; (b) Sunny side

Squares as the Foregrounds for Buildings

Historically the buildings for which a square was the foreground were the important public edifices whose façades were on display. They were town halls, museums and religious buildings such as churches and mosques. Palaces were the focus of attention in many old European squares. The best-known examples are the forecourts of palaces such as that at Versailles and the Royal Palace in Madrid.[8] Today the important edifice is often a substantial commercial building.

The incentive zoning program in New York formulated in 1961, and others like it in the United States, led to the major increase in number of squares that are the forecourts of commercial buildings in the country (New York City Department of City Planning 2007). These plazas may have acted as a precedent for other forecourts as well. The squares in front of commercial buildings tend simply to be set-backs from the property line and remain in private ownership. They make the buildings seem especially important in comparison to those that are built to the property line. If, however, all the buildings are set back, such a differentiation gets lost. The consumption of space by both governmental and commercial enterprises is often regarded as a symbol of their power and wealth but large forecourts can be barren and boring.

The square of the government complex in Chandigarh is hardly a place to be on a summer day. Le Corbusier saw it as a gathering place for large crowds as well as a setting to view the High Court and Legislature (Khilnani 1997). Guildhall Yard in London serves as the foreground for three buildings. Seen from the Library, it is the forecourt for the Art Gallery; seen from the Art Gallery, it is the forecourt for the Library and seen from St Lawrence Jewry, a church on one side of the yard, or as one approaches from Gresham Street, it is the forecourt for the Guildhall seen opposite (see Figure 7.1 (a) on p. 115). The forecourt of the Pittsburgh Plate Glass Building is very different from many deserted forecourts (Figure 5.9 (a)). Piazza San Pietro in the Vatican serves dual purposes; it is the forecourt for St Peter's but also a place that holds large gatherings. Some squares are forecourts

Figure 5.9 Squares as the foreground of buildings: (a) Pittsburgh Plate Glass Place, Pittsburgh, opened in 2003; (b) Federal Plaza, Chicago, with Alexander Calder's 'Flamingo' artwork

of railway stations and although they are primarily links, they can also be designed to be places if provided with seating and other amenities (see Figure 6.6 on p. 110).

In the northern hemisphere, the building on display should be located on the northern side of the square facing south into the sun where it can be best illuminated. The opposite holds for the southern hemisphere. Close to the equator, it makes little difference on which side of a square the featured building lies. Federation Square in Melbourne faces southwest, making the interior somewhat gloomy for much of the day especially in winter. The Seagram Building Plaza, in New York (see Figure 14.4 on p. 273) is spacious but facing west gets little sunlight until noon. It is not a lively place in comparison to that fronting the City Council House 2 building in Melbourne. The Seagram Building Plaza and that at Bilbao's Guggenheim Museum are forecourts from which the buildings, as the works of major architects, Mies van der Rohe and Frank Gehry respectively, can be admired. Such squares often contain a piece of sculpture to give them a central focus.

Squares as Memorials[9]

A number of squares were designed to function primarily as memorials, as the celebration of a person's life or an event. They have little other purpose and maybe need none. In some, however, there seems to be an opportunity cost; they could have been designed to be better places. Others are so located that serving any function other than being a memorial seems impossible; their surroundings do not generate flows of pedestrians onto them. Some squares celebrate not only the person or event but, as works of art, the architect who designed them. Examples are Freedom Plaza in Washington, DC, and the FDR Four Freedoms Park in New York. The first is a memorial to Martin Luther King and the second to Franklin D. Roosevelt.

Freedom Plaza is an open square designed primarily by Venturi and Rauch, built in 1980 (Carr *et al.* 1992). The plaza, 50 centimeters (20 inches) above street level, consists of stone paving inlaid with a map of the central part of L'Enfant's plan for Washington, DC, (see

Figures 0.6 (b) on p. 12 and 11.4 on p. 165). The western end of the plaza has a large fountain, while the opposite end has an equestrian statue of Casimir (Kazimierz) Pulaski. The site is visited by the architectural cognoscenti and is sometimes the site for political rallies and other events but on a day-to-day basis it lies empty. It is not an inviting place. In summer, its floor reflects radiant heat and in winter the wind whistles through it. The US Navy Memorial Plaza that lies just a few blocks to the east of it is different (Figure 5.10). Dedicated in 1987, the enclosing buildings that face it open directly onto the square, helping the south-facing benches to be well used. It serves as both a memorial and an active place.

The FDR Four Freedoms Park, located at the southern end of Roosevelt Island in New York, is a purely contemplative space without any amenity to encourage visitors to linger (see Figure 14.3 (b) on p. 272). Despite lacking visitor parking, a coffee shop, food outlet or public facilities, the memorial is expected to attract 50,000 visitors a year. It consists of a 1.6 hectares (4-acre) park, terminating in a 'room' or square at its tip. The square is framed by large granite blocks on three sides; the fourth is open to views down East River. It is approached from the north via a trapezoidal lawn lined by trees with a larger than life bronze bust of Roosevelt terminating the vista. The memorial's location on a peninsula means that it is surrounded on two sides by water. Along its perimeter are ramped banks with massive wedges of solid granite forming an embankment. The park is seen as a memorial to both Franklin D. Roosevelt and the square's architect, Louis Kahn (Heathcote 2012), although over time we and others suspect that the link with Kahn will be largely forgotten (Iovine 2012). It is a solemn place.

Other memorials have a more local character. Such squares, besides the name, usually include a display and representation of

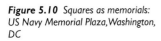

Figure 5.10 *Squares as memorials: US Navy Memorial Plaza, Washington, DC*

artifacts or art works depicting that person or event. Jack London Square in Oakland, California, named after the writer, includes the log cabin he used in the Yukon, statues of London and a wolf. Bronze wolf tracks are inlayed in the floor of the square.[10] The square is closer to popular tastes than Freedom Plaza and Four Freedoms Park. Architectural critics seldom pay any attention to such squares.

Squares as the Setting for Sculptures and/or Memorials

Some squares were designed specifically to be settings for memorials or statues and/or reliefs. Other squares have become memorial squares either because they afforded the placing of an art work in them or because they needed something in them to relieve the monotonous open space. The works may be serious and poignant or playful and light-hearted.

Independence Square in Colombo is a memorial to both Ceylon's independence from British colonial rule and to Don Stephen Senanyake, the Minister for Agriculture under the British, who became the first Prime Minister of independent Ceylon (now Sri Lanka). His statue is placed on a pedestal in the front of the square with a structure representing a traditional pavilion behind him (see Figure 10.3 (b) on p. 152). The sculpture in Chicago's Daley Plaza is very different in character.

The untitled 15 meter-high Cor-Ten steel *Untitled* sculpture, a gift from its artist Pablo Picasso, adds a lively element to the forecourt of the Richard J. Daley Center, a courthouse building (Figure 5.11 (a)). The sculpture is also a conversation piece. The plaza is a major civic open space in Chicago and the place for farmers' markets, and many celebratory events. Without the addition of the sculpture, the plaza would be a largely dull, empty forecourt, despite it containing an in-ground fountain and an ever-burning flame commemorating the fallen Americans of World War II, the Korean War and the Vietnam War. Unlike some modern sculpture that is largely ignored by passers-by, Picasso's work is noticed.

Figure 5.11 Squares as the setting for sculptures and memorials: (a) Daley Plaza, Chicago; (b) Plaza de España, Madrid

Source: (b) Photograph by Renata Sedmakova/Shutterstock.com.

In the center of the Plaza de España in Madrid is a memorial to Miguel Cervantes Saavedra (Figure 5.11 (b)). His life is represented by the two central characters of his most famous novel, *Don Quixote*. The memorial consists of a sculpture of Don Quixote and his faithful squire, the simple farmer, Sancho Panza, astride a donkey. Cervantes looks down on them. It is a light-hearted celebration of the life of the novelist. The square itself has a grimmer history – it was the location of the executions of Spanish patriots by French troops after the 2nd May 1808 uprising.

A number of forecourts of buildings that do not appear to have been designed as settings for sculptures now have them in order to enliven them or because property developers were required to provide sculptures as part of an incentive or an arts promotion program. The forecourts of the Guggenheim Museum in Bilbao is home to *Puppy* (1992) by Jeff Koons, Shakespeare Square in Canberra houses *Two to Tango* (2011) by Michael Le Grand and Scout Place at Circular Quay in Sydney has *Windlines* (2011), the work of Jennifer Turpin and Michaelie Crawford. All sculptures afford an opportunity, especially for designers and artists, to critique the intellectual esthetic nature of the art work.

Squares as Links

Almost all squares contain links. For some, it is the primary purpose that they serve. The pedestrian mall, which falls in between being a street and a square, is an example. Such malls can serve a number of purposes. They can be used as a mechanism to generate pedestrian traffic and/or to make pedestrian movements easier by reducing what are generally regarded as conflicts between vehicular and pedestrian traffic. To fulfill the former function well, a mall needs to have destinations at either end (for, example, the Corso in Manly, Sydney, with the sea at one end and the ferry terminal at the other). The Piazetta in Venice is similar; it links the Piazza San Marco to the waterfront (Figure 5.12 (a)).

Most plazas that are forecourts to commercial buildings, as already noted, offer little more than being a link between a sidewalk

Figure 5.12 Squares that serve predominantly as links: (a) Piazzetta San Marco, Venice; (b) Lincoln Center Plaza, New York

Sources: Both Photographs by Kate Bishop.

and building. Many have been purposefully configured as a link and designed so that there is little temptation for passers-by to linger. Lincoln Center Plaza appears to have been designed to be a place but functions mainly as a link despite recent refurbishments (Figure 5.12 (b)). The raised lawns and flower beds lining the paved walkways of Santiago de Chile's Plaza de la Constitución give a clear message of the expected behavior on them as does the path at the corner of the much less glamorous Wallace Square in Philadelphia and the paving patterns of Albert Luthuli Place in Cape Town (see Figure 2.4 (a) on p. 38). Oxford Square in Sydney and Old Market Square in Nottingham present ways of getting from one street level to another. In Philadelphia's Commerce Plaza, the sight lines from the footpath to the entrances of building are unobstructed. The linkage quality of the spaces is obvious.

Squares as Traffic Circles

Falling somewhere between being a link and a place are squares that have lanes of traffic moving around their edges so that they are difficult to reach. Some squares were designed to be traffic circles (for example, Azadi Square in Tehran) but many have acquired that usage over time as automobile traffic has increased. Their quality as a public place gets lost. There are many examples of such squares.

The Place de la Concorde is perhaps the most famous traffic circle in Paris (Figure 5.13 (a)) although another Parisian example – the Place Charles de Gaulle with the Arc de Triomphe de l'Étoile at its center – may challenge it. The heart of Philadelphia's Logan Square is equally difficult to reach. At its center is the Swann Memorial fountain (1924), designed by Alexander Stirling Calder in honor of Dr William Cary Swann. The square serves as a landmark and a setting for a number of institutional buildings around it. The fountain acts as a playground for children despite the danger in reaching it. The circular square with the Democracy Monument at its center in Bangkok is equally difficult to reach (Figure 5.13 (b)).

Figure 5.13 Squares as traffic circles: (a) Place de la Concorde, Paris; (b) Democracy Monument, Bangkok

Squares as Catalysts for Property Development

Most squares serve a combination of functions. Whether intended or not, a number of those described in this book have been catalysts for the development of adjacent areas.[11] Some critics fear that creating new squares hastens the process of gentrification around them by displacing existing residents, but for municipal authorities that is often exactly their purpose. During the twentieth century and into the early twenty-first, squares have been designed to act as catalysts to spur the revitalization of locales, sometimes with success and sometimes not. The Campus Martius in Detroit is one that is reported to be highly successful in an otherwise hard-pressed city. The Water Gardens in Fort Worth, Texas, and the Plaza d'Italia in New Orleans have yet to play significant catalytic roles.

At Battery Park City in New York, the open spaces – the promenade and the squares terminating the east–west streets – were designed and implemented first to act as a catalyst for the development of high quality buildings (Gordon 1997). Also in New York, a 3.4 hectare (8.5 acre) plaza with green spaces, shopping arcades and cafés is being designed in 2015 as part of the Hudson Yards office development. Granary Square in London is the centerpiece of the redevelopment of a whole new precinct.

Conclusion

Squares can and do serve a variety of purposes. Few, if any, serve only one of the instrumental functions that we have identified in this chapter. Many squares that are visually distinctive and/or create an open space in high-density cities may be important only to serve as landmarks for both tourists and locals. Others may be the focus of attention for photographers but those that serve a multiplicity of purposes are those that function as true cores of cities and districts and become well loved and well used.

The general public does not think about how well a square works on the dimensions discussed here but they notice it when it does not function well. Municipal authorities, architects, landscape architects and city planners may look at squares critically to understand how they function. They consider how congruent the square is with the variety of purposes its overall layout needs to serve and its relationship to its surroundings.

When designing new squares or redesigning existing ones, a series of questions arise: How does their size affect their potential functions? How do their shapes, their degree of enclosure and amount of sunlight affect their qualities for potential users? Ultimately the question of what each square's internal organization should be arises. Implicit in that observation are questions about the appropriate planning and design brief, or program, and the resultant design of the square. It is easy to state the obvious but these concerns are complex.

Notes

1 See Lang and Moleski (2010) for a discussion of various interpretations of the term 'function.' In this book, the symbolic purposes of a design are considered as much a function of a square as any other purpose that it might serve.

2 For a full description of the original planning of Philadelphia, see Reps (1956).

3 See Suttles (1972), Gottschalk (1975) and Lang and Moleski (2010).

4 Such deterministic thinking has long been used by architects to support their efforts. Squares may afford the development of a sense of community; they do not cause it to occur. See Lang (1980) and Harvey (1997).

5 See Lydon *et al.* (2010, 2012) for current examples.

6 See Chapter 6 for further discussion.

7 Kevin Lynch in *The Image of the City* (1960) found that people's cognitive maps of a city consist of schema comprised of paths, landmarks, districts, nodes and edges. A number of other studies have corroborated his work although edges are only important when they are highly distinctive (for example, a river, railway line or mountain range).

8 Werner Hegemann and Elbert Peets present many historical examples in their book, *The American Vitruvius: An Architect's Handbook on Civic Art* ([1922] 1972).

9 In squares as memorials and settings for memorials, their instrumental and symbolic functions overlap. See also Chapter 10.

10 Jack London was the pseudonym of John Griffith Chaney (1876–1916), writer of *The Call of the Wild* among other books. He once worked on the Oakland waterfront.

11 Squares as catalysts function in much the same way as urban architecture as described by Wayne Attoe and Donn Logan (1989). See also Tiesdell and Adams (2011) and Adams *et al.* (2013).

References

Adams, David, Steve Tiesdell and James T. White (2013) Smart parcelization and place diversity: Reconciling real estate and urban design priorities. *Journal of Urban Design* 18(4): 459–477.

Attoe, Wayne and Donn Logan (1989) *American Urban Architecture: Catalysts in the Design of Cities*. Berkeley, CA: University of California Press.

Carr, Stephen, Mark Francis, Leanne Rivlin and Andrew M. Stone (1992) *Public Space*. Cambridge: Cambridge University Press.

Cooper Marcus, Clare and Carolyn Francis (1990) *People Places: Design Guidelines for Urban Open Space*. New York: Van Nostrand Reinhold.

Crouch, Dora and Axel I. Mundigo (1977) The city planning ordinances of the Laws of the Indies revisited. Part II: Three American cities. *The Town Planning Review* 48(4): 397–418

Crouch, Dora, Daniel J. Garr and Axel I. Mundigo (1982) *Spanish City Planning in North America*. Cambridge, MA: MIT Press.

Gordon, David (1997) *Battery Park City: Politics and Planning on the New York Waterfront*. Amsterdam: Gordon and Breach.

Gottschalk, Shimon S. (1975) *Communities and Alternatives: An Exploration of the Limits of Planning*. Cambridge: Schenkman.

Harvey, David (1997) The New Urbanism and the communitarian trap. *Harvard Design Magazine* (Winter/Spring): 68–69. Available at: http://wsm.wsu.edu/stories/2008/Spring/1harvey.pdf.

Heathcote, Edwin (2012) Shared memorial: A monument to Franklin Delano Roosevelt also serves as a fitting tribute to its late architect Louis Kahn. *Financial Times*, November 24–25, p. 15. Available at: www.ft.com/intl/cms/s/2/83409ca6-333c-11e2-aa83-00144feabdc0.html.

Hegemann, Werner and Elbert Peets (1922) *The American Vitruvius: An Architect's Handbook on Civic Art*, reprinted 1972. New York: Benjamin Blom.

Iovine, Julie V. (2012) Louis Kahn's four decades to freedom. *Wall Street Journal*, October 23. Available at: www.wsj.com/articles/SB10001424052970203630604578075044182524.164.

Jacobs, Jane (1961) *The Death and Life of Great American Cities*. New York: Random House.

Khilnani, Sunil (1997) *The Idea of India*. Harmondsworth: Penguin.

Lang, Jon (1980) The built environment and social behaviour: Architectural determinism re-examined. In *VIA IV*. Cambridge, MA: MIT Press, pp. 146–153.

Lang, Jon and Walter Moleski (2010) *Functionalism Revisited: Architectural Theory and Practice and the Behavioral Sciences*. Farnham: Ashgate.

Lydon, Mike, Dan Bartman, Ronald Woudstra and Aurash Khawarzad (2010) *Tactical Urbanism Beta Short-Term Action||Long Term Gain*, vol. 1. New York: The Street Plans Collaborative.

Lydon, Mike, Dan Bartman, Ronald Woudstra and Aurash Khawarzad. (2012) *Tactical Urbanism Beta Short-Term Action||Long Term Gain*, vol. 2. New York: The Street Plans Collaborative.

Lynch, Kevin (1960) *The Image of the City*. Cambridge, MA: MIT Press.

New York City Department of City Planning (2007) Privately owned public plazas: text amendment. Available at: www.nyc.gov/html/dcp/pdf/priv/101707_final_approved.text.pdf.

Reps, John W. (1956) William Penn and the planning of Philadelphia. *Town Planning Review* 27(1): 27–39.

Stein, Gertrude (1937) *Everybody's Autobiography*. New York: Random House.

Suttles, Gerald D. (1972) *The Social Construction of Communities*. Chicago: University of Chicago Press.

Tiesdell, Steve and David Adams (eds.) (2011) *Urban Design in the Real Estate Development Process*. Chichester: Wiley-Blackwell.

Further Reading

Carmona, Matthew (2010) Contemporary public spaces, part two: Classification. *Journal of Urban Design* 15(2): 157–176.

French, Jere S. (1978) *Urban Spaces: A Brief History of the City Square*. Dubuque, Iowa: Kendall-Hunt.

Gehl, Jan (2010) *Cities for People*. Washington, DC: Island Press.

Janicijevic, Aleksandar (n.d.) Urban Squares. Available at: www.urban_squares.com

Moughton, Cliff (2003) *Urban Design: Street and Square*, 3rd edn. Oxford: Architectural Press.

San Francisco Urban Planning and Research Association (SPUR) (2013) *A Guide to San Francisco's Privately-Owned Public Open Spaces: Secrets of San Francisco*. San Francisco: SPUR.

Zucker, Paul (1959) *Town and Square: From the Agora to the Village Green*. New York: Columbia University Press.

CHAPTER 6

TYPES BASED ON SIZE

Implicit in the discussion of the instrumental functions that squares can serve is the fact that purpose and size are interrelated. Whether a square is perceived to be large or small, too large or too small, is relative. A square's 'appropriate' size depends on the purposes that it serves – on whether its form fits its instrumental or symbolic function – and the context within which it sits. Squares certainly come in a range of sizes. In this chapter we distinguish among mega-large, large, medium and small squares, based on our perceptions of what constitutes a particular size.

Mega-Large Squares

A number of the extremely large squares – those over 30 hectares (about 74 acres) – are part of governmental complexes, national, state or municipal around the world. The Medan Merdeka in Jakarta, the Praça dos Tres Poderes in Brasília and Sükhbaatar Square in Ulaanbaatar in Mongolia are among them. The largest square of them all appears to be Medan Merdeka (Independence or Freedom Square) which is approximately 100 hectares (250 acres) in size. Other renowned squares are small in comparison. Palace Square in St Petersburg is 50 hectares (123 acres) and Tiananmen Square covers 44 hectares (110 acres); Red Square in Moscow, at 23 hectares (57 acres), is smaller but we still consider it to be a mega-large square.[1]

Medan Merdeka started as Koningsplein, a sports complex, in the nineteenth century during the Dutch colonial administration of Indonesia. Today it is surrounded by government buildings such as the Supreme Court of independent Indonesia. At the square's center is the National Monument from which diagonal lines radiate out. A paved area around the National Monument is used for parades and celebrations. The remainder of the square is used for both active and passive leisure activities. In 2002, a gated fence was erected around it to keep beggars, the homeless and vendors out.

The largest paved square in the world appears to be Praça dos Girassóis, in Palmas, the capital of the state of Tocantins in Brazil. Not a complete rectangle, It measures approximately a mammoth 800 by 700 meters in size. It is the site of the state's legislative, administrative and judicial buildings. The Bangkok Metropolitan Square, another

Figure 6.1 *Mega-large urban squares: (a) The Grand Parade, Cape Town; (b) Tiananmen Square, Beijing*

Source: (b) Photograph by golddc/ Shutterstock.com.

very large governmental open space, was designed specifically to house large markets and celebrations.

Mega-large squares can serve all the functions identified in Chapter 5 except being outdoor living rooms. Many have served and still serve as parade grounds and most act as the foreground to important religious or government buildings. Tiananmen Square (Figure 6.1 (b)) is 880 meters by 500 meters (2890 feet by 1640 feet) in size. It has the Gate to the Forbidden City to the north, the National Museum of China and the Great Hall of the People on the sides and Mao Zedong's Mausoleum on the south. The square was enlarged in 1958–1959 reputedly to fulfill Mao Zedong's desire for China to possess the largest square in the world. It was further enlarged to take on its present form in 1976. The square hosts military parades, and is the site for political events and where students hold protest meetings. It is also a main tourist destination. Another mega-large square is Grand Parade in Cape Town which held a crowd of 250,000 people gathered to hear Nelson Mandela's address on his release from prison in 1990 (Figure 6.1 (a)).

Large Squares

To us, large squares are those that range in size from about 30,000 square meters (about 7.5 acres) to approximately 10,000 square meters (about 2.5 acres). Large squares are those capable of acting as parade grounds and hosting large political or social gatherings with ease. Paved squares can do so more easily than garden squares. The apparent size of a number of large squares is mitigated by the degree to which they are enclosed by surrounding buildings. Poorly enclosed squares appear to be larger than they are.

The Christian Science Center Square, in Boston, falls into our class of large squares (Figure 6.2 (a)). It is long in comparison to its width, being 374 meters in length (1230 feet) and 85 meters (280 feet) wide. Its character makes it seem even larger than it is. Built in the 1960s, it is an amorphous square reflecting contemporary Modernist design attitudes; its surrounding buildings were regarded as objects in space rather than space makers. The seven buildings include the Mother Church of the Faith, the Mary Baker Eddy Library and the

26-story high former Christian Science administration building. Rows of trees bound the square on one side and offer a weak feeling of enclosure. In the center is a large reflecting pool. The place is one of contemplation, although traffic sounds intrude, and it is not a place for large-scale gatherings. With a perimeter of almost a kilometer, the square presents an uninterrupted circuit for joggers. Its size is impressive.

Times Square in New York, which because of its bow-tie configuration is difficult to measure, is a large square – a mega-large square to some observers – but the height of the surrounding buildings and their being built to the property line without set-backs give it a sense of being smaller. The number of people in the crowd that it attracts on New Year's Eve, for example, nevertheless, attests to its grand size.

Figure 6.2 Large squares:
(a) Christian Science Center, Boston;
(b) Praça dos Tres Poderes, Brasília

At the upper end of the scale are squares such as Rittenhouse Square in Philadelphia (31,700 square meters or almost 8 acres) and the Praça dos Tres Poderes in Brasília (26,000 square meters or 6.4 acres) in size and used as a parade ground. Located on three of its sides are Brazil's legislative, administrative and judicial buildings. The square held 200,000 people when the city was inaugurated as the country's capital in 1960 and is now the setting for the annual Independence Day celebrations. While it is a good place from which tourists can view and photograph Oscar Niemeyer's capitol complex, they do not stay for long. As a large paved amorphous square, it offers little attraction. It lies empty in the hot sun and even on a temperate winter's day. At the lower end of the scale are places such as the Plaza Mayor in Madrid (12,128 square meters or 3 acres) and Piazza San Marco in Venice which is about the same size but has a very different configuration. Trafalgar Square and Granary Square, both in London, are other large squares of about the same area.

Perhaps the best known and most venerated large square is indeed Piazza San Marco in Venice. It is an average of 175 meters (574 feet) in length and about 80 meters (263 feet) across at its widest point. The surrounding buildings are about 17 meters (56 feet) high while the existing Campanile reaches 80 meters (262 feet) into the sky. Boston's City Hall Plaza, which is generally regarded as too large for any function it might serve, is about the same dimension in width across the face of the City Hall as the length of the Piazza San Marco but the open space spreads around the building.

The Piazza del Campo in Sienna is small in comparison. The horse races it hosts twice per year are accommodated in a space that is only 137 meters (450 feet) by less than 100 meters (328 feet) in size. It is a tight fit. The surrounding buildings are generally about 20 meters (65 feet) in height, giving it a sense of enclosure. The Piazza del Popolo in Rome is also considered to be a large space. It is 150 meters (500 feet) by 170 meters (560 feet) in size on its longest dimensions (see Figure 8.9 (b) on p. 131).

Of the squares in the United States, Copley Square, in Boston, is at the lower end of the size of squares we have classified as large. With its stepped floor, it makes a fine place to hold formal gatherings or concerts. Its fountain provides a place for dangling one's feet in cooling water on a hot summer day. It is 83 meters (270 feet) in length at its longest and 148 (485 feet) meters between Trinity Church and the square's edge. The square is surrounded by buildings but the distance between them in the north–south direction is almost 220 meters (721 feet), so the sense of enclosure is lost, a theme considered in greater detail in Chapter 7. The square is the foreground to both the Romanesque Revival Trinity Church and the Italian Renaissance Boston Public Library.

Medium-Sized Squares

Many medium-sized squares – those around 10,000 square meters (about 2.5 acres) down to about 4,000 square meters (1 acre) in size – exist in the world. Medium-sized squares are at the upper extremity of size at which one can recognize a person on the other side of it. The smaller the square, the greater is the likelihood of it becoming a social space. Some such squares are regarded as outdoor living rooms.

Many old squares – well known and unheralded – in European cities fall into this category. Some are relatively quiet places while others are very busy. The Piazza del Campidoglio in Rome is an example of the former although it is becoming a tourist spot. An odd-shaped square, it is narrower at the entrance than at the face of the dominant building. It is about 45 meters (147 feet) wide at the top of the Cordonata (the sloping, staircase-like way leading up to it) and 55 meters (180 feet) wide in front of the Palazzo Senatorio. The buildings surrounding the Campidoglio are about three stories high, so it possesses a real sense of enclosure.

The appearance of size can, however, deviate from these figures based on what is happening around a square. Schouwburgplein in Rotterdam is only 12,250 square meters (a little over 3 acres) in size but appears to be a larger square because so little borders onto it. George Square in Glasgow, which is about the same area, appears to be much smaller because it is enclosed by buildings and has a number of elements in it (Figure 6.3 (a)).

Medium-sized squares can accommodate pop-up events such as the information tent for the 2014 Commonwealth Games in George Square, Glasgow. Larger gatherings including protests can also be housed in medium-sized squares, if the square is not a privately owned open space (POPS), but not on the scale of those held in Trafalgar Square or Times Square.

The instrumental function of many, if not most, medium-sized squares depends on what surrounds them. Many are the forecourts of buildings, governmental, institutional or commercial. Some are the central squares of cities or neighborhoods. Raffles Place in Singapore, 4,200 square meters in size (about 1 acre), consists of paved and grassed areas (see Figure 5.4 (a) on p. 88). Surrounded by food outlets, the ledges that demarcate the lawns are used as seats. The square is the heart of the city-state's financial district and is full of workers from the surrounding buildings at lunchtime and is criss-crossed by people using it as a link for much of the day. The Campo Santa Margherita in Venice is about half the size of Piazza San Marco

Figure 6.3 Medium-sized squares: (a) George Square, Glasgow; (b) Plaza de la Platería, Madrid

Source: (a): Photograph by Kate Bishop.

and somewhat off the beaten tourist track. Surrounded by buildings that include residences, restaurants and shops, it is the heart of the Dorsoduro district of the city. The nearby university further adds life to the square.

Asan Square in Kathmandu, before the earthquake of 2015, was constantly busy. It will be again. Located at the intersection of six streets, it is used as a major link. The bazaar sells a wide range of goods from spices to electronic equipment; the banks and restaurants attract shoppers and clients from all over the city. Its architectural features as well as the general liveliness of the square make it a major tourist attraction. The square appears to be chaotic with people, motorcycles and cars intersecting at different places in the square (see Figure 3.2 (b) on p. 49). A local understanding of how the square operates keeps the various activities under control.

Rockefeller Center Plaza is another square that is the heart of the surrounding district. A major attraction for tourists, the square consists of a small square (the Lower Plaza) within a medium-sized one (the Upper Plaza). The Lower Plaza is just 37 meters by 17 meters (122 feet by 59 feet) in size and large enough to house a winter ice-skating rink; in summer, it becomes an outdoor café. Many sunken squares as small as the Lower Plaza are gloomy, lifeless places but the configuration of the buildings around Rockefeller Center Plaza enables the space to be brightly lit, particularly in the morning to midday.

Small Squares

To us, a small square is one under 5,000 square meters (a little over 1 acre) in size. They vary in the purposes they serve from simply being large light wells to places to sit for a moment to being genuine outdoor living rooms in high-density urban areas. Again, the degree and nature of the way they are enclosed affect the veridical perception of a square's size. Some squares are so hemmed in by buildings that they seem smaller than they are.

Figure 6.4 A small square: Herald Square, New York

Small squares come in all shapes and sizes. Herald Square with nearby Greeley Square in New York are triangular and form a bow-tie shape. The square is lined by trees and has the James Gordon Monument, consisting of the Goddess of Wisdom, Minerva, with her owls in front of a bell, flanked by two bell ringers, mounted on a Milford pink granite pedestal, as its focal point. The square is simply a resting point (Figure 6.4). Place Général Girard in Aups in Provence, France, is irregular in form (see Figure 5.4 (b) on p. 88). It is almost totally taken up by a café and serves as an outdoor living room but one has to make a purchase to use it. Mechanics Monument Plaza is a more vibrant small square in the heart of San Francisco. It has been recently refurbished with moveable tables and chairs and a recharge station for mobile devices. Monument Square in London is simply a paved open space with a pavilion at one end at the base of the column commemorating the 1666 Great Fire in the city.

Pocket Squares

At the lowest end of the size scale is what are called vest pocket parks in North America. They are tiny when compared to the mega-squares. They have proliferated because they serve an essential purpose: a place to take a break in public open space and to have visual relief where property values or densities are high. Those in neighborhoods have their habitués; those in the hearts of the downtown cores of cities serve local workers, shoppers and tourists.

Pocket parks are small squares usually located in the center of city blocks, often between the walls of adjacent buildings, and are about 400 square meters (1/10 acre) large which is about the size of a tennis court. They can serve a number of purposes: a playground for children, a lunchtime or coffee-break spot or simply a quiet sitting area. Most are places to relax away from a city's pedestrian or vehicular traffic.

Paley Park in New York, an endowed, privately owned space open to the public at specific hours, is without doubt the best-known pocket

Figure 6.5 A pocket square/park: Coxe Park, Philadelphia, with a playground at the rear

park.[2] With its waterfall that drowns out the traffic and air-conditioner noises of Manhattan, its moveable tables and chairs and food outlet, it has become a model for squares in many other cities even though it is shadowed by surrounding buildings for much of the time. Opened in 1967, it has functioned in the same manner for almost 50 years although at the time of writing this book, it was showing signs of wear and tear and was undergoing refurbishment.

Coxe Park in Philadelphia is different in nature (Figure 6.5). It is open to the public all day, every day throughout the year. It is divided into two parts: one part is a simple seating area under trees and the second is a playground. Parents can sit in the former and watch their children play. Oxford Square in Sydney, although also small in size, offers little to make a person desire to linger and acts primarily as a link.

The Appropriate Size of Squares

Many authors agree that squares need to be in human scale. Whether or not a square is in human scale visually relates to a person being in control of their own activities and feelings in dealing with the environment at eye-height. From a behavior point of view, it relates to a space being at an appropriate capacity for the events or activities taking place within it. Squares need to be appropriately 'manned' in nautical terms for the activities to function well (Schoggen 1989).[3] If the behavior setting has too few people, it does not function well although passers-by may be enticed in because people attract people (Whyte 1980). If too many people are involved in an activity, others tend to avoid entering because of a feeling that the space is over-crowded. Human scale in this sense is related to concepts of appropriate levels of privacy, which is a concept that is culturally relative (Lang and Moleski 2010).[4] Sometimes a crowded square is in human scale and sometimes not. It depends on what is happening in the square – the activities or events taking place – and who is engaged in them.

We suspect other variables such as the quality of light – sunlight and shade – have an impact on perceptions of whether a square is in human scale or not. They add to the feeling of being comfortable, of not having to 'fight the elements' or circumstances. We know of no research that considers this topic but there appears to be a general agreement among scholars on what the appropriate size of any square is. It is, first, related to the activity it is to accommodate. Second, many observers believe that the size should be related to the height of the enclosing elements. The first is the necessary condition and the second is a possible intervening variable.

A square that serves as a parade ground is very different from those that house smaller ceremonies and to those that act as outdoor living rooms. One of the major issues in designing squares, as already mentioned, is how to cater to infrequent large, formal gatherings while making squares people-friendly or even looking good when empty. The station squares at Shanghai Station are designed for holiday crowds but are empty concrete spaces for 51 weeks a year. Station Square in Cape Town was purposefully designed to be

large enough to handle the anticipated crowds during the Football World Cup of 2010 (Figure 6.6 (a)). The railway failed to receive the ridership expected. Now authorities are discussing what can be done to enliven the space.

Figure 6.6 Station squares: (a) Station Square, Cape Town; (b) Place Charles Béraudier, Lyon

The Cape Town urban design team could learn much from squares such as Place Charles Béraudier – the Part-Dieu station square – in Lyon (Figure 6.6 (b)), as authorities consider proposed changes. It has a much greater degree of enclosure and its surroundings generate much local pedestrian traffic. Its proposed development changes will enlarge the square for reasons not obvious and a sense of enclosure will be lost. This action may well end its present character as a pleasant place to linger while waiting.

Appropriate Size and a Sense of Enclosure

The size of a square in order to obtain a sense of enclosure – of making a square a room – is the focus of Chapter 7 but is touched on here because it has much to do with the perceptions of the appropriate size of squares. For outdoor living rooms, the size, it has been argued by many (Sitte 1889; Sitte and Stewart 1945; Zucker 1959; Gehl 1987, 2010), should be related to the height of surrounding buildings and, in particular, to the height of the featured building. Scholars agree that the surrounding buildings should not be so low in height that a sense of enclosure is lost. They also agree that the ratio of size to height should be around 3:1.

To Zucker (1959), the cross-section of a square should be three to four times the height of the surrounding buildings. This height is based on studies that show that the view corridor of a standing person spreads to about a 60° horizontal angle and vertical vision to a 27° angle. We can and do turn around and raise our heads to look at objects in the world around us, but the 27° angle holds for a person's everyday core of view from a station point. Sitte (cited in Zucker 1959) believed that the cross-dimension of a rectangular square should be between one and two times the height of the adjacent buildings and no more than three times their height. The height of the sun in the sky does not seem to have featured much in his thoughts.

Many of these conclusions about the height of surrounding buildings are based on the analyses of Hermann Maertens (1877) who, drawing on the work of perception psychologist Hermann von Helmholtz,[5] recognized that with an angle of 27°, the top of a building or a monument was perceivable at a distance of twice its height; with an angle of 45°, its height is equidistant from the observer (Figure 6.7).[6] The breadth of the building does not matter as a person can move around to select the desired view. Sitte (1889), focusing on the sense of a place, considered the height of the featured building to be the main determinant of a square's size, not the instrumental function it was supposed to fulfill. The distance across the square from the building that is the focus of attention, he believed, should be over one but less than two times the building's height. Squares, in his view, should be tight spaces. If necessary, well-attended events should be 'shoehorned' into them and people should feel crowded in the space.

To Jan Gehl (2010), a person should, ideally, be able to recognize another on the far side of a square so it should not be more

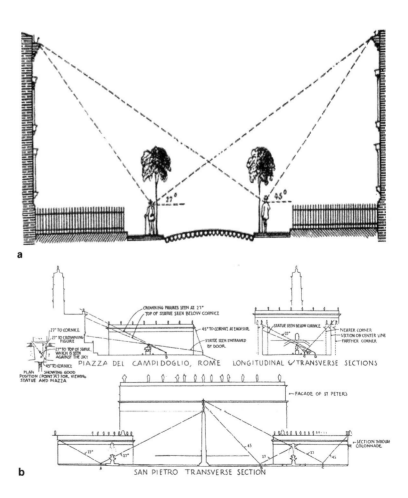

Figure 6.7 Hermann Maertens's viewing angles: (a) Viewing angles of façades as perceived by Maertens (cited in Moravanszky 2012: 657); (b) An analysis of viewing angles in Piazza del Campidoglio and Piazza San Pietro in Rome as perceived by Maertens (cited in Hegemann and Peets ([1922] 1972: 43)

than 30 meters (100 feet) to 35 meters (115 feet) across but many squares need to be larger.[7] The size fundamentally depends on the intended daily activities and events that a square is being designed to accommodate.

Conclusion

A number of observations can be made when comparing traditional Italian squares with the many recently completed squares. The first is that the traditional squares are generally smaller and more tightly enclosed by buildings than their newer counterparts. The modern ones tend to be amorphous, being surrounded by individual buildings vying for attention. Although built over time, the owners and creators of the buildings around the traditional squares showed a sense of decorum rather than competition in designing their buildings.[8] They followed the formal precedents set by earlier buildings.

Large squares can denote prestige but visitors may feel lost in them despite being impressed by their magnitude. The use of the size of squares as a mechanism to establish status may well be sought by decision-makers striving to enhance their city's social status in much the same manner that competing municipalities around the world strive to have the tallest buildings within their boundaries.[9] There are, however, other ways of establishing status, as we explore in Chapter 10.

Critics over time make one consistent observation about the appropriate size of squares. They consider many squares to be simply too large for the purposes they are supposed to serve and state they are over-designed (Balint 1955; Franck and Stevens 2013). Much of the time they end up being windswept, empty voids in the city's urban fabric. One architect, Christopher Alexander (Alexander et al. 1977), suggests that squares should be designed for their perceived instrumental function and then halved in size to get the correct dimension. Certainly, many twentieth-century squares seem to be over-large for anything but photographic purposes and for generating a 'wow' response from visitors. Perhaps the collective need in cities is to have small, medium and large squares. This specification does, however, depend on the social needs of a particular city.

Notes

1 The sizes we provide for the squares in this chapter are drawn from many different sources. While their veracity has not been tested by us, the sizes provided are certainly indicative of the reality.
2 Paley Park has been extensively described. A detailed study of the squares can be found in Whyte (1980). Iwashita (1988) and Surhone et al. (2010) provide other descriptions.
3 For a full discussion of the concept of 'manning,' see also Barker (1968) and Schoggen (1989).
4 Privacy relates to the control of information into and out of a behavior setting. The level of desired control depends on the publicness of the activity taking place. See also Altman (1975).
5 See Hegemann and Peets ([1922] 1972) for cross-sections through well-liked Renaissance plazas that reinforce Maertens' observations.
6 See Hegemann and Peets ([1922] 1972) and Ladd (1987).

7 See also Maertens (1877) and Hall (1969).
8 See Kohane and Hill (2001) for a discussion of the concept of decorum.
9 See Lang and Moleski (2010) for a summary of the recent research on the relationship between built form and social status.

References

Alexander, Christopher, Sara Ishikawa and Murray Silverstein (1977) *A Pattern Language: Towns, Buildings, Construction*. New York: Oxford University Press.

Altman, Irwin (1975) *Environment and Social Behavior: Privacy, Personal Space, Territory, Crowding*. Monterey, CA: Brooks/Cole.

Balint, Michael (1955) Friendly expanses – horrid empty spaces. *International Journal of Psychoanalysis* 36(4–5): 225–241.

Barker, Roger (1968) *Ecological Psychology: Concepts and Methods for Studying the Environment of Human Behavior*. Stanford, CA: Stanford University Press.

Franck, Karen A. and Quentin Stevens (eds.) (2013) *Loose Space: Possibility and Diversity in Urban Life*. New York: Routledge.

Gehl, Jan (1987) *Life between Buildings: Using Public Space*. New York: Van Nostrand Reinhold.

Gehl, Jan (2010) *Cities for People*. Washington, DC: Island Press.

Hall, Edward T. (1969) *The Hidden Dimension*. New York: Anchor Books.

Hegemann, Werner and Elbert Peets (1922) The modern revival of civic art. In *The American Vitruvius: An Architect's Handbook on Civic Art*, reprinted 1972. New York: Benjamin Blom, pp. 7–28.

Iwashita, Hajime (1988) *Pocket Park*. Tokyo: Process Architecture.

Kohane, Peter and Michael Hill (2001) The eclipse of the commonplace: Decorum in architectural theory. *ARQ: Architectural Research Quarterly* 5(1): 63–77.

Ladd, Brian K. (1987) Urban aesthetics and the discovery of the urban fabric in turn-of-the-century Germany. *Planning Perspectives* 2(3): 270–286.

Lang, Jon and Walter Moleski (2010) *Functionalism Revisited: Architectural Theory and Practice and the Behavioral Sciences*. Farnham: Ashgate.

Maertens, Hermann (1877) *Der Optische-Maßstab oder die Theorie und Praxis des ästhetischen Sehens in der bildenden Kunsten. Auf Grund der Lehrer der physiologischen Optic*. Bonn: Cohen. 2nd edn, 1884, Berlin: Wasmuth.

Moravánszky, Ákos (2012) The optical construction of urban space: Hermann Maertens, Camillo Sitte and the theories of 'aesthetic perception.' *Journal of Architecture* 17(5): 655–666.

Schoggen, Phil (1989) *Behavior Settings: A Revision and Extension of Roger G. Barker's Ecological Psychology*. Stanford, CA: Stanford University Press.

Sitte, Camillo (1889) *Der Städtebau nach seinen künstlerischen Grundsätzen*. Vienna: Karl Graesser.

Sitte, Camillo and Charles T. Stewart (1945) *The Art of Building Cities: City Building According to its Artistic Fundamentals*. New York: Reinhold.

Surhone, Lambert M., Mariam T. Tennoe and Susan F. Henssonow (2010) *Paley Park*. Mauritius: Betascript Publishing.

Whyte, William H. (1980) *The Social Life of Small Urban Spaces*. New York: The Conservation Foundation.

Zucker, Paul (1959) *Town and Square: From the Agora to the Village Green*. New York: Columbia University Press.

Further Reading

Caniffe, Eamonn (2008) *The Politics of the Piazza: The History and Meaning of the Italian Square*. Farnham: Ashgate.

Jenkins, Eric J. (2008) *To Scale: One Hundred Urban Plans*. New York: Routledge.

Koolhaas, Rem (1995) Bigness and the problem of large. In *S, M, L, XL*, edited by Rem Koolhaas and Bruce Mau. New York: Monacelli Press, pp. 494–517.

CHAPTER 7

TYPES BASED ON DEGREE OF ENCLOSURE

Paul Zucker (1959) considered squares to be made up of three space-defining elements: the surrounding structures, the floor and the sky. Perhaps the most important variable in giving a square its character is the way it relates to its surrounding buildings and, particularly, the way in which it is framed, or not, by them. Indeed, the surrounding buildings should always be seen as part of a square and the nature of their ground floors adds much to a square's character.

While recognizing that few squares are pure types and that many are hybrids, Zucker differentiated between two types of squares in terms of their degree of enclosure: the closed square and the amorphous square. It is still a useful distinction. Many squares, however, fall in between the two types; some are closer to being closed squares while others are so poorly enclosed that they hardly even warrant being classified as amorphous squares.

Closed Squares

Two ways of using vertical surfaces to enclose squares can be identified: the *classical* and the *baroque*. Classical squares are framed by buildings adjacent to if not abutting each other. The buildings form a clear and strong edge to the square. The Plaza Mayor in Madrid is a good example of being fully enclosed by the walls of buildings on all sides (see Figures 4.7 on p. 79 and 13.1 (b) on p. 257). Baroque types of closed squares (rather than baroque as a style of architecture) are framed by point elements such as columns, trees or even, but less so, buildings separated from each other as individual objects in space. Baroque enclosures often appear to be implied rather than explicit.[1]

The height of the surrounding walls defines the arc of the sky as seen in a square. The ideal size to height ratio in terms of letting sunlight into a square in the temperate climatic zones of the world, as noted in Chapter 6, is about 3:1 but the height of enclosing buildings needs to be lower as one moves away from the equator but then a square starts to lose a sense of enclosure. A trade-off often has to be made between a sense of enclosure and the height required to get high quality light into a square at a particular latitude.

Figure 7.1 Two closed squares;
(a) Guildhall Yard, London –
a traffic-free square; (b) Church
Square, Pretoria – a square
surrounded by roads

Some closed squares form the heart of a city. Those in Latin America that resulted from the application of the *Law of the Indies* are an example. The Grand-Place (Grote Markt) in Brussels, La Place des Terreaux in Lyon and the Piazza San Marco in Venice are widely known. Church Square in Pretoria and more recently, Mandela Square in Sandton, are two very different South African examples. The Grand-Place is surrounded by uniformly high buildings of historical importance including the City Hall and a number of guild halls. Some closed squares are really the courtyards of buildings and were once used by people for their horses and carriages. The square within the bounds of Somerset House in London is a quasi-public example. The public has the right to enter and even to linger but only at certain times of the day. The same observation can be made of the forecourts of mosques.

Closed squares of pure geometric shapes can be considered to be the 'ideal' type although today they are often dismissed as 'old-fashioned.' Other types of squares are a departure from this ideal but they can function as well on almost any dimension of analysis. Squares of highly irregular shapes can also be well enclosed. The use and thus the general character of squares vary considerably based on what uses occur at the ground floor level of the surrounding buildings. They can add to the liveliness of a square if they are the generators of pedestrian traffic or make a square a more peaceful setting if they are not. The ground floor of Madrid's Plaza Mayor is lined by a colonnade behind which are restaurants and shops. Diners can watch the ebb and flow of life in the square and the passing pedestrians can gaze at the diners. Restaurants were added to Mandela Square in Sandton, as noted earlier, to make it a more attractive destination.

Many squares that are surrounded by buildings have lanes of traffic that separate the pedestrian area of the square from the sidewalks in front of the enclosing buildings. Most of London's garden squares are of this type. Squares of this type cannot have cafés and shops spilling onto them from the ground floor of the enclosing buildings. Such amenities have to be based within the square itself as they are in Trafalgar Square.

The sense of separation of the enclosing elements from the square itself very much depends not only on the width of the streets but also on the volume of moving traffic on them. High volumes cut off a square from its surroundings. They make it difficult for pedestrians to reach the center of the square without interrupting the flow of traffic through the use of traffic lights. In extreme cases where traffic volumes are extremely high, the square becomes a traffic circle distributor. Underpasses or pedestrian bridges may be necessary to connect a square to the surrounding sidewalks on the other side of busy streets. These underpasses or bridges are rarely a good solution to the access problem. Underpasses can be difficult to maintain; bridges obstruct views and pedestrians are loathe to use either.

Closed Squares that Surround Buildings

In contrast to those squares that consist of enclosed open space are those, such as the Piazza del Duomo in Florence, which surround buildings. The view of the cathedral is greatly restricted from within the surrounding square. The Market Square in Gouda is another example. In the former the space around the cathedral is tight while in the latter the fifteenth-century gothic Town Hall stands aloof and is easy to see in its entirety from within the square.

A surprising number of such squares in Europe were purposefully redeveloped to enable a view of a key building to be obtained.[2] Tight spaces around churches were altered from their medieval character to become more spacious. The low buildings surrounding Notre Dame in Paris were demolished in the nineteenth century so that the cathedral now stands surrounded by an open space, albeit tight on the sides. The situation in Ulm, Germany, was the reverse. The amorphous open space around the cathedral was filled in with buildings to form a square (Hegemann and Peets [1922] 1972).

Although not exactly surrounding buildings are the examples of Nejmeh Square in central Beirut (see Figure 8.8 on p. 130) and Büyük Han in Nicosia (Figure 7.2 (b)). With its substantial 1930s clock tower at its center, the former is home to the Lebanese parliament, two cathedrals, Art Deco buildings and restaurants. It is frequented by both tourists and locals. It is also an example of a circular square.

Figure 7.2 Closed squares surrounding buildings: (a) Laleli Mosque, Istanbul; (b) Büyük Han, Lefkoþa, Nicosia, Cyprus

Sources: (a) Photograph by Mehmet Cetin/ Shutterstock.com; (b) Photograph by Sengül Öymen Gur.

Figure 7.3 Modernist squares enclosing buildings: (a) The National Museum, Brasília; (b) The SwissRe Building Square, London

Büyük Han was founded by the Ottomans in 1572 as a caravanserai (roadside inn); it has a *masjid* (mosque) with a fountain below it at its center. The square has had many functions. During British colonial days it served as a prison and today it contains shops and restaurants catering to both locals and tourists.

Many Modernist and Postmodernist institutional buildings and high-rise office towers are designed to be objects on display. Some are simply set back from the sidewalk and have a small square, a fore-court, in front of them. Others are completely surrounded by open space of varying sizes. The quality of these open spaces as squares depends largely on whether or not the surrounding buildings offer a sense of enclosure. An amorphous square surrounds the National Museum in Brasília, for example (Figure 7.3 (a)). Much of it is lifeless open space except when special events are held there. The square around the SwissRe building in London is so tight that it hardly warrants being called a square but it is one (Figure 7.3 (b)). The building is surrounded by bollards that provide a measure of security from car/truck rammings.

Sequential Experience in Squares Surrounding Buildings

Some environments are more interesting visually than others and hold our attention to a greater degree when we move through or around them. Those that are rich in detail attract and hold our attention more than those that are plain and have no sculptural qualities. The difficulty is to establish the borderline between richness and chaos especially as one walks through a sequence of spaces. In the squares that enclose buildings, the sequential experience as one walks around the building differs from moving from one space to another past occluding walls and/or arches (Cullen 1961). Both the view of the enclosed building and of the enclosing surfaces change.

In moving through the Piazza del Duomo and around the cathedral or around the SwissRe building in London, the optical transitions are more rapid than when walking around the Town Hall in the

Market Square in Gouda and one would predict it would hold the attention more and be found to be more interesting visually. Such claims have never been verified. The nature of the architecture is probably an intervening variable. Walking around the Town Hall in Gouda, in turn, one assumes would hold one's attention more than walking around the National Museum in Brasília. Although the pure form of the museum (and it being seen as part of the œuvre of Oscar Niemeyer) might be fascinating, the vista hardly changes as one circumnavigates the museum.

Sunken Closed Squares

Sunken closed squares are located below the level of surrounding streets. They can be looked down into, but not out of except skywards. The enclosing walls on their streets sides are usually just one story in height. Sunken plazas seldom attract much activity unless they have restaurants opening onto them or specific events are regularly programmed to take place in them. After much trial and error, the plaza at Rockefeller Center in New York came to life as an ice-skating rink in the winter and an outdoor restaurant/café in the summer.[3] It has the advantage of being tied into an extensive underground passage network linked to the city's subway system.

Citicorp Center Plaza, also in New York is, in contrast to the Rockefeller Plaza, a rather neglected place (Figure 7.4). It is surrounded by tall buildings and is only fleetingly illuminated by the sun.

Figure 7.4 A sunken closed square: Citicorp Center Plaza, New York, at lunchtime on a sunny, spring day

With cafés on its edge, it has its complement of people at lunchtime. The square is, like the Rockefeller Center Plaza, linked to a subway station. One corner is used as a stairway link between station and street and/or adjacent buildings. Other sunken squares such as the John Hancock Center Plaza and the Exelon Plaza, both in Chicago, also have cafés opening onto them. They are alive at lunchtime during the week but empty at weekends. Robson Square in Vancouver is another, very different, example of a sunken square (see Figures 9.4 (a) and 12.8 on pages 139 and 200). It houses an ice-skating and roller-skating rink which generates activity and has an anchor tenant, the University of British Columbia's Continuing Education Centre. Pedestrians tend not to use the sunken part of a square as part of their path. Without activity generators, sunken squares tend to be desolate places where people seldom wish to linger.

Amorphous Squares

Amorphous squares are those that are: poorly defined by buildings or any other feature such as walls, screens or trees or those where the buildings are so low in height that they provide no sense of enclosure to a square. Empire State Plaza in Albany (Figure 7.5 (b)), New York state's capital, Praça Biblioteca Nacional de Brazil in Brasília (Figure 7.5 (c)) and the recently completed Putra Square in Putra Jaya, Malaysia's administrative capital, are amorphous squares. Trafalgar Square, although boldly enclosed on the north by the National Gallery, could be added to the list. None of them possesses a strong sense of enclosure. This lack is partially due to the low height of surrounding buildings in relationship to the size of the square and partially due to the fragmented nature of the enclosing planes formed by the buildings.

Piccadilly Gardens in Manchester, completed in 2001, is an example of a square that is the city's central hub where a range of transport systems come together (Figure 7.5 (a)). It is nevertheless a poorly enclosed square because of the low height of the surrounding buildings in relation to the size of the square. On two sides are lines of buildings, one with cafés and shops on the ground floor but on the other sides it is dominated by a variety of modes of transportation. A building shields the square from a bus terminal, but its height is insufficient to give the space a sense of enclosure. During much of the year it is a large, bleak open space. On sunny summer days in Manchester, the square is, nevertheless, a popular spot where children frolic in the fountains. Few reviewers regard it as an excellent space; many more regard it as poor especially those people who remember the garden that it replaced.

As mentioned, buildings surrounding amorphous squares, even though they may be important, fail to give a sense of enclosure to the squares. They are scattered apart, have substantial spaces between them and/or are separated from the square by roads. Of the squares mentioned here, only Trafalgar Square acts as a true center of life of a city. The others may be grand open spaces but they are largely devoid of people. Piccadilly Gardens, though located in manner to be the heart of Manchester, is more of a link than a place.

Figure 7.5 *Amorphous squares: (a) Piccadilly Gardens, Manchester; (b) Empire State Plaza, Albany, New York; (c) Praça Biblioteca Nacional de Brazil, Brasília*

Source: (b) Photograph by Richard Cavelleri/Shutterstock.com.

Enclosure and the Quality of Light

"Sunlight in cities is an endangered species" (Grabar 2014: website). As buildings in cities are built taller and taller in response to economic pressures to maximize land use and to have contemporary, dramatic skylines, the street level may end up being in "permanent dusk." Sunlight and shade are important aspects of any square's design. Much about the character of a square is based on the way it is penetrated by sunlight; comfort levels depend on it. The people on the steps of New York's Metropolitan Museum on a cool day clearly choose to sit in the sun. The same observation holds for the interior courts, such as the Sculpture Garden at the Museum of Modern Art in New York. In Figure 12.4 (b) on p. 187, showing the Cours Honoré d'Estienne d'Orves in Marseille, the restaurants clearly prefer to be located on the sunny side of the square on a spring day. The seats in the shade on a sunny day are empty. In the summer the situation is different.

Figure 7.6 The quality of sunlight and the quality of squares at midday: (a) Regimental Square, Sydney, Australia, 34°S, summer; (b) Dutch Hospital shopping precinct, Colombo, Sri Lanka, 7°N, in November

Sun angles vary during the course of the year and depend on a square's latitude. In designing squares, the amount of sunlight (and thus warmth) entering a square especially at times when it is likely to be full of people need to be latitude-specific (and sometimes altitude-specific too). In wet, temperate climates, sunlight is highly sought after; in the tropics it is something to be avoided. In temperate climates, squares in business districts need to have good light during the middle of the day, especially at lunchtime (Cooper Marcus and Francis 1990). In the tropics, however, such squares will stand empty during the day as illustrated in Figure 7.6 (b). The square comes to life in the evening when the sun has set. Warmth is modified by high altitudes particularly in the difference between day and night temperatures. At higher altitudes, in cities such as Johannesburg, Lima and Mexico City, the temperature plummets with the sunset.

The quality of light will depend on the orientation of a square, particularly for rectangular squares. The nature of the surrounding buildings, their height in particular, and the sides of the square on which they stand affect the level of light in a square. Tall buildings on the south side of a square in the northern hemisphere, as in Imam Khomeini Square in Tehran (see Figure 0.7 on p. 13) in the southern hemisphere, as in Oxford Square (see Figure 12.12 on p. 213) or Regimental Square in Sydney (Figure 7.6 (a)), cast long shadows over the adjacent open spaces. The nature of the vegetation in the square or in its surroundings also has major consequences for the quality of light and warmth in a square. Regimental Square in Sydney is perpetually in shade and is gloomy. Its location, in a busy area and near a major public train station, nevertheless, makes it a popular place to sit especially during the midday summer heat.

Conclusion

For many critics, the closed square is the 'ideal' type. If it is not cut off from surrounding buildings by traffic and its accompanying odors and noise, it can be a comfortable place to be. If small enough, it can serve as an outdoor room. Sitte (1889) believed that squares should be seen as a room and form an enclosed space. It is not simply that buildings should surround the square; their height is critical. The 3:1 ratio of open space to the height of the surrounding buildings that is repeatedly mentioned in the literature seems about right. It must not be thought, however, that the enclosure in itself will make a square a well-loved place.

The ground floor of the surrounding buildings contributes significantly to the quality of a square. Not all public squares need to be lively. Some closed, dominated squares in Zucker's (1959) terms, need to be sedate settings that do not distract from the elements of a square or its surrounding buildings that are supposed to be the focus of attention. A residential square, in order to be quiet, does not need or want activity to be generated or regular events to be programmed. The requirements to attain a lively public square are different. Many closed squares are surrounded by highly active ground floors with shops, restaurants and people coming and going. Formal gatherings add another layer of life to them. Fountains and other water features, such as those in La Place des Terreaux, Lyon, add a dimension to the experiencing of the visual, sonic and tactile environment. Moving elements whether flowing water, fluttering flags, flying birds, people walking or flashing lights and vivid illuminations as in New York's Times Square also attract attention.

Notes

1 For the implication of the Gestalt 'law of closure' for architecture, see Lang and Moleski (2010).
2 See Sitte (1889) for examples.
3 The history of the development of the plaza is described fully by Alan Balfour (1978) and more briefly by Dennis Sharp (1991) and by Jon Lang (2005:168–173).

References

Balfour, Alan (1978) *Rockefeller Center: Architecture of Theatre*. New York: McGraw-Hill.

Cooper Marcus, Clare and Carolyn Francis (1990) *People Places: Design Guidelines for Urban Open Space*. New York: Van Nostrand Reinhold.

Cullen, Gordon (1961) *Townscape*. London: Architectural Press.

Grabar, Henry (2014) Welcome to permanent dusk, sunlight in cities is an endangered species. *Salon*, April 20. Available at: www.salon.com/2014/04/20/welcome_to_the_permanent_dusk_sunlight_in_cities_is_an_endangered_species.

Hegemann, Werner and Elbert Peets (1922) *The American Vitruvius: An Architect's Handbook on Civic Art*, reprinted 1972. New York: Benjamin Blom.

Lang, Jon (2005) *Urban Design: A Typology of Procedures and Products Illustrated with Over 50 Case Studies*. Oxford: Architectural Press.

Lang, Jon and Walter Moleski (2010) *Functionalism Revisited: Architectural Theory and Practice and the Behavioral Sciences*. Farnham: Ashgate.

Sharp, Dennis (1991) *Twentieth Century Architecture: A Visual History*. London: Lund Humphries.

Sitte, Camillo (1889) *Der Städtebau nach seinen künstlerischen Grundsätzen*. Vienna: Karl Graesser.

Zucker, Paul (1959) *Town and Square: From the Agora to the Village Green*. New York: Columbia University Press.

Further Reading

Carmona, Matthew, Tim Heath, Taner Oc and Steven Tiesdell (2003) *Public Places – Urban Spaces: The Dimensions of Urban Design*. Oxford: Architectural Press.

French, Jere S. (1978) *Urban Spaces: A Brief History of the City Square*. Dubuque, Iowa: Kendall-Hunt.

CHAPTER 8

TYPES BASED ON CONFIGURATIONS

It would be reasonable to expect a square to be square. Although the term 'square' implies that the sides of an open space are of the same length and at right angles to each other, city squares take many forms. Only a minority of squares are actually square-shaped. In this chapter we distinguish primarily between regular and irregular squares, although much of the commentary applies to both. The regular shapes tend to have resulted from advanced planning in response to commercial or esthetic demands whereas the irregular ones have resulted from piecemeal decisions made over time or as the demolition of buildings presented an opportunity to create an open space. Irregular squares can be quite formal in architectural character.

Formal and Informal Squares

Paul Zucker (1959) suggests one should distinguish between formal and informal squares rather than worry if they are square or not. A formal square has a regular shape and the latter an irregular shape. In Figure 8.1 (a), the architecture of the square that is formed by formal buildings is classical. It does not have to be. The key variable is the restrained unity of the character of the architecture of the surrounding buildings. The buildings could be Modernist or even Postmodernist.

The sequence of squares in Montpellier, shown in Figure 8.2, is comprised of a set of formal spaces surrounded by formal buildings. Harvard Square in Cambridge, Massachusetts, is, in contrast, an example of an informal space with informal buildings. Really a traffic intersection, the shape of the square is irregular and each of the

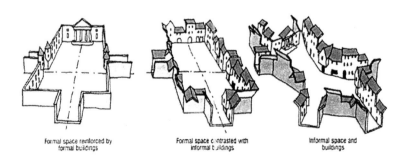

Formal space reinforced by formal buildings

Formal space contrasted with informal buildings

Informal space and buildings

Figure 8.1 *Formal and informal squares: Zucker's distinction between formal and informal squares*

Source: Image Courtesy of Essex County Council.

Figure 8.2 A formal and an informal square: (a) Formal space and formal buildings, Place de Thessalie, Antigone, Montpellier; (b) An informal square: Harvard Square, Cambridge, Massachusetts

Source: (a) Photograph by Blom UK/Getty Images.

buildings has its own character although their heights and materials are similar. The similarity gives some sense of unity to the square.

Regular-Shaped Squares

Square-shaped squares might seem to be the 'ideal' type but there is no reason for it to be seen as such. There are relatively few squares that are exactly a square but Paris has a number: Place des Vosges and the Place de l'Opéra in Paris are examples (Figure 8.3). The Place de l'Opéra was created as part of the revitalization of Paris under the direction of Baron Georges-Eugène Haussmann. Once a quiet square dominated by the Opera, it has become a traffic circle. The Place Vendôme is also square-shaped but has chamfered corners.

Square-shaped squares can be found in a number of other cities. In London, for instance, a number of the garden squares are square in shape. St James's is one. A number of college quadrangles around the world are also square. Christ Church, Oxford, is a British example. The forecourts of mosques, such as the Beyazit Mosque in Istanbul (see Figure 7.2 on p. 116), are often approximately square in form; that at the Jama Masjid in Delhi is a perfect square. Squares that are forecourts to mosques serve a number of purposes: they act as the foreground to the mosque, a place to conduct ablutions before praying and, in the surrounding colonnades, a place to rest. Rectangular squares are, however, more common than square ones.

Rectangular squares come in a variety of forms but there are two basic types: deep squares and broad squares. *Deep squares* are those where the long dimension is more than three times its breadth and the featured building is located on its longitudinal axis. Zucker (1959) refers to such places as "dominated squares." There are many examples: the Place de la Carrière in Nancy, the Place Royale in Valenciennes and Dom Pedro in Lisbon are among them. The core of the University of Virginia with the Library (Rotunda) at one end is an example of a college campus in the United States. In each case the building at the head of the axis is the focus of attention. Nelson A. Rockefeller Empire State Plaza in Albany, New York (Figure 8.4),

Figure 8.3 Square-shaped formal squares: (a) Place des Vosges, Paris; (b) Place de l'Opéra, Paris

Source: (a) Photograph by Stephanie Compoint/4Corners Images.

Figure 8.4 A deep rectangular square: Empire State Plaza, Albany, New York

Source: Photograph by The Albany County CVB.

completed in 1978, has the Old State Capitol at one end of it and the Cultural Education Center at the other end. Other state buildings line the plaza. A very deep, narrow square tends to be similar to an alley or a pedestrian mall.

Broad rectangular squares are similar to deep squares but the featured building lies on its cross-axis. The importance of the featured building is downplayed in this layout. La Piazza dei Signori in Vicenza is an example. The Basilica Palladiana with its tower stands on one side of the square. The Piazza Navona in Rome is similar (Figure 8.5). The church of St Agnes designed by Carlo Rinaldi but completed by Gianlorenzo Bernini stands on the long side of the rectangle. Off the cross-axis in front of the church is Bernini's *Fontana dei Quattro Fuimi* (the Four Rivers fountain – the Ganges, the Danube, the Nile and the Plate) that acts as a nuclear element in the square.

Octagonal squares are unusual but the 1856 plan for a "vegetarian utopia" in Kansas was centered on an octagonal square because it was regarded as a "scientific form" (Gambone 1972). Frederiksplatz (Amalienborg Square) of the palace complex in Copenhagen is a built example; the Octagon in Dunedin on New Zealand's South

Island is another. The two serve two very different instrumental functions. Frederiksplatz is framed by four similar large rococo houses/ palaces built between 1750 and 1758 and four lower sets of buildings and gateways. At the square's center is an equestrian statue of King Frederik V. The instrumental function of Frederiksplatz is as a foreground to the surrounding buildings. Its geometric layout is something for the cognoscenti to savor and the general public to admire. Despite the degree of enclosure, it has no sense of being an

Figure 8.5 A broad rectangular square: (a) Piazza Navona, Rome, aerial view (b) Piazza Navona, Rome, a pedestrian's view

Source: (a) Photograph by Massimo Borchi /SIME/4Corners Images.

Figure 8.6 An octagonal square: Octagon, Dunedin, New Zealand

Source: Photograph by davidwallphoto.com.

outdoor room. The buildings that frame it generate little pedestrian traffic and nobody lingers long in the space. Dunedin's Octagon, in contrast, is the heart of a city (Figure 8.6).

The Octagon in Dunedin was laid out in 1846 during Charles Kettle's surveying of the city. Whether Kettle considered it to be a 'scientific form' is not known. The Octagon, unlike most squares, is on a slope. It is bisected by the city's main streets and framed by some of the city's major buildings: the Town Hall, the Public Library, Public Art Gallery and St Paul's Anglican Cathedral. Covered walkways on its periphery contribute to the comfort of pedestrians. A cinema multiplex, restaurants, bars and cafés on the square as well as it being a transportation hub make the Octagon very much the heart of Dunedin.

Triangular squares are common in cities where grid-iron plans and diagonal streets cross. The Pearl Street Triangle in Brooklyn, New York, is typical of the possibilities to create squares that occur in such situations (Kimmelman 2013). In Manhattan, where Broadway and St Nicholas Avenue cross the north–south avenues, a number of bow-tie squares – two triangular squares with their points facing each other – have been created. Herald Square (see Figure 6.4 on p. 107) with Greeley Square is one of the best known. Rafferty Triangle in Queens, New York, has recently been upgraded to make it a pleasant spot. The triangular area of Vietnam Veterans Plaza in lower Manhattan was built in 1971 by a private/public coalition (Figure 8.7 (a)). It aimed to be a peaceful and dignified memorial space.

Many triangular squares can be found in the old quarters of European and some Asian cities where streets have been created over time in a somewhat haphazard manner. Madrid, for instance, has many small triangular squares that serve as outdoor rooms – they are full of cafés that have outdoor seating during the summer months. Plaza de Angel, Plaza de Mantua (Figure 8.7 (b)) and Plaza de la Platería (see Figure 6.3 (b) on p. 106) are the result of street crossings or the demolition of buildings that once existed at their intersections. Triangular squares are usually small, even the one that acts as the forecourt to St Paul's Cathedral in London is tiny.

Figure 8.7 *Triangular squares:*
(a) Vietnam Veterans Plaza, New York
(b) Plaza de Mantua, Madrid

Circular squares appear in many idealized city plans. Some do exist. Horniman Circle in Mumbai, which was introduced in the Prologue, is one that is full of life (see Figure 0.3 (a) on p. 7). The Place Charles de Gaulle in Paris, with the Arc de Triomphe at its center, is probably the best-known example of a circular area but today it is little more than a traffic circle and a landmark with a memorial arch that is a major tourist attraction (Figure 8.8 (a)). The same observation can be made about the Puerta de Alcala in Madrid. There are many other such squares on a much smaller scale dotted around the world. The Circus in Bath, which is a wooded knoll at the centre of a traffic circle, and Nejmeh Square in Beirut (Figure 8.8 (b)), which has a clock tower at its center, are examples. Hasan Abad Square, a circular square in Tehran, has undergone many changes. A circle of buildings once surrounded a crossroads with a fountain at its center. The fountain is long since gone and one of the crossroads has been lowered into a tunnel so that the square now consists of two semi-circular pedestrian areas bisected by a road. Place du Forez in Lyon is quartered by crossroads but the traffic passing through the square is light, so it is seen as a pedestrian area. The Piazza del Campo in Sienna is often seen to be very roughly semi-circular but it is really irregular in form.

Figure 8.8 *Two circular squares and a semi-circular square: (a) Place Charles de Gaulle, Paris; (b) Nejmeh Square, Beirut; (c) Piazza de la Republica, Rome*

Sources: (a) Photograph by Serge Vero/ Shutterstock.com; (b) Photograph by Mosbah Assi.

Figure 8.9 *Oval squares: (a) Piazza del Popolo, Rome; (b) Roald Dahl Plass, Cardiff*

Source: (a) Photograph by Catarina Belova/ Shutterstock.com.

Oval squares are uncommon. The palace at Caserta built by the King of Naples in 1752 has an oval forecourt but it is not an urban complex (Hegemann and Peets [1922] 1972). The hemicycle at the Place de la Carrière in Nancy is an example, as is the Piazza del Popolo in Rome (Figure 8.9 (a)). In neither case do the surrounding buildings hug the oval, although, in the Piazza del Popolo, the steep hill at one end and the density of the trees at the other end of the oval do give the piazza a sense of enclosure. The size of the square is such that the piazza appears to be a vast urban space that is focused on twin churches – Santa Maria di Montesanto and Santa Maria dei Miracoli.

Completed in 2000 and dedicated two years later, Roald Dahl Plass in Cardiff, located on the site of the historic Oval Basin Plaza, is centered on an oval formed by illuminated pillars (Figure 8.9 (b)). Beyond the oval, however, the square is irregular-shaped with 'nooks' that lend themselves to a variety of instrumental functions. Oval squares of pure geometric forms are the result of self-conscious design. As such, they present architects and designers with places to study. Their geometry makes them almost automatically valuable places.

A number of squares are comprised of a mixture of forms. For instance, an open space may have a rectangular form at one end and a semi-circular or oval row of buildings at the other end that gives them an irregular quality. Other squares are simply irregular in form.

Irregular Squares

Irregular-shaped squares have either been developed over time in response to circumstances and/or have been wedged into existing landholdings and building forms. Two are shown in Figure 8.10. Historical examples are Piazza San Marco in Venice, Neumarkt in Dresden and Mansion House Place in London. A late twentieth-century example is Westlake Park in Seattle.[1] Melbourne's Federation Square is an early twenty-first-century example. Neumarkt in Dresden, destroyed by Allied bombing in World War II, was faithfully but controversially restored to its pre-war state. Empire Square in London, which forms the center of a predominantly residential real estate development, was completed in 2007 (see Figure 14.2 on p. 271).

Some special shapes lend themselves to specific instrumental functions. The predominantly oval Roald Dahl Plass is the forecourt of the Senedd (the Welsh Assembly Hall) and the Wales Millennium Centre. Its bowl form makes it a popular place for celebrations, political gatherings and for concerts because the sight lines formed by the dip in its surface enable any proceedings in the square to be easily watched.

Some squares are simply odd shaped rather than irregular shapes. Consisting of circular and rectangular components, Freedom Square in Kharkiv in the Ukraine is a large square that is dominated by a statue of Lenin. The square was originally named Dzerzhinsky Square after the head of the Bolshevik secret police but received its present name in 1991 on Ukraine's achievement of independence. At the time of writing, its future was uncertain.

Figure 8.10 Irregular-shaped squares: (a) Neumarkt, Dresden; (b) Westlake Park, Seattle

Source: (a) Photograph by Peter Lang.

Grouped Squares

Grouped squares are those which form part of a chain where one square is joined to another. Moving through them can provide a rich visual experience as vistas open up in front of one and close behind. The Place de la Carrière in Nancy is an example already cited. The difference in the spatial quality of each of the enclosed spaces makes them especially interesting as a sequence. In Zucker's (1959) terms, it is a formal set of spaces enclosed by formal buildings. The sequence in Montpellier in France is also a formal composition in his terms (see Figure 8.2 (a)). It is also a single design. Many other grouped squares have resulted from individual decisions made over time.

The Piazza Castelnuovo and Piazza Ruggero Settimo, Palermo, face each other across a street to create one large open space (Figure 8.11 (a)). The same observation can be made about the 'bow-tie' urban open spaces in New York. To get from one to the other means having to cross often busy east–west streets. In 2013, many bow-tie squares were undergoing a major renovation as part of New York City's 'Broadway Boulevard' redevelopment. Times Square in the city is another bow-tie open space being transformed.

Figure 8.11 Grouped squares:
(a) Joined squares: Piazza
Castelnuovo and Piazza Ruggero
Settimo, Palermo; (b) A sequence of
squares: Cinelandia, Rio de Janeiro

Sources: (a) Photograph by Joanne Taylor;
(b) Photograph by Silvio Macedo Soares.

Some grouped squares have resulted from urban renewal projects. The Benjamin Franklin Parkway in Philadelphia consists of a sequential group of partially enclosed squares formed in the era when the City Beautiful paradigm dominated in urban designs. The recent addition of the Barnes Collection Museum with its forecourt does little to enhance the formal qualities of the overall sequence. Cinelandia in Rio de Janeiro is also a loose sequence resulting from piecemeal development (Figure 8.11 (b)). Easy to discern in bird's-eye views, these grouped squares are only fully experienced and comprehended as one walks from one to another. Their relationship to each other and the way that new vistas open up in sequence as one passes occluding elements or surfaces are important to the way we experience and enjoy them as Gordon Cullen explained (1961).

In the older parts of European cities, the emergence of a pedestrian from a narrow street into an open square is a rewarding experience. Irregular-shaped squares offer more potential experiences of this type than regular-shaped formal grouped squares. They, however, lack the unity of design that impresses. Regular-shaped squares appear to offer more in the way of intellectual esthetic analyses. Ultimately, however, a square is enriched by what it offers as a behavior setting or a collection of settings and the opportunities it possesses for observing other people and their activities.

Conclusion

Existing city squares clearly come in an extraordinary range of shapes. Regular-shaped rectangular squares tend to be regarded as more formal than picturesque, irregular ones. The shape itself is of little importance in the contribution a square makes to everyday life. The Street Life Project, conducted by William H. Whyte in New York, strongly supports this observation (1980, 1989). Observations of Roald Dahl Plass in Cardiff and Upper Sproul Plaza in Berkeley also support this conclusion. Sitte believed that irregular-shaped squares work best as urban places because the odd 'nooks' create affordances for many activities (Sitte, cited in Gilbert 2001). The quality of a square ultimately depends largely on how it is linked to streets, how it is enclosed and how the enclosing elements – buildings, columns, or vegetation – meet the ground plane and the setting it forms.

In designing new urban squares in existing cities, the shape is often dictated by the availability of land and its adjacent uses. Many spaces, new and old, result from the demolition of buildings. The shapes themselves dictate the affordances of an open space for instrumental functions but many different types of activities and events can be accommodated in the space available. It depends on the actual design of the square.

Note

1 For a detailed analysis, see Cooper Marcus and Francis (1990).

References

Cooper Marcus, Clare and Carolyn Francis (1990) *People Places: Design Guidelines for Urban Open Space*. New York: Van Nostrand Reinhold.

Cullen, Gordon (1961) *Townscape*. London: Architectural Press.

Gambone, Joseph G. (ed.) (1972) Kansas – a vegetarian utopia: The letters of John Milton Hadley, 1855–1856.*The Kansas Historical Quarterly* 38(1): 65–87. Available at: www.kancoll.org/khq/1972/72_1_hadley.htm.

Gilbert, Helen (2001) A case study in contemporary development: How does it measure up to the principles of classic urban design theorists? Paper presented at the Seventh Annual Pacific Rim Real Estate Society Conference, Adelaide, January 21–24.

Hegemann, Werner and Elbert Peets (1922) *The American Vitruvius: An Architect's Handbook on Civic Art*, reprinted 1972. New York: Benjamin Blom.

Kimmelman, Michael (2013) A street corner serenade for the public plaza. *The New York Times*, May 31. Available at: www.nytimes.com/2013/06/02/arts/design/a-prescription-for-plazas-and-public-spaces.html?pagewanted=all&_r=0.

Sitte, Camillo (1889) *Der Städtebau nach seinen künstlerischen Grundsätzen*. Vienna: Karl Graesser.

Whyte, William H. (1980) *The Social Life of Small Urban Spaces*. Washington, DC: The Conservation Foundation.

Whyte, William H. (1989) *City: Rediscovering the Center*. New York: Doubleday.

Zucker, Paul (1959) *Town and Square: From the Agora to the Village Green*. New York: Columbia University Press.

Further Reading

Hillier, Bill and Julienne Hanson (1984) *The Social Logic of Space*. Cambridge: Cambridge University Press.

Jenkins, Eric J. (2008) *To Scale: One Hundred Urban Plans*. New York: Routledge.

CHAPTER 9

TYPES BASED ON INTERNAL DESIGNS

The way a square is structured by walls, seating (formal as in benches or informal as in steps and ledges), landscaping and the materials of its surfaces creates its affordances for people's activities and emotional experiences. Many squares contain point elements – objects – that can be circumnavigated. Monuments, trees, lampposts, street furniture and fountains are elements that give squares much of their character, both as places to inhabit and as displays to contemplate.

The designs of squares can be classified in a number of ways. At a very general level, one can distinguish between nuclear squares and other types based on their overall organization. Beyond this level, some squares have simple designs; others are highly articulated into a number of parts, sometimes at different levels. The nature and quality of the detailing of a square are always important.

Nuclear and Non-Nuclear Squares

The nuclear square is one of the basic types identified by Paul Zucker (1959). Such squares contain an object that is the focus of attention. Unlike his dominant square type where the feature is one of the buildings that enclose the square, in a nuclear square, the feature is a point element within it. The simplest and boldest type of nuclear square is that with a single focus and a flat surface of a uniform material. The focal element can be a column usually topped by a statue, as in San Francisco's Union Square (Figure 9.1), a statue on a pedestal, a fountain, a sculpture, an obelisk or even a cuboid structure, such as the Kaaba in Mecca. The sculptures most frequently are memorials to famous people or famous events. A very different type of nuclear square is the *chowk* of traditional North Indian cities where a tree is the central focus. It gives shade and creates convection currents that have a cooling effect. Typically, men use the *chowk* for a local meeting point.

To Zucker (1959), the focus had to be in the center but here we take a more relaxed approach to its location. The focus can be located in the center or on one end as in Herald Square, New York (see Figure 6.4 on p. 107) or Heroes Square in Budapest (see Prologue figure on p. 1). The argument for having the point element on one side is that it leaves the center open for events and crowds of people to gather. In squares with a central object, such gatherings can, nevertheless,

still be accommodated although not as well. In Trafalgar Square, the off-center base of *Nelson's Column* is used as the elevated point from which orators can address large gatherings. The square has often been regarded as 'unsuitable' for large groups because of its fragmented nature but the centrality of its location and the ease of access make it the ideal place for a crowd to converge. The gatherings at Tahrir Square in Cairo show that almost any open space can be flooded with protesters.

Although the everyday image of an ideal square may be a nuclear one, many squares are non-nuclear. They have no single element in the center or off-center that acts as a focus for the square. Using

Figure 9.1 *A nuclear square: Union Square, San Francisco*

Figure 9.2 *Two non-nuclear squares (a) Federation Square, Melbourne; (b) Schouwburgplein, Rotterdam*

Zucker's (1959) nomenclature, some are dominant squares where the focus of attention is on a building at one end. Many classical Italian squares were of that nature. Some squares, despite having a major point element at the center, have so many other elements in them that the strength of the nuclear quality is somewhat reduced. Nonnuclear squares come in many forms; Figure 9.2 shows two recently built ones. Federation Square and Schouwburgplein were designed to house gatherings and do so very well.

Plain Surfaced and Articulated Squares

Nuclear and non-nuclear squares may be one way of differentiating between types of squares but the degree to which their internal design is divided into components may say more about their character and the instrumental functions they afford. Many traditional European squares have very simple layouts but recently designed squares tend to be more complex in character. Design paradigms seem to switch between simple and complex forms over time.[1] Plain surfaced squares are differentiated from each other by their enclosing elements. Articulated squares come in many forms.

Plain Surfaced Squares

The basic plain square has a uniform flat surface, a single paving material and no objects within it (Figure 9.3). There are many examples of such squares in Italy. Tiananmen Square is a Chinese example

Figure 9.3 *A uniform surface square: Caixa Forum, Madrid*

(see Figure 6.1 (b) on p. 103). In the Praça dos Tres Poderes in Brasília, the uniformly flat but vaguely patterned surface is largely unbroken by any elements. The surface materials employed in plain surfaced squares vary considerably. Some squares have a simple asphalt surface, like George Square in Glasgow (see Figure 6.3 (a) on p. 106), while in others the surface has a design in expensive materials. Yet others, such as Parliament Square in London, are grassed (see Figure 9.5 (b) on p. 140). The ground surface is either flat or only gently sloping. Depending on their size, plain surfaced squares accommodate events and gatherings very well.

Many flat-surfaced squares have patterned paving. The pavement of the Piazza del Campo in Sienna is divided into central and peripheral areas by a difference in surface hues. Guildhall Yard in London has a uniformly flat but highly patterned ground plane (see Figure 7.1 (a) on p. 115). The curving line cutting across the surface in Guildhall Yard is a reminder of the Roman amphitheater that once existed there. In Rome's Piazza Navona, the floor is uniform in nature but the square contains a number of point elements, fountains and an obelisk. Uniform surface squares are often devoid of formal, built-in seating which allows restaurants to spill out into them with ease.

Articulated Squares

Articulated squares are those that are divided into a number of components by low walls, benches and/or by having their floors at different levels. They come in an extraordinary variety of forms. Their organization can be analyzed using the same categorization of elements of people's cognitive maps that Kevin Lynch (1960) applied to cities: squares have their paths serving as links, nodes (localized behavior settings where paths come together), districts (behavior settings with a similar character), edges (boundaries) and landmarks, such as point elements or curiosity objects. There was a period where designers tried to make squares lively by having many of these elements. In many cases they overdid it; the squares lacked clarity and were seen to be cluttered.

There is no commonly accepted way of differentiating among articulated squares based on the type of their internal organization but here is one effort to identify different types: those that have multiple levels, those that are treed and/or landscaped and those centered on bodies of water.

Squares with multiple levels may have been designed to follow a slope but often they are designed to add variety to a flat piece of land. In Robson Square, Vancouver (see Figure 12.8 on p. 200), the aim is to act as an underpass below a busy road. Changes in surfaces levels are used to form settings for different activities or to form small, partially enclosed spaces that have a clear identity. Amphitheaters, such as that in the Praça Mário Lago in Rio de Janeiro (Figure 9.4 (b)) or the Olympic Plaza in Calgary (see Figure 12.9 on p. 203), provide a clear image of the potential activities that can take place there. There appears to be a world-wide tendency for designers, when they do not know what to do with a large paved area, to include an amphitheater rather than leave the space flat.

Figure 9.4 Squares with multiple levels: (a) Robson Square, Vancouver (b) An amphitheater, Praça Mário Lago, Rio de Janeiro

The danger is that when squares are broken up into a number of levels in order to give them some visual variety, many potential uses are precluded (Franck and Stevens 2007). Indeed, much of the de-cluttering of squares that has taken place in recent years has removed levels that serve little purpose. In Sydney, both Martin Place and Pitt Street Mall were recently de-cluttered.

Treed and landscaped squares can be divided into four types. The first consists mostly of paving with lines of trees or vegetation on the periphery. The second category consists of squares that are flat, grassed, open space. The third is a square that is predominantly a lawn with extensive vegetation including trees on the periphery. The fourth is even more a mixture of pavement, grassed areas and land-scaping. Examples are illustrated in Figure 9.5.[2]

The Place de la République in the village of Villecroze in France is an example of the first. Parliament Square in London is primarily a lawn surrounded by a paved footpath and statues of statesmen and an example of the second type. Copley Square in Boston and many of London's garden squares fit into the third category. They all have a park-like quality. The fourth type includes those, such as Piccadilly Gardens in Manchester (see Figure 7.5 (a) on p. 120) and TransAmerica Plaza (also known as Redwood Park) in San Francisco, that are a real mixture of hard and soft surfaces.

Although no census has been compiled on the types of changes that have been made to urban squares in recent decades, anecdotal infor-mation suggests that a disproportionate number of paved squares have been planted with vegetation. Plaza des Armas in Santiago is an example of a product of the *Law of the Indies* that over the years has been changed from an open plain-surfaced nuclear plaza to one with trees. The same type of change occurred in St James's Square in London. Jacob K. Javits Plaza in New York, completed in 2013, is a very recent example of a change from a plaza largely without trees to one replete with them.

Squares centered on bodies of water are those that surround water features that vary in size from fountains to reflecting ponds, to what might be described as lakes. Cabot Square, at Canary Wharf

Figure 9.5 Treed and landscaped squares: (a) Paved and lined by trees: Place de la République, Villecroze; (b) Flat, grassed surface: Parliament Square, London; (c) Lawn with vegetation on the periphery: Copley Square, Boston; (d) Mix of pavement, grassed and treed areas: TransAmerica Plaza, San Francisco

in London, has a raised two-level pool that fills much of the plaza with places for people to sit located on its periphery. A number of water squares have highly articulated surfaces that create waterfalls and channels of flowing water, such as the Keller Fountain Square in Portland and the Water Gardens in Fort Worth (see Figure 5.5 on p. 89). BBD (Benoy-Badal-Dinesh) Bagh in Kolkata is an example of a square that is organized around a body of water known in India as a 'tank.' Historically, it acted as the water reservoir for the city. It is partially enclosed by the Writers Building on its north and has colonial-era Neoclassical buildings such as the Post Office and St Andrew's Church as important historical elements on its borders. The square is the center of the 'Office Para,' the city's business district.

City Park in Bradford, completed in 2012, is a recent example of a square focused on a large 28 cm-deep (8 inches) mirror pool (Figure 9.6). With laser light projections, mist effects, over 100 fountains, including a central one spouting higher than any other in Britain, the square itself is a major attraction. Linked with Centenary Square outside the City Hall, it forms the heart of Bradford. The pool is drained for large events. Olympic Plaza in Calgary is a more conventional square with a large shallow pool at its heart in summer (which is also drained for special events) and an outdoor skating rink in winter.

Figure 9.6 A square around a body of water: City Park, Bradford

Detailing

The quality of workmanship in the finishing of paving, retaining walls and furnishings, as much as its overall design, distinguishes one square from another.[3] The difference is often perceivable at a glance and consciously or subconsciously registers in the observer's mind. One of the most important characteristics of the pavement of a square is the quality of the materials of which it is constructed and the workmanship it displays. The spate of new, paved squares in Europe designed without due consideration for their appearance has turned many public places into unpopulated, hard, gray-stone, unsustainable deserts (Green 2012).

In the recent design of Yerba Buena Gardens in San Francisco (Figure 9.7 (b)) and Guildhall Yard in London, particular attention was paid to the floor tiling. The Plaza de Oriente in Madrid, in contrast to the hard paving in many squares, has a very fine gravel base that grinds a little underfoot. In general, the less elaborate the pattern, the better, but certain materials and patterns are clearly associated with specific cultures and sometimes specific designers. The floor of the Praça Floriano in Rio de Janeiro is typical of plazas and sidewalks in Brazil. They have rough textured, multi-colored surfaces (Figure 9.7(a)); some are the work of the great Brazilian landscape architect,

Roberto Burle Marx. The rough surfaces can, however, be a tripping hazard for people with mobility issues. Paving details are another consideration (Figure 9.8).

The attention paid to the ratio of risers to treads in steps, the height of seating and the amount of sunlight and shade appropriate to the latitude of a location all add to perceptions of the care put into the design and construction of a square. The design of seating is almost as basic to the quality of a square as is its paving. People entering squares scan the environment to see where they can sit. In general, they like to have moveable chairs, as shown in Figure 9.9 (d) in San Francisco or in New York's Paley Park. They, however, will sit on whatever solid surface is located at seat height. Benches, berms and bollards all afford seating with different levels of comfort.[4]

A tremendous variety of seating arrangements have been employed in squares around the world. The photographs in Figure 9.9 only hint at the range of places people choose to sit and the patterns of built form that afford it. Fixed seating can be arranged to make conversing easier (see Figure 2.1 on p. 35) or more difficult (Figure 9.9 (c)). Although not specifically designed as seating, steps, grassy slopes, bollards, and edges of fountains are used for seating all over the world. Temporary furniture can also be used in squares to provide places to sit when the square is not needed for an event as part of an everyday place activation strategy.

Figure 9.7 *Paving materials and patterns: (a) Praça Floriano, Rio de Janeiro (b) Yerba Buena Gardens, San Francisco*

Figure 9.8 *Paving details: (a) A tree grid, Rockefeller Center, New York; (b) A directional sign, Union Square, San Francisco; (c) A drain, Piazza Farnese, Rome*

Source: (c) Photograph by Alix Verge.

Figure 9.9 *Seating: fixed and moveable: (a) Fixed features: bollards and ledges, Square René-Viviani, Paris; (b) Fixed features: benches and balustrade, Rittenhouse Square, Philadelphia; (c) Fixed features: high-end benches, 425 Market Street Plaza, San Francisco; (d) Moveable tables and chairs, Fremont Street Plaza, San Francisco*

The same observations can be extended to garbage bins, lighting standards, other types of furniture and to signage (Figure 9.10). They need to be of high quality and be well maintained which usually means they must be robust and easy to maintain. The integration of these elements into an overall design is essential to the perceived esthetic quality of a square. Some street furniture is designed following a theme, often historic, to match its context. Otherwise it tends to be Modernist. In the Cours Honoré d'Estienne d'Orves in Marseille, the lamp shades are in the form of a gull's wings (Figure 9.11 (a)). Garbage bins are built into the bases of the lamp poles. In Bradford's Centenary Square the elements are more geometrical. The general requirement to achieve a sense of order is to have a uniform and consistent design or, alternatively, to get a unity through diversity, although this latter approach can result in a chaotic appearance.

Pop-up electric outlets are now standard equipment for squares where flat floors provide for weekly markets and occasional events or concerts. They can be popped up when needed and retracted when not. At Granary Square, London, the size of the pavers covering these outlets fits into the overall design pattern of the floor (Figure 9.12 (b)). They are only discernible by the keyholes required to give access to

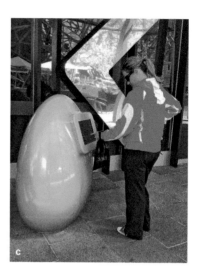

Figure 9.10 *Furniture: (a) Chess/checker table, Yerba Buena Gardens, San Francisco; (b) Garbage bin, Bryant Park, New York; (c) Digital, interactive information booth, Federation Square, Melbourne*

Figure 9.11 *Lighting standards: (a) Cours Honoré d'Estienne d'Orves, Marseille; (b) Centenary Square, Bradford*

Figure 9.12 *Pop-up electrical outlets and toilets: (a) Built-in power sources, Federation Square, Melbourne; (b) Floor paver outlet cover, Granary Square, London; (c) Pop-up toilet in ground; (d) and when above ground*

Source: (c) and (d): Photographs by Albin Olsson/Flickr.

the outlet below. At Federation Square, they are built-in (Figure 9.12 (a)). Toilets can also be pop-up features (Figures 9.12 (c) and (d)).

The Use of Water Features

Fountains often act as the central feature of a square. The sound of falling and splashing water almost inevitably adds to its ambient quality. Active fountains and water installations change the sonic environment and the humidity of a place. On the odd occasion, the sound levels of falling water can be so high they are overwhelming. The City Square in Melbourne, as already mentioned, is such a case. It was redesigned in 2001 to reduce the noise level of the water gushing out from below a statue. The sound level in the square is still high but it now originates from the passing traffic.

Water features can serve many functions. They can, for instance, be part of a city's drainage system as well as functioning as esthetic elements in the landscape. They can add an element of continuity, joining a series of linked squares into a unified design. They can reflect the heritage of a locale or provide a place in which people,

Figure 9.13 Fountains: (a) Logan Square, Philadelphia, with the Swann Memorial Fountain; (b) Civic Plaza, Roseville, California; (c) One of the world's many non-functioning fountains in a public space, Water Tower Park, Chicago

especially children, can play. They can simply be an artistic installation to add visual and sonic interest to a square.

Fountains come in many forms. Two in city squares are shown in Figure 9.13. Some fountains, for example, in Jamison Square in Portland, Oregon, are designed specifically for wading and splashing in. The square attracts visitors from well beyond its immediate neighborhood. The urge to play in the fountains of Roseville's Civic Plaza in California (Figure 9.13 (b)) or in the many other similar fountains across the world, is strong; they are both child- and adult-friendly on a hot summer day. The urge to swim in Philadelphia's Swann Fountain, which is classified as 'child-friendly,' is strong despite the traffic swirling around Logan Square (Figure 9.13 (a)). Playing in such fountains is banned in many places in order to preserve a sense of decorum.

Many nuclear squares have fountains as their focal element. Their style reflects the era in which they were designed. Rome's Trevi Fountain was designed by Nicola Savi in 1732. The Bartholdi Fountain in Lyon's La Place des Terreaux, although in its present location for only a little over two decades, was designed in 1888. The Swann Fountain dates from 1929. The Roseville water feature dates from 2013 and is a type almost automatically specified for new squares today. The photographs show these fountains active and full of life but a disproportionate number of fountains in squares are not spouting any water. Some are turned off during the winter to prevent pipes from freezing; others are simply broken. Fountains need to look elegant when they are not functioning but few do. They also need to be so designed that they do not become garbage bins when idle.

All of the detailing mentioned thus far includes physical infrastructure. New and future squares will undoubtedly cater for technology and personal mobile devices. Many squares are already hot-spots with free access to Wi-Fi and have power points for recharging devices. Old telephone booths are currently being reconfigured in New York to be free Wi-Fi kiosks with touch screens and recharging docks. No doubt digital infrastructure in squares will increase and be improved.

Conclusion

Each type of internal structuring of a square described here has its utility. It may seem that highly articulated squares are the most visually interesting not only because of the variety of their physical components but because of the variety of activities the settings can accommodate. A square with many different internal spaces offers potential places for active or passive activities. Squares can easily be designed to offer many potential behavior settings in the hope that visitors will perceive the opportunities provided and will use them. The question is: To what extent should a square provide for different possibilities?

The uniform surface seems more appropriate for small squares; endless plain surfaces can, however, be boring. Parade grounds and places designed for large events, however, require them. Designers today tend to create squares of multiple levels in order to make them more visually interesting. Doing so has both advantages and disadvantages. Many observers feel that too many squares are being over-designed and cluttered. They argue for "loose spaces" – ones that are adaptable rather than tight squares where the layout is tailored to accommodate a very specific range of activities (Franck and Stevens 2007). Certainly, in recent years, many highly articulated squares have been de-cluttered. They are much simpler in their refurbished form. The relatively contemporary design paradigm favors greater clarity but the desire for simplicity and complexity seems to occur in a cycle across time (Tyng 1975). It is unclear what the next paradigm will specify – it will likely include technological opportunities.

Notes

1 Anne Tyng (1975) traced the changes in preference for simplicity versus complexity over time in building design. Such a cycle in tastes for geometric complexity is likely for the design of squares too.

2 For comprehensive statements on how to use trees in urban design, see Laurie (1978) and Arnold (1993) among others.
3 A number of authors give extensive descriptions of the range of detailing approaches that add to the quality of squares. See Halprin (1963) and Ryan *et al.* (2011) among others.
4 See Savić and Savićic (2013) on design techniques that deter 'undesirables' from using public spaces. See also Figure 14.6 on p. 278.

References

Arnold, Henry F. (1993) *Trees in Urban Design*, 2nd edn. New York: Van Nostrand Reinhold.

Franck, Karen A. and Quentin Stevens (eds.) (2007) *Loose Space: Possibility and Diversity in Urban Life*. New York: Routledge.

Green, Jared (2012) Paver power. *The Dirt*. American Society of Landscape Architects. Available at: http://dirt.asla.org/2012/07/05/paver-power.

Halprin, Lawrence (1963) *Cities*. New York: Reinhold.

Laurie, Ian C. (1978) Overdesign is the death of outdoor liveliness. *Landscape Architecture* 68(6): 485–486.

Lynch, Kevin (1960) *The Image of the City*. Cambridge, MA: MIT Press.

Ryan, Thomas R., Edward Allen and Patrick J. Rand (2011) *Detailing for Landscape Architects: Aesthetics, function and constructability*. Hoboken: John Wiley.

Savić, Selena and Gordan Savićic (eds) (2013) *Unpleasant Design*. Belgrade: G.L.O.R.I.A.

Tyng, Anne (1975) *Simultaneous Randomness and Order: The Fibonacci-Divine Proportion as a Universal Forming Principle*. Unpublished dissertation, University of Pennsylvannia, Philadelphia.

Zucker, Paul (1959) *Town and Square from the Agora to the Village Green*. New York: Columbia University Press.

Further Reading

Cooper Marcus, Clare and Carolyn Francis (1990) *People Places: Design Guidelines for Urban Open Space*. New York: Van Nostrand Reinhold.

Gehl, Jan (2010) *Cities for People*. Washington, DC: Island Press.

Parker, Simon (2002) New zip code for London: WC2. *The Guardian*, November 1. Available at: www.theguardian.com/society/2002/nov/01/local government.publichealth.

CHAPTER 10

TYPES BASED ON SYMBOLIC FUNCTIONS

People are symbol mongers, as noted by Susanne Langer ([1953] 1979). The symbolic functions of squares are those concerned with their meanings as displays, as the communicator of a sense that a place belongs to a group of people. Two aspects of this sense of belonging are reviewed here: first, squares as part of a culture or subculture and, second, as a mark of social status.[1] Although some meanings seem to be understood universally, most are culture-bound. They depend on the associations that individuals or groups of people make between the object, people or event which the square symbolizes (the referent) and the layout of a square and/or with the artifacts that it contains.[2] The referent is part of a community's memory and may relate to past events or people of historical importance or elements of a society that are considered to be markers of socio-economic status. The viewer's associations may be conscious but they are often subconscious.

As works of art, the referent may be the œuvre of the designer of the square or its style of design. The designer may strive to create a shock value, in which case viewers would have to adjust their thinking or reject the square as balance theory would suggest. This topic is an intellectual esthetic concern of interest almost entirely to the cognoscenti and is discussed more fully in Chapter 11. The concern here is more closely focused on the role of squares in contributing to a sense of self-worth or of social status in the minds of their users.

Symbolic Esthetics and the Sense of Belonging to a Locale

City squares possess and can be created to possess specific symbolic meanings. A square or set of squares, as in Savannah, Georgia, can give a precinct or even a whole city an identity that differentiates it from other places. Many municipal officials are, at times, building or renovating squares in order for their cities to be identified as a 'global city' and part of the world economy. The result is often that squares are becoming so similar in character, they could be anywhere, or as Edward Relph (1976) suggests, they are "placeless." Other authorities want the squares in their city to have a clear identity rooted in their locale; they want their cities to be seen to belong to the local people. Designing to instantaneously make a square appear to belong to a specific locale and be simultaneously modern is no easy task because meanings are often only acquired through use over time.

In designing buildings, architects have relied on a Neotraditional approach to locate their buildings in their social and geographical context. They have adapted traditional forms whose patterns communicate a sense of their locale to the inhabitants of a locality. That approach may also be the best way forward for the designers of squares. Some other architects, for example, Kenneth Frampton (1982),[3] however, are advocates of a "critical regionalism" in which traditional forms are used in an abstract manner but few lay-people recognize the message implicit in such forms (Groat and Canter 1979).

Culture-Based Esthetic Character

Predicting accurately the meanings that people will read into specific patterns of built form is difficult because the patterns carry associational meanings in many ways (Appleyard 1979). One way is through its general character. Certain styles, or design paradigms, are associated with specific cultural groups: the Japanese landscape tradition, the Classical style of continental Europe and the English landscape garden tradition are examples. All three traditions have, however, been used outside the context in which they were developed because they are perceived to be fashionable and prestigious.

The Japanese garden is widely recognized by most people to be, if not Japanese, to be East Asian. In Japan, it may be used to instill a sense of locality and pride in their own heritage by landscape architects. Elsewhere it may be used as an exotic mark of status. The Classical design paradigm has been applied so often that, although it may be associated with the high status Beaux Arts tradition of France and what was perceived to have its ancestry in Rome and Greece, it is not closely associated with a specific culture today but with a variety of political stances. The Classical has been used to signify democracy but also by authoritarians to demonstrate their high cultural status.

The garden square as a design paradigm, while not uniquely English, is particularly associated with London. The picturesque English landscape garden approach to squares is associated with England in the minds of the experts. The tradition presents a pattern of landscaping that can be used to reinforce the self-image of people. The garden squares of London, like St James's Square, are very different to the garden squares of Paris, such as the Place des Vosges (Figure 10.1).

Many squares could be anywhere in the world. They have no sense of locale because their layouts are global in character and the qualities of the buildings around them are international. Such designs are widely seen as prestigious. To indigenize them, local artifacts and details are added to give the squares a sense of that particular place or country in which they are located. In Bangkok's Metropolitan Authority Square, a large anonymous space, the fountain with its sculpture adds a local decorative element (Figure 10.2).

Figure 10.1 *Garden squares: London and Paris: (a) St James's Square, London; (b) Place des Vosges, Paris*

Figure 10.2 *Bangkok Metropolitan Authority Square: (a) The square as a space for large events (b) The fountain*

The contents of a square, the objects it contains, probably have stronger associations in the general public's minds with who they are than any overall design qualities that the square possesses. The meanings of objects such as memorials are more directly understandable by the public, particularly if the symbols are literal rather than abstract.

Squares as Symbols of Self

The style of squares and what they contain communicate meanings about who we are. Memorials to famous people and/or to famous victories in battles remind people of their heritage and who they are (or, rather, who they believe themselves to be). Dolores Hayden (1989) believes the reminder raises their self-esteem. This observation does not mean that such memorials are non-controversial as the qualities of almost any person or any event is open to individual interpretation. Many squares have, nevertheless, been designed to instill a sense of identity and pride in the local people.

National Identity

Memorials and the decorative elements and detailing of a square can clearly be a statement of who we are and raise our pride in ourselves. Independence Squares around the world attest to this observation. That in Colombo, Sri Lanka, clearly belongs to that place. The statue

Figure 10.3 Squares reinforcing national identities: (a) St Andrew's Square, Edinburgh; (b) Independence Square, Colombo; (c) World Trade Center Memorial, New York

Source: (a) Photograph by Gail Johnson/ Shutterstock.com.

of the country's first prime minister after independence is a reminder of the country's history and pride in establishing its place among the nations of the world. The Singhalese lions and the pavilion that dominates the square are clearly of the nation. The patterns of the square make literal references to traditional Sri Lankan forms (Figure 10.3 (b)).

Trafalgar Square is generally regarded as a great square. To many Britons, it is a reminder of a famous British naval victory and it gives them a sense of nationhood and pride. People unaware of the Battle of Trafalgar may not consider the square's intended symbolic meaning at all. They see it in terms of their own experiences. Place Charles de Gaulle with the Arc de Triomphe, which was built to commemorate those who died for France in the Revolution and the Napoleonic Wars, serves much the same purpose but for France. St Andrew's Square in Edinburgh is named in honor of Scotland's patron saint. The Melville Monument in it celebrates the life of Hendry Dundas, a major figure in Scottish history (Figure 10.3 (a)).

The World Trade Center Memorial Plaza in New York was created to remember the almost 3,000 people who died in the attacks on September 11, 2001, at the site, at the Pentagon in Washington and near Shanksville, Pennsylvania, as well as the six people killed in the bombing of the Center in 1993. It is as much as anything, a memorial giving identity to the United States (Figure 10.3 (c)). The plaza gives a sense of a common cause and unity to a highly diverse nation.

The associations that memorials evoke and the consequent feelings that they arouse can change over time. These changes often depend on the political values held in a society at a particular time. Toopkhaneh Square (see Figure 0.7 in the Prologue on p. 13) is one example but others abound. Walery Godowski's 1887 monument to Mikolaja Zyblikiewicz (Mayor of Krakow in Poland from 1874 to 1880) was removed by the Communists from All Saints' Square in 1954. In 1985, with the demise of Communism, it was reconstructed.

Group Identity

In many pluralistic societies, each group may want to be recognized as being important in that society. As the ethnicity of populations around squares changes, the new local population often seeks to have their heroes replace those of the previous residents. Mount Morris Square in Harlem, a predominantly African-American part of New York, is now named Marcus Garvey Park in honor of the staunch proponent of Black Nationalism. Nelson Mandela Square, formerly Sandton Square, is, as already mentioned, a European-style square in Sandton, the major business hub of South Africa located near Johannesburg. In Johannesburg proper, the former Van der Byl Square (earlier Government Square) is now, after the end of apartheid in South Africa, Mahatma Gandhi Square. It is a reminder of his long residence in the city and recognition of the importance of the Indian South African community to the country. Naming or altering the name of a square is a regular occurrence. The examples here indicate how changes often seek to remove a country's colonial past. Dalhousie Square in Kolkata (formerly Calcutta) is now BBD

(Benoy-Badal-Dinesh) Bagh. Independence Square in Colombo was once Torrington Square.

Beyond renaming of locations is the designing of places to symbolize something or somebody of importance to a specific group. The Plaza d'Italia was designed purposefully to demonstrate a pride in the achievements of the Italian Americans of New Orleans to the broader community (Figure 10.4 (c)). In the eyes of the cognoscenti, at least, it is more closely associated with its architect, Charles Moore, than what it was intended to communicate to the public.

In recent years, a number of squares honoring African Americans have been built as part of the community's continuing struggle for self-esteem and recognition. The Dr Martin Luther King Jr Memorial in Washington, DC, is an example (Figure 10.4 (a)). While representing

Figure 10.4 Squares reinforcing group identity: (a) Dr Martin Luther King Jr Memorial, Washington, DC; (b) Biddy Mason Park, Los Angeles; (c) Piazza d'Italia, New Orleans

Source: (c) Photograph by Daniel Lobo/ Flickr; (b) Photograph by Laurie Avocado/ Flickr.

TYPES BASED ON SYMBOLIC FUNCTIONS

the life of a leader of importance to all the people of the United States, it is especially important to African Americans. The Biddy Mason Park commemorates the life of an African-American woman who was born into slavery in 1818 and freed in 1856 (Sims 1993). She subsequently became a midwife, an entrepreneur, a philanthropist and a leading figure in the African Methodist church in Los Angeles. She represents the importance of the African-American people of Los Angeles. The park consists primarily of a wall with aspects of her life portrayed on it and is a reminder to African Americans and the general public that the inhabitants of the city have overlapping histories (Figure 10.4 (b)). Harriet Tubman Square in New York's Harlem serves essentially the same purpose.[4] Savannah, Georgia, has a square named after General Casimir Pulaski, a Polish-born hero of the Revolutionary War.

A duality of meanings is communicated in all these examples. While they celebrate specific groups of people, they recognize, implicitly at least, that each group is embedded in the larger society of which it is a component.

Multicultural Identity

Designing a square to represent a number of groups simultaneously is not easy. The obvious way is to create something neutral, usually something Modernistic, but in some multicultural societies the attempt has been made to combine elements that symbolize various communities that the square is honoring. The goal of the 1994 renovation of Pershing Square in Los Angeles was to create a design that represents both the Latino and Anglo populations of the city. The design by Ricardo Legorreta and Laurie Olin strove to create a *zócalo*, the square at the heart of many Mexican cities. In the center of the square is an orange grove that recalls the importance of orange farming in the history of Los Angeles County. The geological fault line that runs through Los Angeles is represented by a jagged line cutting across the square. The square also has a ten-story purple bell tower, a 'Mayan style' amphitheater, benches on which images of Los Angeles are imprinted, works of art and mementos of the past. The public has little difficulty in interpreting the symbolism of these various components of the park. If they need help, signs explain the meanings to them.

The Design of Squares Representing Taste Cultures

In a study of houses conducted during the 1980s, Jack Nasar (1988) showed that both architects and the general public infer social meanings from a building's character. Based on house style, people assigned personalities to a house's owners. Nasar's study also showed that there is a major gap between architect's tastes and the tastes of various sectors of the general public.[5] Herbert Gans, a sociologist, boldly divided the general population of the United States into a number of groups based on shared values (1975).[6] People belong to different taste cultures. Despite the limitations of Gans' generalizations, there is considerable merit to his key notions. Gans (cited in Lang and Moleski 2010: 215) identified:

a high taste culture whose concerns are intellectual, academic and avant-garde, an upper middle class taste culture whose concerns are self-conscious about current fashion, a lower-middle taste culture whose concerns are eclectic, democratic and popular and tend towards the traditional, a lower taste culture whose concerns are largely unself-conscious and anonymous and a quasi-folk taste culture whose concerns are communal and ad hoc.

The squares that are regarded as important, tasteful and of artistic value are similarly biased by the tastes of any evaluator.[7] Whatever their status, people relate positively to those squares that meet their tastes and disparage those that do not. While the members of the high taste culture, including many architects and architectural critics, may hold squares with heroic intellectual esthetic underpinnings in high esteem, those with popular tastes will prefer more traditional squares while those whose tastes are unself-conscious may prefer those where they can enjoy spending time being with friends and acquaintances in comfortable surroundings. Implicitly the qualities of a square are inevitably associated with status. Status, in turn, is related to the education, financial success, culture, age and interests of individuals and groups of people.

Some squares acquire a high status because they display the ideas of an architect or landscape architect who is held in high esteem by his or her professional peers. Although the topic is the focus of attention in Chapter 11, it is mentioned here to place it in an intellectual context. Piazza d'Italia in New Orleans is regarded as an exemplar of postmodern public space design. Both the architect and the work are of more interest to architects than the general public. Freedom Plaza in Washington, DC, has a similar status. It is of great interest to architects as a representative example of the work of its designers, Venturi, Rauch and Scott Brown with George Patton, architects.

Freedom Plaza is a good place to hold protest rallies but it plays little role in the everyday life of people in the surrounding area, even though it is bounded by important buildings (Carr *et al.* 1992). The National Theater and the John A. Wilson Building, which is the seat of the District of Columbia's government, face the square, and the Willard Hotel where Martin Luther King wrote his "I have a dream" speech is nearby. The design does not reflect much of King's life or beliefs. As such, it has little in the way of an association, apart from its name, with the African-American or the American experience. The square's role in commemorating the civil rights leader has been eclipsed in Washington by the Dr Martin Luther King Jr National Memorial that was dedicated in 2011. Although the statue of King at the National Memorial site is regarded by many design experts as inappropriate in style, the general public seems to like its grand scale.

High quality design work is much appreciated by the cognoscenti. This embrace is seen in the attitudes of design professionals to Federation Square in Melbourne, designed by Lab Architectural Studio and Bates Smart, architects. The square has been in place since 2002. It is certainly a singular heroic design whose esthetic qualities relate to contemporary deconstructivist architectural ideology.

The architecture fits the taste culture of avant-garde architectural crit-ics perhaps more than the public who just enjoy the square for what it has to offer. Over time people become habituated to and accepting of architecture that they might not have liked in the first instance.

Social Status and the Design of Squares

The design of a square can denote the social position of the peo-ple who live in or use the surrounding area and vice versa. Those squares, such as London's garden squares, Gramercy Park in New York and Louisburg Square in Boston, that are in the ownership of the people whose houses face them and who have sole access to them, are associated with high socioeconomic status. They make the surrounding neighborhood one in which people may aspire to live. The arrangement is thus reciprocal: the type of square is prestigious which makes the neighborhood prestigious which makes the square prestigious. Property values often reflect the relationship.[8] Many studies have shown that well-maintained, attractive squares sig-nificantly enhance property values in the areas that surround them. Squares can thus be seen as status symbols in much the same way as other possessions. Two of the aspects of high status squares are ownership and size.

While the size of a square may be impressive and may raise the self-esteem of the people of a nation, it may not be admired by others. Mao Zedong sought to have the largest square in the world to elevate the perception of China in his own eyes, the eyes of the Chinese peo-ple and of visitors from abroad. Naghishi-i Jahan Square in Isfahan, Iran is another large square.[9] It has undergone several changes over the years to accommodate new instrumental functions. Its interna-tional importance is now recognized by it being designated a World Heritage Site by UNESCO. The designation gives both the city and Iran world-wide recognition of the importance of their heritage.

While large squares may be seen as prestigious, many other fac-tors play a role. It is not only the size that gives these two squares prestige but what borders them. In the case of Naghish-i Jahan Square, the buildings that surround it, its overall internal geometry and detailing contribute to its status. It is not a blank open space. Many Chinese appear to take pride in Tiananmen Square's existence but it is hardly a luxurious place, despite its surrounding buildings being of significance.

The quality of its detailing gives a square much of its perceived status. High status squares have fine furnishings constructed of high quality materials. What are regarded as high quality materials differ, however, from society to society. In reality, there are no high status materials *per se*; their perceived quality depends on their expense, on how well they fit their instrumental purpose and how they are used (Jacobs 1993). The table tops in Paley Park, New York are not made of cheap materials but of marble. People notice the details.

In many societies trees and lawns are regarded as high status items. The presence of ponds with carp and working fountains are the types of additional items that, as long as they are working, add to the perceptions of the quality of a place. The degree of maintenance required for a square is one indicator of the influence people have who reside or work nearby. Squares in 'posh' areas are usually well kept. Poorly maintained squares may, nevertheless, be highly frequented because of their location in a city. Such squares enhance the general welfare of their visitors by providing them a place for public life (Marshall 2016). Regular users of a square seem to accommodate poor maintenance but these squares fail to raise the esteem of those people who frequent them.

Conclusion

The desire to make the urban public realm a symbol of progress and social importance is a motivating force behind many urban design decisions. One well-proportioned and detailed square does not, however, make a city prestigious. What is important at an urban scale is that squares are designed as part of an overall unified and integrated public environment. No single attribute of a square in communicating messages about the status of people to themselves or others is all that important. In combination, they are. Many factors, including the design of a square, its location and maintenance, contribute to a person's sense of belonging and community esteem. Their participation in the design process and seeing their views adopted in the eventual design of the square is one such factor. Being involved in a square's development can contribute to a sense of ownership of it.[10] This latter observation is particularly important at the local neighborhood level. Without local participation a new square may not be well received in a community even if it is replete with symbols of importance to it.

A participatory process needs to be employed in the design or redesign of a square. City planners and designers can help the stakeholders involved in the design to be aware of the design options and consequences of choosing some features over others. To achieve this end, the professionals need to be knowledgeable about how squares function both as behavior settings and displays. They also need to understand community engagement strategies and techniques that are required to enhance a community's understanding of how squares function (Marshall *et al.* 2012). This view stands in contrast to squares designed as pure works of art – as intellectual esthetic displays where the public is rarely brought into the design process.

Notes

1 These concerns have been discussed at greater length in Lang (1994) and Lang and Moleski (2010).
2 The role of Balance Theory in attitude development was briefly described in Chapter 1.
3 See also Lefaivre (2003).
4 Harriet Tubman (*ca* 1822–1913) was a leading African-American abolitionist and civil rights activist.
5 See also Michelson (1968) and Meade (2012).
6 See also Mann (1979).
7 See Duncan (1973) on landscape tastes and group identity.
8 No. 3 Louisburg Square sold for US$11 million in early 2012 (Acitelli 2012). See also Woolley and Rose (2004).

9   *Landscape Architects Network*'s list of "Top 10 public squares" in the world regards this square as the world's greatest. See Jackett (2014).

10 A designer can play a number of different roles in the design of a square from an independent expert to a facilitator of community engagement in the design process.

References

Acitelli, Tom (2012) $11M for 3 Louisburg Square: Boston's 2nd biggest deal of 2012. Available at: http://boston.curbed.com/archives/2012/04/another-big-one-3-louisburg-square-trades-for-11m.php.

Appleyard, Donald (1979) The environment as a social symbol within a theory of environmental action and perception. *Journal of the American Planning Association* 45: 143–153.

Carr, Stephen, Mark Francis, Leanne Rivlin and Andrew M. Stone (1992) *Public Space*. Cambridge: Cambridge University Press.

Duncan, James S. Jr (1973) Landscape taste as a symbol of group identity: A Westchester village. *Geographic Review* 63(3): 334–355.

Frampton, Kenneth (1982) Towards a critical regionalism: Six points for an architecture of resistance. In *The Anti-Aesthetic: Essays on Postmodern Culture*, edited by Hal Foster. Port Townsend: Bay Press, pp. 16–30.

Gans, Herbert J. (1975) *Popular Culture and High Culture: An Analysis and Evaluation of Taste*. New York: Basic Books.

Groat, Linda and David Canter (1979) A study in meaning: Does Post-Modernism communicate? *Progressive Architecture* 60(12): 84–87.

Hayden, Dolores (1989) *The Power of Place*. Los Angeles: The Power of Place, Inc.

Jackett, Sonia (2014) Top 10 Public Squares. *Landscape Architects Network* May 9. Available at: http://landarchs.com/top-10-public-squares-world/

Jacobs, Allan B. (1993) *Great Streets*. Cambridge, MA: MIT Press.

Lang, Jon (1994) *Urban Design: The American Experience*. New York: Van Nostrand Reinhold.

Lang, Jon and Walter Moleski (2010) *Functionalism Revisited: Architectural Theory and the Behavioral Sciences*. Farnham: Ashgate.

Langer, Susanne (1953) *Feeling and Form: A Theory of Art Developed from 'Philosophy in a New Key'* (republished 1979). New York: Routledge & Kegan Paul.

Lefaivre, Liane (2003) Critical regionalism: A facet of modern architecture since 1945. In *Critical Regionalism: Architecture and Identity in a Globalized World*, edited by Liane Lefaivre and Alexander Tzonis. London: Prestel, pp. 22–55.

Mann, Dennis A. (1979) Architecture, aesthetics, and pluralism: Theories of taste as a determinant of architectural standards. *Studies in Art Education* 20(3): 15–29.

Marshall, Nancy (2016) Urban squares: A place for public life. In *Place and Placelessness Revisited*, edited by Robert Freestone and Edgar Liu. New York: Routledge, pp. 186–203.

Marshall, Nancy, Christine Steinmetz and Robert Zehner (2012) Community participation in planning. In *Planning Australia*, 2nd edn, edited by Susan Thompson and Paul Maginn. Sydney: Cambridge University Press, pp. 276–293.

Meade, Jonathan (2012) Architects are the last people who should shape our cities. *The Guardian*, September 19. Available at: www.theguardian.com/artanddesign/2012/sep/18/architects-cities-jonathan-meades?newsfeed=true.

Michelson, William (1968) Most people don't want what architects want. *Transactions* 5(8): 37–43.

Nasar, Jack (1988) Architectural symbolism: A study of house style meanings. In *People's Needs/Planet Management – Paths to Co-Existence: Proceedings of EDRA 19*, edited by Denise Lawrence and B. Wasserman. Riverside: EDRA, pp. 163–169.

Relph, Edward (1976) *Place and Placelessness*. London: Pion.

Sims, Oscar L. (1993) Profile of Biddy Mason. In *Epic Lives: One Hundred Black*

Women Who Made a Difference, edited by Jessie Carney Smith. Canton: Visible Ink Press.

Woolley, Helen and Stan Rose (2004) *The Value of Public Space: How High Quality Parks and Public Spaces Create Economic, Social and Environmental Value*. London: CABE Space.

Further Reading

Becker, Franklin (1972) A class-conscious evaluation: Going back to Sacramento pedestrian mall. *Landscape Architecture* 64: 295–345.

Dovey, Kim (1999) *Framing Places: Mediating Power in Built Form*. London: Routledge.

Duncan, James S. Jr and Nancy Duncan (2001) The aestheticization of the politics of landscape preservation. *Annals of the Association of American Geographers* 91(2): 387–409.

Fleming, Ronald L. and Renata von Tscharner (1987) *Place Makers: Creating Public Art that Tells You Where You Are, with Essays on Planning and Policy*. Boston: Harcourt, Brace, Jovanovich.

Groat, Linda (ed.) (1995) *Giving Places Meaning: Readings in Environmental Psychology*. London: Routledge.

Lawson, Laura (2007) Parks as mirrors of community: Design discourse and community hopes in East St. Louis. *Landscape Journal* 26(1): 116–133.

Norberg-Schulz, Christian (1980) *Genius Loci: Towards a Phenomenology of Architecture*. New York: Rizzoli.

Rapoport, Amos (1982) *The Meaning of the Built Environment: A Non-Verbal Communications Approach*. Beverly Hills, CA: Sage.

CHAPTER 11

TYPES BASED ON DESIGN PARADIGMS

Squares, we have asserted, are frequently considered to be works of art; they carry the meanings that an artist-designer wants to communicate to the world. The squares so designed self-consciously represent his or her work and values. They possess an intellectual esthetic quality.[1] To most people, the design of a square as an expression of an artist's intent does not matter much, but to the cognescenti the designer's story often transcends the importance of any other function that a square serves. They are interested in the design paradigm used and how the personal values of the designer are manifested in physical form.

Paradigms, Design Paradigms and Designers

A design paradigm refers to ways of thinking, or mindsets, of a group of designers at any particular time. A paradigm in the design fields thus consists of the patterns of built form that are held up as exemplars of good professional practice. The history of the design fields consists of the simultaneous or sequential development of design paradigms and the work of individuals working within them.

Competing paradigms often, if not always, co-exist in the design fields.[2] At present, the architecture and urban design of global, commercial libertarian Modernism competes with the Neotraditional movements, such as 'new urbanism' and 'smart growth.' Understanding the design paradigms, why they exist, and seeing one applied enhances the experience of those who understand a particular paradigm and what it affords. Their responses to a square are likely to be positive if they appreciate the paradigm and see it well applied, and negative if they see it poorly applied. They will also have a negative response if they disparage the paradigm ideologically, as explained by Balance Theory in Chapter 1.

Design paradigms change, often abruptly, in response to changing sociopolitical circumstances and architects' desires to create novel designs for the sake of being unconventional and attracting attention. Sometimes these changes are subtle, such as the replacement of the Classical with the Baroque and sometimes substantial as in the displacement of the Neoclassical by Modernist ideas. These changes

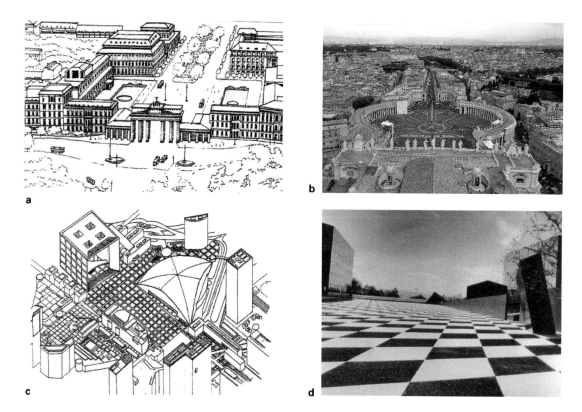

may be associated with a breakthrough attributed to an individual architect, but even then there are usually other designers working along similar lines.

The traditional medieval Italian piazza can be regarded as a product of unself-conscious design even though the buildings around it were self-consciously designed. The squares in Figure 11.1 are clearly self-conscious designs. The Classical, derived from Greek and Roman antecedents, gave way to the Baroque during the sixteenth century although practitioners of the Classical, or more correctly the Neoclassical, persist to this day. The Baroque was a more theatrical version of the Classical. The switch to Modernism was abrupt. Postmodernist design concepts emerged later as a response to the perceptions of the increasing fragmentation of the world and its intellectual underpinnings and to the 'boringness' of much Modernist design.[3] Neotraditional squares are increasingly being developed; they follow the design principles implicit in the layout of traditional squares but have contemporary buildings enclosing them.

The Focus on the Individual Designer

Although the work of particular designers is unique, most of them work within a contemporary paradigm; specific designs are variations on a generic stylistic theme. Jean Philippe Cret's design for

Figure 11.1 Four design paradigms: (a) The Classical: Pariser Platz, Berlin before World War II; (b) The Baroque: Plaza San Pietro, Rome; (c) The Modernist: La Défense, Hauts-de-Seine, Paris (1970s); (d) The Postmodern: Harlequin Plaza, Denver (1990)

Sources: (a) Drawing by Thanong Poonterakul; (b) Photograph by Jarrett Dragani; (c) Drawing by Chao Wang; (d) Collection of Jon Lang.

Rittenhouse Square in Philadelphia was carried out firmly within the classical Beaux Arts tradition but had simpler forms than the work of his contemporaries. It was shaped by his desire to adapt Classical forms to the emerging Modernist innovations appearing at the beginning of the twentieth century. His work thus has a more streamlined look and today appears to be considerably progressive for its time. The square also shows his interest in working closely with sculptors. The result is that Rittenhouse Square has strategically placed sculptures by such luminaries as Antoine Louis Barye and Paul Manship.

The other designers included in this selection are more recent. Dublin's Grand Canal Square (10,000 square meters; 2.47 acres) was designed by Martha Schwartz who is known for her individualistic design expressions. It contains bright red resin-glass paving and glowing sticks and bright green planters that illustrate her bold use of colors in landscape design (Figure 11.2 (a)). Much the same observation can be made about the now removed bright green benches that she designed for the Jacob K. Javits Center Plaza in New York. She had two objectives in the design of the plaza: to create a lively place and to create a work of art. Her goal was partially fulfilled. The plaza was primarily a work of pop-art; only a few workers from the adjacent federal buildings and a handful of other people sat in the square. Despite all the pedestrian traffic through it, the square did not appear to have been a lively place.[4]

The Piazza d'Italia in New Orleans illustrates Charles Moore's often exuberant Postmodernism.[5] The design's elements have strong associations with Italy. Although they are presented in abstract form, the patterns of columns and arches employed in the design are easily recognized as Italianate. Architectural experts are likely to understand the abstractions and the motives of the designer. The Garden of Australian Dreams at the National Museum of Australia is also a Postmodern work, but is, perhaps, best regarded as an extensive deconstructivist sculpture (Firth 2001). The garden is a highly sophisticated map of central Australia with lines crossing it (Figure 11.2 (b)). These lines represent surveyors' reference marks, road maps, dingo fences, and Indigenous Australian national and linguistic boundaries. It is a highly intellectual installation.

Figure 11.2 The intellectual esthetic quality of squares – expressive displays representing the ideas of their designers: (a) Grand Canal Square, Dublin 2008, Martha Schwartz, landscape architect; (b) Garden of Australian Dreams, National Museum of Australia, Canberra, 2000, Howard Ragatt of Ashton Ragatt McDougall, architect, Richard Weller, landscape architect

Source: (a) Photograph by kDamo/Flickr; (b) Photograph by John Benwell/Flickr.

The firm of William Whitfield, architect, is very competent and the task of relating Paternoster Square in London to the adjacent St Paul's Cathedral was not easy. Glancey (2003) suggests that as a work of pure fine art, it fails to raise the enthusiasm of architectural critics; it is not the avant-garde work that is often admired. The Neotraditionalists among the critics are more sympathetic because the square functions well as a place for people and programmed events.

Most architects and landscape architects work within a currently prevailing design paradigm, even though the patterns and materials they employ may be unique and clearly identified with them. They have their own style; they repetitively use specific design patterns and their work is recognized by these patterns. Also clearly identified with individual designers are works which are deviant from contemporary work. Parc Güell in Barcelona (1900–1914) is an example of the work of an architect (Antoni Gaudí) while Nuestro Pueblo (Watts Towers, 1921–1954) and the Rock Garden of Chandigarh (1957–1996) are by lay-people (Figure 11.3).

Although the two places illustrated in Figure 11.3 are public spaces, neither of them is a true square in the way we have used the term here but they illustrate the points being made. The first was the piece-by-piece work carried out by a layman, Sabato (Simon) Rodia over many years. Although it contains built-in seating, it is really a true display to look at. Nek Chand's work in Chandigarh, like Rodia's, was literally built out of junk accumulated over a lifetime. The Rock Gardens is a winding sequence of large and small squares/courtyards containing scenes that hold the visitor's attention. It was threatened with demolition as a junk heap until the Chandigarh authorities realized that it attracted many, many more visitors than Le Corbusier's work in the city (Lang and Moleski 2010). It is both a place to enjoy as well as a work of art to contemplate.

Figure 11.3 Idiosyncratic displays: (a) Nuestro Pueblo, Watts, Los Angeles (b) The Rock Garden, Chandigarh

Sources: (a) Photograph by Lucien den Arnen; (b) Photograph by Worldgraphics/ Shutterstock.com.

Intellectual Esthetics and the Experiencing of Squares

Many Philadelphians recognize the Beaux Arts nature of Rittenhouse Square, but few will know that it is the work of an architect held in high regard by his contemporaries. The square is a much-loved place for the general public because of what it affords: a place to sit, to meet, to watch others, as a short cut and as a sensory experience that differs from that of the surrounding streets. Its fountains and sculptures offer play areas for children.

The general public may well recognize the Italianate qualities of the Piazza d'Italia in New Orleans. Italian-Americans certainly do but this observation does not mean that they necessarily like it. In Australia, both the public and the design experts would, however, have to be told about the architect's story in the design of the Garden of Australian Dreams at the National Museum in Canberra. To many, it is simply a strange geometry of patterns and shapes.

Designs which have striven to be works of art can often incur opportunity costs because of that focus. Freedom Plaza, in Washington, DC, as already noted, could have been more than just an object to contemplate. It is a flat square slightly raised above Pennsylvania Avenue. Its floor is a carefully designed and crafted map of Washington in black and white stone (Figure 11.4). A lawn represents the mall. The experts can appreciate the intellectual foundation of the design which is something to look at but there is little reason to return. The square possesses few amenities for the viewer and potential users other than to contemplate the space as an abstract work of art. Other squares such as Boston City Hall plaza are lesser examples of the same phenomena. They represent the works of major architects and can be analyzed as works of art.

Pershing Park in Washington near Freedom Plaza was designed by M. Paul Friedberg and others (Figure 11.5). It works well as a display

Figure 11.4 Square floor pattern: Detail of the floor pattern of Freedom Plaza, Washington, DC

Figure 11.5 Pershing Square (now Park), Washington, DC

of its designers' ideas (as landscape architects and artists) with a statue of General John Joseph (Black Jack) Pershing, Commander-in-Chief of the American Expeditionary Forces in World War I. It is a pleasant place to be when the fountain is functioning but when the fountain is not working, the square can be dirty and somewhat forlorn. Even then, visitors still sit and relax as it is along a major tourist route. The regular users, many of whom are homeless, sit at the edges. The plaza is now undergoing a redesign.

A final example illustrates the intellectual esthetic quality that squares can possess. The Franklin D. Roosevelt Four Freedoms Park is a memorial to the 32nd President of the United States. It was designed by architect, Louis I. Kahn. To the design experts, it is a place to admire as part of Kahn's body of work. The memorial thus serves a dual function. It is a place to remember Roosevelt and it is an object to contemplate as a work of art by Louis Kahn and as a memorial to him (see Figure 14.3 (b) on p. 272).

Conclusion

All squares can be considered to be works of art and many really are when the pattern of a square is considered to be a medium for conveying the designer's message to the critical observer. While all squares are ultimately expressions of the culture of a city or an expression of current values – a contemporary paradigm – a work of art sets out to be a self-conscious communication of its creator's ideas. It is an artificial display. It may enrich our experiences if we understand the thinking behind the designs and designer/s. Some squares function well as both works of art and as places – the two are not incompatible.

The critical observers are more able to understand a designer's intentions and the relationship between intentions and the resulting work within its contemporary times than lay-people. The public's responses to the design of a square will be immediate and largely unself-conscious; they will likely consider what a square offers them as a place more than they consider the square as an object with specific design intentions.

The frequent clash between a designer's ideas and public perceptions of the resulting quality of a square may well persist into the future as theory in the design fields becomes increasingly intellectualized. We are likely to see more squares that represent their designer's stories. If a paradigm shift in the design of squares occurs towards a larger consideration of the public's views and their involvement in the design process, this prediction will be incorrect.

Notes

1 The concept of intellectual esthetics goes back, at least, to George Santayana's *The Sense of Beauty* ([1896] 1955).
2 See the collections of such statements assembled by Broadbent (1990) on urban design and Conrads (1970) and Hayes (1998) on architecture, for examples of twentieth-century paradigms.
3 See Habermas (1981) and McHale (2007) on postmodernism and Broadbent (1990) on postmodernism in urban space design.
4 For a fuller analysis of the square as designed by Schwartz, see Hill (2007).
5 Allen Freeman (2004) provides a history of the design, demise and restoration of the square.

References

Broadbent, Geoffrey (1990) *Emerging Concepts in Urban Space Design*. New York: Van Nostrand Reinhold International.

Conrads, Ulrich (ed.) (1970) *Programs and Manifestoes on 20th-Century Architecture*, trans. from the German by Michael Bullock. Cambridge, MA: MIT Press.

Firth, Dianne (2001) Extract from Rom 4.1.3's design for the Australian Museum. *Landscape Australia* 3: 45–46.

Freeman, Allen (2004) That 1970's show: In New Orleans, the third act begins on a famous outdoor stage. *Landscape Architecture* May. Available at: www.asla.org/lamag/lam04/may/feature3.html.

Glancey, Jonathan (2003) It's a jumble out there. *The Guardian Weekly*, November 3. Available at: www.theguardian.com/artanddesign/2003/nov/03/architecture.regeneration.

Habermas, Jürgen (1981) Modernity versus Postmodernity. *New German Critique* 22(Winter): 3–14.

Hayes, Michael K. (1998) *Architectural Theory since 1968*. Cambridge, MA: MIT Press.

Hill, John (2007) Jacob Javits Plaza: Reconsidering intentions. Prepared for *Anthropology of Place and Space: Locating Culture*, edited by Setha Lowe and Denise Lawrence-Zúñiga. Malden, MA: Blackwell.

Lang, Jon and Walter Moleski (2010) *Functionalism Revisited: Architectural Theory and Practice and the Behavioral Sciences*. Farnham: Ashgate.

McHale, Brian (2007) What was Postmodernism? *Electronic Book Review*, December 20. Available at: www.electronicbookreview.com/thread/fictionspresent/tense.

Santayana, George (1896) *The Sense of Beauty*, reprinted, Dover, 1955. New York: Charles Scribner's Sons.

Further Reading

Broto, Carles (2000) *New Urban Design*. Barcelona: Arian Mostaedi.

Carr, Stephen, Mark Francis, Leanne Rivlin and Andrew M. Stone (1992) *Public Space*. Cambridge: Cambridge University Press.

Weiss, Morris (1956) The role of theory in aesthetics. *Journal of Aesthetics and Art Criticism* 15(1): 27–35.

PART III

LEARNING FROM CASE STUDIES

Westlake Park, Seattle
Photograph by Kate Bishop.

A case study is a detailed examination of an example of a phenomenon.[1] Throughout this book we have drawn on case studies conducted by others, supplemented by our own observations. Stephen Carr and his colleagues (1992) included over 30 case studies of public open spaces in their work. Clare Cooper Marcus and Carolyn Francis (1990) included studies of many squares in their book and Matthew Carmona (2010, 2014a, 2014b) presented a large number from the London metropolitan area. Robert Gatje (2010) described in detail many European and North American squares that he likes. The set of case studies included in Chapter 12 consists almost entirely of generally well-known squares. Each case was chosen on the basis of the information it was likely to yield and its contribution to the series of examples. Each one is importantly different from the others and/or based on different design paradigms.

The 20 squares cover a range of types. Most are relatively recent, self-conscious designs that have been completed or refurbished within the last 30 years. By self-conscious, we mean that they were designed with an intentional goal in mind. Most of the examples (16 out of 20) are European or North American. Two are located in Asia and two in Australia. No case study examples are from Africa or Latin America although examples from both continents have been mentioned throughout the book. In Chapter 12, we have focused on squares that have been the subject of research or studies that are generally accessible or for which we have reliable data.

The exceptions to the recent construction criterion are Rittenhouse Square, Philadelphia, which dates back to the early twentieth century, and Paley Park in New York, the Capitol Square in Chandigarh and Sproul Plaza in Berkeley, all three of which were built in the 1960s. The last case study, Piazza San Marco, was founded in the year 800. The first two are particularly important because other squares have been modeled on them without the same success. The way they function was not fully appreciated and only some of their characteristics were mimicked. Additionally, the contribution of their contexts to the way the square functioned was not fully understood. The third in the list above Capitol Square in Chandigarh, is internationally renowned, while the fourth, Sproul Plaza, has been so very successful as a setting for student protest gatherings that it became, for a while at least, a type that many Californian politicians wanted to avoid being included in any new state university. Sproul Plaza is now being refurbished to meet new demands but it will retain its essential character.

The first 16 squares that we include in Chapter 12 have been in place long enough for 'the honeymoon phase' to have worn off. The penultimate part of the chapter consists of three squares to watch as they mature. The first, Jacob K. Javits Federal Building Plaza in New York, was completed in 2013; the second, Granary Square in London, is only partially completed and its surroundings have yet to be developed while the reconstruction of parts of Times Square in New York, at the time of writing, had not yet started. Much can be learnt in the future about how these squares function once they have existed for a while in their completed state. We conclude Chapter 12 by having a look at Piazza San Marco (St Mark's Square) in Venice, which, for many observers is *the* major square of historical note. It is difficult to think of a discourse on urban squares that would be complete without a review of its present role in Venice as a lived-in museum.

A shortcoming in our selection is that the design of all the squares is based primarily on the behavior, values and esthetic preferences of the middle classes.[2] They are the ones on whom data are available. In some cases the squares have resulted from a partnership between governmental authorities and private industry through a public-private partnership. Paley Park in New York is an exception; it was a philanthropic gesture.

Notes

1 For a thorough examination of the utility of case studies, see Flyvbjerg (2006) and for case studies in the design fields, see Francis (2001).
2 See Boyer (1992) and Duncan and Duncan (2001) on esthetic preferences in the design of public and quasi-public spaces.

References

Boyer, M. Christine (1992) Cities for sale: Merchandising history at South Street Seaport. In *Variations on a Theme Park: The New American City and the End of Public Space*, edited by Michael Sorkin. New York: McGraw-Hill, pp. 181–204.

Carmona, Matthew (2010) Contemporary public space: Critique and classification, part one: Critique. *Journal of Urban Design* 15(1): 123–148.

Carmona, Matthew (2014a) The place-shaping continuum: A theory of urban design process. *Journal of Urban Design* 19(1): 2–36.

Carmona, Matthew (ed.) (2014b) *Explorations in Urban Design: An Urban Design Primer*. Farnham: Ashgate.

Carr, Stephen, Mark Francis, Leanne Rivlin and Andrew M. Stone (1992) *Public Space*. Cambridge: Cambridge University Press.

Cooper Marcus, Clare and Carolyn Francis (1990) *People Places: Design Guidelines for Urban Open Space*. New York: Van Nostrand Reinhold.

Duncan, James S. Jr and Nancy Duncan (2001) The aestheticization of the politics of landscape preservation. *Annals of the Association of American Geographers* 91(2): 387–409.

Flyvbjerg, Bent (2006) Five misunderstandings about case-study research. *Qualitative Enquiry* 12(2): 219–244.

Francis, Mark (2001) A case study method for landscape architecture. *Landscape Journal* 20(1): 15–29.

Gatje, Robert F. (2010) *Great Public Squares: An Architect's Selection*. New York: Norton.

CHAPTER 12

A SCORE OF CASE STUDIES

In this chapter we identify a number of squares that work on many dimensions, those that have mixed results and others that function well on only a handful. This discrimination does not mean that those that work on many dimensions are necessarily better. Our goal is to point out the differences between types of squares. Trade-offs between achieving one goal or another would have been made in the making of all squares. Not one of the squares that we review is actually a failure on all dimensions of functionality, nor is any a complete success on every criterion. Whether a square is seen as a good or poor place depends on the criteria applied in the evaluation. There are many 'favorite squares' or 'top 10' lists compiled by both scholars and practitioners (e.g. Gatje 2010; Jackett 2014; Project for Public Spaces n.d.).

For city planners and urban designers involved in the development of cities and the design of squares, many questions arise. What is the main purpose of the square? Some serve many purposes reasonably well; other squares serve only a few functions but serve them extremely well. Which is better? Does the square serve 'public life' (Marshall 2016)? Ultimately we leave much to the reader to decide which aspects of a square's performance should be evaluated more highly than others and which values should be contested. We believe that the way to develop the knowledge base required to design squares well is to develop theory from practice and ultimately to learn from example.

In chronological order the squares that are multifunctional consisting of many behavior settings and that work well on many dimensions of esthetic analysis are Case Studies 1–8. None of these squares are perfect but they do serve their purposes very well.

1. Rittenhouse Square, Philadelphia, USA, 1913
2. Sproul Plaza, University of California, Berkeley, USA, 1962, renovated in 2014–2015
3. Paley Park, New York City, USA, 1967
4. Cours Honoré d'Estienne d'Orves, Marseille, France, 1987
5. La Place des Terreaux, Lyon, France, 1994
6. Federation Square, Melbourne, Australia, 2002
7. Paternoster Square, London, UK, 2003
8. Robson Square, Vancouver, Canada, 1979, upgraded in 2009

Two squares that we have deemed to have mixed results are success-ful as places for events and/or as displays, but have less of a sense of enclosure and/or are less successful as settings for everyday life are Case Studies 9 and 10. Such squares may nevertheless be regarded as great places because they are loved. Trafalgar Square is the prime example of the pair we consider. It is widely regarded as one of the world's great squares.

9. Olympic Plaza, Calgary, Canada, 1988
10. Trafalgar Square, London, UK, 1845, refurbished in 2003

The third group consists of squares that work well on only a few, but different, dimensions. They, it can be argued, work well enough. These satisficing squares are Case Studies 11–16. All of these squares are well located in terms of their access as paths for pedestrians. All but Oxford Square are large. They have, in common, opportunity costs; they could have been more than they are:

11. The Capitol Square, Chandigarh, India, 1965
12. Oxford Square, Sydney, Australia, 1988
13. Pershing Square, Los Angeles, USA, 1866, redesigned in 1994
14. Schouwburgplein, Rotterdam, the Netherlands, 1996, refurbished in 2010
15. The Guggenheim Museum forecourt, Bilbao, Spain, 1997
16. North and South Shanghai Railway Station Squares, People's Republic of China, 2010

Three squares that we should watch and analyze to see whether the investment made in taking them forward has been successful in creating pleasant places, and whether their success as catalysts for development nearby works are Case Studies 17–19:

17. Jacobs K. Javits Federal Building Plaza, New York City, USA, 1969, latest redesign in 2013
18. Granary Square, London, UK, partially completed 2012
19. Times Square, New York City, USA, redesign to be completed in 2016

The list above contains 19 cases. An analysis of what is believed by many people to be the greatest urban square of them all (although some disagree) must be included here. The last case study in this chapter completes the full score of 20.

20. Piazza San Marco, Venice, Italy founded in 800 but, more substan-tially in operation from 1100 onwards

Analyzing and Evaluating Squares

Any analysis is biased by a set of values. Our analysis sets out to be descriptive and explanatory rather than normative. Jay Curlin (2012: 77) may be correct in his observation that "we see what we want to see." We have, however, made every effort to provide a broad interpretation of what works and does not work in each square.

The objective here is not to state whether one square is better than another but rather to place perceptions of strengths, weaknesses, successes and failures into context.

The focus of our descriptions is on what a square is like in terms of its design and its connections to its surroundings and the focus of our analyses on its functions as a place, a set of links and as a display. As a result, the history of a square is described only to the extent that it affects its affordances today. The aim here is not to provide an exhaustive coverage of the details of a square nor to praise or belabor the authorities responsible for the square. It is instead to understand the nature of each square and what it affords. For the cognescenti, focusing on the designer of a square may be important because its design can be scrutinized as part of its creator's œuvre. However, our attention is focused on the performance of a square, not its designer. The emphasis in our reviews is on the qualities of squares for pedestrian life, although vehicular traffic must be considered. Five of our case studies – Sproul Plaza, Cours Honoré d'Estienne d'Orves, La Place des Terreaux, Schouwburgplein and Pershing Square – stand on the roofs of parking garages. Robson Square, in contrast, was created on what was a surface parking lot that presented an opportunity for the development of a public open space for pedestrians.

One of the major issues that must be addressed in designing new squares and retrofitting existing ones is whether they are to serve a single purpose or be multifunctional. The popular conception may be that squares have to be the hearts of cities or neighborhoods but this reason for their existence is not necessarily the prime one. A number of squares are deemed to be great successes simply because they are better than what was there before. Some squares are deemed successful simply because they have actually been built against opposing circumstances and odds.

The Format of the Case Studies

The description and commentary on each square included in this chapter follow the same format. Each review is divided into three parts. The first is a general introduction to the square. A description of its key features follows. An analysis of what works and what does not work completes each case study. The emphasis that we give to each segment depends on the nature of the square. We have avoided discussing the qualities of the encompassing elements of a square in terms of prevailing architectural ideologies because their architectural style is largely irrelevant to the quality of a square. How adjacent buildings do or do not meet a square is what is important.

We have tried to present an accessible description, analysis and evaluation of each square but, as already stated, ultimately we leave the reader to decide which aspects of a square's performance should be evaluated more stringently than others. We point out the elements of success and lack of success in each case based on published studies and personal observations by the authors and other key informants.

I Rittenhouse Square, Philadelphia, USA

A Neoclassical, park-like, closed square that is the heart of a neighborhood and a much-loved place[1]

Philadelphia was laid out by William Penn's surveyor Thomas Holmes in 1683 with Southwest Square – now Rittenhouse Square – as one of the city's five original central open spaces (see Figure 5.2 (d) on p. 85). By the mid-nineteenth century, it was surrounded by a high-income residential area and remains largely so. The square's surroundings today consist of a variety of buildings; most generate pedestrian traffic: hotels, including a five star hotel, commercial buildings, churches, schools, colleges, including the Curtis School of Music, shops, a library, institutions, such as the Rosenbach Museum, and restaurants as well as many apartment buildings. Typical Philadelphia row-house neighborhoods are nearby. A critical mass of people thus exists close at hand. The buildings on the south side of the square are generally lower than those on the north, allowing some sun into the square at mid-winter yet the buildings are tall enough in relationship to the size of the square to provide a sense of enclosure.

During the summer, the square is sunlit, but in winter it receives only sporadic sunlight. Philadelphia is located at latitude 40°N, which means that the noonday sun at the mid-summer solstice is 73° above the horizon to the south but, at the winter solstice, it is very low in the sky, being only 27° above the horizon at midday.

Key Features

Designed in 1913 by French-born Paul Philippe Cret, the square has a classical design. It has tree-lined diagonal walkways that extend from its corners to a central oval. This central area contains flower beds, a reflecting pool and the sculpture *Duck Girl* – a young girl carrying a duck under one arm – by Paul Manship. The core of the square is surrounded by a balustrade that provides favored seating for the students who reside or study in the neighborhood. Classical urns with Greek figures on their sides rest on pedestals at the entrances to this central oval. At one end of it stands the statue *Lion Crushing a Serpent* by Antoine-Louis Barye. It is an allegory of the French July Revolution of 1830 with the lion representing good and the serpent evil. Few passers-by recognize the symbolism but admire the boldness of the work.

The square is crossed by paths that, either by luck or design, follow the desire lines of pedestrians. It has a room-like "there" there quality in the form of its central area that is semi-enclosed by a balustrade. In addition, the square is replete with good seating in a variety of locations that afford visitors of different ages, ethnicities and abilities opportunities to sit comfortably and to watch the activities of other people, squirrels and birds. Many people criss-cross the park at all times; their watchfulness provides a safe haven for the elderly to sit and watch the passing scene.

The variety of sculptures and a fountain provide focal points to the square. They also act as play equipment for children. Children favor

Figure 12.1 Rittenhouse Square, Philadelphia: (a) Overall layout; (b) The square in autumn; (c) The square as a playground

Billy, a bronze goat, the work of Albert Laeselle. *The Frog* by Cornelia Van Auken Chapin is equally popular for climbing on (see Figure 12.1 (c)). Deciduous trees provide shade in the summer and allow the little winter sunlight that there is to penetrate the square. The lawns afford lying on and informal play. Cret's intellectual esthetic ideas have not interfered with the square working as a place with sub-settings in a multifunctional manner. His design ideas are often studied by architectural and design experts and students.

Analysis

Jane Jacobs' (1961) description and analysis of the four central Philadelphia squares, conducted more than 50 years ago, remain largely relevant despite the changes that have taken place in the squares' immediate surroundings and the city in the intervening years. Jacobs showed that the context in which the squares exist, as much as their internal designs, very much shapes the role they play in the city.

Of the other three squares in Philadelphia studied by Jacobs (1961), Logan Square is essentially a traffic circle. The buildings around it are largely institutional in character. They are the destinations for pedestrian traffic rather than generators of life into the square. The center of the square with the Swann Fountain, plantings and seating is a pleasant place to be but is not easy to reach because of the traffic swirling around it. Franklin Square was a strong nuclear square with a fountain at its center. Until recently it was located in somewhat seedy surroundings but the neighborhood has gone through much revitalization. The square was refurbished in 2006 and now has a carousel, a miniature golf course and a food outlet; the fountain remains the square's centerpiece. The square is regarded as a destination and one of the city's major playgrounds. Washington Square, also known appropriately as Washington Square Park, was completely redesigned in the 1950s to improve its character. It is a heavily treed park crossed by diagonal pathways with a circular paved area at its heart. It houses the Tomb of the Unknown Revolutionary War Soldier and has a statue of George Washington as its centerpiece. The square is a tranquil setting adjacent to the Independence National Historical Park.

Rittenhouse Square is different from the other three squares. It combines being a place containing a number of sub-settings while providing a set of links and being a display of artistic ideas. Although the square is surrounded by roads, only one of them, Walnut Street, has heavy, stopping-and-starting traffic on it. The square's ambient quality is high and the sound of traffic not significantly intrusive. The rustle of the breeze through the trees and the scent of flowers add to the qualities of the square. The adjacent streets are relatively narrow and it is easy to cross them to enter the square. The surrounding buildings are major destinations and generators of people through much of the day and well into the evening. Visitors flock into the area and many regular visitors live, study, or work nearby. What really is a drawcard is the combination of a park-like atmosphere with the attributes of a paved square.

The design of the square with its diagonal paved paths provides clear links, while its central area with its fountains and sculptures gives the square a clear focus and accommodation for a variety of behavior settings. People use the diagonal paths as links so there is a steady movement of pedestrians through the square. The level of activity 'ebbs and flows' according to the time of day. The layout of the square and the diagonal paths that are lined with benches give people the opportunity to sit and be within sight of each other.

The square's layout affords the development of many behavior settings. Parents with children, teenagers and young adults tend to use different 'nooks' in the central area while the elderly tend to sit on the diagonal walkways or near the circle at the center of the square. Buskers choose to perform at the crossroads of the pathways to ensure they have, at least, a passing audience. People tend to sit in the northern part of the square where the quality of light is best. While the square attracts some transients who loiter, they are under the surveillance of the many other users of the square.

The square's lawns are popular for lying on and its park-like qualities make seasonal changes easy to discern. The square is a popular dog-walking area for nearby residents. A clash between dog-owners and children's parents was resolved by restricting the presence of dogs to a segment of the lawns. The square's paved surfaces provide for easy walking. Children also use the hard surfaces to ride tricycles or scooters, to draw on with chalk and play informal games. The hard ground materials also provide support for markets, art shows, and other events that occur throughout the year. The trees and lawns help reduce the heat island effect stemming from the paved areas; the grassed areas are permeable so they help rains to replenish the water table.

Security is often a concern in the hearts of American cities. Rittenhouse Square has many of the characteristics of defensible space as defined by Oscar Newman (1972). Its clearly defined territories, considerable, although somewhat distant, overseeing of the square from the surrounding buildings and the presence of people in the square all provide its users with a sense of security. High quality lighting illuminates the square at night. The presence of park rangers in the square also adds to the sense of security felt by people. Vandalism still occurs but the security cameras that have been installed have reduced the amount.

Rittenhouse Square was designed, consciously or fortuitously, to be robust. It has survived in its present state for a century. It, nevertheless, requires constant maintenance. The Friends of Rittenhouse Square, a public-private partnership, help to maintain the square by upgrading the plants, maintaining the lighting and restoring the fountains. The group installed and stocks doggy-poo bag dispensers. It also organizes formal gardening activities. A Christmas tree is placed in the center of the square each December and a special festival is organized around its lighting.

Nancy Heinzen (2009) considers Rittenhouse Square to be "perfect" but no square is perfect. The square, nevertheless, represents the mixture of elements that makes a place well loved. The appeal of the square is apparent in its constant and enduring use and the intellectual thought that it provides design experts. It has also been the catalyst for the proliferation of nearby restaurants that, in turn, have had a catalytic effect on the added activity in the square during the evening hours.

2 Sproul Plaza, University of California, Berkeley, USA

Two closed, linked squares that are places and links and the heart of student campus life

Sproul Plaza was designed in 1962 by Lawrence Halprin, a leading twentieth-century American landscape architect. It was at a time when the University of California, Berkeley, was substantially expanding its campus across Strawberry Creek to Bancroft Road and Telegraph Avenue. The square was designed to be and is the center of student activity on campus. In politically volatile times, it is the location of protest gatherings. These gatherings began with the Free Speech Movement in 1964 which initiated Berkeley's reputation as a center of radical political thinking. On an everyday basis, Sproul Plaza is more generally the location for the recruiting of students by various societies and clubs and the hosting of special events such as concerts. It serves as both a set of links and as a place containing a number of behavior settings and sub-settings.

Located at 38°N, the sun angles are similar to those at Rittenhouse Square in Philadelphia. The climate is mild and the large size of the square makes it a pleasant place to be during most of the year. The square is currently going through a major refurbishment and the surrounding buildings are being replaced or upgraded (University of California, Berkeley 2014). The description and analysis presented here are based on how the plaza functioned between the 1960s and 2015. The redevelopment by moore ruble yudell architects and planners and costing an estimated US$223 million, is scheduled to be completed in 2016 (UCB 2016).

Key Features

Sproul Plaza has upper and lower segments. The two form an L-shape and are linked by steps. The upper plaza is dominated by west-facing Sproul Hall, a key administrative building, and the lower plaza, by Zellerbach Hall. Sproul Hall with its Neoclassical façade is raised above the floor level of the upper plaza and is reached by a broad terraced stairway. To the north is Sather Gate through which students pass to gain access to the upper plaza (Figure 12.2 (a)). The plaza is thus a link between the central campus and busy Telegraph Avenue. It is lined on its north–south axis by double rows of the pollard London plane trees.

The lower plaza is flat and plain-surfaced. It is bordered by buildings that are destinations for students and thus generate movement across the campus. Below it is a parking garage. Except for the link to the upper plaza, the square is enclosed by gray-colored buildings designed in the brutalist style that was favored by many architects in the 1960s. They, nevertheless, make the square a lively place because of what they house rather than what they look like. Eshleman Hall, the home of many student groups, faced and enclosed the plaza to the south. It has now been demolished but will be replaced with a newly developed building. Other important student service buildings will remain. The Martin Luther King Jr Student Union, the home

Figure 12.2 Sproul Plaza, University of California, Berkeley: (a) Looking out to Sather Gates Upper Plaza; (b) Upper Sproul Plaza with Ludwig Fountain; (c) The 'Cal Bears' football team sculpture Lower Plaza

of the Pauley Ballroom, abuts the open space on the east, the César E. Chavez Student Center lies on the north and Zellerbach Hall on the west. Zellerbach contains a large auditorium that hosts major addresses. The Chavez Center contains the university learning center, a small shopping area and the Golden Bear Café.

A circular bronzed plaque lies in the floor of the plaza. It reads: "This soil and air space extending above it shall not be a part of any nation and shall not be subject to any entity's jurisdiction," implying that open beliefs are encouraged and should not be persecuted at UC Berkeley. Additionally, a sculpture of a bear stands on a pedestal in one corner of the lower plaza (Figure 12.2 (c)). It represents the 'Cal Bears' football team and the collegial spirit that exists on most American university campuses.

As mentioned as part of the university's master plan, the parking garage under the lower plaza and the buildings surrounding the square are being renovated. They should make Lower Sproul Plaza more of a place than it was by enhancing the uses of the buildings and the location of their entrances (Straus 2014). The plaza has been operating more as a link than a place for much of the time.

Analysis[2]

Sproul Plaza forms the heart of the student life at UC Berkeley because of its location and the nature of the buildings that surround it and the activities they contain. The square houses many of the facilities that students regularly use, creating recurrent patterns of student pedestrian traffic into it. This is true of the old and upcoming design of the plaza. The specific design of the two plazas and the buildings that form them create many links that are busy throughout much of the day. The buildings around the open space 'funnel' pedestrian traffic and make obvious the spacious linkage routes that cater for large flows of people. The links also create many smaller places. The plaza thus gives the university a core and an identity and students a sense of belonging to campus life. The university is hopeful that the new design will further enhance the student experience and the physical space (UCB 2016).

The broad terraced staircase in front of Sproul Hall on the Upper Plaza forms an excellent dais. This dais affords the addressing of an audience from a raised position. The stairs are also used as seating and as a meeting point. The variety of behavior settings differs during the course of the day, week and seasons. The size of the plaza is sufficient to hold many people. The fountain lies at the extreme western end before the steps lead down to the Lower Plaza. It thus does not interfere with the gathering of people in the plaza. The edge of the fountain is used as seating. The fountain is named after a dog, Ludwig, who used to spend extensive time in the plaza in the 1960s. It now acts as a focal point, a nuclear element, in the plaza. Sadly, the fountain is often not functioning.

Only two years after it was built, the Upper Plaza and the staircase in front of Sproul Hall were the site of the Free Speech Movement protest. Later it was the site of the riots at Berkeley in protest of the US participation in the Vietnam War, the bombing of Cambodia and the invasion of Iraq. More recently the Occupy Berkeley protests of 2011 took place there. It was easy to assign the cause of these events to the design of the campus, which politicians did. The universities of the California state system that were built after the 1960s were consciously designed to contain no such central square where students could easily gather en masse.

The flat surfaces of the plazas afford many activities. In addition to providing for large gatherings, Upper Sproul Plaza has pockets along its sides formed by the pollard planes, benches and bike racks. They afford polychronic standing pattern of behavior very well and as a result often accommodate smaller semi-private gatherings. While they are in open view, they have auditory privacy. The trees are also used architecturally to form a boulevard. As William Whyte noted (1980), food is a catalyst for both creating links and for interactions among individuals. The Golden Bear Café and many food outlets located along Bancroft Way are at the edge of campus and where its pedestrianization begins.

As one might expect on a university campus, the spaces are dominated by students. When the university is on break, especially over the summer months, the plaza is much less used and empty after office hours. Bicycles flying across the campus taking advantage of the smooth surfaces were previously perceived by some to be a hazard, as noted by Cooper Marcus and Francis (1990). Subsequently bike-free zones were established on campus.

Some people may be aware of the plaza being the design of Lawrence Halprin during the period that he was establishing his practice.[3] The work at UC Berkeley was the springboard for his award-winning career. Many of the qualities for student life and particularly movement through the campus that he sought to achieve have been realized. He established a number of precedents that have been implemented at many university campuses around the world. One was the then highly controversial idea of eliminating vehicular traffic from the campus to create a pedestrian super-block. The creation of an outdoor 'auditorium' in the Upper Plaza, the use of trees to create spaces and the subtle use of light and shade were some of the other aspects of his contributions to the design of urban squares.

The buildings surrounding the plaza are dour in appearance but the way they meet the open space is central to the quality of the plaza. It is clearly the heart of the campus for students.

3 Paley Park, New York City, USA

An endowed, quasi-public place, a vest-pocket square, an oasis in a busy city

Located in Midtown Manhattan's cultural district and surrounded by high-rise buildings, this small square was chosen to be reviewed because it is a much-celebrated vest-pocket park that has served as a precedent for many other similar sites. Unlike many other plazas in New York that were legally required as part of the city's incentive zoning program, Paley Park resulted from a philanthropic gesture. A quasi-public space, it was privately financed and is owned by the William S. Paley Foundation and was named by Paley in honor of his father, Samuel Paley. A plaque at the entrance reads: "This park is set aside in memory of Samuel Paley, 1875–1963, for the enjoyment of the public."

Paley Park is located on East 53rd Street in Manhattan, on the former site of the Stork Club. It was designed by the landscape architects Zion & Breen, and opened in May 1967. It is small in size, being only 390 square meters (0.04 hectares or 4,200 square feet; roughly 100 by 42 feet) in area. The square located at latitude 41°N is framed on the south by tall buildings so little sun penetrates it in winter. As a quasi-public space, Paley Park is only open to the public at restricted, although generous hours: 8.00am to 10pm in summer and 8.00am to 8.00pm during the colder months. These hours are typical of many publicly owned spaces. As Paley Park is not publicly owned, it is not required to abide by a number of New York City public space codes.

Key Features[4]

Paley Park is surrounded by red-brick walls on two sides, a waterfall on the back wall and is open to the street on the fourth (Figure 12.3). Rectangular gates that are closed at night face the street. When people cannot enter, at least they can see in. The walls are covered in

green, English ivy that contrasts in the spring and summer with the brightly colored flowers that are grown in planter boxes on both sides of the square. The edges of the planter boxes provide additional seating to the chairs. The key feature and attraction of the park is, without doubt, the rock-faced 6.1 meter-high (20 feet) waterfall that fills the whole of the back wall. The water pours down at 6,800 liters (1,800 gallons) a minute powered by a 50 horsepower pump (Surhone *et al.* 2010). It cascades from the top of the wall, hits a level and splashes into a pool at its base, creating a spray. The waterfall also provides a dramatic focal point and attracts visitors into the square. The sound of falling water at 60–70 decibels blocks out urban noises and creates a tranquil and private locale in the midst of Manhattan. On cold days, the water is heated by a steam pump before being raised up to the top of the waterfall to fall down again. In winter, it is turned off.

Paley Park is furnished with moveable, lightweight, wire-mesh, 'bird chairs' designed by Harry Bertoia, and moveable marble tables that let people configure the furniture to suit the size of their group. People inevitably shift the location of chairs before they sit down. Shade in the summer is provided by the canopy of honey locust trees. Planted at 3.7 meter (12 feet) intervals, they create a dappled effect as light passes between their leaves. The canopy also tends to exclude the view of the adjacent buildings towering above. As these trees are deciduous, they allow the sun to enter Paley Park briefly in the early and the late winter, although in mid-winter the sun is so low in the sky that sunlight is completely cut out by the adjacent buildings.

Figure 12.3 *Paley Park, New York*
Source: Photograph by Kate Bishop.

Next to the entrance on the interior of the square are gatehouses facing inwards. On one side is a food stall, which in 2014 was closed for redevelopment, and the park keeper's shelter; a machine room is on the other. Paley Park is raised four steps above the street level. Very steep but short wheelchair ramps are located on both sides of the steps. The square comprises a blend of synthetic materials, textures, colors and sounds. The paving is made of rough-hewn tiles rather than concrete. They are visually interesting but require some care to avoid trips and falls.

Analysis

Paley Park is solely a place consisting of a nested set of small behavior settings. Unlike many other spaces of its size in New York City, it is neither a link providing access from the sidewalk to a building nor is it part of a mid-block crossing. Many people do cross the square to approach the waterfall before sitting down or exiting once again back to 53rd Street. As a place, it has proven to be enduringly delightful in most people's eyes. Over the years it has been extensively studied because it is regarded as a prototypical vest-pocket park and has been the precedent for many other such small urban places. Few of them have been as successful because they do not possess the combination of urban context and design quality that Paley Park has.

William Whyte (1980) is among many who have studied Paley Park and its users in some depth. Their conclusions are that it is popular because it is located directly off the street so that people are attracted to look into it and enter and that it has carefully considered design attributes. One key to Paley Park's success is the waterfall. The falling water is loud in decibels but the sound is tolerated because of its source. It drowns out much of the noise of urban life although it makes quiet conversations difficult. It improves the ambient quality of such a small space.

The water and its spray, in combination with shade given by the trees, make for a cooler setting than the nearby streets on a summer day. Other key factors are the moveable chairs and the availability of something to eat and drink. The food outlet attracts people who then consequently attract more people. In winter, only a few hardy souls sit in the square when the plaza is open. In summer, the scene is different: the space is active and busy. Despite its heavy use, people who desire to be alone feel that in a lively city they can be in an environment that affords them a restful place to linger away from the vehicular and pedestrian traffic on Fifth Avenue.

On any given day the space is visited by both regular local and one-time visitors. As an observer commented soon after the park was opened, "it is located where people are" (Wagner 1967: 117) – this is still the case. Regulars come from the nearby offices and adjacent neighborhoods. Jerome Kayden (2000: 57) notes on any given day: "the roster might include visitors from New Jersey or Japan as well as landscape architects and designers making an educational journey." The people using Paley Park are adults of all ages and a mixture of men and women – rarely homeless people. Women, especially, are comfortable there on their own or while waiting for friends. Smokers enjoy the park because New York's stringent municipal rules on where one can smoke do not apply to it because it is not a public place. Cigar smokers recognize that Paley Park is one of the few outdoor places in New York where you can legally smoke a cigar (Gardiner 2012). Only a few children accompany their parents to the park, but those who are in the space find the edges of the planter boxes something to climb on and the water something to play in. The park is well maintained and clean, something visitors appreciate. The custodians also provide an extra sense of security although some visitors may find them to be somewhat officious.

In 2014, Amanda Burden, a former Planning Commissioner for New York City, noted in her TED talk that "places like Paley Park didn't happen by accident. Public space has to be fought for to begin with and then to be successful somebody has to think very hard about every detail." The attention paid to the quality of the items in the park is noticed consciously or subconsciously by people. Few will know who the designer of the chairs was but they will notice their quality. The tables tops are marble, not a cheap material. The quality of the trees and even the brickwork is high. The variety of materials adds to the perceived quality of the park and must add to the sense of self-worth of the visitors to the park. The cognescenti appreciate Paley Park's design with the rectilinear geometry of the space as a much enriched version of the Modernist paradigm. They will also appreciate the design's role as a precedent for other squares and as part of the body of work of its designers which has been written about extensively. Casual visitors simply enjoy the space for what it offers.

4 Cours Honoré d'Estienne d'Orves, Marseille, France

A typical rectangular, closed, European square that has been a catalyst for change in its surroundings

Parking is an issue in most cities, and particularly in those urban precincts that were built before the development of the automobile. Parking space, whether in the form of surface lots or structures, has been created wherever space can be accommodated. Often public squares have been turned into parking lots. Although fulfilling the demand for parking, the change has often been accompanied by a loss of a broad range of public amenities in a locality for residents and visitors alike. Today a number of such parking lots have been returned to public open space and pedestrian traffic. The Cours Honoré d'Estienne d'Orves, in Marseille, is an example.[5] What sets this square apart from many others is that it was a substantial parking structure rather than a surface lot that was the location for a square.

The site has had a history of change. It was once the Canal de l'Arsenal des Galleries connected to the Vieux-Port of Marseille. The Arsenal became redundant in the late eighteenth century with the consolidation of facilities at Toulon and the link to the Vieux-Port became a customs canal. It was filled in between 1927 and 1929 when the Vieux-Port lost its role as a commercial harbor. The port, nevertheless, remains important as a place where cruise ships dock, and as the center of tourism in Marseille. When filled in, the canal site became a rather desolate and grubby open space. In 1965, when having to deal with the needs of drivers, the municipal government built a three-level parking structure on the site.

The parking structure operated for two decades until the 1980s. As noted by Espuche (n.d.), pressure from a residents' association, Les Arcenauix, sought to change the character of the precinct. The discussions about the nature of the changes that should take place were prolonged and heated. They reflected debates around the world centered on the role of the car in the city. The contemporary mayor, Robert Vigoroux, supporting Les Arcenauix, was a strong advocate for the demolition of the car park and the creation of a public square. The Marseille municipal government decided to demolish the parking garage and replace it with underground parking. The decision was implemented in 1987 with the construction of a garage for 650 cars. The parking, together with the creation of a public square, was seen as a potential catalyst for the regeneration of the precinct. This has indeed occurred.

Key Features

The square was constructed for €2,674,500 in contemporary terms. At 12,300 square meters (about 3 acres) the Cours Honoré d'Estienne d'Orves is the largest open space in the dense center of Marseille (Espuche n.d.). It was designed to host a variety of events, such as markets and concerts, so its surface is largely a flat area paved with granite and stone. The pattern differentiates the central part of the square from its borders. The square is a simple, rectangular closed type. Only one of the original Arsenal buildings remains but older buildings facing the square were refurbished and the new ones were designed with a sense of decorum, thus maintaining the continuity of the square's visual character. Their entrances line the frontages of the buildings as can be seen in Figure 12.4 (a).

The ratio of width to the height of surrounding buildings is fortuitously close to the ideal as perceived by Sitte (Sitte and Stewart

Figure 12.4 The Cours Honoré d'Estienne d'Orves, Marseille, France: (a) The square looking west (b) The square looking east on a late spring day

1945) and Zucker (1959). It gives the square a fine sense of enclosure, of being an outdoor room. It also allows the penetration of sunlight into the square throughout the year. Marseille's latitude of 43°N and the square's east–west orientation enable the sun to bathe the square's northern side in light while the southern side is in shade as can be seen in Figure 12.4 (b). The northern is the preferred side in spring and autumn but on hot days the shade is preferred. The 1.50 meter-thick (5 feet) ceiling of the parking garage makes it possible to include services and carry the weight of fountains and, if it had been so desired, planting. Pedestrian access via steps and elevators to the parking garage is from the square itself, further increasing the pedestrian traffic through it. At the eastern end of the square are a reflecting pool and a classical statue.

The ground floors of the adjacent buildings open directly onto the open square, in many cases without a single step up. Passers-by can thus look directly into the windows of the shops, galleries and restaurants that line the edges of the square. During the warm months, the restaurants spill out into the open space, almost filling it on occasions. In winter, they withdraw into the buildings.

Considerable attention was paid to the detailing of the square. Designed by architect Charles Bové, the open space is defined not only by the buildings but also by the tall lampposts with lightshades in the shape of birds' wings. Garbage bins are built into their base. The character of the posts is repeated in the railings of the car park exits, helping give a unity to the whole design. Bollards linked by chains close off the two ends of the square. They replicate those of the nineteenth-century triumphal Arch, the Port d'Aix, in the city. A mast covered with flags, the work of sculptor, Daniel Buren, is located on one side of the square.

Analysis[6]

The square has become a major destination for both tourists and locals. It can be analyzed in terms of its affordances for people and in terms of the processes that brought it about. It possesses many of the characteristics required to make squares lively places. It is both a link and a place. Its function as a link can best be seen in the winter photograph of it taken by Gilles Martin-Raget that we have used to introduce Part I of this book on p. 19. The square is located on the daily paths of movement of workers and residents and is a link between the underground parking garage and the surrounding precinct.

As a place, it is full of visitors and behavior settings. Access from the core of the city, from the heart of the tourist destination of the Vieux-Port and from surrounding residential areas, is easy for pedestrians. It is flat and few streets have to be crossed. Nearby streets are narrow. The parking garage below makes the square a destination for drivers. The ground floors of the buildings that line the square are located directly on the square and no cars pass between them and the open area. The windows overlooking the square provide opportunities for natural surveillance although not too much should be expected of the consequences. The large number of restaurants on the square is a natural drawcard as are the bookshops and galleries. Food is clearly the major attraction. The people who frequent the restaurants are of all ages but clearly are middle-class or wealthy. Children are often seen running around and playing on the hard surfaces in its traffic-free space.

Cours Honoré d'Estienne d'Orves is a true closed square with a simple design that is uncluttered by fixed features. The milieu affords the creation of many behavior settings. Such designs serve many purposes. The square shows that parking under a square can work well. Symbolically the square is a meaningful display and place. Its history is explained on a plaque, and for people who are unaware of the square's history, its architecture is clearly related to the Mediterranean and to its city. While few people will know of the architect or of the designer of the furniture, the work of Charles Bové and Daniel Buren will be significant to the cognescenti. The avant-garde among them may be disappointed that the architecture is not more Modernist, reflecting the era in which the square was completed. Ultimately the uniqueness of the open space in the old city of Marseille makes the square especially important.

Procedurally the renovation shows that a powerful, well-organized and well-led residents' committee with a clear sense of its goals can make substantial contributions and changes to the urban environment. The catalytic power for change of such a development is significant. The housing in the area has been much refurbished and new cafés and restaurants line the square and adjacent streets. Art galleries have opened on the square and nearby. While no systematic study of the square seems to have been undertaken, by casual observations and by all anecdotal reports the square is deemed to be a success by municipal officials, the general public and residents of the area.

5 La Place des Terreaux, Lyon, France

A large, refurbished, rectangular, closed, nuclear square that is the heart of Lyon[7]

La Place des Terreaux is located on the Presqu'île between the Rhône and Saône rivers in the old city of Lyon. The zone is classified as a World Heritage Site by UNESCO. The square is Lyon's heart for both locals and tourists. The redesign of the Place des Terreaux was one of seven coordinated projects carried out by Lyon's administration during the 1990s to improve the city. The square has had a long checkered history, including the incident when 79 of the city's citizens were sent to the guillotine after the Siege of Lyon during the French Revolution (Vanario 2002).

The square had a somewhat seedy reputation prior to its recent makeover. The refurbishment involved building an underground garage to solve the parking problem in the center of the city and the revamping of the surface of the square. The design goal was to create a modern place while respecting the heritage of the precinct. *Tout changer sans rien toucher* – change everything without touching anything – was the objective. The design team hired by the city was comprised of Christian Drever as the urban designer and architect, Daniel Buren as the sculptor and Laurent Fachard as the lighting engineer. The layout shows that uncluttered designs afford the development of many formal and communal behavior settings.

Key Features

La Place des Terreaux lies below the foothill of La Croix-Rousse in a busy commercial and shopping area that is also the center of the administration of the city (Figure 12.5). Immediately adjacent to the square are popular shopping streets: Rue de la République, Rue President Éduoard-Herriott and Rue de Brest. Many restaurants are located just off the square on the narrow streets that lead into it.

The square has always been a flat paved area but recently it has had some significant changes. It is still enclosed by the same build-ings, many of which are of historic note. On the west lies the Palais St Pierre and the Musée des Beaux-Arts de Lyon; the Hôtel de Ville de Lyon is on the east and houses that have become banks and other commercial uses lie on the other enclosing sides. The square is a deep one in shape and, in some ways, acts as forecourt for the Hôtel de Ville, a bold building with a central dome and side pavilions. A row of 14 columns crossing the façade of the Palais St Pierre was the only change made to the enclosing elements of the square dur-ing its refurbishment. The narrow street on the shaded south of the square has boundary markers and surface materials that differentiate it from the paving of the rest of the square.

Figure 12.5 La Place des Terreaux, Lyon. View to the Palais St Pierre with the Bartholi fountain on the right

Sixty-nine mini water and light ground fountains were installed orthogonally in the dark square paving in five lines, 5.9 meters (20 feet) apart (Figure 12.5). The fountains were designed to enliven the square by spouting water to various heights. They froze during the bitter winter of 2011–2012 and were not functioning in 2013. The traffic, including trams/street cars, on one side of the square adds a degree of bustle to it. The entrances to the underground car park for both vehicles and pedestrians are outside the square but do not impinge on it as they do at Pershing Square in Los Angeles. The surrounding buildings are subtly floodlit at night, adding a lively ambience to the square.

Place des Terreaux is a closed square with an 1880s fountain designed by, and named for, Auguste Bartholdi[8] as its nuclear element. The fountain was realized by Gaget and Gautier in 1889. At its center is an allegorical statue, representing the Garonne River and its four tributaries flowing down into the sea. The river is represented by a woman leading a chariot. The water flows down the sides of the sculpture into a semi-circular pool that is surrounded by an enclosing wall at seat height. To build the underground parking, the fountain that had been originally located in front of Hôtel de Ville was moved to its current location on one side of the longitudinal axis of the square.

Analysis

While La Place des Terreaux was long the heart of Lyon, its refurbishment has reinforced its centrality for both locals and tourists. Its location in a busy commercial and shopping area creates a critical mass of nearby potential users. It is also well served by public transport. A number of trams and buses pass by the square. Drivers who use the parking garage use the square as a link to reach their other destinations. As a result, the square is both a destination and a link.

The square illustrates a number of other points made earlier in this book. A nuclear element such as a fountain (in this case with a lively sculpture) gives a square a "there" there which provides a point at which people can meet and contributes to its sense of place. Over time it has hosted many different behavior settings. It is also a landmark within the square. The square is surrounded by buildings of note that are destinations in themselves so the square acts as both a place, a set of places and as a series of links criss-crossing it. The quality of light is always important. Located 46°N, the square has an east–west orientation and hence is bathed in sunlight in the morning and evening from May to August but at midday the southern half is in shadow. The sun's presence in winter is, as one might expect, fleeting, so the restaurants line the north side of the square trying to catch the sun.

La Place des Terreaux is famous for the illumination of the façades of the adjacent buildings. While the illumination is important in order to prevent a gloomy night-time atmosphere, the square is better known for being the focal point for the Fête des Lumières for which Lyon is famous. The lighting provides for different light shows playing across the façades of the enclosing buildings each year.

The square's flat surface affords large gatherings. It consists of many changing behavior settings. It is host to markets, concerts and a variety of celebrations. These celebrations include not only the Fête des Lumières but, more particularly, major celebrations after sporting events such as victories in important football games. The flat surface also makes it easy for cafés and restaurants to open directly onto the square. They are major attractions which, in turn, become the major attraction for yet other visitors. At lunchtime, the restaurants are patronized by people who work nearby. In the evening, it is mainly tourists and younger patrons who use the square.

The presence of people gives all those who are there a sense of security. This feeling is enhanced by restaurant owners behaving as if the space outside their restaurants is semi-public and under their control. In addition, the square is naturally surveilled – viewing from the windows of adjacent buildings is part of everyday and night life. The cleaners of the square are ever present and add a sense of security as well as maintaining the square's cleanliness, something that is remarked on by visitors. Although large and clear in the center, the square has much seating on its periphery. Not only are there the chairs in the restaurants but public benches, bollards and the edge of the Bartholdi Fountain are also used by all ages, as seating.

Fountains serve as playgrounds for children, adolescents and even adults. The 69 surface fountains (when working) and the Bartholdi Fountain are a major attraction, especially for children. It has become a tradition for football fans to drench themselves in the waters of the fountain to celebrate a win. As the square is a large one, the sound of splashing water does not carry far but the hum of voices in the background adds a positive sonic quality to the square. The square also shows that traffic sounds are not necessarily detrimental to the ambient quality of a square.

Some renowned designers, such as Gehl and Gemzøe (2000) and Broto (2000), along with the general public, as noted through their use of the square, regard the square as a great success. Unlike Paternoster Square in London where the architecture of the surrounding buildings, rather than the square itself, has been criticized by some (Glancey 2003; Sudic 2003), here it is the square itself and the life in it that have been of concern to critics. The architecture of the surrounding buildings was 'a given' in the redesign of the square. Few people will know of the designers involved in the creation of the square and few will know of the allegorical nature of the sculpture of the fountain. Some may know of Auguste Bartholdi but mostly it is the cognescenti who appreciate the history of the redesign of the square.

6 Federation Square, Melbourne, Australia

An irregular, partially closed square: a created heart for the city

Completed in 2002, at a cost of over AUD$460 million (almost four times the predicted budget), Federation Square is an air-rights development located over train tracks. The cost overrun was due largely to the cost of building the concrete deck[9] while the trains continued to operate but also to significant design changes required by the public in order to maintain views of heritage buildings. The spacing of the columns supporting the deck restricts future track layout options, something of concern to the State Railway Authority.

The square is a collection of open spaces and buildings operated by Fed Square Pty, Ltd, a company wholly owned by the Government of Victoria. It was purposefully planned to be Melbourne's prime urban square. An attempt made in 1968 to create such a place, City Square, was deemed to have failed to achieve that purpose. Its long narrow shape precluded many activities that *the* central square of a city is expected to accommodate. A renovation during the 1990s resulted in little improvement. The Melbourne City Council decided to remedy the situation and selected a site over the Jolimont Railyards leading out of the city's busy Central (Flinders Street) station. Its goal was to connect Flinders Street on one side of the site with the Yarra River on the other and to create vistas of the adjacent heritage buildings including St Paul's Cathedral.

Before the building of Federation Square, the site was dominated on one side by the twin towers of the former Gas and Fuel Corporation that were generally regarded as eyesores by the public. They were demolished. The state government organized a design competition for the site that attracted 177 entries. Several of the designs were put on public display and a jury chose that of Lab Architecture Studio of London and Bates Smart of Melbourne. The landscape architects were Karres+Brand. The winning design was a controversial selection because of its architectural qualities and because one of the 'shards' of the design was deemed to be obstructing the vista towards St Paul's Cathedral.

Key Features

Covering 3.8 hectares (roughly 9 acres; a large Melbourne urban block), Federation Square consists of two open spaces – St Paul's Court opposite the Cathedral and the Square facing the Flinders Street Station – and one covered space – the Atrium. The square has a strong sense of enclosure on three sides provided by three-to-four-story-high buildings but a weaker one on the west where Swanston Street intervenes between it and the station. Although the station is a major historical building and a landmark in the city, its location does not make Federation Square a dominant square. The view from the footpath tends to be in the other direction – into the square.

Federation Square is a mixed institutional-commercial development that forms a roughly U-shaped southwest-facing environment (Figure 12.6). A central feature of the square is a giant screen on which sporting and other events are shown that attracts large crowds. The square has a number of entry points from the streets, and the doorways of its enclosing buildings face onto it. The buildings are primarily cultural institutions such as the Australian Center for the Moving Image, the Ian Potter Center of the Art Gallery of Victoria and the Australian Special Broadcasting Service. The area around the square includes retail and commercial outlets, a hotel and the railway

Figure 12.6 Aerial view of Federation Square, Melbourne

Source: Photograph by Nils Versemann/ Shutterstock.com.

station. Outdoor cafés in the square attract patrons to sit and view their surroundings and the activities that occur within it.

The architecturally bold buildings that form the square are irregular in appearance. They are covered with a complex geometric pattern of triangular tiles composed of five smaller triangular ones. Some of the tiles are made of perforated solid zinc and sandstone, while those of the Atrium facing the square are glazed with a green hue. Each building has a unique surface geometry but the general fractal nature gives a unity to the overall design. The floor of the square is gently sloping and slightly undulating; it affords many activities: primarily formal but also, on its periphery, communal. The surface is partially of bluestone paving that matches that generally used in Melbourne but the floor of the main square is of ochre-colored sandstone. It forms a huge art work, *Nearamnew*, the creation of Paul Carter. The work consists of textural pieces and poetic writing laid in a gently undulating manner. Symbolically the square commemorates the 1901 unification of the states of Australia into a federated nation (Rutherford 2005).

Analysis

The square has been applauded by architectural critics for its adventurous design qualities.[10] It is described by the Victoria Council of the Arts as possessing the world's "most stunning architecture." To many lay-people, the buildings around the square are unattractive (Levy 2012). Over time the public appears to have become used to their esthetic quality but still may not like them. It does not fit in with any popular taste culture. What is important to the public are the variety of behavior settings that occur there and that they can participate in.

For the architectural cognescenti, the deconstructivist architecture of the complex, with its diverse shapes, slots and the unity of the buildings through their materials and geometrical patterns, is of great interest. They might associate the architecture with the Jewish Museum in Berlin and know of the work of the architects, Lab Architecture Studio in London and Bates Smart of Melbourne. The square's value to the experts is indicated by the numerous architectural awards that it has won. The art work of floor of the main square, *Nearamnew*, is also of interest to some but may be largely unnoticed by the general public. Federation Square shows that the image of a square is important but ultimately its quality depends on the nature of the space it contains and its location. The architecture, in itself, is unimportant other than that it acts as a billboard advertising the square. At Federation Square its radical nature is very successful as an advertisement.

The quality of light in a square is always important. The station across a road on the southwest side is relatively low in height as are the buildings on the north so that the square, located at 38°S, is bathed in sunlight from the north for much of the day. It must be remembered that Melbourne is in the southern hemisphere and the noonday sun shines from the north. The very core of the square, however, facing southwest is only well illuminated by the sun on a summer evening. The result is that it is usually a gloomy corner, particularly in winter.

The train station and tram lines empty passengers along two sides of the square and the north-south, Swanston Street is full of pedestrians crossing the adjacent river. On the northern side of the square lies Melbourne's Central Business District with its commercial buildings and major retail shops. On its south across the Yarra River is the Southbank development of commercial and retail activities and restaurants. Federation Square is thus a fulcrum in the link between the activities taking place on either side of the river. The location of Federation Square is at a busy point in Melbourne and the mix of uses in the buildings that form it ensures a steady stream of people passing by and through it. This flow of people and the programming of formal events make the square *the* central place in the city of Melbourne as was intended. Free Wi-Fi access encourages people with computers and other portable devices to linger. The views to St Paul's Cathedral and the station add visual interest on one side of the square.

The success of the square lies in its qualities as a place reinforced by the links that occur across it. As a place it provides for large gatherings; frequent formal events are held in the square. These include protest meetings, celebrations, the showing of major sports events on fixed screens and the presentation of on-stage performances. Federation Square is also a place for communal gatherings; informal performances occur around its periphery where steps leading into the square provide seating for onlookers. People sit at various locations where steps and edges are used for seating, as meeting points, as places to wait for a train or to watch street performances. Visitors of all ages seem to enjoy the space. The square is not located in or near a neighborhood of young families and so it is not a local play area for young children, although school children use the space as a link as they walk to and from school.

The success of the square led, in 2006, to new developments underneath it on the Yarra River side. Steps lead down from the square to the river's edge where old vaults have been converted into cafés. This type of extension suggests that the square will act as a catalyst, spurring further air rights commercial development to the northeast over the rail tracks and along the Yarra River. Such a development would enhance the geographic centrality of the square in Melbourne.

7 Paternoster Square, London, UK

Competing ideologies in the design of a quasi-public, nuclear, closed square in an historic context[11]

Analyzes of Paternoster Square, a privately owned public open space (POPS), show the clash in values as to what is often held to be a good square by avant-garde architects and by the general public. Three schemes that represent different design paradigms are discussed briefly here. The first is the 1956 Modernist proposal prepared and built under the direction of Sir William Holford; the second is a Neoclassical design by Hammond, Beeby & Babke, Porphyrios Associates and John Simpson & Partners. The square built is the third design and the work of Whitfield Partners.

The Holford scheme consisted of narrow rectangular, commercial buildings set in the orthogonal pattern favored by the Rationalists among the Modernists. The height of the buildings was restricted by building codes. The narrowness of the building was a purposeful effort to give the workers in the interiors natural daylight. The buildings, however, soon proved to be less than functional in everyday use. They failed to meet the floor plan requirements of commercial organizations that cared little about daylight penetration into buildings. The external space that the buildings created was regarded as dull because it afforded few pleasant behavior settings. Critics and general public alike considered it to be "a grim piazza" (Watkin 1996: website).[12] Located at 52°N, the height of the noonday sun is only 61° at the summer solstice.

During the 1980s the complex became abandoned step by step. The ownership of the site changed hands a number of times and the search for a new design began in earnest only in the mid-1980s. A competition was held in 1986 but the winning design by Arup Associates was much criticized for being too commercial by people such as Prince Charles who saw himself as an advocate for the general public in their fight against developers and 'starchitects.' He argued for a more classical approach. A new competition was organized by *The Evening Standard*. The winning design by John Simpson in conjunction with a number of other architects was considered to be a pastiche of classical forms by avant-garde critics.

In 1995, the Mitsubishi Corporation bought the site and asked Whitfield Partners to produce the design that was ultimately implemented. The square is an 'all-of-a-piece' urban design which means that although the individual buildings may have been designed by different architects, they conform to a set of design guidelines that gives the square a uniform appearance.

Key Features

Paternoster Square is a closed, nuclear square with a column located off-center. The surrounding buildings are five and six stories in height and with the limited size of the square give it the appearance of an outdoor room. The buildings are occupied primarily by financial service uses such as the London Stock Exchange, Goldman Sachs, Merrill Lynch and Nomura Securities. The ground floor is mixed in use with cafés and shops. The square has several narrow links to its surroundings: to St Paul's underground station via Paternoster Row and Panyer Alley, to Newgate Street via Rose Street and to St Paul's Churchyard, a pedestrian way that runs along the north side of St Paul's Cathedral, via the relocated Temple Bar (Figure 12.7).[13] On one side of the Temple Bar entrance to the square are public toilets.

The square's floor is flat surfaced with a sunburst pattern. The nuclear element is the 23 meter-tall (75 feet) Paternoster Square Corinthian column of Portland stone. It is topped by a gold leaf-covered copper finial (colloquially referred to as a pineapple). It is illuminated at night by a fiber-optic device. The column, designed by the architects, also serves as a ventilation shaft for a service road that runs under the square. At the eastern end of the square is the bronze *Shepherd and Sheep* by Dame Elisabeth Frink. The statue is a reminder of the historical usage of the area (Lang 2005).

Analysis

Figure 12.7 Paternoster Square, London: (a) Aerial view of the square; (b) Temple Bar in its relocated position as an entrance to the square from St Paul's churchyard

Source: (a) Photograph by Luciano Mortula/Shutterstock.com.

The same variables are at play in Paternoster Square as in the multifunctional squares already described in this chapter. It consists of many potential behavior settings. One reason for the square's general liveliness is that it is closely linked to its surroundings and those surroundings are both destinations and generators of people's movements. St Paul's Cathedral is not only a destination for worshippers

but for considerably more tourists. They have to pass by the Temple Bar to enter the Cathedral and can see into the square. The square is easily accessible by public transport – the underground system via St Paul's station and by the buses that ply up Ludgate Hill. The buildings in the neighborhood of the square are full of workers but few residents; the City of London has a residential population of fewer than 8,000 people but the daytime population swells to 300,000. Many commuters into the city, from both the underground and the buses, use the square as a pedestrian link to their destinations.

The square itself, unlike Trafalgar Square or Piccadilly Circus, is not a destination for tourists. It is for local workers but the tourists who visit St Paul's in droves recognize the amenity provided by the square and may enter it. In and around the square are cafés and restaurants, both international chains and local varieties. They attract workers and tourists to have lunch or afternoon tea there or to sit on the stone benches and steps along the north side of the square. The workers are predominantly young middle-class men and women and the services provided on the square cater for that population. The public toilets are an added amenity, mentioned because many squares do not have these facilities. They are clean, have attendants and although an entrance fee is charged, they are well used.

The square is a pleasant place to be. The quality of light makes a difference to the ambient quality of the square. It is a suntrap in summer. The height of the enclosing buildings on the south side of the square, apart from St Paul's to the southeast, is low so the summer sun streams into the square; its north side is fully illuminated and replete with people on a sunny day. In addition, the paleness of the buildings reflects light into the square. In winter the height of the noonday sun is only 25° above the horizon so little sunshine penetrates the square. On weekends outside peak tourist season, the pedestrian zone certainly has fewer people lingering there than on a warm, sunny summer day.

Some critics look at the square in terms of its architecture, as a display, rather than as a place, which to them is banal and disappointing (Sudic 2003). Those critics who respond favorably to the project like the uniformity of its architecture that follows the precedent set by Christopher Wren's chapter house for St Paul's (which is integrated into the plan). They respond warmly to the use of brick and stone. They also praise the scheme for its mixture of offices and shops and its spatial organization with its large central piazza and pedestrian walkways that cut through the block and link the square to the surrounding urban fabric. They praise the square for being a true square and one that has lively settings consisting of links and places. Others dismiss the mixed-use nature of the square because the scheme fails to include any housing. Many critics would have preferred to have had heroic buildings representing the fragmented nature of society of the first decade of the twenty-first century, perhaps something like Melbourne's Federation Square.

The square is administered by the Paternoster Square Management office, owned by the Mitsubishi Estate Company (Vasagar 2012). The nature of quasi-public spaces everywhere is ambiguous and Paternoster Square is no different. Such spaces raise questions about the role of privately owned public open spaces (POPS) in the city. While the square, after the owners having given permission, hosts markets and small concerts, it precludes other activities. Political and protest meetings are barred. In 2012, paper signs in black, enameled metal frames placed at the entrances to the square warned that admission by right to enter could not be assumed (see Figure 4.3 (b) on p. 75). The signs were prompted by the Occupy London actions of October 2011 when police sealed off the entrances to the square to stop protesters from entering it because it is private property. Despite the square always being open to people – it is not gated, although Temple Bar has a gate – the public can still be barred from entering it as it is also private property.

8 Robson Square, Vancouver, Canada

A sunken, linear, dumbbell set of revitalized linked squares

Robson Square is a public plaza located in the heart of Vancouver on the former site of a surface parking lot. It lies across Robson Street running southwest to northeast aligned with the grid street pattern of the city's Central Business District. The square was part of a larger urban design project involving the development of the University of British Columbia (UBC) Continuing Education Centre, the British Columbia provincial government offices, the conversion of the old principal court building to the Vancouver Art Gallery and the creation of links to the Law Courts. It represents an effort by Arthur Erickson Architects and Cornelia Oberlander as the landscape architect to integrate buildings, landscape and sculptures into a unified design.

The square's composition can be traced back to a 1975 proposal to build a tower for the UBC Centre on the southwest of the site that would, given Vancouver's latitude of 49°N, have cast long shadows onto its surroundings. A long, low-rise building designed by Arthur Erickson, architect of the proposed tower, was substituted and completed in 1983 (Schelling 2009). As a result, despite its northern latitude, the square is full of light on sunny days. Running below ground level under Robson Street, the square links the UBC Centre to the Vancouver Art Gallery. The two ends of the square are thus destinations for students and visitors but the amount of movement between them is low. The square is surrounded by government office buildings, including the Law Courts, and by commercial buildings, but they offer little sense of enclosure. The square on the north side of the Gallery – the North Square – is often regarded as part of the overall design.

Considerable thought was given to the design of Robson Square in order to enhance the experience of Vancouver's downtown for both locals and tourists, particularly during the 2010 Winter Olympic Games. One idea was to cover the whole area across Robson Street with a roof, referred to as a clamshell. Instead domes were placed over the two open-to-air portions of the ice-rink that extends under Robson Street to keep rain off them, something highly desirable in

Vancouver's inclement winter climate. Robson Street was closed to vehicular traffic during the Olympics and remained so until reopened to traffic in December 2012. It was, at the time of writing, due to be re-closed during the summer months when it hosts food trucks, art installations and small markets.

Key Features[14]

Robson Square is located at an important spot in Vancouver's CBD; it provides a link between the city's major department stores and the Robson Street shopping area. Underground parking is available nearby and the square is only a block away from the Canada Line City Centre Station. It is thus easily accessible to workers in the CBD and a substantial number of local residents as well as people who come into the city from the suburbs. The square is the location of local markets, special events and protest meetings. On the north side of the Art Gallery away from Robson Square is North Square, which acts as a forecourt to the Gallery. Thus, the ground floor areas, the sunken plaza and North Square, with a little imagination, can be considered to be loosely linked squares.

Robson Square itself is a rather austere, typical gray concrete Modernist design. From both ends, the sunken square is reached by long sets of stairs and ramps. It has been refurbished and it catches the sunlight on a sunny summer day. The south-facing space at the north of Robson Street houses the outdoor café of the Art Gallery at

Figure 12.8 Robson Square looking southwest in 2014

the top of a set of steps that leads down to the ground level and then to the sunken part of the square (Figure 12.8). The steps are extensively used for seating on sunny days.

In summer, the rink accommodates programmed activities and events. Food is available from vendors at street level, intermittent food trucks and an outdoor café on the south side of the provincial offices that catches the sunlight. A number of sculptures enliven the square. The *Bird of Spring* is a bronze sculpture by the Inuit artist Abraham Etunga from Cape Dorset, in Canada's Nunavut Territory. Another sculpture, *Spring* is a large, red steel coil that appears to hold up the roof of the underpass under Robson Street which is the work of Chinese immigrant and artist Alan Chung Hung.

Analysis

Robson Square is another example where the location of a square in relationship to its surroundings and closeness to a critical mass of people is central to what a square can become. The square is located on major paths that people take in moving around central Vancouver so it is much enlivened by their comings and goings. To make a square a destination, it has to have potential behavior settings that attract visitors. Robson Square is rich in them; UBC's Centre, the Art Gallery, the Law Courts and offices as well as commercial buildings that edge the square provide a daily critical mass of people nearby. The square itself has the ice-rink, scheduled activities and nearby shops and restaurants that are themselves attractions.

Formal activities enliven sunken squares. Without the ice-rink or entry to the UBC Centre, few people would go down the stairways; very few would use the sunken part of the square to cross Robson Street. When there are strong magnets at both ends of an underpass – a dumbbell design – it will be used by people. Although that is true of Robson Square, many visitors, nevertheless, prefer to cross Robson Street at street level (Klassen 2012).[15] The stairs down to and up from the sunken portion of the square provide seating as well as enabling movement between levels.

Robson Square is a loosely closed square with dominant buildings at both ends. The surrounding buildings on the north and south abut the square directly, although on the other two sides, busy streets (Hornby Street and Howe Street) come between the square proper and the enclosing buildings. The varying heights of the surrounding buildings mean that in some areas the dimension of the square varies considerably from the 3:1 open area to building height ratio that is regarded as giving a good sense of enclosure. The trees, however, are used architecturally in lines that add to the definition of the square's open spaces.

The history of the development of Robson Square shows the concern for sunlight at high latitudes. In closed squares the quality of light is always important. In Vancouver with its mild, at times cloudy, year-round climate, access to sunlight is crucial to the success of an open space as a place that people want to be. The direction of sunlight illuminating Robson Square was an important part of its design. The northeast–southwest orientation of the square allows sunlight to enter it from the south. Lively open spaces can be created in squares sunken below street level but they require good light and formal activities to succeed. The glass and steel domes allow the light to penetrate to below ground level. When Robson Street is closed to vehicular traffic, food trucks and market stalls locate there spontaneously – they cannot access the sunken portions of the square.

As a work of architecture, Robson Square is a genuine design *tour de force*. Its design has won many awards, including one from the Royal Canadian Institute of Architects who praised it as a "bold contemplative work of urban design" and as "a linear urban park importing nature into the city" (*Globe and Mail* 2011: website). For the cognescenti, there is much to ponder. They may, for instance, recognize the bold horizontal lines and the use of concrete as typical of the work of Erickson. They will also recognize it as a well-functioning facility/infrastructure during and after the Olympic Games.

Although not strictly part of Robson Square, North Square with its fountain acts as the forecourt to the Art Gallery on the other side of the building to that facing Robson Square. Despite the bulk of the Gallery to its southern side, it is well enough lit to be made attractive. It is currently being refurbished. Supporters of that development dismiss Robson Square's claim to be the heart of downtown Vancouver; they believe that the North Square reincarnated will be the downtown's true public space. They claim it is smaller and better defined. Time and patterns of use will tell.

9 Olympic Plaza, Calgary, Canada

An amorphous park-like square and a created heart for a downtown

City of Calgary officials witnessed the outpouring of people's joy and their surging into the streets and squares of Sarajevo to celebrate the winning of a silver medal by a Yugoslavian skier, Jure Franko, at the 1984 Winter Olympics being held in the city. As a consequence they decided to have a proper venue for awarding medals at the 1988 Winter Olympic Games to be held in Calgary. Olympic Plaza was the result (Marr 2013).

Calgary Olympic Plaza was originally designed in 1987 by M. Paul Friedberg and Partners as landscape architects and Gibbs Gage Partnership as architects. It was built at a cost of only CDN$5.5 million to be the venue specifically for the medal presentation ceremonies at the 1988 Olympic Winter Games (Randl 2012). At the time, Calgary had a fairly quiet downtown particularly at night and at weekends, due to the lack of residential areas in its core and few places to hold large gatherings in a pleasant setting that would draw people into the city. A temporary site for such assemblies was created in Olympic Plaza. The square came alive during the presentation of the medals for the Olympics with as many as 30,000 people attending a ceremony, a number really beyond the capacity of the space. The success of the square as a venue during the Olympics showed public officials that the square had the potential for holding future events and other programmed activities that would draw people into the center of the city.

When the Games were over, downtown Calgary reverted to its old self. The core of the city emptied every evening and the plaza became a location for the homeless. It became clear to the city officials and to critical observers that the plaza had to be carefully designed, maintained and activated with programmed events.

Key Features[16]

The 1.2 hectare (3 acre) square lies in Calgary's municipal and cultural district at McLeod Trail and between 7th and 9th Avenues. Adjacent to the plaza across the streets are City Hall, the Centre for the Performing Arts and a number of commercial buildings. These surrounding buildings provide a poor sense of enclosure as they are set well back from the plaza, some across streets. One advantage of the location is that it is easily accessible by Calgary's C-Train that runs along one side of the square and has a stop at City Hall. On three sides the streets are full of traffic and the C-Train especially at rush hours. The fourth side is a pedestrian mall open to vehicular traffic at certain hours.

Today the park-like square has a number of distinct features. At its core is a large open space with a reflecting pool that has a colonnade and Olympic adornments along one side of it. *The Famous Five* sculpture[17] by Edmonton artist Barbara Peterson lies in one corner of the square. Large seating areas, picnic tables and benches, a stage and an open-air amphitheater are its other

Figure 12.9 *Olympic Plaza, Calgary: the reflecting pool on a summer day*

major features. The colonnade provides a backdrop to the reflecting pool when it is used as an ice skating rink in winter and to the events that take place there when it is drained. Directly opposite the reflecting pool is the small amphitheater and its concrete seating. Sponsored pavers with engravings and paths provide links around the periphery of the square. They enable people to cross it from one side to the other or to walk around its central area. The square is surrounded by deciduous and evergreen trees.

Located 51°N (comparable to Paternoster and Trafalgar Squares in London), the city has a continental climate with severe winters and warm summers. The central space, which has the city's only outdoor refrigerated surface, is used as a public ice-skating rink from November to mid-March. In summer it is a wading pool with fountains along its edge spraying water towards the middle (Figure 12.9).[18] As the plaza is large and not closely enclosed by buildings, the sun shines in year-round, although only for a short midday period and at a very low altitude in winter.

Analysis

Despite its limitations, Olympic Plaza is in many ways a successful place and an important location in Calgary. Some of the city's inhabitants argue that it is indeed the city's heart. The plaza contains a variety of settings – paved and grassed areas – and specific attractions such as the reflecting pool that acts as a focal point, the nuclear element, in the plaza. It thus consists of a varying nested set of behavior settings.

Places to hold programmed events are an important feature of life in many cities; squares may exist for no other purpose than to provide space for them. The original intent of the square, to hold a special event means that the design of the space facilitates this use very well. Olympic Plaza's almost flat paved surface of the reflecting pool when drained provides the platform for a range of activities. The easy access by the city's C-Train contributes to the success of these major events and festivals. Having a 'service road' along one edge of the plaza allows major equipment and event-related deliveries and maintenance vehicles to easily access the site. The City of Calgary does extensive work to program and support events in the square – in 2012, 40 events including concerts, plays, markets, festivals and ethnic group celebrations were held in it. The city administration maintains the square to a high standard which enables these events, regular and one-off, to be held throughout the year. They attract Calgarians and visitors, young and old, to the plaza. One major annual use of the square is related to the Calgary Stampede, an annual rodeo and festival held in July, attended by thousands of local and international visitors. This contributes to the profile of the square. Another memorable event was held in 2004, when over 30,000 fans packed the plaza to celebrate the Calgary Flames ice hockey team reaching the Stanley Cup finals.

The Calgary experience offers planners and designers a number of lessons. The limitations of the plaza arise from its surroundings as much as anything else. It is often empty of people. The plaza's size makes it suitable for large events but it lacks a feeling of intimacy due to the absence of a sense of enclosure that would turn it into a large outdoor room. Whatever sense of enclosure it possesses comes partly from the trees located on the sides of the plaza. On three sides of the square, the surrounding buildings and roads do not provide much of a sense of enclosure, nor do the activities they generate spill out directly into the plaza.

When places are not active or activated, transients such as the homeless see the opportunity to move in. This is especially the case with squares located in areas of cities with low night-time populations. Calgary's CBD is only full of people during working hours. What is needed to enliven the plaza is a cluster of residents and late-night activities nearby. They would make the people present in the park feel more secure.[19] The nearby East Village is currently being gentrified and redesigned to activate the east end of the Central Business District. The consequent change in the population composition may see more local residents using the square. Another lesson that is also now being learnt in New York is that temporary design changes or place-making events can illuminate the affordances of a place and lead to permanent changes.

Despite the success of all the events held in the square to date, the square still retains a negative reputation by many locals, especially at night. The plaza is, nevertheless, alive with people during the daytime, especially at midday, when many workers in the urban core come down to eat their lunches there. It also holds many memories for Calgarians, given its special event status.

10 Trafalgar Square, London, UK

A public landmark, a forecourt, an amorphous square, and a setting for events[20]

Trafalgar Square is an internationally known public space and tourist attraction in London's borough of the City of Westminster. The square commemorates the Battle of Trafalgar in 1805, a British naval victory of the Napoleonic Wars off the coast of Cape Trafalgar in southwest Spain. The original name was to have been 'King William the Fourth's Square' but George Ledwell Taylor, a London architect, suggested its present name. While the Greater London Authority manages the square, it is owned by the Queen of England by 'the right of the crown.' The City of Westminster owns the North Terrace, which was a road until 2003, and the roads on the other sides of the square.

Trafalgar Square, as we now know it, dates from the mid-nineteenth century when it was redesigned by John Nash, who was commissioned by King George IV. Sir Charles Barry oversaw the completion of the square in 1845. Small piecemeal additions have taken place over time including the addition of the lions designed by Sir Edwin Landseer in 1868; some statues were removed at that same time.

The square was refurbished in 2003 when the eastward traffic road, Pall Mall East, on the north side was closed and turned into a pedestrian terrace and others of the surrounding streets were narrowed. The retaining wall on the north side of the square was demolished and a broad set of steps installed to lead from the terrace down to the floor of the square. The design was undertaken by W. S. Atkins with Foster and Partners. In 2009, the fountains were fitted with new pumps capable of sending jets 24 meters (80 feet) into the air and an LED system was installed to shine colored lights in the fountains in time for the Summer Olympic Games held in London in 2012.

Key Features

The whole open space, including surrounding streets, is about 2.3 hectares (5.7 acres) in size with the square itself being only roughly 110 meters (360 feet) square in shape. It is easily reached from places throughout London. The Northern and Bakerloo underground lines have a stop at the square and a District Line station is nearby. Nineteen bus routes pass by the square. It is foolhardy to attempt to drive there and expect to easily find parking nearby.

The square itself consists of a large central paved area with *Nelson's Column* guarded by the four lions added in 1868 located off-center to the south on the north–south axis. Pedestals with statues stand in the corners of the square. Three have figures of once famous people on them while the fourth hosts changing contemporary art works. In 2000, the then Mayor of London, Ken Livingstone, wished to replace the statues with ones that had more meaning to today's public but his desire remains unfulfilled.

The square is a strong nuclear one despite the number of components in it that detract from the centrality of *Nelson's Column*. The 51.6 meters (169 feet 3 inches) in height Corinthian column is clearly the focus of attention. Its pedestal has four bronze panels; three depict Nelson's naval victories and the fourth Nelson's death. A sandstone statue of Nelson by Edward Hodges Bailey tops the column. Two fountains complete the composition of the square. They were originally purposefully placed to reduce the amount of space for crowds to assemble. Their location certainly makes for an uncomfortable space for large events to be held to its north but people do squeeze in. On a sunny day, spectators have to look into the sun to watch a performance.

The grand set of steps that leads from North Terrace into the square is paralleled by an elevator that provides access for the less able. A café and public toilets provide amenities for visitors. The National Gallery is the enclosing element along the whole north side. The other three sides are bounded by streets with a variety of buildings on them: the church of St Martin-in-the-Fields and South Africa House being on the east side and Canada House on the west. They provide only a loose sense of enclosure. The square is largely open on the south as a traffic circle handles the vehicles that move down to Whitehall and Westminster. In the circle is an equestrian statue of Charles I. The relationship of the height of surrounding buildings to the square is too low to provide more than a partial sense of enclosure but this lack of enclosure means that the square receives much sunshine on sunny days although it lies 52°N.

Analysis

The square is regarded internationally as the central one in London (Figure 12.10). Many Londoners claim that it is the city's heart; it certainly is for the West End. The layout may not be ideal but it affords the creation of many behavior settings. Probably the factors that make it so important are its size and easy accessibility via underground railway and by bus from all parts of London. This accessibility makes it a good place to meet people and for crowds to gather for political rallies, performances and celebrations. The National Gallery on its north is a major tourist attraction and other attractions lie nearby. The recently created North Terrace acts as a link to the National Gallery. The terrace has a simple design and is crowded with pedestrians on their own or in tour groups even on rainy days. The current director (cited in *The Economist* 2012: 89) of the National Gallery, nevertheless, finds that Trafalgar Square "lacks a sense of decorum as the forecourt to the gallery."

The square's overall composition with its various statues and fountains is fragmented. The lack of a large uncluttered open space does

Figure 12.10 *Trafalgar Square, London: (a) Aerial view, London Olympics celebration 2012; (b) Internal, south view of the square with the North Terrace in the foreground; (c) A view towards the North Terrace showing the new grand stairway and the National Gallery*

Sources: (a) Photograph by Peter Macdiarmid/Getty images; (b) Photograph by Claudio Divizia/Shutterstock.com.

not prevent a great range of events being held in the square. The plinth of *Nelson's Column* becomes a dais for speakers and, with it being at the southern edge of the square, it does provide an area for large gatherings to meet on its north. Each year at Christmas time, a Norwegian Spruce, a gift from Oslo, is set up in the square under the supervision of the city's mayor. The tree-lighting ceremony attracts many spectators. Spontaneous celebrations also occur after major football games, on New Year's Eve, and Canada Day is officially celebrated there.

The square does act as a link especially now that the grand stairway leading up to the North Terrace and the National Gallery is in place. Its utility as a link is, however, marred by the traffic that swirls around it on three sides. It thus is primarily a place with a variety of sub-settings. The traffic noise is a constant presence in the square but does not seem to inhibit activity. To some extent the sound of water splashing in the fountains mitigates the impact of outside sounds.

Although the square has little seating and the ledges around the fountains are generally too high to be comfortable to sit on, they are used as seating. They provide a good vantage point to watch the comings and goings of tour groups or just simply sit and rest or to have one's photograph taken. The fountains attract attention as do the pigeons that remain after a successful eradication program.[21] The lions that guard *Nelson's Column* have been clambered on so much that they are in danger of being damaged because they make an obvious backdrop for photographs. The fourth plinth in the square with its changing displays of contemporary art also attracts attention. The café and toilets located below the North Terrace are added amenities.

Historical celebrations, such as the Allied victory in Europe at the end of World War II, and the many protest meetings that have been held in the square over the years give Trafalgar Square an embedded history. The celebration of Nelson's victory over the French fleet at Trafalgar is meaningful to Britons while others might see the square as a celebration of imperial power of the British Empire. The cognescenti will likely be aware of the square's design history, who its designers are, who the statues are and who their sculptors were. There is also some intellectual historical design interest in its surroundings. The square does provide a place from which to admire the National Gallery and St Martin-in-the-Fields, a church whose design inspired many others, particularly in North America.

Trafalgar Square makes many lists of great public squares not simply because of its character but rather because of the number of events that have taken place there and currently occur there. Its central location and spaciousness are vital to its success. It is a true hard-surfaced urban square; trees only line two edges of the square on its eastern and western sides. Much public life in London is played out in Trafalgar Square as shown in Figure 12.10 (a) with the 2012 London Olympic Games Victory Parade.

11 The Capitol Square, Chandigarh, India

A large dominant and symbolic, Modernist but amorphous, square[22]

Chandigarh is the capital of two Indian states: Haryana and Punjab. It was built to be the capital of Indian Punjab when the state was divided into Indian and Pakistani components at Independence in 1947. Punjab was again reduced in size along linguistic lines with the formation of the Hindi majority area of Haryana from its eastern part. Chandigarh lies on the border between the two. It was designed by Le Corbusier with the collaboration of Maxwell Fry and Jane Drew and his cousin Pierre Jeanerette. It is a Rationalist scheme that marginally changed what Le Corbusier deemed to be an earlier "Anglo-Saxon" design created by Maciej (Matthew) Nowicki and Albert Meyer, by straightening the curving streets into a grid-iron pattern (Mumford 1954; Nilsson 1973). After Nowicki was killed in an airplane crash, Meyer lost interest in pursuing the project. Fry and Drew strongly urged the Indian and Punjab governments to hire Le Corbusier. Designing the city represents a turning point in Le Corbusier's career, forming the intellectual basis for his later work; the capitol complex is regarded as his supreme work. It is the best known and most frequently photographed architectural feature in the city (Lang 2002). The square provides a fine place to take photographs of the buildings.

Key Features

The capitol complex was designed by Le Corbusier, with B. V. Doshi as his site architect, to be a symbol of the new India. It was begun only four years after India gained its independence from British rule. The complex is comprised of three buildings and a large plaza (Figure 12.11). A fourth building, the Governor's palace, was proposed by Le Corbusier but rejected by Jawaharlal Nehru, India's premier, as too grand for a mere provincial administrator. Nehru was a strong supporter of the project because it fitted in with his vision of India's modern, socialist future (ibid.).

The complex sits in isolated splendor, removed from the city. It is surrounded by roughly grassed open space with deciduous trees planted in groups. It is not an urban setting. Passing traffic is not visible from the square as the adjacent roads are in trenches. Food vendors selling chai, coffee, basic foods and cigarettes have set up their stalls behind the buildings but not in the square. Makeshift parking lots are located on the periphery of the complex. In the architectural literature, little attention is given to such details. The complex is usually described in terms of its buildings; scant attention is paid to the square and its utility other than it being part of a grand urban vision of one of the twentieth century's major architects.

The layout of the complex is composed of two cross-axes on a monumental scale. The two most important buildings – the Legislature and the High Court – face each other across the plaza. The third building, the Secretariat is placed to one side behind the Legislature. The

placement is highly symbolic and stands in contrast to the British colonial arrangement at New Delhi where the Legislature was placed behind the Secretariat with the Viceroy's Palace at the head of the complex, signifying the power of the British Crown. Like New Delhi, however, Le Corbusier's proposal had the Governor's building at the head of the scheme. On a clear day the Shivalak Hills can be seen in the distance to the north.

The plaza is a vast space paved with concrete. It is one large behavior setting. It was designed to hold large gatherings and symbolically to 'out-do' the grand axial space of the government complex in New Delhi, designed by Sir Edwin Lutyens and Sir Herbert Baker. Today it contains only one of the three objects that Le Corbusier proposed to be placed in it: the *Open Hand* memorial. It is 26 meters (85 feet) tall, the largest of Le Corbusier's sculptures. The open hand is a recurring symbol in his work. Neither the Tower of Shadows nor the Governor's

Figure 12.11 The Capitol Square, Chandigarh: (a) Legislative Assembly Building; (b) Le Corbusier's **Open Hand** sculpture with the Legislative Assembly and Secretariat in the far distance; (c) The view southeast towards the High Court from the center of the square

Source: (a) Photograph by J. Palys/ Shutterstock.com.

mansion is likely to be built in the near future, if ever. If they were built, they would enhance the composition.

Analysis

It is difficult to assess the utility of the square today; it is surrounded by fencing and is off-limits to visitors, having been caught up in the turmoil of the political conflicts between India and Pakistan. The square is certainly oversized except as a symbolic gesture of grandeur. There is no sense of enclosure nor was one intended; it is an extreme example of an amorphous square. Its main function is to serve as part of an intellectual esthetic composition for the architectural expert's pleasure. It is not a destination in itself except for photographing the buildings. No critical mass of people exists nearby; it lies in an ex-urban setting. That isolation was an intended part of the design. The only people who go to the complex go to work or seek to resolve legal matters and they do not pass through the square. The square has never hosted large gatherings. It could hold spectacular military parades if seating in stands was provided for spectators. Architects and tourists arrive from India and around the world to pay homage to the design.

Chandigarh, at 31°N, is located not all that far from the Tropic of Cancer. In the summer between April and June, the temperature reaches over 40°C; the square is boiling hot not only from the direct rays of the sun but from the radiant heating from the concrete floor. It is impossible for locals to walk on the concrete bare-footed. In winter, chilly winds sweep across the square from the snow-covered mountains in the north. Whether the water runoff from the square during the monsoon rains has a scouring effect on the streams in the area is unknown. Such concerns were apparently not regarded as important; the grandeur of the monumental scale was.

The complex is inspiring to many architects and a source of pride for the general public. Some Indian architects see antecedents to the square in the layout of Fathepur Sikri of the Mughal emperor Akbar but it takes some creative imagination to see the link. Fathepur Sikri's layout consists of broken symmetries; the capitol complex at Chandigarh, with its axial layout, is closer to a symmetrical design. The buildings at each end of the axis that make it a dominant square are exemplars of Le Corbusier's œuvre and an esthetic precedent for his later work.

The architecture is a continuation of a line of thought that began 20 years earlier with his proposal for the League of Nations building (1927). The turning of standard building components into sculpture, the use of bright primary colors, the parasol shell forms and the contrasting of shadow and light were all new to architecture. Concrete was the major material employed, enabling the dramatic roof forms, bold sculptural and vertical elements and the *brise-soleil* to be created. The cognoscenti will know of the impact of his Chandigarh designs on Le Corbusier's architecture and reputation. They may know of the impact of his visits to the power station in Ahmedabad with its cooling towers on the design of the Legislature. They will appreciate, given their own values, the role that design ideas and precedents played in his professional life. Along with the general public and tourists, they may appreciate the significance of the open hand monument and its representation of 'peace' and 'the giving and receiving of ideas' (Lang 2002). Lay-people may not know of this relationship but they will, at least, be awed by the scale of the square and the buildings. The buildings and plaza were designed with an understanding of the quality of materials and workmanship that was available at the time in India. Le Corbusier's work set a precedent for later buildings in Chandigarh based on his forms so much so that the label 'Chandigarh architecture' is applied to them.

The plaza was designed with two functions in mind. The first is to provide a setting for the buildings and be a symbol of the new India. The second was to afford large gatherings. The former is clear in the design, the latter may still occur. What their nature might be is open to conjecture. An opportunity was lost to make the square something that really serves as the heart of Chandigarh. It remains a space isolated from the city waiting to be engaged. Today it is "a desolate, concrete pavement; nobody crosses it and nobody lingers there," as noted by Khilnani (1997: 134). To many of the cognescenti, this quality does not matter; it is the architectural idea of Le Corbusier that counts. To lay-people, the square is an awe-inspiring space. As Nehru said: "The capitol complex will make everybody sit up and think" (Lang et al. 1997: 311).[23]

12 Oxford Square, Sydney, Australia

A partially sunken, pocket, public square that is primarily a link[24]

Oxford Square is located on the northern side of a busy street on the edge of Sydney's Central Business District.[25] It was built to eliminate the awkward intersection that existed between two streets, which meet at right angles, and Oxford Street, which the two meet at a 45° angle. The layout of the square has been altered a number of times since it was first closed to vehicular traffic. The present version was created in 1988.

The neighborhood surrounding Oxford Square is a busy one. Adjacent Oxford Street consists of two-, three- and four-story buildings abutting each other. On the ground floor the street is lined with small shops selling a variety of products and hosting a number of service providers. Above them are apartments and commercial firms. Across Oxford Street from the square are pubs, shops, restaurants and apartment buildings, including one called Oxford Square. The street is a major bus route from Sydney's CBD to the city's eastern and southeastern suburbs; a bus stop is located near Oxford Square. The surrounding area is known for its LGBTI community with an annual Gay and Lesbian Mardi Gras parade occurring alongside Oxford Square in February/March, attracting tens of thousands of spectators. The area's night-time economy, with bars and nightclubs that have both a straight and a gay clientele, is of great importance to the City of Sydney which is investing in this precinct's creative and cultural activities.

The southern, sunny, side of the Riley Street block, next to the site, has a number of cafés that have a substantial patronage, especially on weekend mornings. It is also the location of apartments and subsidized artists' studios. Burton Street consists of three-story terrace/row houses, many of which have been divided into apartments and have small corner shops or cafés on the ground floor. A number of commercial art galleries can also be found in the neighborhood. Given its context, one might expect Oxford Square to be full of people sitting in it, but it is not. It is a weak place but it is an important link. Many people pass through the square. Using behavior mapping techniques, Bishop and Marshall (2014) found that between peak times of 5pm and 7pm on weekdays, more than 4,100 pedestrians passed through this very small square. Even between midnight and 2am on a typical weekend, 300 people were passing through or 'hanging out' in this space.

Key Features

The square consists of three components: the paved area below Oxford Street with circular planter boxes that have broad but sloping edges, a promontory off Oxford Street with an ornate, historical drinking fountain, and a curved link between Oxford and Burton Streets (Figure 12.12). The square's floor level is as much as 3 meters (10 feet) below Oxford Street with a vertical, face-brick lined retaining wall on its southern, Oxford Street, side. A cast concrete balustrade

Figure 12.12 *Oxford Square, Sydney; a view towards Burton Street*

lines part of the top of the retaining wall and provides for the safety of pedestrians walking down the street. It also provides potential seating although the sharp drop for anybody falling off into the lower part of square is a deterrent. A large quarter-circular planter box at the Oxford Street level provides a sunlit place to sit. The other part of the upper edge of the square has an iron fence. In addition, benches lining the Oxford Street sidewalk on the street separate the sidewalk from the square. They face the street, not the square.

The floor of the square is paved with tiles. In addition to the three planter boxes as mentioned, the square contains three spindly plane trees and an ornate light standard. The ground floor of the two-story building on the northern side of the square has a glass-fronted café and doorways that are entrances to the apartments above it.[26] Tables with folding chairs are placed in the square to provide outdoor seating for the café. People sit there from time to time but they do not turn the square into an active place. A nightclub is also located on the north side of the square bringing it to life late at night and in the early hours of the morning, as noted by Bishop and Marshall (2014) above. People do sit on the steps and ledges during the day but they seldom linger. The drinking fountain is a small-scale landmark but is not used as a place to meet; there is no seating there from which people could pause to rest or watch the activity on Oxford Street.

Analysis

As an environment, the square affords a number of behavior settings but little occurs there. The square shows the importance of a number of the features that make for lively squares, not because it possesses them but because it does not. The first has to do with the quality of light. Sydney is located at latitude 34°S and the mid-summer sun reaches a height of 83° above the horizon. Despite this altitude, the square, being small and located to the south of a two-story building, is in shadow throughout the year, except on a late summer afternoon when the setting sun swings over to the southwest. The brick retaining wall reflects very little light into the square. On a hot summer day when one might think the coolness of the square would be an attractive place to sit in the shade, it is still hardly occupied. The sunlit cafés on the south side of Burton Street provide a more pleasant place to linger. The public toilets nearby might be regarded as a positive amenity but the odors that frequently emanate from them do not help.

The square serves primarily as a link between the three streets that meet there. Many people tend to by-pass the center of the square despite the set of steps in the foreground of Figure 12.12. Given the number of pedestrians who do travel through the square itself, many people take the stairway or ramp from Oxford Street to Burton Street and thus do not pass through the heart of the square. The steps are easy to negotiate and follow the desired lines of pedestrian travel. Although a café is located on the square, it does not attract a large clientele at any time so it does not activate the square to any significant degree. Although the rims of the planter boxes afford places to sit, they are seldom sat on as they are uncomfortable for that purpose. In contrast, a single place on the edge of the planter box on Oxford Street is quite frequently used; it provides a better view. It is also a sunnier spot than the edges of the planter boxes in the square itself.

The people walking through the square provide some potential interest to others sitting in it but they do not attract much attention. The square is something to look down into rather than up out of it – even so, few passing pedestrians give it a second glance. The diversity of passers-by on Oxford Street cannot be seen from within the square. The only time the square really comes to life as a place is in the early hours of weekend mornings when the clientele of the nightclub spills out onto the square. The concrete pavers are greatly stained with the residue of chewing gum which is not easy to clean off. The windows in the buildings surrounding the square do afford opportunities for natural surveillance but they are not heavily occupied during the day.

The square acts as a minor landmark on Oxford Street because it provides a break in the line of shop windows and walls that are built to the property line on the south side of the street, all the way from Hyde Park in the city's Central Business District to a more significant open space, Taylor Square, to the east. Oxford Square is not a node in Kevin Lynch's (1960) terms, despite the paths crossing there, so it and its affordances are not really noticed. Passers-by are kept away from the square's edge by the benches on the inside of the sidewalk so they do not automatically look down into it; nor are there any activities in the square to catch their eye. The passers-by probably do not know the name of the square but associate Oxford Square with the tall apartment building across the road from it. The ornate small metal kiosk that houses the drinking fountain is in an isolated position, which makes drinking from it easy (when it is functioning), but it hardly catches the eye as it is not directly in the path of people's movement.

Oxford Square illustrates the difficulty of making a sunken plaza an active one. It has been thoughtfully designed to serve as a link. It has a ramp for bicycles, the less able-bodied, or people pushing baby carriages to move from Oxford Street to Burton Street. The square has been carefully detailed with fine brickwork and paving. It is not, however, a place in which to linger. The square serves its purpose as a link and, unless it was raised to be level with Oxford Street, it will remain simply a public space to pass through. There is neither much to attract people nor is there much about the square for the cognescenti to ponder. Unfortunately, it has been included as a case study to be representative of the many, lesser-known sunken squares found in cities around the world.

13 Pershing Square, Los Angeles, USA

A loosely enclosed, articulated square and a park symbolic[27]

Pershing Square, located in the historic core of Los Angeles's financial district, is the city's major central public open space. The square was founded in 1866 as the Plaza Abaja but was renamed after World War I in honor of General (Black Jack) Pershing, Commander-in-Chief of the American Expeditionary Force. The square has been redesigned several times over the years. For example, as it was regarded as an eyesore, it was renovated for the 1984 Summer Olympic Games that were held in the city. The most recent design was a US$14.5 million complete renovation designed by Ricardo Legoretta and Laurie Olin in 1994. The square they inherited lay above an underground parking garage and consisted of a lawn with trees and diagonal paths that met at a central point where it contained two reflecting pools. They had been donated by a Hungarian immigrant, Kelly Roth, in honor of his wife.

From the 1950s to the 2000s, suburbanization depleted central Los Angeles of its middle-class workers and resident inhabitants and much of its liveliness. The surrounding neighborhoods became heavily populated by men living in single-room occupancy units. The square grew to have an unsavory reputation. By the late 1980s, as noted by Loukaitou-Sideris and Banerjee (1998), it had become a place where many homeless, the poor and some drug addicts gathered. The behavior settings it contained were seen in a negative light by the general public. The square was run-down and the furnishings vandalized. The immediate surroundings of the square, nevertheless, have fine buildings from the 1920s that provide a partial sense of enclosure to it. They are distant enough, given Los Angeles's location of 34°N, for the square to receive sunlight throughout the year.

This review of Pershing Square is important because it illustrates the difficulties of trying to self-consciously communicate specific meanings through design. The goal of the redesign was to create a square with potential behavior settings and meanings that would have a broad appeal to the public. Symbolically, its objective was to represent both the Latino and Anglo populations of the city. It thus had to have positive referents for the two populations. A competition that attracted many entries from prestigious firms was held for the redesign of the square. The winning scheme by Legoretta and Olin was never fully implemented but its major components can be seen in place today (Figure 12.13 (b)). Legoretta attempted to create a *zócalo*, the square at the heart of many Mexican cities, but it is difficult to see the connection in the design of Pershing Square. *Zócalos*

Figure 12.13 Pershing Square, Los Angeles: (a) Pershing Square before revitalization; (b) An aerial view of the redesigned square

Source: (a) The Los Angeles Public Library; (b) Photograph by Alex Bandea/Flickr.

are usually uniform flat surface squares, but Pershing Square is an articulated square with a number of sub-areas at different levels.

Key Features

The square is a full Los Angeles city block; it is 2.2 hectares (5.4 acres) in size. It is bounded on all sides by streets carrying heavy traffic. It is raised 1 meter (3 feet 3 inches) above the street level so that the existing parking garage built in 1952 could be retained without significant changes made to it. The entrances to the parking garage are directly from the adjacent streets somewhat cutting off easy access to the square for pedestrians. In addition to driving there, visitors can reach the square by the two lines of the LA Metro and by buses of the public transportation system.

In the center of the square is an orange grove that serves as a reminder of the importance of orange farming in the history of Los Angeles County. A sculpted court with a fountain occupies the southern end of the square and the fault line that runs through Los Angeles is represented by a jagged line, designed by Barbara McCarren, cutting across it. A starred paving pattern resembles the stellar constellations visible in the city during the winter. The square also contains a ten-story purple bell tower, a 'Mayan-style' amphitheater, benches in which images of Los Angeles are imprinted, planter boxes with ledges at seat height, works of art and mementos of the past. The bell tower, aqueduct and orange spheres were designed by Legoretta to represent the flow of water from the mountain chain, the Sierra Nevada on the east of Los Angeles, down to the orange groves (Olin 2012). The square also houses a statue of Eugene A. Obregon, a Mexican-American hero of the Korean War. The variety of spaces in the square affords the creation of many communal behavior settings. However, it is the formal ones that have proven to be what enlivens the space.

Analysis

Today the square remains largely free of communal behavior settings. The former homeless and transient inhabitants have been moved on by the police but a number still linger in the square. The benches continue to provide places for the homeless to gather. Regular formal gatherings in the form of rallies, the celebration of events, and programs for children are successful in attracting people and temporarily activating the square. In winter, an ice-rink proves to be popular but at a typical midday only a handful of workers in the surrounding buildings eat their lunches in the square. The presence of too many panhandlers makes middle-class people feel awkward or unwelcome in the space. The square remains largely deserted and although it does not possess the unsavory reputation of its past, it is still regarded as an unattractive place to visit.

The presence of the underground garage and the square being 1 meter (3 feet 3 inches) or higher above the sidewalk create a problem difficult to overcome. The reason why the square is seldom lively lies not with the square itself but with its surroundings; the area does not contain the critical mass of people who could potentially enliven the square. Despite the density of buildings, central Los Angeles is remarkably uncrowded. Heavy traffic on nearby roads and the entrances to the underground parking parallel to the square hinder easy access to it for pedestrians.

The square consists of a number of settings. Time will tell whether they hold up well and the design of the square proves to be robust. The public varies in its ability to understand the symbolic meanings of the numerous components of the square even though signs explain the meanings to them. Instead they see concrete spheres, uncomfortable seating and a bell tower that has little significance for them. Other design features of the square are more directly problematic. The raised entryways on the corners are uninviting; it is better to go down 1 meter into a square than up 1 meter into it. Although the entrances are easy enough to negotiate, they seem to convey symbolically a 'keep out' message to any potential visitors. Similarly the 'coercive design' features such as the arched seating and railings that are meant to keep the homeless from sleeping in the square do not have the 'sit-on-me' invitational quality that people generally seek (Lang 2005).

The urine odors in many parts of the square caused, in particular, by homeless men are unpleasant. The area in the northeast of the square that is lined with palm trees is referred to colloquially as "urinal alley." The sonic ambient quality of the square with the cars and trucks driving by, although not overwhelming, is another minor deterrent for middle-class people and children to use the square. There are many elements in the square to climb on that would make it a good behavior setting as a playground for children if it was an attractive place for their parents to visit. The redesign of the square shows that changing a design does not necessarily change the communal use of a square, but that it can be designed to afford formal gatherings in a satisfactory manner.

The Friends of Pershing Square, a public interest group, believes that a number of changes should be made to the square to make it more inviting, as documented by Yen (2013): (1) the surrounding walls should be demolished so that people can see into the square; (2) the long driveways parallel to the sidewalks that are used to get into the parking garage should be replaced with perpendicular ones; (3) the sidewalks around the square should be widened; (4) parallel to these sidewalks should be tables with inlaid chessboards and other similar amenities; (5) the square should be de-cluttered to make it possible to use it as a diagonal link; and (6) the square should have a café or restaurant. As noted by Yen (ibid.), the organization believes that it should be more like New York's Bryant Park (designed by Pershing Square's landscape architect Laurie Olin) or San Francisco's Union Square. Such thinking shows the importance of learning from case studies in the design fields. In the meantime, a US$700,000 renovation paid for by local business interests is underway. It represents another effort to make Pershing Square a meaningful place. It is, however, the surrounding environment that also needs to change.

The nature of central Los Angeles is being upgraded; it is becoming re-inhabited as many people, including families, discover the benefits of central city apartment living. In late 2014, a $2 million proposal to further revamp the square was announced, including two children's playgrounds, each catering to a specific age group (Evans 2014). These playgrounds opened in 2015. A new design competition was also announced in 2015 with the winner to be announced in 2016. The Executive Director of Pershing Square Renew Inc. (2015: website) has stated: "Their challenge isn't to win awards; it's to win over hearts. More than anything else, these groups [the designers] need to focus on the experiences their design will inspire and the memories the Square will create." It will be interesting to see whether the square achieves any goals set for it in this new process. It remains a square in waiting relying on formal programming to temporarily enliven it. It serves such occasions well enough but it could do more (Yen 2013). If it does, the entrance to the Biltmore Hotel that was changed so that it is not facing the square may well be returned to be on it, adding to the activation of the square.

14 Schouwburgplein, Rotterdam, The Netherlands

A large, amorphous civic square and a clash between intellectual and experiential esthetics

Cities of the Netherlands such as Amsterdam, Utrecht, Groningen and Maastricht possess fine closed squares surrounded by three- and four-story, richly surfaced and detailed buildings. These squares are full of daily life and carry symbolic meanings as hearts of their cities. Schouwburgplein, also known as Theater Square, is different. Created as part of Rotterdam's 1985 Inner City Plan, it was designed to be a modern square for contemporary ways of life. Its design was not based on empirical realities but rather on a Rationalist desire to create something new and better. The emphasis was placed on making a setting for large gatherings and a place that was a self-conscious work of art.[28] Schouwburgplein was designed to be a hard urban open area rather than an intimate space or a garden square. Its aim was to reinforce Rotterdam's brand as a modern city.

Completed in 1996, Schouwburgplein was designed by West 8 Urban Design & Landscape Architecture (led by Adriaan Geuze and Jerry Van Eyck) on the site of an earlier square that was dreary and lifeless. The design team embraced "the artificiality of the post-industrial world" (Ouroussoff 2005: website). The square's design was predicated on its use for large events – markets, concerts and rallies – and its presentation as a display, as a work of art. It was partially renovated in 2010 to correct some problems primarily with flooring materials. Time will tell if it needs further renovation.

Key Features

The square is a large open space (12,250 square meters; 3 acres), located in the heart of Rotterdam. On two sides it is bounded by important buildings – the municipal theater, designed by W. Quist, a concert hall and the Pathé Cinema complex, designed by Koen van Velsen. Across Karel Doormanstraat on its east, but separated from it, are restaurants and shopping malls, all of which are potential but not effective, generators of activities in the square. Within an easy radius of the square is a large catchment of people, both workers and residents. The city's central station and bus terminal are located a couple of blocks away and trams and buses pass by the square.

Following the precedent of the great squares of Italy, Schouwburgplein is a hard square; it has no plantings. It deviates from the traditional Italian squares in that it is an amorphous rather than a closed square. Except for a small portion between the theater and cinema, no commercial uses face immediately onto it. The square's surface is raised 0.35 meter (14 inches) above the street level which, while partially segregating it from the surrounding restaurants and shops, allows natural light to penetrate the parking garage below. It also makes the center of the square a very large stage. Much attention was paid to flooring materials and the surface, like that of Federation Square in Melbourne, is a work of abstract art. The square is divided into functional (in a narrow Modernist sense) areas. Each is weakly demarcated into territories by the nature of its flooring material but which are hardly obvious to the casual observer.

Outside the businesses are standard metal panel floors and near the benches and lights the floor is of wood and rubber. In the sun-illuminated areas the surface has mosaics of timber, resin, rubber and metal panels. In 2010, the smooth metal plates were replaced by wood and epoxy resin was roughened to make it easier to walk on, especially for those people with mobility issues or wearing high-heeled shoes.

For the avant-garde esthetic quality of the square, the designers drew their inspiration from the city's industrial and waterfront past. Three ventilation towers line the street edge. At night, they are lit from within. The 35 meter-high (115 foot) hydraulic light masts are colloquially seen to be 'desk lamps.' Their arms go up and down like oil pumps under the control of the public. The Karel Doormanstraat side of the square – the side which has the best sunlight – is lined with narrow wooden benches that are heavily used on a sunny day. In Rotterdam's cool temperate climate with its location 53°N, the benches are welcome. Much of the square, however, can be an unpleasant space when winds channel through it.

The lighting quality of the square is a work of art. Instead of flooding the square in a uniform quality of light or simply highlighting some features, as is common in many squares around the world today, or following the tradition of Times Square or Piccadilly Circus by focusing on the surrounding walls, white/green/black fluorescent panels in the square are lit from below.

Analysis

Schouwburgplein is a large, open area that is bathed in bright light on a sunny day, but even when there are people strolling within it, it seems empty. Even when Karel Doormanstraat, the street that runs down its eastern side, is full of people, few individuals meander across to the square. Its layout affords little for the development of communal behavior settings (Figure 12.14). Seeing the square during a standard week or weekend day reinforces its image as a place for formal, programmed events and little else. There is no reason to linger in the square; nothing holds the attention of a visitor. The concert hall and municipal theater both generate flows of people but only at specific hours. The location of the surrounding land uses and building functions do not make the square a link among them, so few people cross it (Koh 2014). In a study by sociologist Thaddeus Muller (cited in Hoogstad 2009) the regular users of the space have a more positive attitude to the square than most citizens of Rotterdam. It is not, however, a place for people to sit and enjoy the day while watching the passing scene (ibid.).[29]

The business and establishments on the periphery of the square tend to be introverted; life is within them. The square attracts few

Figure 12.14 Schouwburgplein, Rotterdam, in 2013: (a) Children on a school outing; (b) A parking garage entrance; (c) Noon on a sunny spring day looking north; the light masts are on the right

buskers because there are few people there to be entertained. It is not a child-friendly space; it offers them little although children do clamber on the roofs of the entrances to the underground parking garage (Figure 12.14 (b)). The square with its pop-up electrical socket connections providing power to temporary stalls affords the efficient instalment of exhibitions and markets. These types of events contribute a life to the square.

The lamp standards and the entrances to the parking are art works themselves in otherwise stark surroundings – these are of interest to visitors. The composition has been much lauded by leading architectural critics such as Nicolai Ouroussoff (2005) and the late Ada Louise Huxtable (2005) as well as designers such as Helena Gentili (2014) as a work of art. It is also a display of the sculptural elements it contains and the major civic buildings around it. To critics who perceive the design as incurring substantial opportunity costs, the square is an example of architects paying less attention to civic life and more to creating an expressive design.

Designs can be evaluated, first, in terms of their goals, and, second, whether the design has met those goals. The appropriateness of the qualities sought by municipal authorities and the designers in Schouwburgplein is open to much debate. Should Schouwburgplein have been more than a place for large events and a work of art? Should it have been a Trafalgar or Times Square – a true heart of a city? Schouwburgplein certainly caters for large events better than either of those two places. However, observers and critics seeking a lively place on an ordinary sunny day are disappointed. Interestingly, one of its original designers, Adriaan Geuze, recognizes that the square did not turn out as intended. He has been contracted to give the square a facelift (Gentili 2014). It will be interesting to see what it achieves.

The Project for Public Spaces (PPS) group (n.d.) believes that a square should be more than a place to hold programmed events; it should be alive at other times. Critics of PPS such as Schneider (2010) say that it compares Schouwburgplein with an idealized image of what a square should be. The square is primarily a space to be looked at and admired and is indeed a success on this dimension especially at night when it is illuminated. It appeals then to both the general public and the intellectuals (ibid.).

The conclusion one draws from this analysis is that perceptions of what is required of a public space differ. There is a consensus that Schouwburgplein has a dramatic Postmodern design, that it is a showpiece of avant-garde landscape art. It is an original, monumental and elegant, but ultimately, a cold place. Over time the surrounding uses may change when entrepreneurs recognize the opportunities presented by the square and open onto it. The amorphous nature of the square in relation to its immediate context does, however, make it difficult to achieve this without a major reorganization of the whole open area of the square, including its adjacent streets.

15 The Guggenheim Museum Forecourt, Bilbao, Spain

A museum forecourt that is a dominant, amorphous square[30]

The forecourt of the museum was selected for analysis here to see what lessons can be learned from a situation in which a square is dominated by a featured landmark building, or in contemporary architectural terms, an iconic building. Its aim was to help the Basque people communicate its independent identity (Vidharte 2002). The forecourt is one part of the space that surrounds the museum, making the building a 'gem' placed as a display in an open setting.

The decision made in the 1980s to build a prestigious museum was part of the effort to transform Bilbao from being a declining, rusty, industrial river port city into an important cultural center. Along with other major infrastructure developments designed by internationally renowned architects, the museum has had a major catalytic effect on changing the image of Bilbao and on major property investment in the adjacent Abandoibarra area of the city. The museum is the best known of all the developments in the city that formed part of the *Bilbao Ria 2000 Plan* (Lang 2005).

When the Solomon R. Guggenheim Museum was looking for a second European site for a museum (the first is in Venice), the Basque administration was looking for a potential donor for such an institution. An agreement was reached between the two whereby the Basque government would pay for the building while the Solomon R. Guggenheim Museum would provide the exhibitions. The site selected was a former industrial/port area loosely located at the center of a triangle formed by the Arriaga Theatre, the University of Deusto and the fine arts museum. A limited competition was held for the design of the building. It was won by Frank Gehry over Arata Isozaki and Coop Himmelblau.

The museum is a shell consisting of a series of interlocking volumes, some formed of orthogonal coated stone and some of curved forms covered by a titanium skin. The armature consists of a steel framework similar to that provided by Auguste Bartholdi for New York's Statue of Liberty. The interior of the building has linked bridges connecting 18 galleries spread over three floors. Of the 32,500 square meters (345,000 square feet) of the site, 24,000 square meters are occupied by the building, of which 9,066 square meters are devoted to exhibition space (Lang 2005). The building is *the* work of art. It is unusual in that it is lauded by architects, critics, academics and the lay public alike (Paul Goldberger, as reported by Tyrnauer 2010). The setting of the museum has, however, received relatively little attention in the public discourse.

Key Features

The open space in which the Guggenheim Museum sits consists of three main parts. The forecourt is on the southern side facing into the city (Figure 12.15). A set of steps on the west leads down to the

Figure 12.15 The forecourt of the Guggenheim Museum, Bilbao, 2008

Source: Photograph by Corkery Consulting.

Nervión River. An esplanade running along the south bank of the river leads to a northern forecourt to the museum where its group entrance is located. This base level is well below that of the city center, enabling the top of the museum to be level with that of the city's buildings. As Bilbao is located 43°N, the southern face of the museum is illuminated by the sun, when it is shining, throughout the year.

The southern forecourt in front of the Guggenheim is the largest of these spaces. It extends over two roads and so provides a direct pedestrian link to the old city. It now houses Jeff Koons' mammoth sculpture, *Puppy*. Some seating on the periphery of the forecourt is provided as a place for a few visitors to rest. As a link, the forecourt provides a clear view of the building from the city side, but not of the entrance to the building. The entrance is tucked away down a sloping set of stairs. Unlike most museums there is no grand staircase to the museum's portal. The 1 meter (3 foot 3 inches) treads of the stairs are long in comparison to their risers. They require some attention when one goes down them as the spacing is unusual. On the left of the forecourt as one faces the museum is the café; it is the only part of the interior that in any way looks out onto the forecourt. It is richer in potential behavior settings than the museum's forecourt.

The open area at the northern façade of the museum faces the Nervión River and tends to be the place to where visitors to the museum find their way. It provides a space for visiting groups to gather and get organized when they arrive or depart from the museum. When waiting they either sit and enjoy the views of the river or walk along the esplanade. Although it faces north, more places exist where people can sit either on the grass, on ledges or on the benches than in the museum's forecourt.

Analysis

The museum, along with other major investments in Bilbao, has had a major catalytic effect on property development in the city and thus on its income through an increase in its tax base. The visitors to the museum have generated a considerable further income to the city by their day-to-day expenditures. The investment by the Basque government has indeed transformed the city. It has, however, focused on enhancing the city's infrastructure and buildings rather than on the quality of the city's public realm. The Guggenheim was supposed to "integrate into the city's urban structure" and the forecourt could have been used to do that (Lang 2005: 123). A chance to create a well-detailed urban design that enhances the life of Bilbao was lost. The museum remains an object in space detached from the city.

The building is said to be sensitive to its urban environment because of its height and the materials of which it is made. The height difference between the river and the city made it possible to have a taller building on the site than the norm in the city's center and still have its apex no higher than those of the buildings opposite. Limestone with a sandy hue was selected especially for the Guggenheim to make it similar to the materials of the buildings of the city. The forecourt meets the city well but is not part of it.

There is little in the design of the forecourt that makes it a great asset to the city. It functions well enough as a forecourt but it also represents an opportunity cost. It lacks detail and contains no attractions to make it a place that people want to be other than to view and take photographs of the museum and gain access to it. It is not a 'place' or an urban square that attracts locals as it provides no amenity for them. The blank walls of the Guggenheim provide neither signs of life within the building from the outside nor do they afford any natural surveillance opportunities from within the building of the spaces around it. The forecourt simply provides a link from the sidewalk to the building and a location from which to contemplate the museum's sculptural qualities. *Puppy* certainly helps reduce the visual size of the forecourt and adds an element of interest to it. The complex contains a cutting-edge building that is setting a precedent for new early twenty-first-century 'signature' buildings which may also stand alone as objects in space.

What, then, are the limitations of the forecourt as a place rather than simply a link? As a place and as part of the city, the forecourt breaks the rhythm of the existing blocks and follows the Modernist paradigm of setting buildings as objects in space rather than as space makers. This observation can be regarded in positive terms as breaking from the shackles of the city's industrial past, or in negative terms, as an over-bearing display. In either case the forecourt fails to enhance the quality of the pedestrian experience of the city's inhabitants. The unassuming stairs from the forecourt to the entrance of the museum are a unique contribution to museum design.[31] Although architecturally provocative, the stairs provide neither a comfortable walkway going down or up nor a comfortable place to sit. People, primarily young people, nevertheless, do sit on them. They tend to be in the way of those people seeking to enter the museum but cause no hardship.

The forecourt as a work of art might be regarded as a great Minimalist success; as a link it is fine although few people approach the museum from the city side. As a place for people to be, the forecourt offers very little. *Puppy*, as a nuclear element in the square, does give the square some focus. The forecourt has little sense of enclosure; there are no structures other than the museum opening onto it. No amenity, such as a café or shop that would generate life, spills out onto the forecourt. There are no eyes looking down into it providing people with a sense of security. The forecourt has the reputation, deserved or not, of being a place where muggings occur (PPS n.d.). It certainly possesses none of the characteristics of a "defensible space" in Oscar Newman's (1972) terms. The same observation holds for the river side of the building although with its varied types of seating, the river and people walking along the esplanade, it is a more pleasant space to be in than the forecourt. As a behavior setting, the forecourt, itself, is a link not a place.

16 North and South Shanghai Railway Station Squares, Shanghai, People's Republic of China

Two contrasting closed squares designed to hold masses of travelers a couple of times a year[32]

Many railway stations have squares in front of them. Some are of historical note, others are more recent.[33] Some, such as Place Charles Béraudier in Lyon, are closed squares and lively places through much of the day (see Figure 6.6 (b) on p. 110); others are amorphous squares and boring spaces. Most station squares act as reception areas and, when the buildings are grand edifices, as foregrounds to them. They are dominant squares. Some act solely as links between sidewalks and station; others are places full of life with hotels, shops, cafés and restaurants nearby. They see waves of people ebb and flow over the course of a day, week and year. Some stations handle a vast number of people on specific days and are empty otherwise. The Shanghai Railway Station Squares are examples of this. Their dilemma is even greater than most. The demand for travel at the Chinese New Year is huge as urban residents return to their regional homes but for the rest of the year the squares lie relatively vacant.

Shanghai Railway Station, located on Moling Road in the Zhabei District of Shanghai, is one of three major stations in the city. It is administered by the Shanghai Railway Bureau. The station was reconstructed in 1987 to be the city's main station and handle the

Figure 12.16 North and South Squares at Shanghai Station: (a) South Square: view of the station from the square; (b) North Square: view of the station from the square

Source: Both photographs by Cheng Ma.

largest amount of traffic of all the stations in the city. Locals refer to it as the New Station because it replaced the Shanghai's old North Station. It is the terminus of the main Beijing to Shanghai route and many other long-haul trains that go to the Jiangshu and Anhui provinces as well as to the north. On the north and the south of the station are large open spaces – North Square and South Square – that are connected by a tunnel that lies to the east of the station (Figure 12.16). Both are served by metro stations and both provide access to the stations' ticketing booths and to the stations' platforms.

In 2008, in order to handle the increased load of passengers arriving for the 2010 World Exposition, the station was further increased in size. North Square was redeveloped in order to reduce its congested nature and opened to the public in May 2010. Before redevelopment it contained a bus station and was the entrance to the railway station for working-class people. The north building was extended from 10,000 square meters (108,000 square feet) to 15,560 square meters (167,000 square feet) and the south building was refurbished. The North Square was then constructed. Not only is the railway station a destination but also the long distance bus station that is located off North Square draws additional travelers into the area.

Key Features

The two squares differ in character. South Square is a paved, nuclear square with a four-faced clock tower in the center as its focal point. The clock tower is raised three steps up on a circular platform. The steps act as seating. The station building is a dominant structure on its north. The square is a very loosely closed one with the enclosing buildings creating a fragmented façade around it. This fragmented character is reinforced by the flow of traffic around the open space of the square on all four sides. A number of covered entrances at its corners link the concourse below to the square. On the east and west of the square are rows of trees with seating below them. A row of seating also exists along the northern edge of the square and a number of food stalls are located on the periphery of the square.

North Square is large, being almost 4 hectares (about 10 acres) in size. It is considered to be the center of the surrounding business district as well as a forecourt for the station. The Zhabei Government District around the square was redeveloped in the 1980s from being an area of low-rise apartment buildings to a high-density, mixed-use precinct. Today the square is surrounded by restaurants, shops, entertainment facilities and many hotels but they, like those at Schouwburgplein in Rotterdam, do not open directly onto the square. The square is a flat paved area with very few trees and relatively little seating. Like South Square, vehicular traffic moves around it on all four sides to provide a drop-off point at the entrance to the station for people arriving in cars and taxis. The bus station is adjacent. Below the square is a level that provides pedestrian access to the station. For much of the time the square is a deserted hardscape but during the New Year holiday season it is crammed full of people.

Analysis

Unlike Schouwburgplein, no significant intellectual esthetic ideas are obvious in the design of the two station squares. They function well on some dimensions of evaluation and not on others. The two are really pragmatic solutions to the need to handle large flows of people which they do efficiently. The South Square is the livelier space because more facilities and services are located adjacent to it.

Both squares are isolated from the surrounding buildings by the heavy traffic on the roads around them. Neither is an integral part of their neighborhoods and neither square is itself a destination. The surrounding neighborhoods house a critical mass of people, but this factor alone is an insufficient reason for a square to be used as an outdoor space. It has to provide some amenity level – some attraction for people to use it. The Shanghai Station squares only serve the station and the travelers who use it. They could also have been an asset to the precincts in which they are located. If that was the intention to make them so, they have not succeeded.

The entrance to Shanghai Station from South Square is in the center of the building facing the square. The exit is separate and towards the east of the entrance. A giant electronic board above the entrance shows the schedule of trains departing and arriving each day. It is easily seen from the heart of the square. Turning to the right from the exit leads to the taxi rank and bus station that serves local destinations in Shanghai. The entrance to the metro station is also adjacent. The constant movement of vehicles adds to the activity around the square but not in it. In pleasant weather the square could be a place for people to relax in the open air and watch the passing scene.

The center of South Square is an uncluttered space that could be used to host large events and handle the flow of people at holiday time. The clock tower acts as a nuclear element in the square and as a landmark and a meeting point. The seating on the periphery of the square and the steps around the clock tower are behavior settings of people waiting to catch a train or to greet arrivals. The trees provide some shade on a hot summer day. People also sit on the floor of the square, often in small clusters and of all ages, young and old. There is simply not enough seating to accommodate all the people waiting. The North Square is very different in character.

The design of North Square is even more utilitarian as a link than South Square. Its design takes simplicity to the extreme. The square is an almost entirely paved open space. The lack of seating or any other amenity means that it is an unattractive place to wait or to linger. North Square illustrates the difficulty of having to accommodate crowds of people waiting for buses and trains at some times of the year but also be a pleasant place during most of the time when it is not being heavily used. With the buildings and hotels facing directly onto the square, one might expect that locals and visitors would find the square a place to relax and animate the space. People's activities, however, do not spill from the surrounding buildings onto it. The square is certainly no heart to the business area around it.

The conclusion one draws is clear. North Square has almost no amenity value for people other than travelers using it as a link to the station. South Square, although more cluttered in design, offers more amenities than its northern counterpart. North Square is simply a link; South Square to some extent is a place as well as a link. The question in designing such squares is: Should these squares provide amenities that would afford people in their surroundings some utility when the instrumental function of the squares is to be a heavily used link on one or two days a year? Maybe the Shanghai Railway Bureau does not want to have people loitering in the square. The squares, especially North Square, offer almost no amenity as places to wait. If one observes the behavioral tendencies of the people who are there, maybe the squares should offer them more potential behavior settings.

17 Jacob K. Javits Federal Building Plaza, New York City, USA

Shifting design paradigms in the search for an appropriate government building forecourt

Jacob K. Javits Federal Building Plaza[34] in the Civic Center district of Manhattan is the forecourt to the 41-story Federal (office) Building constructed between 1963 and 1969 and named after the former US Senator. A western addition was added in the mid-1970s. The building's forecourt is partially enclosed on the east side by the James L. Watson Court of International Trade building. Javits Plaza is included as a case study here because it has had five iterations since 1968.[35] It is an exemplar of shifting landscape design paradigms. Its original design was added to by an art work that proved to be disliked by the users of the plaza (Deutsche 2003). The work was removed and replaced by a supplemented version of the original layout. That design gave way to another art work consisting of curving benches. It was regarded as dull (Hill 2007). The latest design is in the prevailing landscape architectural design paradigm.

The plaza that was completed in 1968 consisted of a fountain, planter boxes in two corners and a patterned floor. One stepped up into it from the street. In 1981, a work of art, *Tilted Arc* by Richard Serra, was installed across the plaza as shown in Figure 12.17 (a). It was a 3.66 meters high (12 feet), 36.6 meters wide (120 feet),

62.5mm-thick (2.5 inches) solid, and unfinished, self-oxidizing Cor-Ten steel plate, and slightly tilted. Designed specifically for the plaza, its placement created two separate potential behavior settings. Costing US$175,000 in 1981, it was commissioned under the General Services Administration's Art in Architecture Program (Weyergraf-Serra and Buskirk 1991). When in place, it was not liked by the federal employees who used the square. They felt that it made a poorly functioning plaza worse and they found it made them uneasy; the latter being purported to be one of the artist's intentions. *Tilted Arc* was removed as the result of a court order despite strong opposition from the fine arts community – artists, museum curators and art critics – who felt that the removal infringed the rights of expression of an artist (Deutsche 2003). After the removal of *Tilted Arc*, the raised flower beds in the corners of the square and the fountain remained as temporary design measures. Trees in planter boxes were added to give some greenery to what was deemed to be a harsh square.

The next design to be implemented was the work of the office of landscape architect Martha Schwartz. Schwartz's goal was to create a lively place as well as a work of art. The planter boxes and the

Figure 12.17 The Jacob K. Javits Federal Building Plaza: (a) **Tilted Arc** (artist Richard Serra) in the plaza, 1981; (b) Seating in the Martha Schwartz design, 1997; (c) The Van Valkenburgh design, 2013; (d) Seating in the Van Valkenburgh design, 2013

Sources: (a) Photograph by Robert R. McElroy/Getty Images; (b) Photograph by jphilipg/Flickr.

fountain that had long ceased to function were removed and replaced with bright green, curving benches that provided both sociopetal and sociofugal seating arrangements as shown in Figure 12.17 (b). The plaza was regarded as a 'clever design' of engaging graphic patterns that were of interest to the design experts. It won an American Society of Landscape Architects professional design award in 1997. The fifth and current effort at designing the plaza was initiated in 2010 and completed in 2013. The Schwartz-designed plaza was demolished, the leaking roof of the parking garage below was repaired and a new design by Michael Van Valkenburgh Associates, Inc. was constructed as shown in Figure 12.17 (c) and (d).

Key Features

The Van Valkenburgh design, while retaining the curving character of its predecessor, recognizes the plaza's primary use as a link. A grand set of steps and accompanying ramp from the street afford easy access to the square and the Federal Building. The paving pattern reflects that of the Federal Building. Marble rectangular and circular benches echo those of the Schwartz design. The northern portion of the square is ringed by deciduous Chinese magnolia trees that provide shade for those seated under them. Indigenous evergreen shrubs and ground cover make for a garden-like quality to the design. A grid of ground fountains with programmed water patterns, a feature of many contemporary designs, such as the Place des Terreaux in Lyon and Granary Square in London, adds life to the open space, when they are working.

Analysis

The Jacob K. Javits Federal Building Plaza is located opposite Foley Square in an area with a substantial number of federal, state and local government buildings and thus employees. A few residential neighborhoods, including Chinatown and a series of new apartment buildings, are nearby. Despite the residential population of the area, the plaza is not a destination in itself. It is the link between the sidewalk and the federal building. The several designs of the plaza have sought to make it something more – a place and a display to be admired. Indeed, the three designs considered here, the *Tilted Arc*, the Martha Schwartz design and now the Van Valkenburgh creation, have all been highly lauded by contemporary professionals (Hill 2010).

The 1968 Plaza served primarily as a link to the Federal Building from the street although the seating was used by federal workers at lunchtime. It was, nevertheless, a bleak space considered to be one of many "bad plazas in front of bad skyscrapers" (Hill 2010: website). Whether intended or not as a critique of the plaza, *Tilted Arc* was widely regarded as a sculpture that added no amenity to the open space. The artist argued that the sculpture did not interfere with the functioning of the plaza and indeed it enhanced its quality by dividing it into two components, each of which afforded different behavior settings. Supporters of the *Tilted Arc* saw it as giving "an incoherent, intractable space a focus and a sense of possibility" (Brenson 1985:

website). Those in opposition to its removal seldom, if ever, used the square. Very few federal employees who worked in the building lamented its departure. The court trial that followed the removal resulted in the *Visual Artists Rights Act of 1990* protecting the rights of artists of "recognized stature"[36] from destruction (Weyergraf-Serra and Buskirk 1991).

The curving benches of the design by Martha Schwartz allowed people to choose whether they wanted to sit in the sun or shade and they provided the affordances for sitting alone or the formation of group behavior settings, although the concaves were too large for easy conversation for more than three people. The benches were described by some as a more publicly acceptable design intervention in the plaza than Serra's *Tilted Arc*. In reality, the two designs show an affinity. Both were minimalist designs and made the plaza displays to contemplate as much as places to inhabit. Workers did use the benches in the Schwartz design for lunch or coffee breaks and some residents drifted down from Chinatown but it was seldom, if ever, a lively place. The latest design has greener credentials and complies with the contemporary tendency to turn paved squares into parks. Many professionals who identify themselves as landscape urbanists believe that this type of action is part of a new "urban design with nature paradigm" (Koh 2009).[37]

The current design of Jacob K. Javits Plaza with its magnolia trees and fountains is closer to popular tastes than either of its predecessors and more generally fits in with the anti-urban character of much thinking in the design fields that Steve Conn (2014) writes about. This plaza is an articulated, amorphous square, with considerable vegetation on a street that is busy on weekdays. It possesses places to sit in a variety of forms and locations but the seating is cold, hard and not particularly comfortable. The pockets in the square formed by the landforms create a number of smaller potential behavior settings where communal gatherings can occur. The plaza now sets out to be a place as well as a link. Its instrumental function, nevertheless, remains primarily to provide a passageway between street and building. It is in shadow much of the day because it has tall buildings on the south and west of it but it catches some morning sun as the more distant New York City Supreme Court building to the east lies behind Foley Square. As a display, the Jacob K. Javits Plaza and its past forms give artists, architects and landscape architects much to contemplate about the politics and ideologies of landscape and urban design.

We can learn much from the shifting history of the plaza. Primarily, forecourts of buildings present a tricky design problem and a disproportionate number are uninspiring empty spaces as Jerold Kayden's (2000) analysis of the results of New York's incentive zoning program showed. As links, they work well enough; they are satisficing solutions but their configurations make it difficult to make them more than that. Second, it is near impossible to create a lively square when the surrounding buildings generate few people with time to linger. They are almost all office workers rushing to get to work on time and rushing to get home again in the evenings. It will be interesting to see whether the increase in the residential population of the area results in more use of the plaza as a place outside the lunch hour. It would require a café opening on it to provide an amenity that would draw people to it. It is not clear that the federal government wants it used other than as a decorative link. Third, it takes courage for designers to break away from the prevalent contemporary design paradigm held in high esteem by their peers to deal directly with the problems at hand.

18 Granary Square, London, UK

A large privately owned public open space designed to be a catalyst for the regeneration of and the heart of an urban precinct

Granary Square is the central feature of the private estate that forms the development of King's Cross Centre in London's Borough of Camden. The borough's goal for the whole project is to regenerate a neglected and abandoned part of London and for the developers to make a profit. Funded by King's Cross Central Limited Partnership and designed by Townshend Landscape Architects, the development is being built on a 27.5-hectare (68-acre) site. A sign at the entrance states: "Welcome to King's Cross. Please enjoy this private estate considerately" (Vasagar 2012: 16). Thus, from the outset when entering the square, the visitor who reads the sign knows that he or she is not entering a publicly owned and administered space. The developers say that they are providing a new element to the city and that it will be clean, safe and well maintained. Critics believe that the spaces are designs based on a commercial model.

The site, which once was King's Cross Railway Lands, lies to the north of King's Cross and St Pancras railway stations. From the 1850s until the 1970s, the lands were a major railroad cargo route into London. Barges too once unloaded their goods from the Regent's Canal that runs through the site. When abandoned, the site became an industrial wasteland with some of the derelict buildings occupied by squatters.

Granary Square stands at the heart of the area and is comparable in size to Trafalgar Square. It is part of a group of squares – Station Square, St Pancras Square, Cubitt Square and North Square – designed to be a catalyst spurring the development of new buildings in the precinct and also to serve as an open space to them. Granary Square, in particular, provides an outdoor open space for the staff and students of the University of the Arts but it has also been designed to be a regional drawcard.

Key Features

The surroundings of Granary Square consist of the Granary Building, which has been refurbished to house artists' studios, a major restaurant, the Central St Martins (art college) and the University of the Arts, commercial office space and retail outlets (Figure 12.18). Some of the buildings that form part of the whole development are historic but much is of recent development and even more is under construction. Old railway lines and a glass-topped locomotive turntable are reminders of the peculiarities of the site's history. The reuse of the

Figure 12.18 *Granary Square, London; (a) A view from the southeast in 2013; (b) The south-facing terraces leading down to the Regent's Canal in 2014; (c) The fountains as a play area*

Source: (c) Photograph by Ron Ellis/ Shutterstock.com.

setts from the old site is another less obvious reminder of the past. Otherwise the floor of the square is paved with stone from Italian quarries. It is uniformly flat and designed with enough uncluttered open space and pop-up electric outlets to cater for events throughout the year but particularly during the summer months. In winter, the square is intended to have an ice-skating rink.

The most notable feature of the square is the fountains (Figure 12.18 (c)). They consist of 1,080 individual jets rising from the floor in front of the Granary Building (Carrier 2012). They are programmable and can shoot up in spouts of assorted heights and in patterns with varying colors of light; each jet is individually lit. They are thus designed to be entertaining day and night. The fountains are fed from underground tanks holding 105,000 liters of filtered recycled water (ibid.). The fountains can be turned down to provide a splashing area for children and turned off to allow for major events such as concerts to take place in the square. On a warm sunny day, children love to play in the water. The fountains and the use of squares as ice-skating rinks in winter are typical of recently developed squares with winter climates.

On the square's western side is a sculptured grove of pleached lime trees, clipped into cubical form. Moveable tables and chairs are placed under them. A four-story building housing restaurants is proposed for the square's eastern side. Regent's Canal forms the southern boundary of the square. Broad terraces and a stairway lead down from the square to the canal (Figure 12.18 (b); see also Figure 1.1 on p. 27). Joggers and walkers stride along the towpath and narrow boats are moored nearby. The terraces face directly into the sun and so allow visitors to lounge in a sun-bathed environment when the weather is good. A busy road, Goods Way, lies on the southern side of the canal. It will be lined in the future with commercial buildings. One hopes that they will not cast shadows onto the terraces and the square.

Analysis

Granary Square is a private development with a focus on providing for commercial activities and obtaining a return on the capital invested. It appears to have been designed primarily to be a central focus for a major property development and for holding large events that would draw outsiders into it. The uniformly flat, paved expanse of the square affords such occasions very well. Events are widely advertised and attract people from across London. At the same time it does, however, appear that the square will also be a place for nearby residents to use as a playground for their children who are especially attracted to the fountains. When the fountains are turned off and the space is turned into a large open expanse, it can host 2,000 people sitting on deck chairs watching films and sporting events on a large screen (King's Cross Central Limited Partnership 2014). The square is full of people then. As an ice-skating rink in winter, it will attact skaters if the success of other squares such as Robson Square in Vancouver, Calgary's Olympic Plaza and Pershing Square in Los Angeles are reliable indicators.

The square contains little fixed seating because it would get in the way of catering for large gatherings. The row of fixed concrete backless benches that line the northern and southern sides of the square facing the fountains are used by students and visitors, even on bleak days. The way the benches are configured does not make conversation easy for more than a couple of people. They are places to sit in solitude.

A noticeable feature of the square is that it is well lit. Despite its 52°N location, the size of the square allows the sun to shine into it from the south for most of the year. The southern edge of the square is defined by the terraces leading down to the Regent's Canal and Goods Way, the four-laned street south of the canal, meaning that the buildings on the south are at some distance from the square. The same observation can be made about the buildings on its east and west. It also means that the square has and will have little sense of enclosure and the uses that surround it do not spill directly out into it.

The Granary Building, being on its northern side of the canal, catches the sun and reflects some warmth into the open space as well. The building does not, however, open up onto the square nor can one see into it from the outside to get a sense of the life within it. Although anybody can enter the front part of the building, the entrance has no invitational quality and, once inside, farther entry is restricted to only those with authorization.

Like many privately owned squares, the presence of security guards, while unobtrusive, is, nevertheless, obvious. They add a sense of security to the area but also a sense of limits on allowable behavior. The comings and goings of students to Central St Martins mean that people are present in the square or crossing it for much of the day and into the evening. Restaurants in the Granary Building and in adjacent buildings, as they open up, will provide an added sense of people's presence in the square and casual public surveillance on it.

The square at the time this book was written was new. While there are elements on the site that remind the visitor of its past, it has no history in its present guise. Its role in the lives and its meanings for the people of London will evolve. At present, few Londoners know of its existence. Its location means that it is unlikely to attract tourists in the way Trafalgar Square does other than to organized events. Questions to ask once the excitement of the new square has worn off and the claims of the designers and the marketing language of the developers have subsided include: Is the square as comfortable to be in when no event is being held as the landscape architects claim it will be? Is it a lively square or mainly a large, mostly empty space? Is the square a destination attracting people from the neighborhood or will it be used mostly for scheduled events? Is it as heavily used by students and staff of the University of Arts as predicted? If the square is well used, what places in the square do people frequent?

As the square is not public space, political demonstrations or rallies are unlikely to be welcomed if the Paternoster Square experience is a precedent. Injunctions against them taking place will no doubt follow the announcement of any such planned activities. What can actually take place is up to the management of a private company, not an elected municipal authority. The management of the square will likely be transformed over time to deal with political activities, impromptu meetings and pop-up events. The response will determine how 'public' the square will actually be. Time will tell.

19 Times Square, New York City, USA

A large, informal, irregular, bow-tie square that is the heart of a city and a square in transition[38]

Times Square is an example of a place whose open space, really a bow-tie traffic intersection, is dissimilar to any image one has of an ideal square. The square does, however, possess many of the qualities that one associates with well-functioning squares. It is certainly replete with a variety of behavior settings. Orginally called 'Longacre Square,' it received its current name in 1904 when The New York Times moved its headquarters into what is now One Times Square.

Described often as New York's agora, the square is a brightly illuminated node where pedestrian paths cross in the city's Theater District. As a major north–south, east–west link in midtown Manhattan, an estimated 300,000 people pass through the square each day. Events frequently take place in the square which is large enough to hold 500,000 people. The primary occasion is the annual ball drop on New Year's Eve but many other celebrations drawing people together in their thousands take place in Times Square. They are as varied as watching the results of presidential elections or celebrating sporting championships. All, however, has not always been well in the square and its surroundings.

During the 1920s, the precinct was a center of crime and corruption. From the 1960s to the 1990s, it developed a further seedy reputation because of its 1960s go-go-bars, and more recently, its adult entertainment premises. Efforts to make the square a more popular place for the general public began in the 1990s under the direction of Mayors Ed Koch and David Dawkins. Advocates for remodeling the square wanted the area to be safe and clean. Those people opposed to this idea were worried that the whole precinct would become 'Disneyfied' and lose its distinctive urban grunge look and feel. In 1992, The Times Square Alliance, a public-private partnership and advocacy group, which was dedicated to having a cleaner Times Square with more family-friendly attractions, was founded. New uses were sucessfully attracted to the area and the added security personnel on almost on every corner, made the area feel safer.

During the first decade of this century, under the leadership of Mayor Michael Blumberg, the vehicular traffic lanes on Broadway from 42nd Street to 47th Street were temporarily transformed into a pedestrian plaza filled with inexpensive multicolored plastic deck chairs that were later replaced by more sturdy metal furniture. The aim was to reduce the air and noise pollution in the square and to test the impact that the road closure would have on traffic flows. Although the effort was initially opposed by business people who feared a loss of trade, none occurred. Additionally, injuries to pedestrians decreased while the number of pedestrians passing through the square increased. The impact on the movement of vehicular traffic in the precinct has been mixed. The largely successful experiment with the square has led to a new plan. In the summer of 2015, Mayor Bill Blasio was on record as suggesting he is not yet convinced about the new plan and entirely pedestrianizing Times Square (Nahmias and Pybarah 2015).

Key Features

An area stretching from West 42nd Street to West 47th Street, Times Square consists of a number of components. It is first of all a traffic intersection where Broadway crosses Seventh Avenue. At its northern end is a triangular plaza, Duffy Square, containing a memorial to Chaplain Francis P. Duffy along with a statue of George M. Cohan (Figure 12.19 (c)). A TKTS discount theater ticket booth is also located there. The booth has a stepped red roof that provides seating from which events in the square can be viewed (Figure 12.19 (a)).

The original 2011 proposal will likely turn the temporary changes of street closures (seen in Figure 12.19 (b)) into permanent ones. The

Figure 12.19 *Times Square, New York: (a) Times Square: TKTS booth red platform seating; (b) Moveable sidewalk chairs and benches; (c) Times Square in the spring of 2013. The Francis Duffy memorial is in the immediate foreground*

Sources: (a) Photograph by Lissandro Melo/Shutterstock.com; (b) Photograph by Andrew F. Kazmierski/Shutterstock.com.

proposal prepared by Snøhetta Design, an international architectural and landscape architectural firm led by Craig Dykers and Kjetil Trædal Thorsen, is expected to cost US$29 million. Some of the funds will be spent on dealing with the ageing infrastructure below Broadway; the remainder will be spent on the square itself.

The surface across the plaza will first be leveled to create a continuous flat area. The surface finish of the new plaza will consist of two tones of dark concrete pavers arranged in an alternating brick pattern so that it will be different in color from the street's pavement. Small stainless steel 'pucks' about a centimeter (1/3 inch) in diameter will be placed in some sections to reflect the light from the surrounding signs. The aim is to avoid too sanitized an image by retaining a 'gritty' atmosphere in the square. Large benches will be used to make distinct potential behavior settings and make the pedestrians (and bicycle) links clearer. New infrastructure elements that better provide for large events will be added to the square.

Despite the city's commitment to the Snøhetta design, other proposals keep being put forward. One of them, at least, suggests a very different future for Times Square. It strips the walls of all their lighting and advertising displays, closes the whole present bow-tie area of the square to vehicular traffic and plants trees, turning the square into a large green oasis (Pham 2015). Such proposals fit in with a current landscape architecture paradigm that advocates turning squares into parks.

Analysis

Times Square is as much a symbol of New York as the Empire State Building or the Brooklyn Bridge. It is a place fully activated daily by thousands of people using it as a link and by those visiting it as a destination either to shop or simply to people-watch and enjoy the atmosphere. The Theater District, which is part of the precinct in which the square is located, is an attraction in itself. The square is a major node in Kevin Lynch's (1960) terms and a significant tourist hub attracting American visitors and sightseers from around the world. Pedestrian and vehicular paths cross there and create a chaotic multi-behavior setting environment that is part of a vibrant city's life. In addition to the theaters, the square is surrounded by an area of late-night activities that generate people well into the small hours of the morning.

An x-shaped space, Times Square is crossed longitudinally by Seventh Avenue. The streets from 43rd to 47th Streets all cross the square. Each carries one-way traffic that moves in stops and starts along it. As noted already, until recently, the square was also crossed by traffic on Broadway but, as an experiment, it has been closed to traffic to create a more pedestrian-friendly space. Nevertheless, as a result of all the traffic, the ambient quality of the square is still not high. With the traffic still passing along one side of the square its sonic qualities are poor. The air quality is also poor. New York's latitude and the height of the enclosing buildings mean that that the square is only sunlit during the middle of the day. During the winter, chilly winds are channeled up the streets. Times Square is a great place not because of its attributes but because, as G. K. Chesterton (1908) noted of great squares, it is much loved. If Rockefeller Center is for the middle class, Times Square is for everybody. It is a place to mix, vicariously at least, with people from all walks of life and from around the world. The one forgotten population in Times Square are children – this place is not child-friendly.

Times Square is an informal, closed square with buildings built to the property line on all of its sides. The character of its enclosing walls, if not unique, is unmatched outside of Tokyo. The requirement that building owners display illuminated neon or LED signs called 'spectaculars' or 'jumbotrons' on a proportion of the façades of their buildings makes the square a symbol of lively urban life. Zipper news crawls add to the stroboscopic effect of the square. Visitors captured by video cameras can and do watch themselves pass by or perform on large screens. In November and December, Christmas decorations add a level of festivity to the square. The brightly colored flashing walls at night are a tourist attraction but they do seem a little tawdry in daylight. It is also a somewhat grubby place despite being constantly swept.

The ground floors of the buildings are lined by shops, restaurants, fast food outlets and theater entrances. The sidewalks are frequented by vendors of tourist trinkets, clothing and street food. Hawkers sell tickets for guided bus tours and for admission to major tourist attractions and are the true habitués of the square. They keep an eye on what is happening as much as do the formal security personnel on site.

The TKTS booth is an added attraction because it draws a crowd looking for theater tickets at discounted prices. The grandstand that is provided by its roof is often packed with sightseers. Neither fixed benches nor any other fixed elements that can be used as seating can be found in the square. As can be seen in Figure 12.19 (b), the square is replete with moveable tables and chairs provided by the city (see also Figure 2.6 (a) on p .40). They are used by people to sit and watch public life on display, rest or eat. Much is attractive about Times Square as witnessed by the number of people who frequent the place but there is also much that is simply tolerated because it is a place to have been and to have seen. In support of William Whyte's famous quote, public spaces provide entertainment, which is usually provided by the people themselves: "what attracts people most, it would appear, is other people" (1980: 19).

Many lessons can be learnt from Times Square. Political leadership and popular support are vital to obtaining change. Both the politicians and the general public need to be convinced that change could have a positive impact on their city. Temporary measures can be used to test design ideas and to show the public what the intentions of a design are, as was done in Vancouver's Robson Square and Calgary's Olympic Plaza. Simple designs offer much; the proposed changes for Times Square are designed to enhance the ambient quality of the square for pedestrians. Time will tell what the impacts are of the changes on the utility of the square and whether they will enhance its 'iconic' status. There appears to be no reason for that image to change although some New Yorkers will no doubt miss its traditional gritty nature.

A remaining question is: Will the popularity of Times Square as a destination result in the square becoming an unpleasantly over-crowded place? To some, it already is (Pham 2015). Visitor numbers have reached as high as 480,000 people on a single day up from a high of 350,000 a decade ago. The result has been a boom in retail sales and hotel occupancy but some commercial enterprises are beginning to ask whether they want to be permanently located on the square. Landlords are creating building entrances and internal facilities are located so that employees can avoid entering the square. They worry that a tipping point might be reached when companies no longer wish to be located on the square (Bagli 2015).

20 Piazza San Marco, Venice, Italy

A large irregular, multifunctional, dominant, closed square[39]

Piazza San Marco with the Piazzetta form linked squares that are the heart of Venice. San Marco is the only one of the many squares in the city called 'piazza'; the others are called 'campi.' The Piazza is a dominant square with St Mark's Basilica (Basilica Cattedrale Patriarcale di San Marco) at its eastern end. The Basilica is the exemplar of Venetian-Byzantine architecture; its golden appearance gives it an aura of opulence. The Piazza is also a closed square forming a large outdoor room; Napoleon is reputed to have regarded it as "Europe's most beautiful drawing room." Today some critics are less enthusiastic. Bayley (2008: website) describes it as an "undisciplined, overpriced, fatigued international playpen."

Being an irregular, trapezoidal form, the length of the square is visually changed when seen from the Basilica because of the convergence of its two sides. This design was not a Renaissance intellectual design playing with the optics of texture densities but a response to land ownership patterns. Over the centuries the various developers

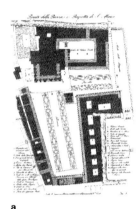

Figure 12.20 *Piazza San Marco: (a) The plan; (b) An inside view towards the Basilica; (c) Aerial view*

Sources: (b) Photograph by chaoss/ Shutterstock.com; (c) Photograph by DEA/ PUBBLI AER FOTO. Getty Images.

a   b

and designers of the buildings that enclose the square have had to deal with the given characteristics of the site.

Key Features

At 1.3 hectares (about 3 acres) and 1.7 hectares (4.2 acres) with the Piazzetta, Piazza San Marco is a large square (although small in comparison to the world's largest) but in good weather it is crowded with tourists. It has been estimated that there is a 175:1 tourist to resident ratio in the center of Venice during the height of summer (Ivanovic 2008). The Piazza and the centerpiece of the Piazza, the Basilica, are on different axes. The Basilica's bell-tower, the Campanile, is a separate 98.6 meter-tall (323 feet) structure that is a prominent landmark located where the Piazza and Piazzetta meet. Its origins date back to the ninth century but the current structure was built in 1912, a decade after its predecessor was destroyed by an earthquake.

The Piazza is also an example of a square where the buildings around it, built over five centuries by different developers, were designed by a number of architects but with a sense of decorum.[40] New buildings were designed to respect rather than compete with the buildings already there. The square is surrounded by arcades and although they differ in height and, to architects at least, create some awkward angles, a uniformity of design is maintained. Jacopo Sansovino designed the two-story Biblioteca Marciana in 1536 but it was further developed by Vincenzo Scamozzi. The Procuratie Vecchie that forms the north side of the square was designed by Bartolomeo Bon the Younger in 1520. The Piazzetta has the *Doge's Palace*, a Gothic structure that faces the lagoon on one side with the National Library of St Marks on the other. At its lagoon end are two columns memorializing two of Venice's patron saints: St Mark and St Teodoro of Amasea. While the architecture is much admired, it also has its critics. Edward Gibbon (cited in Bayley 2008: website) described it as "a large square, decorated with the worst architecture I ever saw."

The floor of the Piazza makes a major contribution to the perceived quality of the square. It is almost completely flat and paved in a simple pattern. The flat surface affords many activities and makes the square a robust space. A comparison between the paving materials, the people and their activities in 1723 and 1730 as presented by Canaletto and the square today (Figure 12.20 (b)) attests to the robustness of its spatial configuration and the enclosing elements of the square. Awnings are still in use and the Campanile, although bolder today than in 1723, remains an important focal point. Pigeons are a dominant presence in the square. Venetian authorities have been less successful in getting rid of them than the City of Westminster in London's Trafalgar Square. In winter, the square often floods (see Figure 2.8 (a) on p. 41). The flooding results from a combination of high tides, strong southerly winds and wave action that causes water to flow into the lagoon and then into the city. In response, municipal authorities place raised platforms along the main streets and across the Piazza and Piazzetta. It might be fun for some people to see and use in this state but for others it is a condition that creates hardships and needs correcting. At times during the summer, pungent smells make the square an unpleasant place. Visitors adapt to the odors but it is hardly a desirable attribute.

Analysis

Piazza San Marco's history, configuration and the activities that take place there make it a much-admired place. Its eastern end acts as a link from the portal under the clock tower through the Piazzetta to the lagoon. Today the Piazza and the Piazzetta rely on tourists to give them life. The resident population of Venice has dwindled from 171,000 in 1951 to only a little over 60,000 today and it continues to decline. Eighteen million visitors come into the city each year and experience Venice as a living museum. Tourists form the primary group of people who visit the square either to look at and/or photograph it and the Basilica. Some of them will stop and have a meal or a drink in one of the restaurants that line it and while doing so, they can watch the activities in the square. Until recently, people were allowed to feed the pigeons.

The Basilica gives a strong focus to the square. Without it the Piazza would be a less interesting place. The edifice is also a significant destination for tourists. A bronze replica of *The Horses of St Mark* adorns the balcony but it is the mosaic work that is the major attraction.[41] In addition, the Campanile is a point element in the square but because it is well off to one side, it does not make the square a strong nuclear one. It is, nevertheless, a major landmark not only in the square but for Venice. It is also a destination. Tourists can take an elevator to the top of the tower and obtain great views over Venice. Queues of people waiting to ascend to the Campanile are a feature of the life of the square during the tourist season.

Piazza San Marco is a closed square. The enclosed space is overlooked from the second and third stories of the surrounding buildings. The proportion of width to the height of the surrounding buildings adheres to the relationship that many scholars feel gives a square the qualities of an outdoor room. Napoleon was correct in his observation. The width of the square to its height varies from 2:1 to 3:1. Over the course of the day the height of the surrounding buildings allows users to have a choice of sunlight or shade in which to sit. Most of the restaurants are located on the northern, sunlit, side of the square.

Located at 45°N, the Piazza is a sunny space throughout the summer and into the early winter because the buildings around it are relatively low and the Piazzetta is open on the south. The square can be quite hot and humid in mid-summer but the configuration of the Piazzetta and Piazza allows breezes to waft in from across the lagoon. The heart of the square is sheltered against strong winds but not gales. In winter months, the *aqua alta*, the high water, is a regular occurrence.

The uniformly flat, paved surface of the Piazza affords the many activities associated with celebrations and festivals. Its pattern gives some interest to the surface. Children can follow its lines and chase the pigeons. The Piazza contains no fountains, no trees and no fixed benches. To sit in the Piazza, one either has to sit on the floor or sit on a chair in one of the cafés that surround it. There are no ledges on which to sit. The Piazza is a place where very few Venetians gather. The Piazzetta comes to life at the edge of the lagoon, the Molo San Marco. It is where the behavior settings are heavily nested and the polychronic activities take place.[42] The steps around the two columns at the head of the Piazzetta are regularly used for sitting on and have been for centuries, as Renaissance paintings show.

Many architectural features of the square attract attention, as mentioned. One is the way in which the sequences of spaces open up as one moves through them. Entering the square from the water or, particularly, from the land through the entrance of the Torre dell'Orlogio, the visual transition when moving from a narrow space as it opens to a large vista creates an element of surprise even for the residents of Venice. For the cognescenti, the intellectual esthetic quality of the square with its asymmetries as a display is important. The richness of the architectural history and detailing is available for their appreciation. The square and Basilica are a reminder of Venice's past and its links to Byzantium and to the Church of the Apostles in what is now Istanbul. For the lay-person, the richly decorated Basilica, which dates from the eleventh century, is of historical interest. The combination of the spaces in the Piazza and Piazzetta seems to offer something for everyone.

Conclusion

All the squares included here were analyzed at a particular point in time but the contexts of squares change. For example, Pershing Square in Los Angeles may be perceived to be a disappointment now but as the Central Business District of the city is revitalized, it may well be regarded as a major asset to the area. Granary Square may develop into a true heart of its precinct as buildings around it are completed. Some of the squares we have included in this chapter are being looked at anew as municipal authorities and/or advocacy groups seek to eliminate opportunity costs. Much of the commentary presented in this chapter will, however, be able to be replicated in many years' time as most of the squares we have reviewed are robust places.

Notes

1 For a photographic essay on Rittenhouse Square, see Scavo (2009); for histories and analyses, see Jacobs (1961), Skaler and Keels (2008) and Heinzen (2009).
2 Clare Cooper Marcus and Carolyn Francis provided an analysis of the affordances of Sproul Plaza some 25 years ago (1990).
3 See Ness (2009) on Halprin's work and life.
4 For general descriptions and reviews of Paley Park, see Iwashita (1988), Tate (2001) and Surhone et al. (2010). Jerome Kayden (2000) provides some additional details. Reviews also appear in Wagner (1967) and Johnson and Frankel (1991). For a thorough analysis of the square, see Whyte (1980).
5 The square was named in honor of French naval hero of World War II and a martyr of the Resistance.
6 This analysis is based on the authors' personal observations and general enquiries rather than on a set of systematic research studies.

7 For a fuller description of the square, see Lang (2005 : 94–97). For an analysis of the square when first refurbished, see Broto (2000) and Gehl and Gemzøe (2000).

8 Frédéric Auguste Bartholdi (1834–1904) is best known in the United States as the sculptor of the Statue of Liberty in New York and the Bartholdi Fountain on Independence Avenue in Washington.

9 The deck is supported on steel columns and beams with vibration-absorbing spiral springs and rubber padding.

10 For reviews of the design of the square, see Brown-May and Day (2003) and O'Hanlon (2012).

11 For an earlier case study, see Lang (2005: 248–252). For a general history of the scheme written on behalf of the property developers, Mitsubishi Estate Co., Ltd, see Jackson (2003). For a critical architectural review before the square was completed, see Glancey (2003).

12 See Watkin (1996) for a statement on the early planning of Paternoster Square.

13 In 2004, Temple Bar, a Wren-designed archway that once stood on Fleet Street to mark the western boundary of the City of London, was rebuilt as the cathedral-side entrance to the square. The expense of the relocation was borne by The Corporation of London, the Temple Bar Trust and by a number of the city's livery companies.

14 This analysis is based on the authors' personal observations and general enquiries rather than on a set of systematic research studies.

15 The debate as to whether or not to close Robson Street to vehicular traffic permanently or seasonally continues, see Klassen (2012).

16 This analysis is based on the authors' personal observations and general enquiries rather than on a set of systematic research studies.

17 The sculpture commemorates the five Alberta women who sought to have women regarded as persons in the Canadian Constitution and thus eligible to vote. Although at first unsuccessful, the five were successful in a ruling by the Judicial Committee of the British Privy Council in 1929.

18 See Figures 2.8 (a) and (b) on p. 41 for the seasonal change and the change in the nature of the behavior settings.

19 See Oc and Tiesdell (1997) on the subject and the experience in the United Kingdom.

20 For additional photographs of Trafalgar Square, see Hargreaves (2005) and Hood (2005); for a detailed history, see Mace (2005).

21 A ban on feeding pigeons and the presence of trained Harris's hawks have reduced the number from an estimated 35,000 down to a handful.

22 Probably the most thoughtful description of Le Corbusier's work in India appears in Nilsson (1973). Other books that discuss the capital complex are Evenson (1966), written in happier times, and Kalia (1999). Bahga et al. (1993) describe the capitol complex and Khilnani (1997) provides a brief non-architect's critique. See Lang et al. (1997) and Lang (2002) to understand the importance of Le Corbusier's design in the history of modern architecture in India.

23 The full text of Nehru's statement can be found in Lang et al. (1997: 311).

24 The observations made and the conclusions drawn from them are based on a detailed study sponsored by the City of Sydney and conducted under the direction of Kate Bishop and Nancy Marshall of the Faculty of the Built Environment at the University of New South Wales. See also Bishop and Marshall (2014) for a systematic review of Oxford Square.

25 In reading this study, it must be recalled that, like Federation Square, the noonday sun shines from the north in Oxford Square.

26 At the time this book was being edited, the café had ceased to operate.

27 For a fuller description of the functioning of the square before and after renovation, see Loukaitou-Sideris and Banerjee (1998). See Olin (2012) for one of its designer's views on the shortcomings of the square. This review relies heavily on Lang (2005: 90–94).

28 A number of discussions of Schouwburgplein as a work of art can be found, see, for example, Ouroussoff (2005), Huxtable (2005) and Gentili (2014). Mark Hoogstad (2009) summarizes the views of the square held by different people. Ben Schneider (2010) provides a simple description of the square.

29 The study involved 80 hours of observation and 120 interviews; reported in Hoogstad (2009).
30 Much has been written on the museum (see Vidharte 2002, for instance) and on its catalytic effect on the development of Bilbao. See Segal (1999) and Lang (2005: 120–123), for instance. Few observers have looked at the functioning of the space in which the museum is set.
31 Earlier the direct entrance off the street was an innovation at the Museum of Modern Art in New York.
32 Little has been published on the performance of the squares. Pu Miao (2011) reviews the performance of recent urban spaces in China at a more general level, including the Shanghai Station squares. Many of his observations about them have universal application.
33 Dam Square in Amsterdam and Rossio Square in Lisbon are examples of the former and the square at King's Cross in London and the Carrefour d'Europe in Brussels are examples of the latter.
34 Often referred to simply as the Jacob Javits Plaza but also as the Javits Center Plaza and Federal Plaza. It should not be confused with the Jacob K. Javits Convention Center in Midtown Manhattan and its plaza areas.
35 See Hill (2007) for a comparison of the plaza when it housed Richard Serra's work and when it housed the benches designed by Martha Schwartz. See Weyergraf-Serra and Buskirk (1991) and Senie (2001) for a discussion of the controversy regarding *Tilted Arc*'s removal. See Hill's three articles (2000, 2007, 2010) for a detailed history of the plaza.
36 "Recognized stature" has yet to be defined.
37 Landscape urbanism can trace its roots back to Ian McHarg's *Design with Nature* (1969). Possibly the best explication of the paradigm was written by Koh (2009).
38 For histories that present the colorful life of Times Square prior to its gentrification, see Rogers and Weston (1960), Traub (2004) and Friedman (2007). See Boyer (1992) and Sagalyn (2001) for an analysis of the taste culture to which the redesign appeals.
39 Much has been written on the Piazza. Most of it is descriptive history. For an analysis of its changing shape and the activities that take place in the square, see Fenlon (2009). Foscari (2014) puts the square into its context. For a recent architect's view, see Gatje (2010).
40 For a discussion of the concept of "architectural decorum," see Kohane and Hill (2001).
41 See Demus (1988) for a full description of the mosaics.
42 See Chapter 2 for a description of this term.

References

Bagli, Charles V. (2015) Times Square's crushing success raises questions about its future. *The New York Times*, January 26. Available at: www.nytimes.com/2015/01/27/nyregion/times-squares-crushing-success-raises-questions-about-its-future.html?_r=5.

Bahga, Sarbajit, Surinder Bahga and Yashinder Bahga (1993) Capitol complex (1951–62). In *Modern Architecture in India: Post-Independence Perspectives*. New Delhi: Galgotia, pp. 24–27.

Bayley, Stephen (2008) Venice is the only city on earth going backwards. *The Spectator*, February 8. Available at: www.spectator.co.uk/features/488691/venice-is-the-only-city-on-earth-going-backwards

Bishop, Kate and Nancy Marshall (2014) Towards an evidence-based model for assessing urban squares as social place. *International Journal of Interdisciplinary Social and Community Studies* 9(1): 1–10.

Boyer, M. Christine (1992) Cities for sale: Merchandising history at South Street Seaport. In *Variations on a Theme Park: The New American City and the End of Public Space*, edited by Michael Sorkin. New York: McGraw-Hill, pp. 181–204.

Brenson, Michael (1985) Art view: The case in favor of a controversial sculpture. *New York Times*, May 19. Available at: www.nytimes.com/1985/05/19/arts/art-view-the-case-in-favor-of-a-controversial-sculpture.html?pagewanted=all.

Broto, Carles (2000) La Place des Terreaux. In *New Urban Design*. Barcelona: Arian Mostaedi, pp. 26–33.

Brown-May, Andrew and Norman Day (2003) *Federation Square*. South Yarra: Hardie Grant Books.

Burden, Amanda (2014) How public spaces make cities work. A TED talk. Available at: www.ted.com.talks/amanda_burden_how_public_spaces_make_cities_work.

Carrier, Dan (2012) Property: Spectacular fountains provide centrepiece to King's Cross development close to university. *Camden New Journal*, June 7. Available at: www.camdennewjournal.com/news/2012/jun/property-spectacular-fountains-provide-centrepiece-king%E2%80%99s-cross-development-close-univ.

Chesterton, G. K. (1908) *Orthodoxy*. London: Bodley Head.

Conn, Steve (2014) *Americans against the City: Anti-Urbanism in the Twentieth Century*. New York: Oxford University Press.

Cooper Marcus, Clare and Carolyn Francis (1990) *People Places: Design Guidelines for Urban Open Space*. New York: Van Nostrand Reinhold.

Curlin, Jay (2012) The evidence of things not seen. *The New Yorker*, July 30, p. 77.

Demus, Otto (1988) *The Mosaic Decoration of San Marco Venice*, edited by Herbert L. Kessler. Chicago: University of Chicago Press.

Deutsche, Rosalyn (2003) *Tilted Arc* and the uses of democracy. In *Designing Cities: Critical Reading in Urban Design*, edited by Alexander R. Cuthbert. Oxford: Blackwell, pp. 160–168.

The Economist (2012) Between the buildings: London's public spaces have got better but not good enough. *The Economist*, June 30, pp. 88–89. Available at: www.economist.com/node/21557741.

Espuche, Albert Garcia (n.d.). Cours d'Estienne d'Ovres, Marseille (France) (1989). Available at: www.publicspace.org/en/works/z012-cours-d-estienne-d-orves

Evans, Donna (2014) Two playgrounds, other improvements coming to Pershing Square. *DT News*, September 18. Available at: www.ladowntownnews.com/news/two-playgrounds-other-improvements-coming-to-pershing-square/article_2c68d9f2-3eca-11e4-aeb4-bb3b8c2dd0dc.html.

Evenson, Norma (1966) *Chandigarh*. Berkeley and Los Angeles: University of California Press.

Fenlon, Iain (2009) *Piazza San Marco: Wonders of the World*. Cambridge, MA: Harvard University Press.

Foscari, Giulia (2014) *Elements of Venice*. Zurich: Lars Müller Publishers.

Friedman, Josh A. (2007) *Tales of Times Square: Expanded Edition*. Portland, OR: Feral House.

Gardiner, Ralph, Jr (2012) Puffing freely courtesy of Paley. *The Wall Street Journal*, May 29. Available at: http://online.wsj.com/news/articles/SB10001424052702303807404577434592256330010.

Gatje, Robert F. (2010) *Great Public Squares: An Architect's Selection*. New York: Norton.

Gehl, Jan and Lars Gemzøe (2000) *New City Spaces*. Copenhagen: Danish Architectural Press.

Gentili, Helena (2014) Moving lights: Schouwburgplein in Rotterdam. *Gizmo*. Available at: www.gizmoweb.org/2014/02/moving-lights-schouwburgplein-in-rotterdam.

Glancey, Jonathan (2003) It's a jumble out there. *The Guardian*, November 3. Available at: www.theguardian.com/artanddesign/2003/nov/03/architecture.regeneration.

Globe and Mail (2011) Arthur Erickson landmarks awarded prestigious architectural award. *The Globe and Mail*, May 4. Available at: www.theglobeandmail.com/news/british-columbia/arthur-erickson-landmarks-awarded-prestigious-architectural-award/article578658/.

Hargreaves, Roger (2005) *Trafalgar Square through the Camera*. London: National Portrait Gallery Publications.

Heinzen, Nancy M. (2009) *The Perfect Square: A History of Rittenhouse Square*. Philadelphia, PA: Temple University Press.

Hill, John (2000) Jacob Javits Plaza. *A Weekly Dose of Architecture*, April 10. Available at: http://archdose.org/wp/2000/04/10/jacob-javits-plaza.

Hill, John (2007) Jacob Javits Plaza: Reconsidering intentions. Prepared for *Anthropology of Place and Space: Locating Culture*, edited by Setha Lowe and Denise Lawrence-Zúñiga. Malden, MA: Blackwell.

Hill, John (2010) Plaza redo, again. *The Architect's Newspaper*, January 2. Available at: http://archpaper.com/news/articles.asp?id=4208.

Hood, Jean (2005) *Trafalgar Square: A Visual History of London's Landmark through Time*. London: B. T. Batsford.

Hoogstad, Mark (2009) Een 'podium' om te mijden. *NRC Handelsblad*, 25 Februari: Achterpagina, 18.

Huxtable, Ada Louise (2005) Down-to-earth masterpieces of public landscape design. *The Wall Street Journal*, May 5: D10. Available at: www.wsj.com/articles/SB111515970031423786.

Ivanovic, Melena (2008) *Cultural Tourism*. Johannesburg: Juta and Company, Ltd.

Iwashita, Hajime (1988) *Pocket Park*. Tokyo: Process Architecture.

Jackett, Sonia (2014) Top 10 public squares. *Landscape Architects Network*, May 9. Available at: http://landarchs.com/top-10-public-squares-world/.

Jackson, Nicola (2003) *The Story of Paternoster: A New Square for London*. London: Wordsearch Communications.

Jacobs, Jane (1961) *The Death and Life of Great American Cities*. New York: Random House.

Johnson, Jory and Felice Frankel (1991) *Modern Landscape Architecture: Redefining the Garden*. New York: Abbeville Press.

Kalia, Ravi (1999) *Chandigarh: The Making of an Indian City*. New Delhi: Oxford University Press.

Kayden, Jerold S. (2000) *Privately Owned Public Space: The New York City Experience*. New York: New York City Department of City Planning and the Municipal Art Society.

Khilnani, Sunil (1997) *The Idea of India*. Harmondsworth: Penguin.

King's Cross Central Limited Partnership (2014) Home page. Available at: www.kingscross.co.uk/

Klassen, Mike (2012) Re-think Robson Square without permanent closure. *Huffpost British Columbia*, October 31. Available at: www.huffingtonpost.ca/mike-klassen/vancouver-robson-square_b_1844575.html

Koh, Anemone Beck (2014) Landscape Architect, Interview by Jon Lang, *Oikos*, Wageningen, The Netherlands.

Koh, Jusuck (2009) Articulating landscape urbanism: Ten defining characteristics. In *Green Infrastructure: High Performance Landscape. Proceedings of the International Federation of Landscape Architects*. Rio de Janeiro. ABAP, 19+.

Kohane, Peter and Michael Hill (2001) The eclipse of the commonplace: Decorum in architectural theory. *ARQ: Architectural Research Quarterly* 5(1): 63–77.

Lang, Jon (2002) *A Concise History of Modern Architecture in India*. New Delhi: Permanent Black.

Lang, Jon (2005) *Urban Design: A Typology of Procedures and Products Illustrated with Over 50 Case Studies*. Oxford: Architectural Press.

Lang, Jon, Madhavi Desai and Miki Desai (1997) *Architecture and Independence: The Search for Identity – India 1880 to 1980*. New Delhi: Oxford University Press.

Levy, Megan (2012) How ugly? Fed Square ranked amongst the worst ever. *The Age*, April 4. Available at: www.theage.com.au/victoria/how-ugly-fed-square-ranked-among-worst-ever-20120404-1wbum.html.

Loukaitou-Sideris, Anastasia and Tridib Banerjee (1998) *Urban Design Downtown: Poetics and Politics of Form*. Berkeley, CA: University of California Press.

Lynch, Kevin (1960) *The Image of the City*. Cambridge, MA: MIT Press.

Mace, Rodney (2005) *Trafalgar Square: Emblem of Empire*, 2nd edn. London: Lawrence and Wishart.

Marr, Norma (2013) This month in history; February 1988 – The Olympic Plaza. *Calgary Herald*, February 7. Available at: http://blogs.calgaryherald.com/2013/02/07/this-month-in-history-february-1988-the-olympic-plaza/.

Marshall, Nancy (2016) Urban squares: A place for public life. In *Place and Placelessness Revisited*, edited by Robert Freestone and Edgar Liu. New York: Routledge, pp.186–203.

McHarg, Ian L. (1969) *Design with Nature*. Garden City, NY: The Natural History Press.

Miao, Pu (2011) Brave new city: Three problems in Chinese urban public space since the 1980s. *Journal of Urban Design* 16(2): 179–207.

Mumford, Lewis (1954) Nowicki's work in India. *Architectural Record* 116(3): 153–159.

Nahmias, Laura and Azi Pybarah (2015) Advocates slam proposal to shut plazas at Times Square. Available at: www.capitalnewyork.com/article/city-hall/2015/08/8574863/advocates-slam-proposal-shut-plazas-times-square.

Ness, Carol (2009) Landscape designer who built Sproul Plaza leaves a national legacy. *U.C. Berkeley News*. Available at: http://berkeley.edu/news/media/releases/2009/10/30_halprin.shtml.

Newman, Oscar (1972) *Defensible Space*. New York: Macmillan.

Nilsson, Sten A. (1973) *The New Capitals of India, Pakistan and Bangladesh*. London: Curzon.

Oc, Taner and Steve Tiesdell (eds.) (1997) *Safer City Centres: Reviving the Public Realm*. London: Paul Chapman.

O'Hanlon, Seamus (2012) *Federation Square, Melbourne: The First Ten Years*. Melbourne: Monash University Publishing.

Olin, Laurie. (2012) Q+A> Laurie Olin. *The Architect's Newspaper*, June 15. Available at: www.archpaper.com/news/articles.asp?id=6117.

Ouroussoff, Nicolai (2005) Confronting blight with hope. *New York Times*, February 24. Available at: www.nytimes.com/2005/02/24/arts/design/24moma.html?pagewanted=all&position=&_r=0.

Pershing Square Renew Inc. (2015) Homepage. Available at: http://pershingsquarenew.com/competition/.

Pham, Diane (2015) Four architects reimagine Times Square as a place you actually want to visit. *Landscape Architecture, Midtown*, January 12. Available at: www.6sqft.com/4-architects-re-imagine-times-square-as-a-place-you-actually-want-to-visit/.

Project for Public Spaces (n.d.) Hall of Shame: Available at: www.pps.org/great_public_spaces/list?type_id=2.

Randl, Chad (2012) Biography of M. Paul Friedberg. The Cultural Landscape Foundation. Available at: http://tclf.org/pioneer/m-paul-friedberg/biography-m-paul-friedberg.

Rogers, William G. and Mildred Weston (1960) *Carnival Cross Roads: The Story of Times Square*. New York: Doubleday.

Rutherford, Jennifer (2005) Writing the square: Paul Carter's Nearamnew. *Portal Journal of Multidisciplinary International Studies* 2(2): 1–14.

Sagalyn, Lynne B. (2001) *Times Square Roulette: Remaking the City Icon*. Cambridge, MA: MIT Press.

Scavo, Armond (2009) *Through an Artist's Eye: Philadelphia*, vol. 1: *Rittenhouse Square*. Philadelphia, PA: Blurb Inc.

Schelling, Steven (2009) Arthur Erickson, 1924–2009. *DailyXtra*, May 21. Available at: http://dailyxtra.com/canada/news/arthur-erickson-1924-2009-52673.

Schneider, Ben (2010) Schouwburgplein. Landscape Architecture Study Tour by Professor Jack Ahem. Available at: http://people.umass.edu/latour/Netherlands/schneider/.

Segal, Arlene (1999) Turning the tide: Guggenheim, Bilbao. *Planning: Architectural and Planning Review for South Africa* 163(May–June): 4–9.

Senie, Harriet F. (2001) *The Tilted Arc Controversy; Dangerous Precedent?* Minneapolis, MN: University of Minnesota Press.

Sitte, Camillo and Charles T. Stewart (1945) *The Art of Building Cities: City Building According to its Artistic Fundamentals*. New York: Reinhold.

Skaler, Robert M. and Thomas H. Keels (2008) *Philadelphia's Rittenhouse Square*. Charleston, VA: Arcadia Press.

Straus, Jacob (2014) Lower Sproul Plaza transforming into a hub of student life. *The Daily Californian*, August 29. Available at: www.dailycal.org/2014/08/29/lower-sproul-plaza-transforming-hub-student-life/.

Sudic, Deyan (2003) If only Sir Christopher were alive today. *The Guardian/The Observer*, January 19. Available at: www.theguardian.com/theobserver/2003/jan/19/2.

Surhone, Lambert M., Mariam T. Tennoe and Susan F. Henssonow (2010) *Paley Park*. Mauritius: Betascript Publishing.

Tate, Alan (2001) *Great City Parks*. London: Spon Press.

Traub, James (2004) *The Devil's Playground: A Century of Pleasure and Profit in Times Square*. New York: Random House.

Tyrnauer, Matt (2010) Architecture in the Age of Gehry. *Vanity Fair*, August. Available at: www.vanityfair.com/culture/features/2010/08/architecture-survey-201008.

University of California, Berkeley (UCB) (2016) The Lower Sproul Redevelopment Project. Available at: http://lowersproul.berkeley.edu/home.

Vanario, Maurice (2002) *Rues des Lyon à travers les Siècles*. Lyon: ELAH.

Vasagar, Jeevan (2012) Public spaces fall into private hands. *The Guardian Weekly*, June 22: 16–17.

Vidharte, Juan Ignacio (2002) The Bilbao Guggenheim Museum. In *Euskal Hiria*. Victoria-Gasteiz: Central Publishing Services of the Basque Government, pp. 153–158.

Wagner, Walter F. Jr (ed.) (1967) In Manhattan a small park located where people are. *Architectural Record* 142(9): 117.

Watkin, David (1996) It's back to the future in the heart of London. *City Journal* (Winter). Available at: www.city-journal.org/html/6_1_its_back_to.html.

Weyergraf-Serra, Clara and Martha Buskirk (eds.) (1991) *The Destruction of Tilted Arc: Documents*. Cambridge, MA: MIT Press.

Whyte, William H. (1980) *The Social Life of Small Urban Spaces*. Washington, DC: The Conservation Foundation.

Yen, Brigham (2013) 'Friends of Pershing Park' reimagines downtown LA's faded historic park. *DTLA Rising*. Available at: http://brighamyen.com/2013/02/04/friends-of-pershing-square-reimagines-downtown-la-greatest-faded-public-space/.

Zucker, Paul (1959) *Town and Square: From the Agora to the Village Green*. New York: Columbia University Press.

Further Reading

Balfour, Alan (1978) *Rockefeller Center: Architecture of Theatre*. New York: McGraw Hill.

Brill, Michael (1989) Transformation, nostalgia and illusion in public life and public places. In *Public Spaces and Places*, edited by Irwin Altman and Erwin H. Zube. New York: Plenum Press.

Carmona, Matthew (2014a) The place-shaping continuum: A theory of urban design process. *Journal of Urban Design* 19 (1): 2–36.

Carmona, Matthew (ed.) (2014b) *Explorations in Urban Design: An Urban Design Primer*. Farnham: Ashgate.

Carmona, Matthew, Tim Heath, Taner Oc and Steven Tiesdell (2003) *Public Places – Urban Spaces: The Dimensions of Urban Design*. Oxford: Architectural Press.

Carr, Stephen, Mark Francis, Leanne Rivlin and Andrew M. Stone (1992) *Public Space*. Cambridge: Cambridge University Press.

Duncan, James S. Jr and Nancy Duncan (2001) The aestheticization of the politics of landscape preservation. *Annals of the Association of American Geographers* 91(2): 387–409.

Feraboli, Maria Teresa (2007) *City Squares of the World*. Vercelli: White Star.

Jenkins, Eric J. (2008) *To Scale: One Hundred Urban Plans*. New York: Routledge.

Whyte, William H. (1989) *City: Rediscovering the Center*. New York: Doubleday.

PART IV

WHAT WORKS AND
WHAT DOESN'T WORK

The Museum Quarter, Vienna
Photograph by Jude Stoddart.

Any presentation claiming to deal comprehensively with what works and what does not work in the design of urban squares has to be treated carefully. The reasons are threefold. First, it is easy to draw [false] conclusions from correlations between variables; there may well be intervening variables that impact on apparent patterns of causes and effects.[1] Second, the totality of a square and its set of individual aspects are at work simultaneously and disaggregating them to ascertain what factors are at play is difficult. Finally, people who set out to assess urban squares have different values and motivations and evaluation criteria. Our own assessments draw on many studies and reviews, sometimes contradictory, as well as our own research.

A number of worthwhile attempts have been made to list the factors that make for successful urban squares based on the assumption that a square has to be lively to be regarded as successful.[2] Some cities have developed detailed guidelines for the design of public squares or at least open space. These guidelines can be highly specific in detailing the requirements for any new urban space. They are based on the assumption that good design can be achieved by following a formula. New York's City Department of City Planning (2007) guidelines, for instance, detail the number of linear feet of seating and number of trees that are required by the size of the square. Its focus is understandably on the privately owned public spaces, given the disappointing results of the city's incentive program formulated to achieve more public open spaces, as Gilbert notes (2001). Many architects, who may want to do things their own way, believe that these guidelines can hamper innovation.

Assessments and conclusions about urban squares are biased by the assessors' beliefs about what qualities a square should possess "How strong the lens, how keen the eyes . . . to see what we hypothesize" (Curlin 2012: website). What is perceived to be successful depends on one's sociocultural character. To act as outdoor living rooms in the right neighborhood setting, we also recognize the diversity of instrumental purposes that squares can serve as outlined in Chapter 5.

This fourth part of the book is divided into two closely related chapters addressing the functioning of squares. They both specifically deal with what works and does not work; Chapter 13 deals with the qualities of lively places and links while Chapter 14 considers what makes squares quiet places. The latter chapter covers the attributes of squares that are simply boring as well as places that were intentionally designed to provide visitors with a sense of peace and quiet. Both chapters deal with the issue of how best to meet the objective that a square is intended to serve but implicit in the discussion is that the objectives are worthwhile. The requirements presented in Chapter 14 may well seem to be the opposite of those presented in Chapter 13 but, as will be shown, the story is not quite that simple. The chapter also serves as a caution. However well-meaning a designer may be, it is easy to end up with public spaces that fail to meet their intended purposes if the assumptions on which their designs are based are erroneous.

We acknowledge that our approach is biased by assuming that the aim of many designs is to create squares that are well loved by people of different ages, cultures or socioeconomic groups engaged in a variety of activities. One should not, however, believe that a diversity of people will fill the square if the principles laid out in Chapter 13 are followed. It depends on the location and context of the squares and the attitudes and predispositions of potential users.

Notes

1 The authors are well aware of the Hawthorne effect although it is not directly relevant to this review. The effect states that changes perceived in people's behavior as the result of the redesign, in this case, of a square may be related only to the special social situation and social treatment they received and not the pattern of built form.
2 Project for Public Spaces (n.d.), for example, suggests a list of 10 principles for the design of successful squares.

References

Curlin, Jay (2012) *The Evidence of Things Not Seen.* Available at: www.new-yorker.com/magazine/2012/07/30/the-evidence-of-things-not-seen.
Gilbert, Helen (2001) A case study in contemporary development; how does it measure up to the principles of classic urban design theorists? Paper presented at Seventh Annual Pacific Rim Real Estate Society Conference, Adelaide, January 21–24. Available at: www.prres.net/papers/gilbert_a_case_study_in_contemporary_development_how_does_it_%20 measure_up_to_the_principles_of_classic_urban_design_theorists.pdf.
New York City Department of City Planning (2007) Privately owned public plazas: text amendment. Available at: www.nyc.gov/html/dcp/pdf/priv/101707_final_approved.text.pdf.
Project for Public Spaces (n.d.) 10 principles for successful public squares. Available at: www.pps.org/reference/squaresprinciples/.

Further Reading

Engwicht, David (1999) *'Street Reclaiming': Creating Liveable Streets and Vibrant Communities.* Gabriola Island, BC: New Society Publishers.

CHAPTER 13

THE QUALITIES OF LIVELY URBAN SQUARES

'Fitness for purpose' is still the worthy goal for a designer, whether designing a new square or redesigning an existing one. Purpose just needs to be defined in broad terms rather than in the way the concept of function that we inherited from the Modernists is understood.[1] Jan Taugh (cited in Engwicht 1999) believes that the urban environment should provide the affordances for looking, listening and talking to people, walking about and sitting down – to be the outdoor rooms within a city. Many public authorities clearly do not want to have squares with the characteristics Taugh regards as good; they fear that the space will be taken over by transients, the homeless and other segments of the population whose presence is deemed to be less than desirable (Savić and Savićic 2013).[2] The impact of the redesign of Bryant Park in New York suggests, however, that well-located and well-designed public open spaces attractive to the general populace are not places desired by the homeless (Weber 1995). Where they are, transients are accepted as legitimate users of the square and interfere little with how a space works for others.

One approach we could have taken for this book would be to simply describe the squares that we like.[3] A second approach would have been to consider squares as self-conscious works of art.[4] The qualities of an urban square can certainly be analyzed in terms of how well it meets the principles of the design paradigm employed, or how well it meets its designer's goals. Finally any statement on what makes a square desirable can be based on how well it functions as a place and a display not only for the experts but as part of people's life in a city.

From the observations made in the past twelve chapters it can be concluded that the qualities of a square depend as much on what is around it as on the design characteristics of the square itself. As outlined in Part II of this book where types of squares were described, squares can serve many functions simultaneously and/or sequentially in time. In this chapter we take the position that a square should be an attraction and a lively place. Gertrude Stein (1937: 289) once remarked that her hometown, Oakland, California, had no "there" there – no spot that was a landmark and a node, so no sense of presence for her. Lively squares need to have a sense of presence but not all squares need to be full of people, as we discuss in Chapter 14.

Our observations of what makes squares lively places are intended to be indicative and not prescriptive. In application, they have to be adjusted for their cultural and climatic, indeed microclimatic, conditions (Zacharias *et al.* 2001). The broad categories of connectivity and linkages; surrounding uses; degree of enclosure; and the affordances of the square itself are always important when considering which characteristics make for lively squares.

Contextual Concerns

The context in which a square is located greatly affects its usage and meaning for both the inhabitants of a city and for visitors. To be a pleasant place, the quality of light and sound in a square and its degree of enclosure explain much about a square's quality. To be a destination, a square needs to be linked into the pedestrian flows of a city. The surrounding buildings and the activities they house, and the way the square is related to them are important.

The number of people living or working in nearby buildings affects the use of squares because they are the potential passers-through or visitors to them. To be used by people with any frequency a square needs to be located within easy walking distance (that is 200–300 meters or 220–330 yards) of a critical mass of people. The distance depends on the degree to which pedestrian routes (to a square) require crossing major roads or transit lines. The greater the frequency of street crossings, the shorter is the distance that people are prepared to walk. Ideally, the approaches should have no more than slight gradients especially up-slopes in the walk to the square (Hewasam *et al.* 2012).

As Hillier and Hanson (1984) and others note, the manner in which streets and/or passageways open off a square has a consequence for the life of a square. If a square is part of a pedestrian network (as many classical European squares are) and there are destinations before and after it that generate traffic (a dumbbell pattern of attractors, or anchors), then people will use the square as a link and simultaneously add life to it and provide the people within the square something to watch. Camillo Sitte (1889; Sitte and Stewart 1945) believed that squares served by many narrow entrances – his "turbine" squares – function best because they give a sense of arrival when moving from a tight space into a large one (Figure 13.1 (a)). Such a sense is engendered if the entry to a square is through a narrow passage that opens into the square as when approaching the Plaza Mayor in Madrid from any of its portal entrances (Figure 13.1 (b)) or entering the Piazza San Marco in Venice, especially from the land side along Mercante and under the Torre dell'Orologio (the clock tower).

Good connections to a public transport system are necessary, particularly for those squares where large events are held. London's Paternoster Square and Trafalgar Square and New York's Times Square, among others we have mentioned, are well used partly because they are closely linked to an underground railway station and to pedestrian paths as well as the nature of the buildings that surround them. Calgary's Olympic Plaza is next to the city's Light Rail Transit, making major events easy to access.

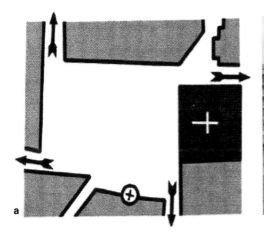

Figure 13.1 Camillo Sitte's Turbine plan: (a) The general concept; (b) Two of the "turbine" entrances to Plaza Mayor, Madrid

Source: (a) Collins and Collins (1965: 34).

The greater the diversity of uses occurring in the surrounding buildings, the more likely a square will be used as a link and as a set of places, provided its design accommodates both. In fully enclosed squares, the frequency of entrances directly onto the square enhances the coming and going of people, especially if the entrances are to busy shops and restaurants. Squares surrounded by houses are quieter places and may serve as outdoor rooms especially in high-density neighborhoods where residential apartments are small.

Blank, textureless walls make dull surroundings. A problem arises when the desire is to create a lively square and its enclosing building's internal uses demand blank walls. This clash can be partly negated by turning the walls into green walls as in the Caixa Forum in Madrid or having murals or reliefs on them, as specified in the building codes of the City of Bellevue (1989) in the state of Washington, USA, or in the town of Chemainus in British Columbia, Canada (Figure 13.2).

Although there are some fine squares that are cut off from the buildings around them by heavily used traffic lanes on all four sides, it is not an ideal arrangement. Squares that have no moving cars, buses and trucks between the open space in their centers and their enclosing buildings tend to work well as outdoor living rooms, provided they are not too large. Busy streets present a daunting challenge for pedestrians to reach a square. Azadi Square in Tehran (see Figure 4.7 (b) on p. 79) is surrounded by moving cars and buses. Unless such

Figure 13.2 Green walls and murals: (a) Caixa Forum, Madrid, Patrick Blanc, botanist; (b) 'Logging with Oxen' mural, Chemainus, Canada, Harold Lyon, artist

squares have a major attraction within them, they will be little used. Place Charles de Gaulle in Paris, a traffic circle, which is reached by underpasses, has the Arc de Triomphe as a major destination which provides fine views of Paris from its roof.

Traffic lights help people cross a street to reach a square but waiting for them to change is as tedious for pedestrians as it is for drivers. Pedestrian underpasses are not a good solution as they are usually gloomy, or may be perceived to be unsafe and difficult to access, although they do not have to be either. Unless barriers prevent pedestrians from jay-walking, overpasses seldom, if ever, are well used in providing a safe passageway. Pedestrians will reluctantly use them if there is no alternative means of getting access to a square. The square has to be a major attraction for people to bother. In villages the traffic volumes may be so low that the vehicles are not intrusive and, indeed, add vitality to a place. Busy streets also affect the sonic quality of the square. A steady hum of traffic may provide white noise and a sense of the people in a square being part of a busy city, but constant or extreme traffic noise intrudes on conversations, programmed events or simple solitude (Cogger 2016).

Any transition from a sidewalk to a square needs to be level or to have low, easy steps or ramps linking the two. The number of steps into Paley Park is about the maximum that one should have to go up or down between street and square (see Figure 12.3 on p. 184). Squares raised more than 0.5 of a meter (20 inches) above the street level are less attractive than those at the same height or below the surrounding street level. Stepping down tends to give a square a basic level of enclosure but a square loses a comfortable connection with the surrounding buildings and streets if it is more than 1 meter (3 feet) below street level. Squares at basement level are seldom lively unless they are the location for very specific activities organized in them as, for example, in Rockefeller Center, New York during both summer and winter (see Figures 2.2 (a) and 2.2 (b) on p. 36).

The quality of light in a square is, as described in Chapter 7, fundamental to the perceived quality of a square. Dark and gloomy squares are seldom lively places. Trees and plants find it difficult to thrive without sunlight. The height of surrounding buildings in relation to the latitude of a square is the major factor in shaping the quality of light in a square. The location and height of the buildings surrounding a square also have other important consequences. The height of the surrounding buildings determines the perceived sense of enclosure; this variable is one of the most important in defining the quality of a square. To obtain a strong sense of enclosure for the people within the square, the width to height ratio seems to be about 3:1 (Maertens 1877; Sitte 1889; Sitte and Stewart 1945; Zucker 1959; Gehl 2010). The height affects the amount of sunlight directly penetrating a space or being reflected off walls and windows. At the higher latitudes a trade-off has to be made in the design of a square between obtaining a strong sense of enclosure and having a significant amount of sunlight penetrating into it.

The Characteristics of the Square Itself

No square, even the most lively and lauded, possesses all the characteristics that we identify in this chapter. Taken one by one, none of the requirements we specify are crucial to the performance of a square in anybody's eyes. Added together, they make a significant difference. As will be clear, the requirements listed are neither independent nor mutually exclusive.

Basic Requirements

Many concerns have to be addressed in the design of the internal layout of a square in order to make it a place. Almost everything depends on its instrumental purpose. While this observation is a platitude, it still needs to be stated. The challenge is for policy-makers, planners and designers to decide on the set of purposes that a square is expected to fulfill. The floor of the square has to be designed with the square's instrumental purpose in mind. A flat uniform surface is the fundamental requirement for most activities and events. If it is to house formal gatherings, a raised area that can act as a platform needs to be incorporated.

Designers must beware of making squares too large. It is better to have to 'shoehorn' some events in rather than making the square large enough to accommodate major events spaciously. The objective is to make the square appear to be inviting when few people are there. Throughout this book, we have considered squares to consist of places and links. The requirements of the latter are easier to list so we begin with them.

Links

People generally walk in approximately straight lines between points of origin and destination across a square unless there are obstacles in the way. Links should, ideally, be flat, smooth and barrier-free to accommodate the movement of people of all abilities. Links need to have comfortable walking surfaces. Some tiled surfaces become very slippery in wet conditions and uneven through wear over time, which can make them hazardous for walkers. To function well, the routes through squares need to be obvious. They can be demarcated by symbolic gateways (for example, gaps between raised planter boxes) at the entrances to the square, or by changes in the hue or texture of the floor material of the square. If the square is of different levels, there should be ramps as well as steps between the levels. Obstacles in the form of street furniture, bollards and posts in the line of movement should be avoided. At night, good illumination is necessary. Lights should line paths that are clearly demarcated; otherwise light should enfold the square.

Using Abraham Maslow's hierarchy of human motivations as an organizing model, the requirements of squares in relationship to their surroundings and as links themselves can be summarized in Table 13.1.[5]

Table 13.1 The basic requirements for lively squares as links

Design factor	Basic requirements	Comfort	Safety and security	Belonging and esteem	Experiential esthetics
Relationship to surroundings	Close to activity generators	No steep slopes on approach roads; well-kept, smooth pavements to cater for all abilities	Clear sight line into the square; street furniture located out of the paths of movement; passive surveillance	Surfaces, materials and detailing with positive associations for the users*	Positive sequential experience when moving through spaces on the route to the square
As passageways	Clear and direct points of entry and exit; smooth surfaces; understandable signage, multi-lingual in some places	Smooth ground surfaces for walking (by all abilities), moving in wheelchairs, pushing baby carriages, pulling trolleys, etc.	Good lighting; clear and visible way-finding signage	Indigenous vegetation border; local decorative features in light standards and other street furniture or the esthetics of Modernist globalization*	High quality, robust materials providing high levels of rich sensory experiences

Note: *There is likely to be a clash between advocates for local character to be represented in the square and those people who favor more global designs.

Places

The quality of the square's paving is fundamental to making it a good place. The paving, as for links, needs to be easy and safe to walk on and have a simple, geometric pattern that is meaningful for the population of concern. In almost all squares the location and quality of seating are important if it is to be a space where people can linger. There needs to be a range of options from which people can choose without the square becoming cluttered with 'bits and pieces' of street furniture.

A square should contain sociofugal and sociopetal seating arrangements (Osmond 1966). Convex patterns of seating afford the former and concave the latter. The latter affords easy verbal and visual communication between people and the former the opportunity to be left alone. The distance apart for face-to-face communication should be at a socio-consultative distance (about 2 meters; 6 feet 6 inches) to create sociopetal spaces as defined by Hall's (1969) *proxemic* theory which studied human perception and use of space based on cultural norms. The dimensions of the spaces in the benches in Barcelona's Parc Güell are fixed at an appropriate socio-consultative distance (see Figure 2.1 on p. 35). The curving benches that used to exist in the Jacob K. Javits Center Plaza in New York (see Figure 12.17 (b) on p. 230) created concave and convex forms of varying dimensions giving individuals and groups of visitors a choice of places to sit, depending on their level of need for privacy. The convex shapes created the sociofugal spaces that are important in assisting people to achieve privacy in a public space.[6]

A well-located and well-designed square with links running across it and good seating will need no special features to attract or entertain visitors (Lindsay 1978). Apart from good seating and opportunities to watch other people and their activities, a square often needs to have some catalyst to attract people. Features that add to the quality of a square for people are a café or food/refreshment outlet, art installations and programmed performances (Whyte 1980; Mehta 2013b). Sonic levels need to be low or obscured by white noise (Cogger 2016, 2011; Kang 2006). Traffic passing along one side of a square can add to its life although it can also impact negatively on the ambient quality of a place.[7] Clean well-managed toilets provided in or nearby a square add to its basic amenity level. The presence of other people (including buskers), birds (even crows, pigeons and ibis that are generally regarded as a nuisance) and smaller animals such as squirrels, depending on the location and cultural context, adds to the general attractiveness of a square as a place. The use of native vegetation increases the possibility of attracting indigenous species of birds and adds to a square's sense of locality.

People need to feel comfortable if they are to linger in a square. There are two major dimensions to feeling physically at ease: (1) being metabolically comfortable; and (2) being ergonomically comfortable. For the former, a square needs to provide options to sit in the sun or shade, under cover or, in winter, near a heater and either in or out of breezes. Wind tunnels and downdrafts from surrounding buildings detract from the quality of any open space. While people are less demanding in their requirements for outdoor furniture than indoor, benches and ledges need to be at sitting heights. The expectations of comfort are higher for chairs and benches than for ledges and higher for ledges than for steps. Some chairs should be moveable as it provides users with choice and autonomy, as Whyte (1980) noted in his research. Lawns are popular places to sit and new designs such as 'grass chairs' offer unique seating in some climates and contexts.

People who visit squares, whether local or tourists, also need to feel psychologically comfortable when in them. They need to feel safe and physically and mentally secure. If a square has the reputation, earned or not, of being dangerous, few people will enter it. A feeling of physical security comes from perceiving that others lack the opportunity to engage and are not engaging in antisocial behavior; mental security from having a sense of control over one's social environment. In many cities the fear of crime has been a leading reason that people cite for not using public open spaces (Miethe 1995). It is a major reason why privately owned public spaces (POPS) that are well patrolled by security personnel are popular. The presence of a caretaker or guard as in Paley Park in New York or the Praça de Ludo in Rio de Janeiro has mixed reviews. Whyte (1980) noted that guards add to the sense of security people feel when they are in public open spaces. Unfortunately, the notion that a guard is needed in that space suggests that the space is in fact, unsafe. In some places such as Granary Square in London, Constitution Square in Berkeley and Times Square in New York, the 'security guards' may also act as ambassadors and tourist guides. In all these cases there is a loss of individual privacy but it is generally agreed that this loss is something that people have to accept in order to feel safe (Jacobs 1961). A sense of safety also comes from the presence of at least some other people

similar to oneself in terms of age, gender or ethnicity. This requirement is a reality for many people, although it is not widely regarded
as an ideal situation by those who prefer to see individuals happy
to share public spaces with a diversity of people unlike themselves.

To enhance a sense of security in any square, Crime Prevention
Through Environmental Design (CPTED) principles should be applied
(Atlas 2008). They include a square being overlooked by people
from windows that they frequently use.[8] The square also needs to
be visually open without objects or some types of vegetation which
people can hide behind (although for children such places add to the
playground quality of a square). Freeway Park in Seattle, as noted,
although an attractive and interesting design with many 'nooks and
crannies' became notorious for the antisocial behavior that took place
there because its intricate design obscured views (Mudede 2002). At
night, good lighting and no dark corners in a square are important
requirements. The façades of adjacent buildings should also be at
least partially illuminated which helps avoid the square appearing
to be gloomy.

Popular additional features that people find attractive in a square
include point elements that make it a nuclear square. They act as
reference points and places to meet. These features can be obelisks,
statues, clock towers, fountains or even a tree. Almost anything associated with water seems to be an attraction, especially for children.
Ponds or other water features can give a focus to a square as can
memorials, sculptures or art installations. Objects that move – performers, flags, birds flying and branches of trees that rustle with
the wind – enhance the general atmosphere of a place (Figure 13.3).
Finally, programmed events such as festivals and markets attract
locals and visitors to almost any urban open space.

Sense of Place

The often expressed worry that recently designed squares could be
anywhere because they follow prestigious, international stylistic patterns is misplaced.[9] All squares have a sense of place by the nature

Figure 13.3 Performers attract
attention: (a) Piazza della Rotunda,
Rome; (b) Quincy Market, Boston

of them being in specific contexts and geographic localities (Marshall 2016). The characteristics of the people who are in a square contribute to its sense of place immediately, regardless of how similar the square is to those in other countries. In addition, designing with the climate in mind locates a square within a geographic context.[10] Having native vegetation for its own sake as well as to attract local birds adds a dimension to establishing a sense of locale. Using or representing local decorative features, indigenous art work and local variations of international themes helps to establish a clear identity to a square and also a sense of pride in the people who use or observe a square. The cognoscenti often deplore the use of such decorative features in a literal sense. They prefer to see them applied as abstractions. Pershing Square in Los Angeles represents one such effort. It does not appear to have been too successful.

Many sociopolitical factors in everyday life and the teaching of histories are more important than the physical design of places in establishing a group's unique identity, for example, by gender, socioeconomic status or ethnicity. In many places, signage needs to be bilingual or even multi-lingual. Creating well-designed places will partially meet people's need to see themselves held in esteem by others. In addition, memorials to the heroes and positive historical events associated with a group help build the esteem in which they

Table 13.2 The basic requirements for lively squares as places

Design factor	Basic requirements	Comfort	Safety and security	Belonging and esteem	Experiential esthetics
Getting access to a square	Continuous, unfragmented access routes; clear way-finding signage; easy links to surrounding streets; legislated accessibility requirements; free entry	Ramps for people of all abilities to have easy access; smooth floors and well-designed steps with broad treads, handrails other inclusive features	Ideally, no streets to cross between the enclosing elements and the surface of the square; smooth ground surfaces; no tripping hazards; good lighting	Patterns of surfaces with positive associations for people; diverse and many programmed events aimed at different user populations	Positive sensory experiences: visual, olfactory, haptic and auditory
Sitting	Variety of seating options: benches, ledges and, ideally, moveable chairs, lawns and/or sloping grassed areas; being able to choose one's own seat	A variety of seating heights for people of all abilities; sunlight and shade levels appropriate for the climate; gentle flushing breezes; Wi-Fi; electric outlets for personal technological devices near seating; heating and cooling systems	Well-maintained landscaping; clear sight lines; sociofugal seating for people seeking solitude; sociopetal seating for groups wanting to talk	High quality furnishings, materials and good workmanship; well-maintained seating; native trees and other local vegetation	Pleasant odors; rich and comfortable tactile experiences; a quiet sonic environment; understandable and positive symbolic meanings

Table 13.2 continued

Design factor	Basic requirements	Comfort	Safety and security	Belonging and esteem	Experiential esthetics
Talking	Sociopetal seating; low levels of sound from passing traffic or other sources	Lack of sun glare; range of seating options	Clear sight lines; good lighting at night; no dark corners	Freedom to be their authentic self and to talk freely in the public space	Quiet movements to look at (e.g. flowing water)
Watching and being watched	Clear sight lines for seeing into and out of a square; the presence of people; activities, nature to watch; good, durable lighting	No obstacles in performance zones; climbable features for children	Natural surveillance from surrounding buildings and from people in the square; although not ideal, security guards and/ or surveillance cameras	A diversity of regular and pop-up events to provide services or entertainment on occasions; infrastructure and amenities appropriate for different groups	Positive sensory experiences; moving elements such as flags or birds to watch; people carrying out activities; organized performances
Performing/ self-testing	Performance zones; climbable seats and benches; sculptures, art installations; water features on site	The comfort level of children being challenged through climbable objects*; digital challenges such as installations, games, hubs	Non-slip surfaces; soft surfaces to avoid injury; durable sculptures, and furniture	Inclusive performance zones (e.g. including, seniors' fitness equipment or allowing teens to skateboard)	A range of different experiences on site across different times of day, seasons or year
Eating	Tables, chairs, benches; accessible food outlets within or on the periphery; garbage bins	Comfortable table height levels; moveable chairs; drinking fountains	Sturdy, durable and maintained tables and chairs; long and regular food outlet hours	Clean surroundings; a variety of foods at affordable prices in or near the square	High quality food; fresh, clean odors; no odors from toilets
Events/ programming	Flat surfaces; flexible space; power outlets; water supply; sewer links; nearby public transport; nearby public toilets; free entry	Ample space; storage for needed equipment (e.g. chairs, ice-rink Zambonis); raised platforms for performers and orators; acoustical comfort levels	Clear boundary markers for event zones; good lighting; marked surface changes; safe access for individual pedestrians and crowds; crowd control and medical services for large events	Regular and diverse programmed events; informal events welcomed; community and its members involved in events; local artworks / productions (temporary and permanent)	Lighting for the events; positive multisensorial experiences

Note: *Fear of litigation resulting from injuries makes this requirement unacceptable to many municipal authorities.

hold themselves. Members of these groups see that contributions to society are recognized and valued.

No single factor, apart from having a solid surface, is necessary to make a square into one that is potentially well used. Several factors, in conjunction with each other, are necessary to make a lively square. The essential ones are listed in Table 13.2 but not all these factors are required in every square. Table 13.2 should be regarded as a menu from which to choose the range of characteristics appropriate for the instrumental purpose(s) a square is to serve.

Requirements of Squares as Artistic Displays

Inevitably all squares are displays. They have a design and usually objects within them that communicate meanings or, more correctly, have meanings read into them. The general public will often have very different feelings about the design of a square compared the design, architecture and art cognescenti. The public will interpret the layout of the square based on their own experiences while the latter groups will analyze the square based on design and art theories.

Designing a square with a layout and objects that fit the taste culture of the users is a difficult task, conceptually and physically. A popular square will be used by people with very different values. Avant-garde designs may amuse the average user but providing the square meets their basic requirements, it will be unlikely to cause offense although it might be seen as a waste of money. The general public is not habituated to modern artistic forms. Literal art works, whereby meanings are easy to interpret, may well cause more problems due to conflicts of opinions. Modern art works are seen to be gender and ethnically neutral although they are generally specific to a taste culture. Once viewed carefully, they are often disregarded thereafter as objects in space to glance at in passing.

The style of the architecture of the surrounding buildings of a square has little effect on the performance of the square. The buildings in Federation Square in Melbourne are regarded by some of the public as "ugly," as noted by Levy (2012), although they appeal to the cognescenti who understand and appreciate the cleverness of the architects' argument for their design. The square itself is a successful place in most people's eyes. Although it has a somewhat gloomy interior, it possesses many of the characteristics we identify as the basis for creating lively urban places and links.

The requirements of squares as displays are summarized in Table 13.3. It is clear that the characteristics required to make squares artistic displays can easily contradict some of the requirements to make squares lively. To be lively, squares have to serve well as places and links otherwise they remain displays to contemplate. As such, many architects argue, they attract certain types of visitors (Carmona 2014a). As displays, squares may also boost the self-image of nearby residents and workers even if the squares' esthetic character deviates from their tastes.

All designing requires trading-off one design objective with another. Designing is, after all, a contested process, as we make clear in the Epilogue, Notes on the Designing and/or Upgrading of Squares. If squares are artistic displays as well as places and links, it is an added bonus.

Table 13.3 The requirements of squares as displays

Design factor	Basic requirements	Comfort	Safety and security	Belonging and esteem	Esthetics
In the users' eyes	Patterns of enclosing elements; objects to fit the users' tastes; literal rather than abstract forms for sculptures, design features, installations	Objects or installations that do not cause physical or emotional harm	The qualities listed in Table 13.2 to be implemented	Symbols used in the statues, sculpture and furnishings in accord with the user population's values; native vegetation	Multi-modal, sensory complexity; formal order; symbols of belonging
In the eyes of the cognoscenti	Freedom of artistic expression for the designers; patterns associated with a design paradigm or ideology	Furnishings primarily as works of art, but they have to fulfill their instrumental functions as well	The designer's personal attitudes towards comfort, safety and security, and belonging and esteem should be clear in the design; furnishings are the designer's tastes	Patterns to represent avant-garde tastes; starchitect's works/style on display	Overall design and objects within it to be 'heroic' and avant-garde; furnishings are works of art

Maintenance Concerns[11]

Although there are many examples of run-down squares that are well used, particularly by nearby residents and local workers, a very detailed and well-maintained square attracts people more than one that is not. It may also raise the spirits of locals when a council or business commits money to the maintenance of a square. Such actions demonstrate that the square and its users are valued and worth investing in. The construction and furnishings should be robust as well as finely detailed. They need to retain their quality over time and in changing weather conditions with infrequent maintenance.

Squares need to be clean. While pigeons add life to a square, they are generally regarded as undesirable when they are present in large numbers. Garbage bins need to be provided and emptied regularly. Although there is no conclusive evidence that it works, the "broken window hypothesis" that fixing small acts of vandalism reduces vandalism is widely considered to apply to open spaces in cities (Kelling and Coles 1997). Fixtures and furnishings, trees and plants require constant maintenance and the cost of doing day-to-day maintenance and refurbishments needs to be considered before designing begins.

Conclusion

All the generalizations presented in this chapter are just that, generalizations. They assume that the design goal is to create a meaningful square that provides a place for people to enjoy themselves. The generalizations as summarized in Tables 13.1–13.3 parallel the efforts of Jan Gehl (2010), Matthew Carmona and his colleagues (2003, 2014a, 2014b), Vikas Mehta (2013a, 2013b), John Montgomery (1998) and Charles Landry (2006), to mention but a few. The overlaps are not coincidental as we are all looking at the same phenomena.

Robert Gatje (2010: 11) writes: "Twenty centuries ago, the Roman architect Vitruvius gave us the best criteria for judging architecture. The functions are usually rendered in English as 'Commodity, Firmness and Delight'. Squares too can be judged à la Vitruvius by their 'utility, integrity and delight'."

The general design goals that are established to guide the design of a square are likely to be as universal in character as Vitruvius's statement. Identifying the specifics should be guided by the generalizations presented in this chapter if the goal is to create lively, well-loved squares. The generalizations we present need to be adapted to the patterns of behavior and esthetic values that exist within specific cultural frames. The Epilogue, Notes on the Designing and/or Upgrading of Squares addresses the issues involved in doing so. The attempt will be made in Chapter 14 to do the reverse of what we have presented here. Its purpose is to point out how to design quiet, restorative squares but also to explain why some squares that were supposed to be lively have not turned out that way.

Notes

1 See Lang and Moleski (2010) for a broad definition of the purposes of buildings and open spaces in a city.
2 See Savić and Savićic (2013) and Chapter 14 for the techniques used to deter people from lingering.
3 Robert Gatje's book *Great Public Squares: An Architect's Selection* (2010) is an example of this type of analysis.
4 Nicolai Ouroussoff's (2005) and Ada Louise Huxtable's (2005) assessments of Schouwburgplein in Rotterdam are an example.
5 See Maslow (1987) and Huitt (2004) on the hierarchy of human needs. The model is widely used in thinking about the functions of the built environment. See Lang and Moleski (2010).
6 Irwin Altman (1975) provides a clear explanation of the nature of privacy.
7 Jack London Square in Oakland has a train line and La Place des Terreaux in Lyon has trams and cars along one side while buses, cars and other vehicular traffic swirl around three sides of Trafalgar Square in London.
8 Oscar Newman's (1972) concept of defensible space, while much challenged, has stood up well over time.
9 See Relph (1976) for a discussion on place and placelessness.
10 Prominent Indian architect, Charles Correa, is among those who stress this requirement in establishing a sense of place.
11 For general commentaries on the management of public spaces, see Department of the Environment (1997) and Carmona *et al.* (2008).

References

Altman, Irwin (1975) *Environment and Social Behavior: Privacy, Personal Space, Territory, Crowding*. Monterey, CA: Brooks/Cole.
Atlas, Randall (ed.) (2008) *21st Century Security and CPTED: Designing for Critical Infrastructure Protection and Crime Prevention*. Boca Raton, FL: CRC Press.
Carmona, Matthew (2014a) The place-shaping continuum: A theory of urban design process. *Journal of Urban Design* 19(1): 2–36.

Carmona, Matthew (2014b) *Explorations in Urban Design: An Urban Design Primer*. Farnham: Ashgate.

Carmona, Matthew, Tim Heath, Taner Oc and Steven Tiesdell (2003) *Public Places – Urban Spaces: The Dimensions of Urban Design*. Oxford: Architectural Press.

Carmona, Matthew, Claudio de Magalhães and Leo Hammond (eds.) (2008) *Public Space: The Management Dimension*. London: Routledge.

City of Bellevue (1989) Ordinance Number 4108. Available at: www.bellevuewa.gov/Ordinances/Ord-4108.pdf.

Cogger, Rachel (2011)The urban symphony, are you listening? Unpublished thesis, University of New South Wales, Sydney.

Cogger, Rachel (2016) Tuning in and out of place. In *Place and Placelessness Revisited*, edited by Robert Freestone and Edgar Liu. New York: Routledge, pp. 120–137.

Collins, George R. and Christiane Crasemann Collins (1965) *Camillo Sitte and the Birth of Modern City Planning*. New York: Random House.

Department of the Environment (1997) *Managing Urban Spaces in Town Centres: Good Practice Guide*. London: HMSO.

Engwicht, David (1999) *'Street Reclaiming': Creating Liveable Streets and Vibrant Communities*. Gabriola Island, BC: New Society Publishers.

Gatje, Robert F. (2010) *Great Public Squares: An Architect's Selection*. New York: Norton.

Gehl, Jan (2010) *Cities for People*. Washington, DC: Island Press.

Hall, Edward T. (1969) *The Hidden Dimension*. New York: Anchor Books.

Hewasam, Chamali, Saman Bandara and S. C. Wirahsinghe (2012) Identifying quantifiable measures of walkability. Paper presented at FARU Symposium, Galle, Sri Lanka, August 24.

Hillier, Bill and Julienne Hanson (1984) *The Social Logic of Space*. Cambridge: Cambridge University Press.

Huitt, William G. (2004) Maslow's hierarchy of human needs. *Educational Psychology Interactive*. Valdosta, GA: Valdosta State University. Available at: www.edpsycinteractive.org/topics/regsys/maslow.html.

Huxtable, Ada Louise (2005) Down-to-earth masterpieces of public landscape design. *The Wall Street Journal*, May 5, p. D10. Available at: www.wsj.com/articles/SB111515970031423786.

Jacobs, Jane (1961) *The Death and Life of Great American Cities*. New York: Random House.

Kang, Jian (2006) *Urban Sound Environment*. London: Spon.

Kelling, George L. and Catherine M. Coles (1997) *Fixing Broken Windows: Restoring Order and Reducing Crime in Our Communities*. New York: Simon & Schuster.

Landry, Charles (2006) *The Art of City Making*. London: Earthscan.

Lang, Jon and Walter Moleski (2010) *Functionalism Revisited: Architectural Theory and Practice and the Behavioral Sciences*. Farnham: Ashgate.

Levy, Megan (2012) How ugly? Fed Square ranked amongst the worst ever. *The Age*, April 4. Available at: www.theage.com.au/victoria/how-ugly-fed-square-ranked-among-worst-ever-20120404-1wbum.html.

Lindsay, Nancy (1978) It all comes down to a comfortable place to sit and watch. *Landscape Architecture* 68(6): 492–497.

Maertens, Hermann (1877) *Der Optische-Maßstab oder die Theorie und Praxis des Ästhetischen Sehens in der bildenden Kunsten. Auf Grund der Lehrer der physiologischen Optic*. Bonn: Cohen, 2nd edn, 1884, Berlin: Wasmuth.

Marshall, Nancy (2016) Urban squares: A place for public life. In *Place and Placelessness Revisited*, edited by Robert Freestone and Edgar Liu. New York: Routledge, pp. 186–203.

Maslow, Abraham (1987) *Motivation and Personality*, 3rd edn. Revised by Robert Frager, James Fadiman, Cynthia McReynolds and Ruth Cox. New York: Harper and Row.

Mehta, Vikas (2013a) *The Street: A Quintessential Social Public Space*. London: Routledge.

Mehta, Vikas (2013b) Evaluating public open space. *Journal of Urban Design* 19(1): 53–88.

Miethe, Terance D. (1995) Fear and withdrawal for urban life. *Annals of the American Academy of Political and Social Science* 539: 14–27.

Montgomery, John (1998) Making a city: Urbanity, vitality and urban design. *Journal of Urban Design* 3(1): 93–116.

Mudede, Charles (2002) Topography of terror. *The Stranger*, August 22. Available at: www.thestranger.com/seattle/topography-of-terror/Content?oid=11685.

Newman, Oscar (1972) *Defensible Space*. New York: Macmillan.

Osmond, Humphrey (1966) Some psychiatric aspects of design. In *Who Designs America?* edited by Laurence B. Holland. New York: Doubleday, pp. 281–318.

Ouroussoff, Nicolai (2005) Confronting blight with hope. *New York Times*, February 24. Available at: www.nytimes.com/2005/02/24/arts/design/24moma.html?pagewanted=all&position=&_r=0.

Relph, Edward (1976) *Place and Placelessness*. London: Pion.

Savić, Selena and Gordan Savićic (eds.) (2013) *Unpleasant Design*. Belgrade: G.L.O.R.I.A.

Sitte, Camillo (1889) *Der Städtebau nach seinen künstlerischen Grundsätzen*. Vienna: Karl Graesser.

Sitte, Camillo and Charles T. Stewart (1945) *The Art of Building Cities: City Building According to its Artistic Fundamentals*. New York: Reinhold.

Stein, Gertrude (1937) *Everybody's Autobiography*. New York: Random House.

Weber, Bruce (1995) Town square of Midtown: Drug dealers' turf is now an office oasis. *The New York Times*, August 25. Available at: www.nytimes.com/1995/08/25/nyregion/town-square-of-midtown-drug-dealers-turf-is-now-an-office-oasis.html.

Whyte, William H. (1980) *The Social Life of Small Urban Spaces*. Washington, DC: The Conservation Foundation.

Zacharias, John, Theodore Stathopoulos and Hanqing Wu (2001) Microclimate and downtown open space activity. *Environment and Behavior* 33(2): 296–315.

Zucker, Paul (1959) *Town and Square: From the Agora to the Village Green*. New York: Columbia University Press.

Further Reading

Burden, Amanda (2014) How public spaces make cities work. A TED talk. Available at: www.ted.com.talks/amanda_burden_how_public_spaces_make_cities_work.

Cerver, Francisco A. and Michael Webb (1997) *Redesigning City Squares and Plazas*. New York: Hearst Books International.

Cooper Marcus and Carolyn Francis (1990) *People Places: Design Guidelines for Urban Open Space*. New York: Van Nostrand Reinhold.

Forsyth, Ann and Laura Musacchio (2005) *Designing Small Parks: A Manual for Addressing Social and Ecological Concerns*. Hoboken, NJ: John Wiley & Sons, Inc.

Francis, Mark (2003) *Urban Open Space: Designing for User Needs*. Washington, DC: Island Press.

Francis, Mark (2012) Mixed life places. In *Companion to Urban Design*, edited by Tridib Banerjee and Anastasia Loukaitou-Sideris. London: Routledge, pp. 432–446.

Lennard, Suzanne C. and Henry L. Lennard (2007) *Genius of European Squares*. Carmel, CA: Gondolier Press.

CHAPTER 14

THE QUALITIES OF QUIET URBAN SQUARES

Almost all proposed designs for public spaces get contested by individuals and groups with a diversity of partisan interests. The objectives for a square to be a lively or a quiet place are often the subject of intense debate. While some squares were purposefully designed to be quiet, tranquil places of retreat, that was not the intention for other squares. They have simply turned out to be very quiet, unused and disappointing places. We can learn much from both.

Tranquil Squares

Some squares were purposefully designed to be quiet places. This observation is particularly true of squares in residential areas. The semi-private garden squares of London fall into this category. They provide an outdoor space for the square's surrounding residents who hold a key that enables them to obtain access to the open space. The general public is not admitted. Nevern Square Gardens in the Earl's Court area of London is an example (Figure 14.1 (a)). Built in the 1880s,

Figure 14.1 London's Garden Squares: (a) Nevern Square, Earl's Court; (b) Russell Square, Bloomsbury

Figure 14.2 Empire Square, London Bridge area, London, 2007

the garden within the rectangular square is about 3,000 square meters (3/4 acre) in size. It has a central lawn with gravel paths and borders planted with trees, shrubs and flowers on its periphery and scattered benches. The surrounding fence has four Victorian wrought-iron locked gates supported on decorative piers. The garden is administered by the Nevern Square Garden Committee. Many of London's squares are similar in character. Some (for example, Russell Square, Figure 14.1 (b)) are open to the public. The City of London commissioned a comprehensive policy and practice document *Quietening Open Spaces* (Environmental Protection UK 2010) which provides guidance on how to transform public spaces into quiet places.

A number of recently built squares, either paved or with lawns and landscaping, have been designed to be quiet places. Some are the center of new residential developments; others are in the heart of cities. Empire Square in south London (Figure 14.2), although open to the public at all hours, has the attributes of a place designed not to entice passers-by to enter.[1] Apartment buildings and a gym open onto the square. At lunchtime on a lovely sunny summer's day, the square is a very quiet place but it does offer a place for nearby residents to meet and relax.

Contemplative Spaces

Some public spaces that have been called squares have been purposefully designed to afford quiet contemplation. They have little

opening onto them, are located away from large numbers of people and have little in the square to attract people apart from the square itself. They do not act as links between destinations. Some are garden-like while others are hard places. Some are memorial squares and some are simply works of art.

Figure 14.3 Open spaces as places for contemplation: (a) Pope John Paul II Prayer Garden, Baltimore; (b) Four Freedoms Park, New York

Pope John Paul II Prayer Garden is one of the few garden spaces in central Baltimore, Maryland (Figure 14.3 (a)). The garden is open from 9.00am to 3.00pm when the weather is good. Dedicated in 2008, it commemorates the visit of the Pope to the city. Its layout is in the form of a fish, an image associated with Christianity. It is a nuclear place with a statue by Joseph Sheppard of the Pope holding two children. To create this place, which has a spiritual meaning for some and is a garden retreat for others, the historic Rochambeau, a Renaissance-revival apartment building, was demolished. It exemplifies the trade-offs that often have to made in developing new squares in the built-up inner areas of cities.[2]

Four Freedoms Park in contrast to the Pope John Paul II Prayer Garden is a hard place. The square at its tip is partially enclosed by granite blocks. It is a place to contemplate the contribution of Franklin D. Roosevelt to the USA, and its architect Louis I. Kahn to architecture.

Links

The squares, or plazas, in front of significant commercial buildings were purposefully designed to serve as a link between sidewalk and building and to put the building on display. These squares do not provide for any function other than supplying a place for the workers in the building and visitors to come and go or, now, to smoke outside. Implicit in their design is the desire to deter loiterers. These squares stand in strong contrast to the traditional Italian piazzas that acted as the foreground for important edifices such as churches and palaces.

The recently designed forecourts to commercial buildings have the characteristic of good links presented in Table 13.1 but few of the features that would make them lively places. The forecourts themselves are seldom bold displays even when they are designed to be works of art; the commercial buildings are what are on display.

The design of the forecourt to the Seagram Building in New York (Figure 14.4) is one that has attracted much attention because it is regarded, with the building, as an outstanding work of modern architecture and an example of the œuvre of its architect, Mies van der Rohe (Dimendberg 2004; Jordy 2005; Burden 2014). Considerably more thought was given to the design of the building than the plaza. Similarly, as another example, more attention was paid to the buildings of Der Neue Zollhof in Düsseldorf than to the space between them. A number of well-known urban commentators have wondered if such forecourts could have been designed to offer more to pedestrians (Kayden 2000; Burden 2014). If, however, they were designed to be places, the commercial building's dominating presence at the end of the forecourt would be diminished as in the forecourt to the Ch2 Building in Melbourne.

Figure 14.4 *The forecourt to the Seagram Building, New York*

Inadvertently Dull Squares

A number of squares mentioned in this book are widely perceived to be dull places that represent lost opportunities in enhancing the life of a city. The objective here is not to criticize the designers but rather to show that even highly respected architects, and/or the circumstances they found themselves in, have created squares that have proved not to be places but to be simply links and not even busy links.

A number of possible explanations for the state of these squares can be identified. They may be away from the movements of pedestrians, devoid of sunlight, in a wind tunnel or suffer from air pollution and/or unpleasant odors or are bombarded by loud traffic noise. They may simply be located as the result of road closures or on left-over parcels of undeveloped land without much thought of what the site offers for its use as a square. There might be 'unfriendly' adjacent uses at the site. In addition, the neighbors may not want a lively square on the site. In some cases in seeking to make 'a work of art,' the sponsor/administrator of a square and its designers did not care that the square should be a public space to be potentially enjoyed by a diversity of people.

As examples, Stamford Square in Putney, London, completed in 2014, has what seems today to be the obligatory (and design trend) ground fountain. It faces north and, even on a sunny day, it is bleak and the café on its eastern side does not open out onto it. The square is simply not an inviting space. In contrast, a square in an arid subtropical climate, the central square in Chandigarh's Sector 17 is sundrenched and boiling hot on a summer's day and equally uninviting. Unlike the central squares of many cities, it is not listed in travel brochures as a place to visit although local shoppers do bring some life to it in the evenings.

Squares are often large for prestige reasons. The squares at the Capitol complex and the Sector 17 Market in Chandigarh are highly prestigious not only because of their size but also because they are displays/works of art. The Sector 17 square is certainly the more interesting of the two. Neither, however, is climatically sensible if pedestrian comfort is a consideration. They have, in common, a bold design and are displays of Le Corbusier's virtuosity as an architect. The city square, as would be expected, given its latitude of 31°N, is almost deserted under the summer noonday sun, but even in the cool of the evening, it is hardly a busy place by Indian standards.

A number of squares are simply large open spaces devoid of anything interesting in them. They are full of life during events and rallies but are otherwise empty and dull places. This criticism has been directed at Schouwburgplein in Rotterdam, as noted earlier in Chapter 12 of this book. It was developed in the 1990s and has been already reworked and further design changes are planned (Schneider 2010). The square is surrounded by a number of building types: a theater, concert hall, restaurants, shopping malls and Rotterdam's Central Station, and so one might expect it to be a busy place every day. Its layout was based on a strong intellectual esthetic idea – it was to be a space from which the panorama of the city skyline would be visible. In its design much attention was paid to the sun angles (the square is located at 53°N) and the various times that different activities would occur around the square. It provides good open space for these busy times and for markets, fairs and other special events. Despite the efforts made to improve on its dull predecessor, it is still as lifeless for much of the time. If it is evaluated as a work of art, it is seen to be a great success, according to critics.

Chinggis Khan Square in Ulaanbaatar in Mongolia is a grand open space where celebrations, parades and other formal events are held. Motivated protestors see the affordances of the site for organizing gatherings to vent their political frustrations. Purposefully or not, it was designed for large gatherings and as a forecourt to government buildings and not to be a multifunctional place. These types of squares would have been more active places if designed to serve a greater range of purposes and their internal organizations designed to afford more and varied activities. This goal has been set in the redesign of a number of similar but smaller squares around the world. Queen Elizabeth Plaza in Vancouver primarily services the theatre on site, but is left empty most other times, unless rented out (CDN$3000/day for special events (Figure 14.5 (b)). The City Hall Plaza in Boston is one of them that will have incremental changes made to it to transform its character over ten years (Ross 2011).

City Hall Plaza is a forlorn open space for much of the time, as has been noted by any number of observers (Figure 14.5). I. M. Pei, an architect as renowned as van der Rohe and Gehry, was the designer of the plaza, Boston's City Hall and the other structures of its Government Center. The plaza was constructed between 1963 and 1968 at the height of the influence of the Modernist design paradigm. It is located on the site of the former Scollay Square, a vibrant public space of historical interest. Scollay Square was, however, run-down and located in an area regarded as undesirable by middle-class people. As in many cases where a new square is being designed, Pei was inspired by an historical precedent. In this case it was the Piazza del Campo in Sienna. The problem with drawing directly on precedents in design is that the context in which the precedent works can be very different from the context faced locally.

Figure 14.5 Two squares that are generally regarded as having incurred significant opportunity costs:
(a) City Hall Plaza, Boston;
(b) Queen Elizabeth Plaza, Vancouver

Like so many Modernist designs, Boston's City Hall Plaza is a more sanitized place than its predecessor, but it is lifeless except when events such as markets are held. Evaluations of the utility of the plaza do differ. It is often praised simply because it exists, given the political struggles required to get it built. Others dislike the plaza because of the harshness of the contemporarily fashionable esthetic paradigm in which the new buildings were built and for the plaza's lack of any amenity for potential users. The Project for Public Spaces (n.d.) ranked it at the top of its list of squares "Most dramatically in need of improvement" in the United States. The space is cold, wet and very windy in winter, and dusty and unpleasantly hot in the summer heat. Lighter, quicker and cheaper place activation strategies are now being tested in the space.

It can be argued that Schouwburgplein, Chinggis Khan Square and Boston's City Hall Plaza were designed to be simply large, grand open spaces; Pershing Square in Los Angeles is different. It was designed to be a lively place. Like Boston's City Hall Plaza and Schouwburgplein, it superseded an earlier square that was seen to be malfunctioning. It has the difficulty of being above the street level as well as consisting of a variety of levels that serve little purpose. It does, however, have a high intellectual esthetic content that can be appreciated by the layperson and cognecenti alike. The layout of the square also contains many potential behavior settings. They, however, remain potential. The population who might avail themselves of the square's opportunities is simply not there. The utility of the square would undergo a substantial transformation if its surroundings were to change in character and become generators of pedestrians with some leisure time. This change now appears to be underway.

Often to enliven non-nuclear squares, an art installation is added. Picasso's *Untitled* sculpture enlivens Daley Plaza in Chicago and Koons' *Puppy* has been a positive addition to the forecourt of the Guggenheim Museum in Bilbao. Schouwburgplein has 15 meter-high ventilation shafts activated by LED displays that are important elements in the square. Such squares tend to have elements of interest but most have a poor degree of enclosure; they are amorphous squares. As a single criterion, this lack of enclosure is not a serious drawback, but the cumulative effect of a series of deviations from the 'ideal' type results in opportunity costs in their designs. They could have been designed differently with greater effect.

Drawing on these examples and many others with similar characteristics, a number of conclusions can be reached about why some squares are neither well used nor held in high esteem. The reasons have to do with the location of the square, the design of the square itself and/or with the management and financing of the square.

Contextual Concerns

The buildings that have forecourts are often located in the very dense cores of cities with a large number of people living and working nearby. They are usually purposefully designed to serve no more than a link between street and building. It is their internal design not context that leads to their single-function nature. For squares that are poorly used, inadvertently, it is a different matter.

If a square is not functioning well as a place where people want to be and wish to spend time, it is likely located away from centers of activity. It will relate poorly to its surrounding areas with few or no links to buildings that are normally generators of pedestrians and the square may be surrounded by vehicular traffic (for example, Place de la Concorde in Paris, Logan Square in Philadelphia, and Public Square in Cleveland). In addition, if it is located where crime levels are high or perceived to be high (as was the case of Freeway Park in Seattle or even Pershing Square in Los Angeles), its reputation will deter people from going there.

Areas with perceived loud noise levels are undesirable even though some lively squares have high sound levels. An example of this is Paley Park in New York where the waterfall produces loud sounds at 60–70 decibels, but they are perceived as pleasant sounds. People accommodate to the sound level because of the square's positive features. People accommodate to odorous places too. Squares will, nevertheless, be unpleasant if they are located near the source of unwanted smells so that odors waft into the space and breezes do not flush pollutants out of them. Some squares have none of these negative attributes, but are still accruing opportunity costs. In this case, it has to do with either their design or how the square is administered or both.

The Characteristics of the Square Itself

The single most important problem with many squares is that they are simply too large for their purposes. They appear to be empty even when there are people in them. In some cases this situation is tolerated by a city's establishment because a square hosts one important event a year for which a large space is needed. The Praça dos Três Poderes in Brasília serves well as a place to celebrate Brazil's independence from Portugal but otherwise only provides photographers with enough space to compose their photographs of the buildings around it that were designed by Oscar Niemeyer.

More generally, squares that possess no catalyst to attract people such as food outlets, pop-up events, or regular activation strategies either in them or adjacent to them tend to be quiet places. They also tend to have undifferentiated asphalt or paved concrete surfaces, with no "there" there – not a sculpture, art feature, nor fountain. These factors again are not the sole reasons for a square being quiet. They may contain no place to sit, for example, the renovated Shanghai Railway Station North Square, as Miao (2011) notes. The ledges may be uncomfortably high or low for sitting on even though people will strive to do so with dangling legs if too high or with legs scrunched up if too low. Seats that are fixed in location, facing vehicular traffic with their backs to any activities that might take place in the square are not good places to sit. A square enclosed by untextured and uninteresting blank walls is simply boring. Signage that is haphazardly placed, poorly lettered and difficult to read hardly makes a square legible or an attractive place.

Squares with an orientation and layout that make it a suntrap in hot weather and a cold dark place in winter and with surrounding buildings that create unpleasant downdrafts into the space are uncomfortable places to be, unless artificial mechanisms are used to ameliorate conditions. Plazas that are poor places for most people may attract the homeless or transients who have to tolerate environmental hardships. Their presence will be encouraged if a square has neither natural surveillance nor good lighting at night. As reported by Grenfell (2012), the area around the Guggenheim Museum in Bilbao is reputed to be crime-ridden and was dull until *Puppy* was added to it. The squares both at the front and rear of that building have almost no possibility of being naturally surveilled by other people in them. Perhaps the forecourt's lack of a sense of enclosure detracts from the possibility of it being a vibrant place rather than simply a forecourt that is a link between the city and the Museum. The forecourt of the Guggenheim Museum is, however, a good place from which to photograph the building on display.

Designing to Deliberately Exclude Specific Behaviors

The underlying theme of this book is that we know what the characteristics are of lively squares. In order to make them pleasant for the majority of people, squares have often been made unpleasant for groups of people or configured and detailed to preclude specific behaviors that are regarded as undesirable. The groups of people who are designed-out are not necessarily seen as threatening but consist primarily of the homeless, the unemployed, the poor and teenagers. To make a place clean and friendly for the 'right' type of people, public authorities include coercive devices in the layout of squares that deter specific behaviors. In addition, some may have restricted hours of entry. These approaches challenge the ideas of 'inclusivity' and all people having a 'right to the city.'[3]

A number of coercive tactics for preventing specific actions from taking place in a square, or any public space, without the presence of a controlling official can be found around the world. A sample is shown in Figure 14.6. They are regarded as 'silent agents.' Benches that are uncomfortable to sit on for more than 10 minutes because of the slope of their seating or ones that have armrests to make rough

Figure 14.6 Coercive design: (a) Do not lie down here; (b) Do not sit here

sleeping on them impossible, the ledge that is made of boulders, the sticking of non-drying paint on fences to discourage climbing on them, are regular features in many urban public places. Some such devices are very effective: the spiked aluminium bars that deflect urine streams onto the feet of urinating men is an example. More common devices include metal rungs or spikes on ledges to prevent skateboarders from skating on them or spikes to dissuade anybody from sitting on them.[4]

Conclusion

Cities should have a mix of both lively and quiet squares that cater to a variety of public needs (Marshall 2016). To that end, some squares need to be quiet, elegant places. Unfortunately other squares that were designed to be lively vibrant places are quiet by default. All the squares mentioned in this chapter are well maintained. Maintenance levels cannot be blamed for the marginal performances of squares. In the case of other quiet squares, the administrators have not worried about maintenance and these squares become dirty and unkempt. Designers incorporate, purposefully or not, the characteristics that make squares dull places because priorities other than to make them beloved public places were deemed to be of greater importance.

Notes

1 Matthew Carmona regards Empire Square as an example of a place where esthetic values overrode use values (2014: 19).
2 See Carmona (2014); see the Epilogue of this book, Notes on the Designing and/or Upgrading of Squares.
3 Much has been written on this topic. Scholars and practitioners have considered this topic from design, legal, social, ethical and practical perspectives.
4 Unpleasant Design has become an umbrella term for devices that preclude specific actions. See Davis (1990) and Savić and Savićic (2013).

References

Burden, Amanda (2014) How public spaces make cities work. A TED talk. Available at: www.ted.com.talks/amanda_burden_how_public_spaces_make_cities_work.
Carmona, Matthew (2014) The place-making continuum: A theory of urban design. *Journal of Urban Design* 19(1): 2–36
Davis, Mike (1990) *The City of Quartz*. London: Verso.
Dimendberg, Edward (2004) *Film Noir and the Spaces of Modernity*. Cambridge. MA: Harvard University Press.
Environmental Protection UK (for the City of London) (2010) *Quietening Open Spaces: Towards Sustainable Soundscapes for the City of London*. Brighton: City of London.
Grenfell, Milton (2012) Rybczynski is wrong on the Eisenhower Memorial. *Better Cities and Towns*, April 20. Available at: http://bettercities.net/news-opinion/blogs/milton-grenfell/17804/rybczynski-wrong-eisenhower-memorial.
Jordy, William H. (2005) *'Symbolic Essence' and Other Writings on Modern Architecture and American Culture*. New Haven, CT: Yale University Press.
Kayden, Jerome S. (2000) *Privately Owned Open Space: The New York City Experience*. New York: The New York City Department of City Planning and the Municipal Arts Society.
Marshall, Nancy (2016) Urban squares: a place for public life. In *Place and Placelessness Revisited*, edited by Robert Freestone and Edgar Liu. New York: Routledge, pp. 186–203.

Miao, Pu (2011) Brave new city: Three problems in Chinese public open space since the 1980s. *Journal of Urban Design* 16(2):179–207.

Project for Public Spaces (n.d.) Hall of Shame: Available at: www.pps.org/great_public_spaces/list?type_id=2.

Ross, Casey (2011) A 10-year plan for City Hall Plaza: New incremental approach starts with remodelled T-Station, trees. *The Boston Globe*, March 16. Available at: www.boston.com/business/articles/2011/03/16/after_many_false_starts_a_new_city_hall_plaza_plan/.

Savić, Selena and Gordan Savićic (eds.) (2013) *Unpleasant Design*. Belgrade: G.L.O.R.I.A.

Schneider, Ben (2010) Schouwburgplein. Landscape Architecture Study Tour by Professor Jack Ahem. Available at: http://people.umass.edu/latour/Netherlands/schneider/.

Further Reading

Garvin, Alexander (1995) *The American City: What Works and What Doesn't*. New York: McGraw-Hill.

Lang, Jon (1994) *Urban Design: The American Experience*. New York: Van Nostrand Reinhold.

Mehta, Vikas (2013) Evaluating public space. *Journal of Urban Design* 19(1): 53–58.

EPILOGUE

Praça dos Tres Poderes, Brasilia

NOTES ON THE DESIGNING AND/ OR UPGRADING OF SQUARES

The designing process followed in creating squares, or any other arti-fact, often seems to be irrational. "The pseudoscience of planning seems almost neurotic in its determination to imitate empiric fail-ure and ignore empiric success," as Jane Jacobs noted (1961: 183). Municipal officials and designers are seduced by bold images of what they have seen or read about. "Why don't we create a place like Paley Park in New York?" or "We need to have something like Piccadilly Gardens in Manchester." They consider squares as products and seek to adapt prestigious examples to an available site. Following such a process can lead to a successful result if the climatic, sociocultural, urban and economic context of the precedent is close to the situation in which it is being applied. Many ideas are indeed transferable across sociocultural and even climatic boundaries because of unrecognized latent demands. The High Line in New York has a precedent in the Promenade Plantée in Paris; the Goods Line in Sydney has a precedent in the High Line. Outdoor cafés work as well, with some climatic man-agement techniques, in Copenhagen as in Rome. The latent demand for such places existed in New York and Copenhagen respectively. The case studies in Chapter 12 were not presented as precedents but rather as a basis for the design principles presented in Chapters 13 and 14. Much can be learnt from specific cases but designers need to retain a critical attitude in considering whether a potential precedent or some aspect of it is applicable in the situation they face.

The General Structure of the Design Process

The logical first step in the designing of squares involves the setting of general goals. The process can involve different stakeholders and local community members to a greater or lesser extent.[1] The ques-tion that first needs to be addressed is: Is a square needed? If it is, then another question arises: What is the instrumental purpose or purposes that the square is to serve? The next step is to turn these goals into specific objectives. This step is followed by focusing on the identification or creation of the patterns of built form that meet these diverse objectives. Synthesizing these often contradictory patterns into a concrete proposal is no easy task. The steps involved in implementing the design then represent a design process in itself. Ideally, once built, there is a phase of rigorous post-occupancy evaluation that would feed into our knowledge base to aid future decision-making.

It would be wonderful if the design process was a logical, sequential step-by-step progression but that is not the case. As many say, design problems are 'wicked.'[2] They consist of components that are known and can be measured but also much that is unknown. What one needs to know is not obvious. Wicked problems are never completely resolved, so no proposal can be regarded as perfect but one potential design can be considered to be better than the others in addressing the specifications of its locality and socioeconomic and political context.

Each step of each phase of the design process involves thinking both divergently – the act of generating ideas – and convergently – the act of synthesizing parts into wholes. The process is one of continuous conjecturing about what should be done and how it should be done. These conjectures are very much affected by our knowledge of case studies and functional theory – empirical generalizations about how the built environment works in affording activity patterns and associational meanings. These conjectures are tested against a set of evaluation criteria that are derived from the goals set for a square.

The whole process is one of continuous debate – discussions are held among designers and between designers and clients as well as with those people who control the budget, consent authorities and, in best practice, the proposed space's potential users. Each of these individuals or groups may have different objectives and different levels of knowledge about how squares function and have different expectations and levels of investment for the outcomes. Evidence drawn from case studies and patterns of built form based on empirical evidence (as presented in Chapters 13 and 14) can provide strong support for a designer arguing that one proposed scheme is more desirable than another. As Jane Jacobs (1961) noted, evidence is, however, often eschewed and the proposal proceeds based on precedents that have captured the imagination and that may or may not be working well. Their functioning has never been thoroughly evaluated.

Approaches to Designing

The decision to build a square or redevelop one should begin, as we (and others such as Gehl (2010) have advocated, with establishing a set of general goals that define the desired nature of the space available. The next step is to define these goals in terms of how they dovetail into more encompassing city plans and visions. When designers are working under strict time and budgetary constraints, it is tempting to by-pass these early steps and simply look at what is believed to be a successful design elsewhere and adapt its patterns to the situation at hand. This short-cutting of the process has led to many design failures because the social and physical context of the precedent being used is misunderstood and/or the assumed latent demand for a new square did not exist. In addition, acclaimed designs often function considerably less well than their reputation would suggest or how they are described in architectural and other professional journals. Rigorous case studies are few and far between because observers fear costly litigation if they expose what does not work. A number of approaches to the setting of goals and conducting the design process co-exist; they all follow approximately the model described at the outset of this chapter. At the most general level, when designing a square, it is possible to distinguish between the Rationalist and the Empiricist schools of thought.

The Rationalist approach to designing a square involves the creation of a proposal based on images of an ideal future. The aim is to get beyond the mundane realities of the present world. The approach is based on a set of assumptions of what is good: good people, good sensible behavior and the 'right' ways of life. Good designs then follow from logical thinking. The approach works well if the assumptions are rooted in potential users' predispositions. Very often, however, the argument is based on the designer's desire to depart from the norm and his or her own feelings about what will be good for others in the future. The assumption is that once the square is built, the public will recognize that the resulting built forms, from the large scale to the detailed, are good places for them. Many architects prefer to work this way based on their own assumptions about what is ideal; in doing so they feel unconstrained by the way the world actually works. What the leading Rationalists have produced over the past century is a number of highly innovative designs. The results are generally thought-provoking, either as great successes establishing bold new ideas or as abject failures.

Designing squares to be displays often follows a broad Rationalist approach where a designer (or, more likely, design team) as an artist, expresses a view or critique of the world and then decides what should be designed based on that view. The design, nevertheless, has to receive the approval of those in power: specific decision-makers who include politicians, property developers and public authorities. They are guided by some image of public, private and personal interests and by the designer of a square claiming superior insights and the right of self-expression as an artist.

Empiricists, on the other hand, advocate creating designs based on actual, not imagined, places and displays that they believe do work and that they like. Two observations raise questions about this approach: (1) perceptions of places that work differ from observer to observer although there is often a surprising consensus among people of diverse backgrounds; and (2) the examples of good squares that can be used as precedents are inevitably drawn from the past and present. Designs are for the future. The Empiricist assumption is that much is stable in the world and that the past is a predictor of the future. This position has much to support it. Many squares have been functioning well for two or more centuries. They have been robust enough to continue to serve important purposes despite a changing world. The argument for designing city squares following an Empiricist line of thought is thus based on the observation that what has worked well for people in the past, and works well today, will function well in the future. The limitation of the Empiricist approach is that it tends to be failure-avoiding. Empiricist designs work well enough but seldom break new geometric or symbolic grounds. They are adequate (or in economic terms, satisficing) solutions. Design-conscious scholars and practitioners expect more.

Much design is indeed based on the adaptation of precedents (either the idealized designs of Rationalists or existing designs) to the situation at hand. The design process tends to be a mimetic one in which existing or generic solutions are adapted to the situation faced by designers. As Jane Jacobs (1961) noted, the problem is that the hearts and minds of both designers and decision-makers are captured by dramatic, bold designs that do not necessarily work well. They reuse those patterns rather than repeating the principles of less bold designs that do work well. This book is based on the assumption that there is an alternative approach.

A Normative, Evidence-Based Approach to Designing Squares

In an evidence-based approach to design, the whole process begins with a decision to create or redesign a square based on the perceptions of opportunities to improve a current situation. The identification of the need for a square may come from the general public, designers, a community group, property developers, politicians or a perceptive individual. Often it is indeed a single person who perceives an opportunity and argues for it tenaciously.[3] A detailed program, or brief, specifying the qualities sought for the square is then developed as a major step towards achieving a good design. While this process is generally seen as an analytic one, it is really a design one; it is a creative "act of will" as Bacon (1967) discussed many years ago. A stand is taken on the direction to pursue.

The quality of any self-consciously designed square, when functioning on a day-to-day basis, depends heavily on the quality of the goals and objectives established at the outset and the design program. It is not, however, until proposed designs are open to evaluation that the issues that ought to have been considered in developing a program are understood. The act of designing is used as an analytical tool. Just as frequently it is not until the square has been built and its performance can be seen and evaluated that the issues that should have been resolved are fully clear as was the case in the 1994 design of Pershing Square. By then it is often too late to do more than make slight adjustments to a square's layout and to rely on actively programming events that fit the space to make it come alive.

As design problems are 'wicked,' decisions about the future and designs that will work in that future always have to be made under a cloud of uncertainty. Empirical evidence reduces the uncertainty but does not eliminate it. This reality is compounded by the need to identify the latent demands of potential users. What would people enjoy that they cannot articulate but would recognize as what they want if it were built? On the other hand, potential users may believe that they would use a square with particular characteristics but when such a place is built, they do not use it.

Creating the Program

Much of the negative commentary on new public spaces is a criticism of the goals set by public officials and designers. Perceptions of what the function of an open space should be inevitably differ.[4] We take the position that the goal of any design is to create a place that is congruent with people's behaviors and values, not what they believe their behaviors and values to be. The program is thus a conjecture about what should be done.

A number of concerns arise during the setting of goals and operationalizing them in terms of attainable ends: Who sets the program? Who makes the decisions? How does one rank the importance of the various objectives and what design features are people willing to trade off to attain other benefits? How are the designers selected? How are the general public and/or specific interest groups to be involved in a collaborative design process or making decisions? Further questions arise: Who are to be regarded as the potential users and what kinds of experiences do designers want them to have in the square? Do users have a role in determining those experiences? Is the square to be primarily an artistic display or a place and/or a link? Is it to be a square that attracts tourists or a place primarily for locals? In other words what is the instrumental function to be? Is it to house special events? How much space is required for them? What kinds of facilities should be provided in the square? What is the budget? Are the designers to worry about the budget available at the outset or should they come up with the 'best' design and let the public officials find the funds required to get the design built – or to what extent is there middle ground? How healthy is the maintenance budget for the short and long term? The list of questions could go on and on.

The program is usually created by the designers selected for the project or a specialist consultant based on deliberations with the various stakeholders. Alternatively, a public design charrette process can be employed to ensure the public and stakeholders have a voice in the design at very early stages in the discussion of ends and means.[5] Setting the goals for any public space is always a political act open to debate because it depends on competing images of what the future is likely to be and how a design should function in that future. The goals and ultimately a proposal to build a square – whether it is a new scheme on a brownfield site as part of an urban renewal scheme or part of a new property development on a greenfield site – are indeed statements of will on the part of decision-makers. The same holds true when refurbishing an existing square. The decision-makers will be acting, explicitly or implicitly, on behalf of those who have a stake in the project. These stakeholders may be property owners, politicians and public administrators but we argue they should certainly include the people who are likely to use the square or those for whom the square is specifically being created. Almost inevitably a design is targeted, usually implicitly rather than explicitly, at a specific population. Who should it be? Who is it likely to be? The decision is often made by default and is ultimately implicit in the implemented design itself. Managing access, which very often means excluding the homeless and other 'undesirables,' is often a higher priority than seeking a good square for all.

The people with a stake in the design of any square will be varied. Each stakeholder group or individuals involved will strive to get their own self-interests met. Politicians will worry about being re-elected, property developers will seek to maximize their profit, non-profit organizations and public agencies want their voices heard and designers will usually want to strongly influence the final design. The decision to empower one group rather than another needs, we argue, to be made for the public good. The public good is, however, notoriously difficult to define. At the least, designers should seek a solution that, although it may serve one group better than another, should not disadvantage any one group. The design that is put in place should be what is called a Pareto Optimal solution.[6]

Moving from a broad vision and a set of goals to measurable objectives and the application of design principles (that is, statements that link objectives with patterns of built form) is a technical concern based on empirical functional theory (that is, descriptions and explanations of how different patterns of built form function) (Lang and Moleski 2010). The process is, as has been noted, an argumentative one because the same goal can be achieved by meeting different design objectives. The end product of this phase of the decision process is a program specifying the performance requirements of the patterns that will ultimately form the design of the square. Illustrations of the individual patterns that are required to meet the objectives should be included in the program. Doing so helps designers focus on the pertinent concerns and opportunities. The design of the program has to be recognized as the central creative act in the entire decision-making process.[7] In a pluralistic and collaborative world, the public and community stakeholder groups can and should assist in developing and determining the program.[8] Many designers, however, believe that the public and other stakeholders simply get in the way of striving to create a good design (Hayes 1998).

Synthesizing Individual Patterns into Potential Solutions

Program development and the creation of a specific design proposal are iterative processes. The act of design reveals previously unidentified issues that have to be resolved and hence the program gets adjusted accordingly. Designing involves identifying/creating a proposal that meets the program, based, we argue, on evidence such as that presented in the chapters of this book. Knowing how specific squares and the patterns of built form within them work is one basis for evidence. The other is to understand how specific design principles work in context.

The creative acts in developing a design proposal, as in the development of the program, involve both divergent and convergent thinking. The generation of different means of attaining specific ends requires the constant evaluation of what is being proposed. This evaluating forms part of the iterative process of making conjectures about what should be done, predicting their performance and testing them logically. Almost inevitably designers have to face the reality that the design objectives established in the program contradict each other. The patterns of built form used to achieve one objective may not be compatible with the patterns required to achieve another. Trade-offs are inevitable. Convergent thinking in designing a square is the act of synthesis, of drawing patterns that resolve particular problems together to form a coherent whole. It is a highly value-laden process because it involves weighing one pattern against another and thus one objective versus another. How should the designer/design team proceed? Two approaches are possible.

A *breadth-first approach* is one in which as many options as possible are generated thinking divergently. These options are left open at the outset. No decision about which is the best option is made in this brainstorming phase. The purpose is to avoid prematurely truncating, or closing, lines of thought that at the outset may seem unwise but, if carried further, work well in conjunction with other patterns of built form.

A *depth-first approach*, in contrast, is one in which design decisions are made rapidly in order to achieve a single proposal. It involves selecting the one design pattern that seems to be the best at each stage of the process and then going on to the next until a completed potential solution is created. This design can then be evaluated, lessons learnt from it and the process repeated based on different assumptions until a set of designs is available for the decision-makers to consider. It is an efficient process but design possibilities that might have worked well can easily get by-passed because they were discarded before they were combined with other patterns. In addition, some designers may be reluctant to discard their first design even though it is patently insufficient; they may have an intellectual and emotional investment in it.

Whether one follows a breadth-first or a depth-first approach, the designer has to decide whether to start with the large-scale concerns or the smaller-scale details. The argument for dealing with the large-scale patterns first is that they establish the parameters that constrain what follows and in so doing simplify the design process and make it more efficient. Thus, in designing squares, the design decisions involving the overall configuration and instrumental purposes a square is to fulfill are resolved first before any concerns about its internal design are addressed. The argument for the reverse approach is that the details simply have to work well for a square to work well so they need to be considered first. What actually seems to be best is to move back and forth from a breadth-first to a depth-first approach and from making the small-scale to the large-scale decisions and then back again – an iterative process.

The depth-first approach, while maintaining a quasi-breadth-first attitude in generating a number of designs, seems to be the most logical way of proceeding. Different design teams can generate their own designs. The set of designs so created can then be subject to open examination. Inevitably a number of questions and issues arise in this phase of the decision process. The broadest of all is: If the square is to be primarily a lively place, what is the role of the designer's desire for freedom of expression in its design to be? Then: Does one use case studies (as in Chapter 12) or the type of evidence summarized in Chapters 13 and 14 as the basis for developing the patterns to be used in synthesizing a solution? Or both?

The question of when to consider economic and political feasibility is also an issue open to debate. Here too there are advocates for opposing approaches. The first is an *ideals approach* in which the best possible design is created and then gradually reshaped and redesigned until an economically and politically feasible one is achieved. The second is a *realist approach* in which economic and political feasibility issues are imposed as constraints from the very beginning. An economically feasible design is sought and then incrementally improved until the design is no longer financially viable. Either way, the process is not only a debated and defended one but is often also highly emotional. It is no wonder that many designers prefer to take standard solutions and adapt them as a package to the situation at hand. It saves time and money and the result may work to some degree.

It is clear that the architect or landscape architect, while designing, is constantly making predictions of how a proposed design will work and evaluating those predictions. The most important evaluation comes at the end of the design phase, and that is to evaluate the proposal or competing proposals. Ideally several proposals based on different assumptions should be available for evaluation. Each proposal should explain its inherent biases in its attempt to fulfill any given program.

Evaluating Competing Designs

If the design results from a competition, a panel of experts or a jury selects the best one, based on the consent authority's evaluation criteria combined with their own value judgments. In some contexts the jury's decision is final, but in others it is open to challenge. Given the values of the authors of this book, once potential designs have been produced, the evaluation process should involve the broader local community, architectural critics and those who have the power to make the decisions to implement one proposed design rather than another. If no design is regarded as good enough, either the patterns that meet specific objectives of the project have to be rethought or the design objectives, themselves, need to be reconsidered.

A number of issues arise in evaluating designs: What assumptions does one make about the future context in which the square will operate? Whose and/or what evaluation criteria should one use in evaluating possible designs? Does one worry about the multiplier and side effects of the square on its surroundings when it is completed? Sometimes the main reason for building a square is for it to be a catalyst for development in adjacent areas – what will this area look like and be like in the future?

How does one establish what the most important criteria are and what are the lesser ones to use in evaluating competing design proposals? To what extent does one play safe or gamble on whether a completely new design idea will function as predicted without any evidence to support it? We believe that the way a decision is made needs to be transparent and the decision criteria understandable. Not everybody involved in making a choice has to agree about the decision criteria but they do need to understand them. Using evidence of what works and does not work, both at the broad scale and at the detail level, adds some rationality to the evaluation process although political processes and ends often overrule empirical evidence. Designers need to draw on case studies and empirical functional theory if they are to convince themselves and then others about what makes for a good design. The application of this knowledge contributes to their political power and influence.

A Brief Note on Implementing a Design

Moving from a design on the drawing board or on the computer screen to getting it built often results in changes to the design and thus implicitly to the program. Often it is not until the process of implementing a design begins that unforeseen design questions arise. Almost inevitably partial redesigns occur during the construction of a square which implies that the program gets altered and the whole design process gets partially, at least, revisited.

Conclusion

Planning and design goals establish the general purpose a square is to serve. Such statements are usually so general that they are seldom disputed. Debate begins when translating these goals into operational objectives. These objectives and the patterns of built form that meet them need, we believe, to be based on evidence. There is now a considerable body of knowledge which enables us to develop design principles that link objectives with design patterns.

Designers need to keep an open mind in addressing the situations they face. Most, however, are creatures of habit. They have developed a set of patterns of form for which they have a preference and that defines their style. We recognize the work of individual designers in their repeated use of specific patterns of built form. Often they are hired because of the perceived compatibility between their style and the values of the clients/authorities who hire them. The alternative is to use a creative, evidence-based approach to design in which standard ways of working are challenged. Applying such an approach requires considerably more intellectual energy than designing by habit. It must also be recognized that in designing for the future, indeed, in creating the future, much is uncertain. The evidence presented in this book provides the basis for making sensible conjectures about how to design squares with confidence while recognizing that uncertainty.

Notes

1 See Healey (2003) and Innes (2010) on the collaborative planning process.
2 See Bazjanac (1974), Schön (1983), Rittel and Webber (1984), Hamilton and Watkins (2009) and the essays in Herbert and Donchin (2013) on the complexity of the design process. See Alexander *et al.* (1977) on the nature of patterns.
3 Riverwalk (Paseo del Rio) in San Antonio in Texas is an example of a highly successful public realm development that resulted from the foresight, initiative and perseverance of a single individual. See Lang (2005: 350–353).

4 If one considers a design such as that of the Seagram Building Plaza in New York, the goals implicit in its design were very different from what critics such as Dimendberg (2004), Jordy (2005) and Burden (2014) believe they should have been.
5 See Batchelor and Lewis (1985) for an explanation of how to run design charrettes. See also the National Charrette Institute in the USA (2015).
6 A Pareto Optimal design solution is one that, after a search, is the best among other options in making at least an individual or set of people satisfied without being detrimental to others. See Mathur (1991) for a discussion of the concept.
7 Even the architects who are renowned for the forms that deviate from the norm that characterize their work recognize this reality. Le Corbusier (1923) is a prime example.
8 See Marshall et al. (2012) for a broader discussion of public involvement in the planning and design process.

References

Alexander, Christopher, Sara Ishikawa and Murray Silverstein (1977) *A Pattern Language: Towns, Buildings, Construction*. New York: Oxford University Press.
Bacon, Edmund (1967) The city as an act of will. *Architectural Record* 141(1): 113–128.
Batchelor, Peter and David Lewis (eds.) (1985) *Urban Design in Action*. Raleigh, NC: North Carolina State University and the American Institute of Architects.
Bazjanac, Vladimir (1974) Architectural design theory: Models of the design-process. In *Basic Questions of Design Theory*, edited by W. R. Spilliers. New York: American Elsevier, pp. 3–20.
Burden, Amanda (2014) How public spaces make cities work. A TED talk. Available at: www.ted.com.talks/amanda_burden_how_public_spaces_make_cities_work.
Dimendberg, Edward (2004) *Film Noir and the Spaces of Modernity*. Cambridge, MA: Harvard University Press.
Gehl, Jan (2010) *Cities for People*. Washington, DC: Island Press.
Hamilton, D. Kirk and David H. Watkins (2009) *Evidence Based Design for Multiple Building Types*. Hoboken, NJ: John Wiley & Sons, Inc.
Hayes, Michael K. (1998) *Architecture Theory since 1968*. Cambridge, MA: MIT Press.
Healey, Patsy (2003) Collaborative planning in perspective. *Planning Theory* 2(2): 101–123.
Herbert, Gilbert and Mark Donchin (eds.) (2013) *The Collaborators: Interactions in the Architectural Design Process*. Farnham: Ashgate.
Innes, Judith (2010) *Planning with Complexity: An Introduction to Collaborative Rationality for Public Policy*. London: Routledge.
Jacobs, Jane (1961) *The Death and Life of Great American Cities*. New York: Random House.
Jordy, William H. (2005) *'Symbolic Essence' and Other Writings on Modern Architecture and American Culture*. New Haven, CT: Yale University Press.
Lang, Jon (2005) *Urban Design: A Typology of Procedures and Products Illustrated with Over 50 Case Studies*. Oxford: Architectural Press.
Lang, Jon and Walter Moleski (2010) *Functionalism Revisited: Architectural Theory and Practice and the Behavioral Sciences*. Farnham: Ashgate.
Le Corbusier (1923) *Vers une Architecture*. Trans. from the French as *Towards a New Architecture* by Frederick Etchells, reprinted 1970. New York: Praeger.
Marshall, Nancy, Christine Steinmetz and Robert Zehner (2012) Community participation in planning. In *Planning Australia*, 2nd edn, edited by Susan Thompson and Paul Maginn. Sydney: Cambridge University Press, pp. 276–293.
Mathur, Vijay K. (1991) How well do we know Pareto Optimality? *Journal of Economic Education* 22(2): 172–178.

National Charrette Institute (USA) (2015) NCI Charrette System. Available at: www.charretteinstitute.org/

Rittel, Horst and Melvin M. Webber (1984) Planning problems are wicked problems. In *Developments in Design Methodology*, edited by Nigel Cross. New York: John Wiley & Sons, Inc., pp. 135–144.

Schön, Donald (1983) *The Reflective Practitioner*. New York: Basic Books.

Further Reading

Alger, John R. M. and Carl V. Hayes (1964) *Creative Synthesis in Design*. Englewood Cliffs, NJ: Prentice Hall.

Lang, Jon (1994) *Urban Design: The American Experience*. New York: Van Nostrand Reinhold.

Lawson, Bryan (1999) *How Designers Think: The Design-Process Demystified*. Oxford: Architectural Press.

INDEX